JOANN SFAR

VAMPIRE LOVES

Color by Audré Jardel

Translation by Alexis Siegel

:01

First Second

New York & London

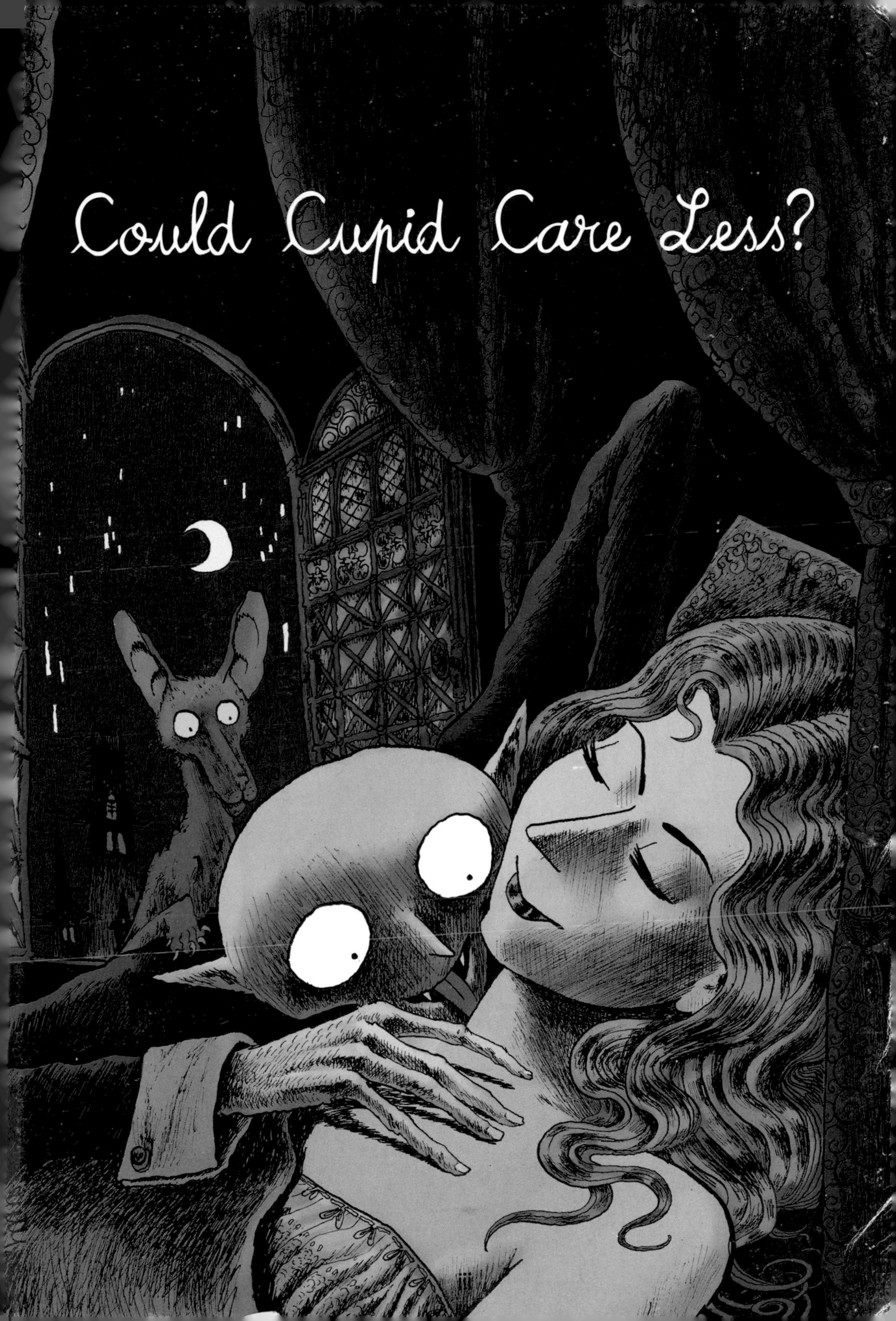
Could Cupid Care Less?

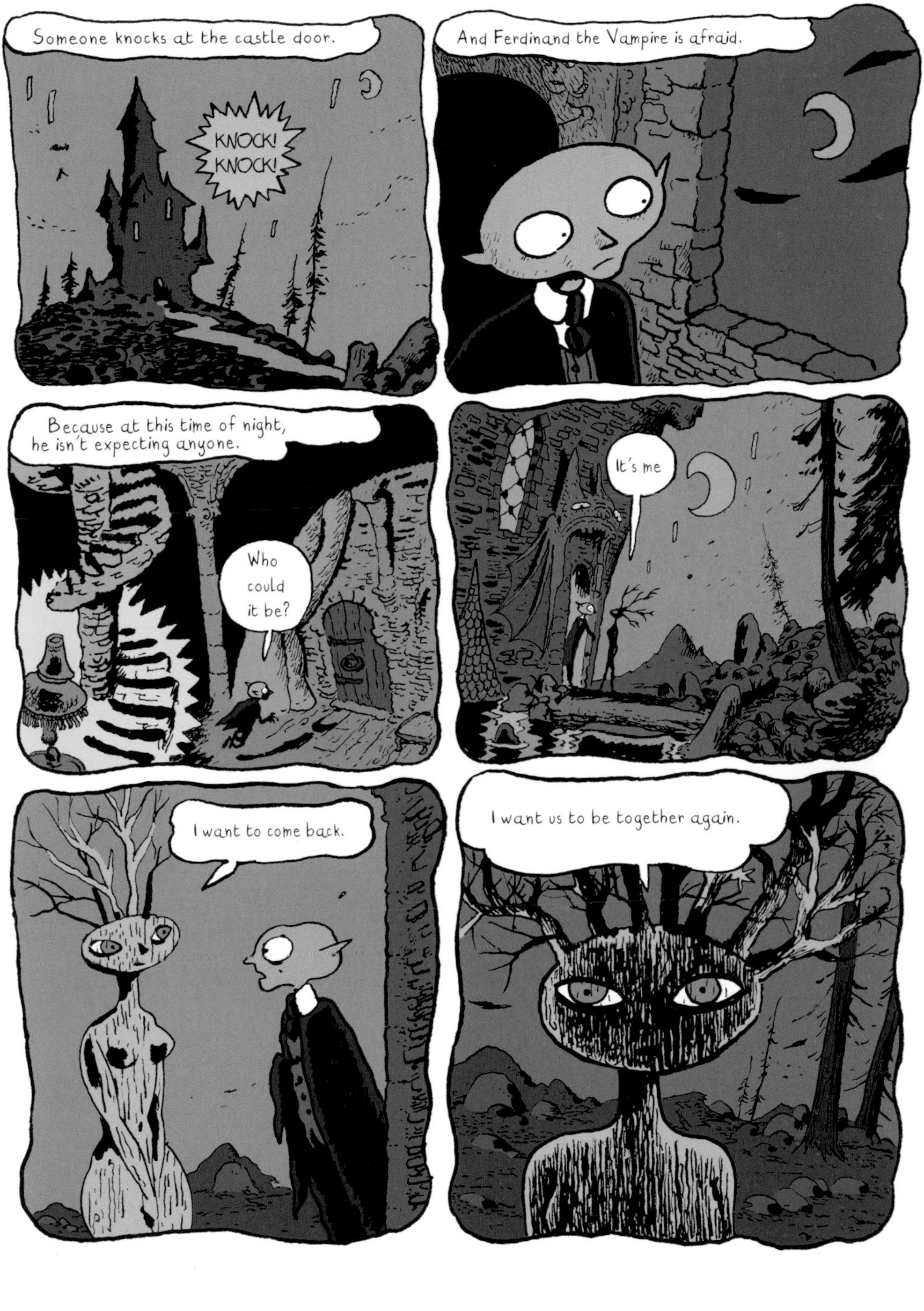
Someone knocks at the castle door.
KNOCK! KNOCK!
And Ferdinand the Vampire is afraid.
Because at this time of night, he isn't expecting anyone.
Who could it be?
It's me
I want to come back.
I want us to be together again.

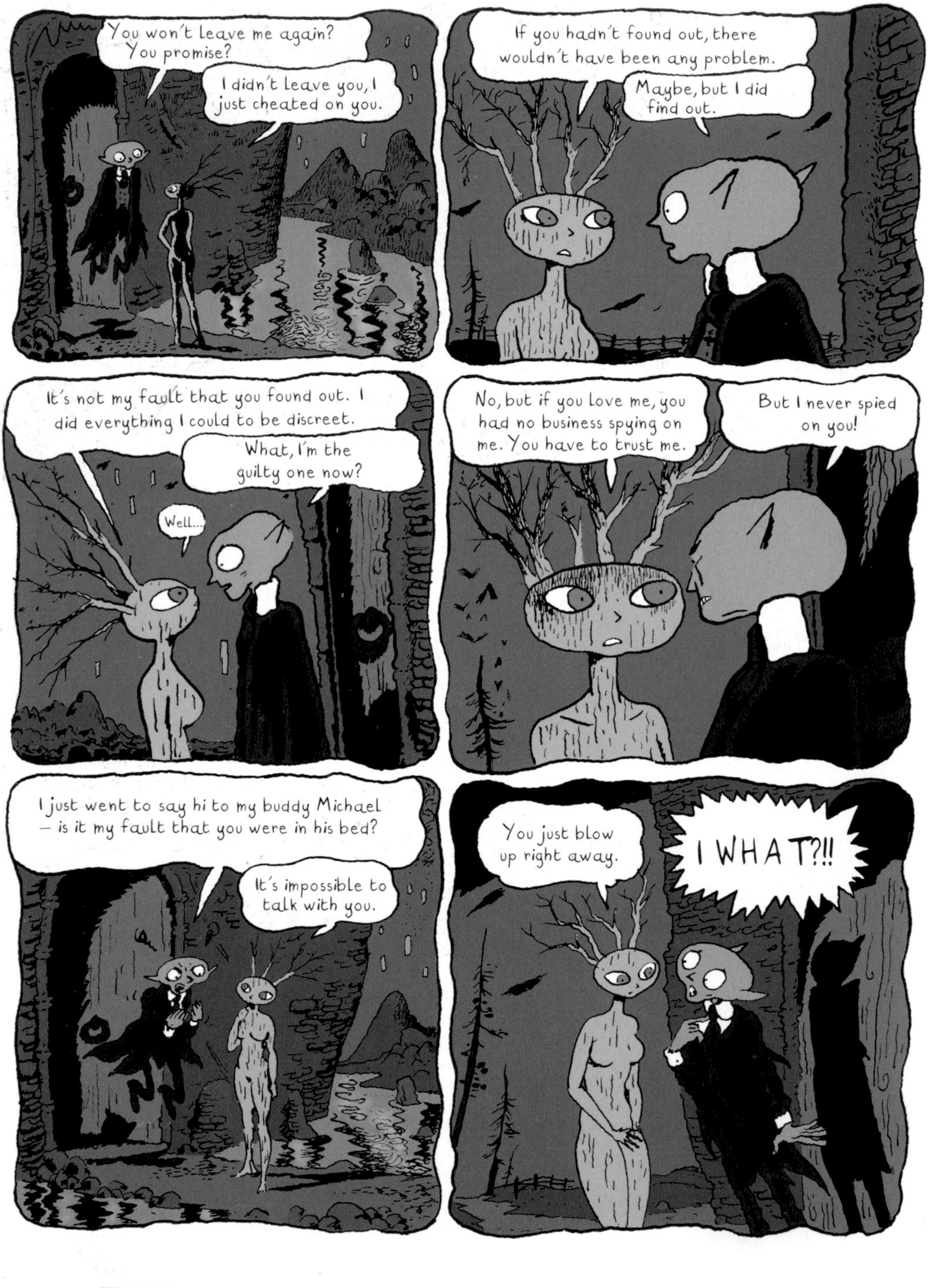
You won't leave me again? You promise?
I didn't leave you, I just cheated on you.
If you hadn't found out, there wouldn't have been any problem.
Maybe, but I did find out.
It's not my fault that you found out. I did everything I could to be discreet.
What, I'm the guilty one now?
Well...
No, but if you love me, you had no business spying on me. You have to trust me.
But I never spied on you!
I just went to say hi to my buddy Michael — is it my fault that you were in his bed?
It's impossible to talk with you.
You just blow up right away.
I WHAT?!!

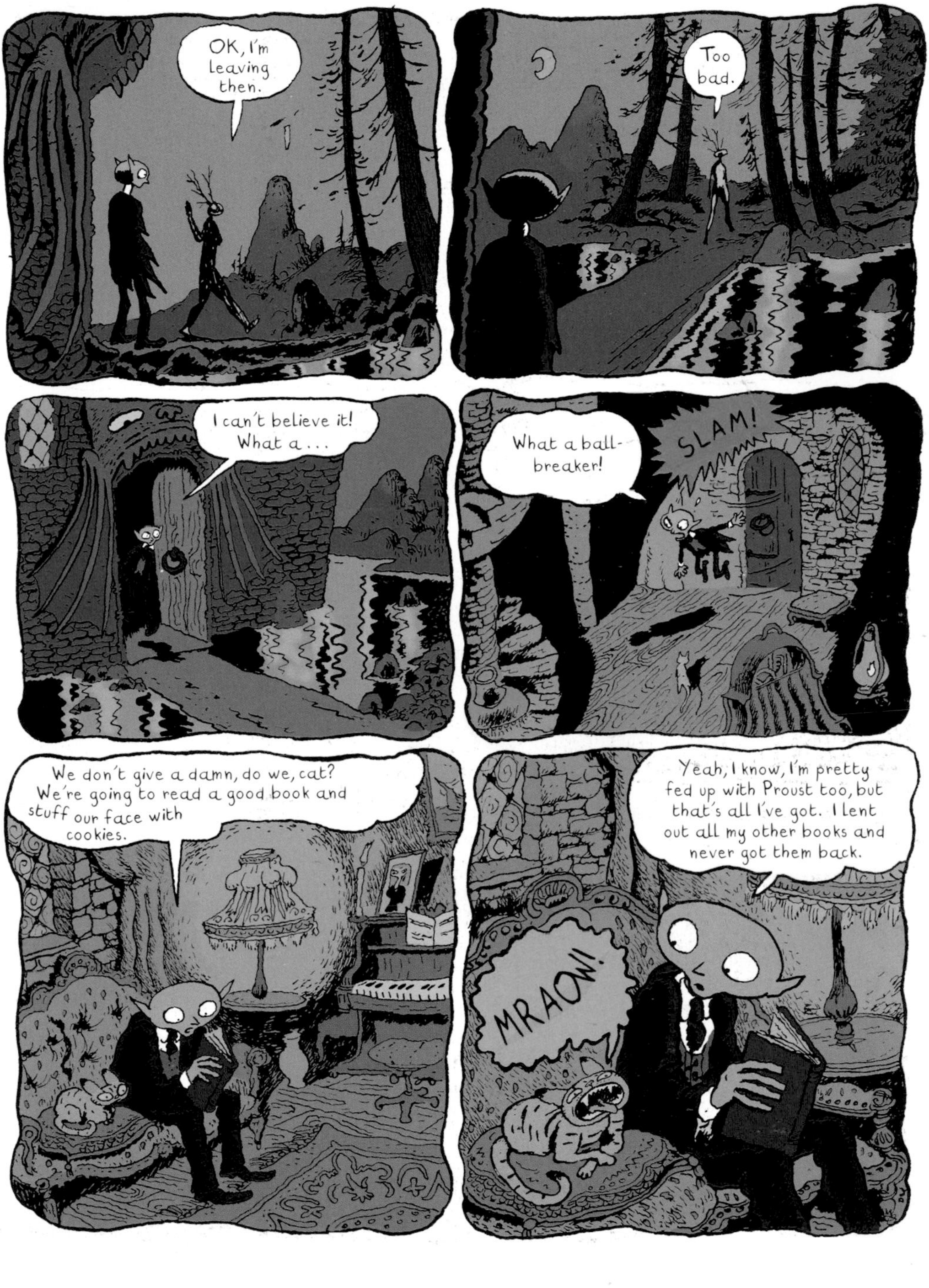
OK, I'm leaving then.
Too bad.
I can't believe it! What a . . .
What a ball-breaker!
SLAM!
We don't give a damn, do we, cat? We're going to read a good book and stuff our face with cookies.
Yeah, I know, I'm pretty fed up with Proust too, but that's all I've got. I lent out all my other books and never got them back.
MRAOW!

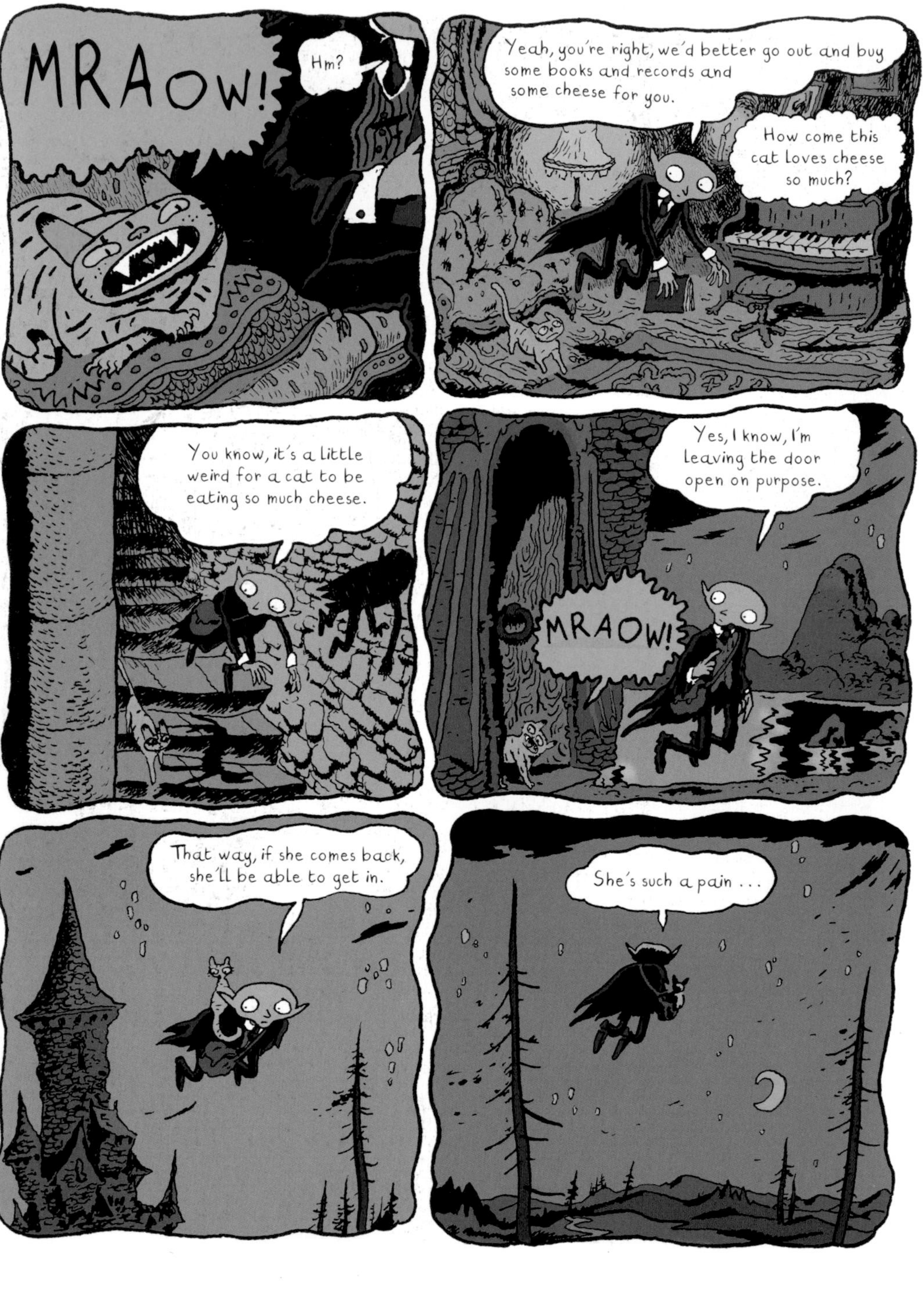
MRAOW!
Hm?
Yeah, you're right, we'd better go out and buy some books and records and some cheese for you.
How come this cat loves cheese so much?
You know, it's a little weird for a cat to be eating so much cheese.
Yes, I know, I'm leaving the door open on purpose.
MRAOW!
That way, if she comes back, she'll be able to get in.
She's such a pain . . .

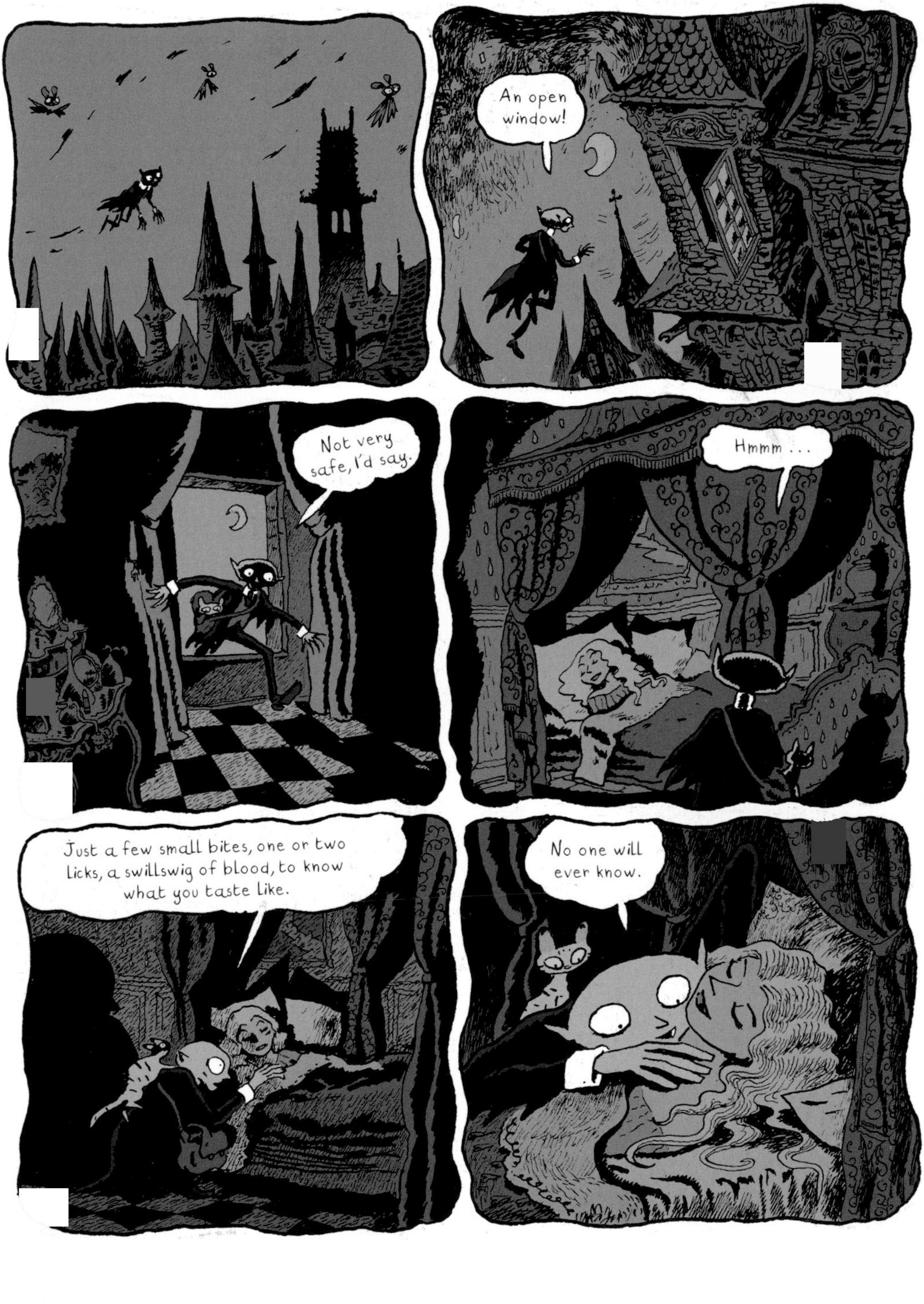
An open window!
Not very safe, I'd say.
Hmmm . . .
Just a few small bites, one or two licks, a swillswig of blood, to know what you taste like.
No one will ever know.

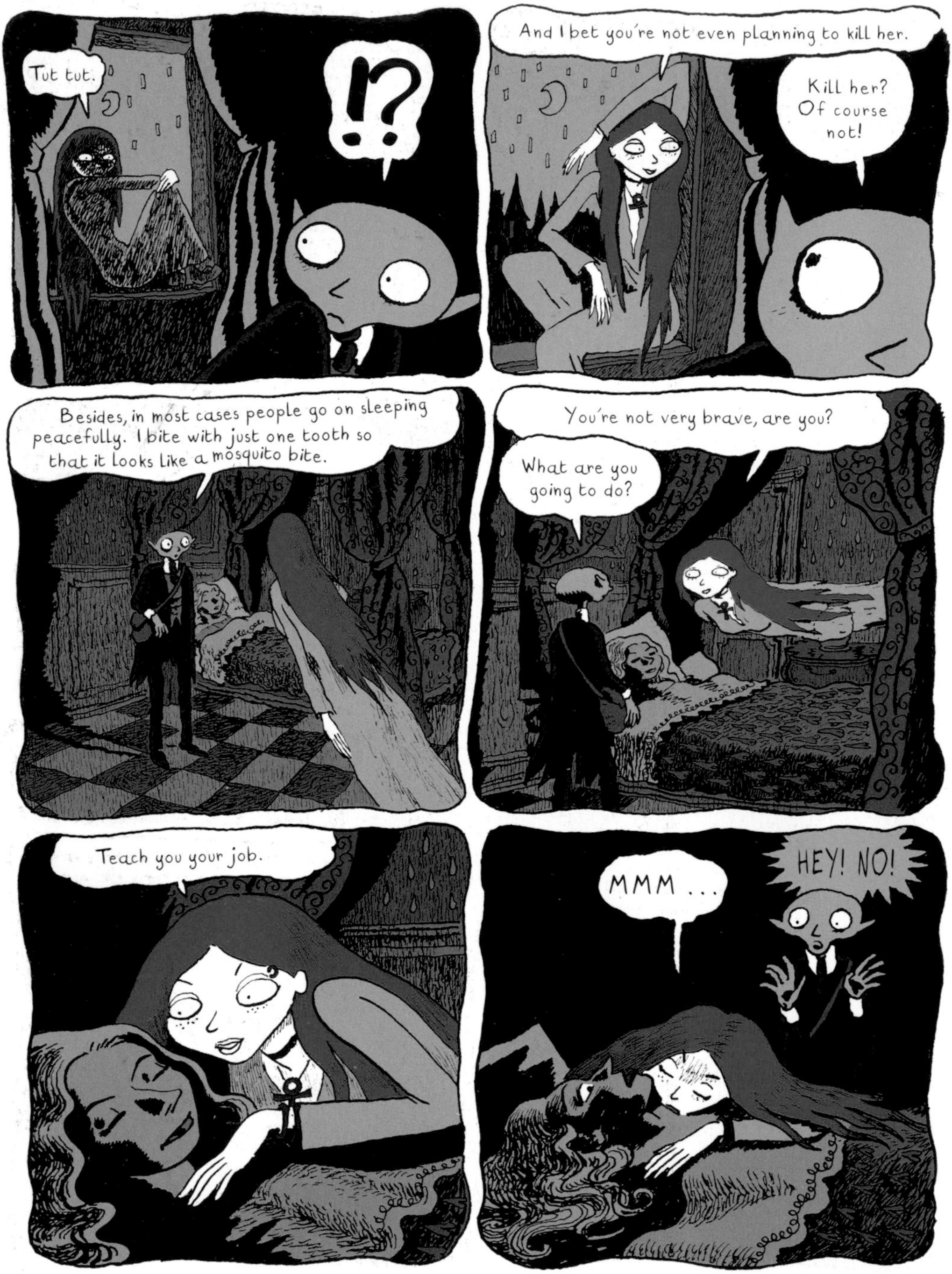

Tut tut.
!?
And I bet you're not even planning to kill her.
Kill her? Of course not!
Besides, in most cases people go on sleeping peacefully. I bite with just one tooth so that it looks like a mosquito bite.
You're not very brave, are you?
What are you going to do?
Teach you your job.
MMM ...
HEY! NO!

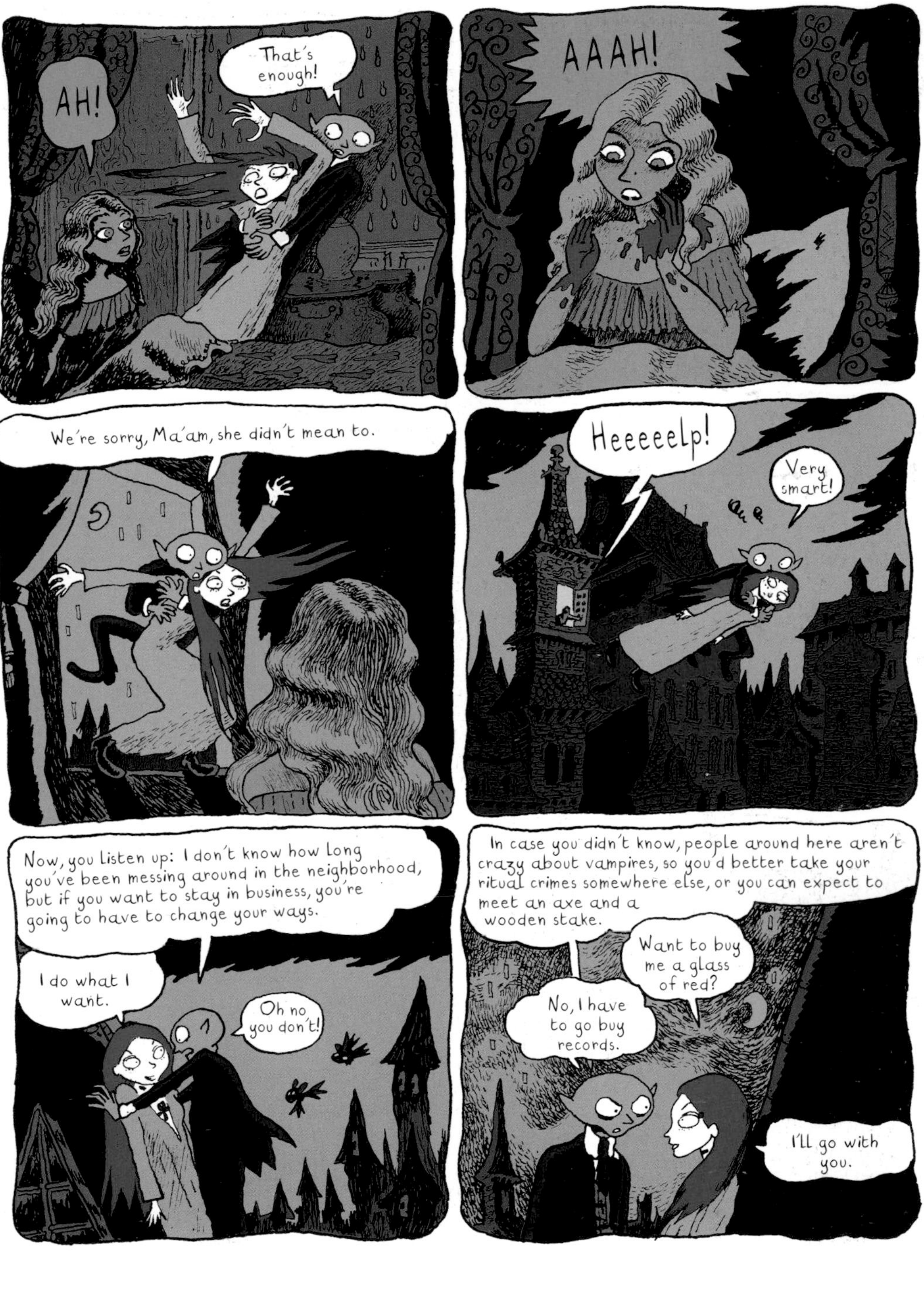
AH!
That's enough!
AAAH!
We're sorry, Ma'am, she didn't mean to.
Heeeeelp!
Very smart!
Now, you listen up: I don't know how long you've been messing around in the neighborhood, but if you want to stay in business, you're going to have to change your ways.
I do what I want.
Oh no you don't!
In case you didn't know, people around here aren't crazy about vampires, so you'd better take your ritual crimes somewhere else, or you can expect to meet an axe and a wooden stake.
Want to buy me a glass of red?
No, I have to go buy records.
I'll go with you.

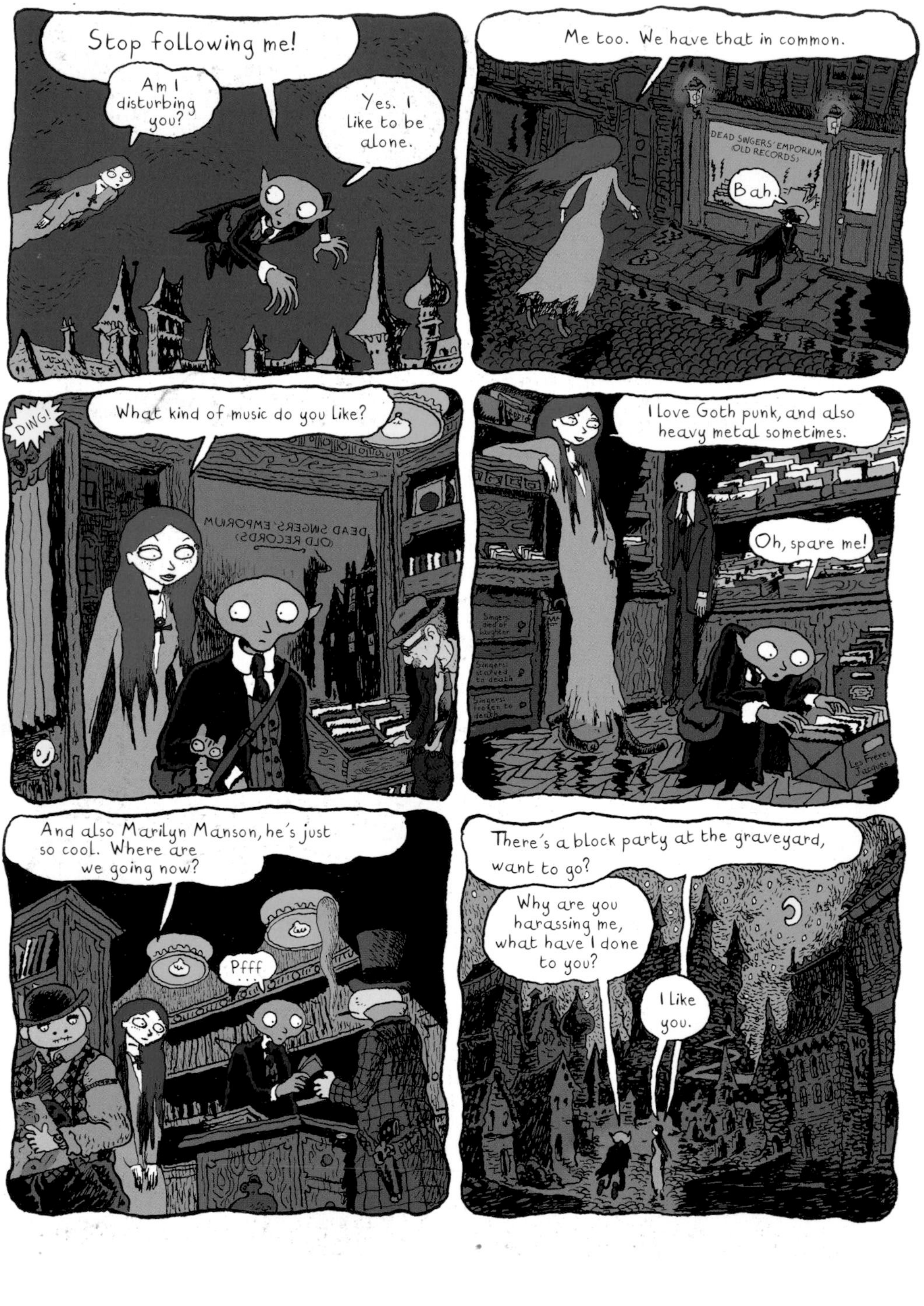
Stop following me!
Am I disturbing you?
Yes. I like to be alone.
Me too. We have that in common.
DEAD SINGERS' EMPORIUM (OLD RECORDS)
Bah.
DING!
What kind of music do you like?
I love Goth punk, and also heavy metal sometimes.
Oh, spare me!
And also Marilyn Manson, he's just so cool. Where are we going now?
Pfff...
There's a block party at the graveyard, want to go?
Why are you harassing me, what have I done to you?
I like you.

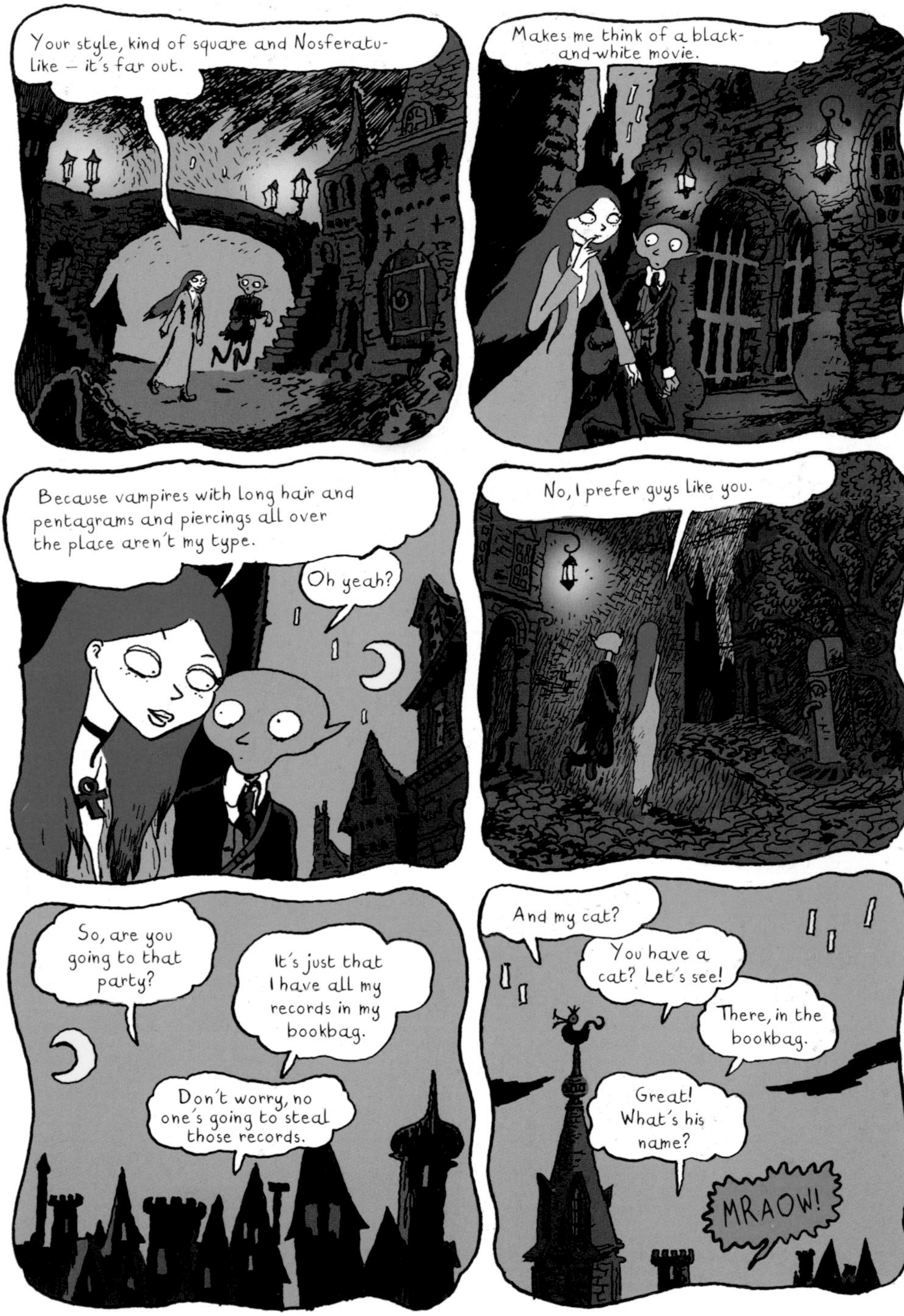
Your style, kind of square and Nosferatu-like — it's far out.
Makes me think of a black-and-white movie.
Because vampires with long hair and pentagrams and piercings all over the place aren't my type.
Oh yeah?
No, I prefer guys like you.
So, are you going to that party?
It's just that I have all my records in my bookbag.
Don't worry, no one's going to steal those records.
And my cat?
You have a cat? Let's see!
There, in the bookbag.
Great! What's his name?
MRAOW!

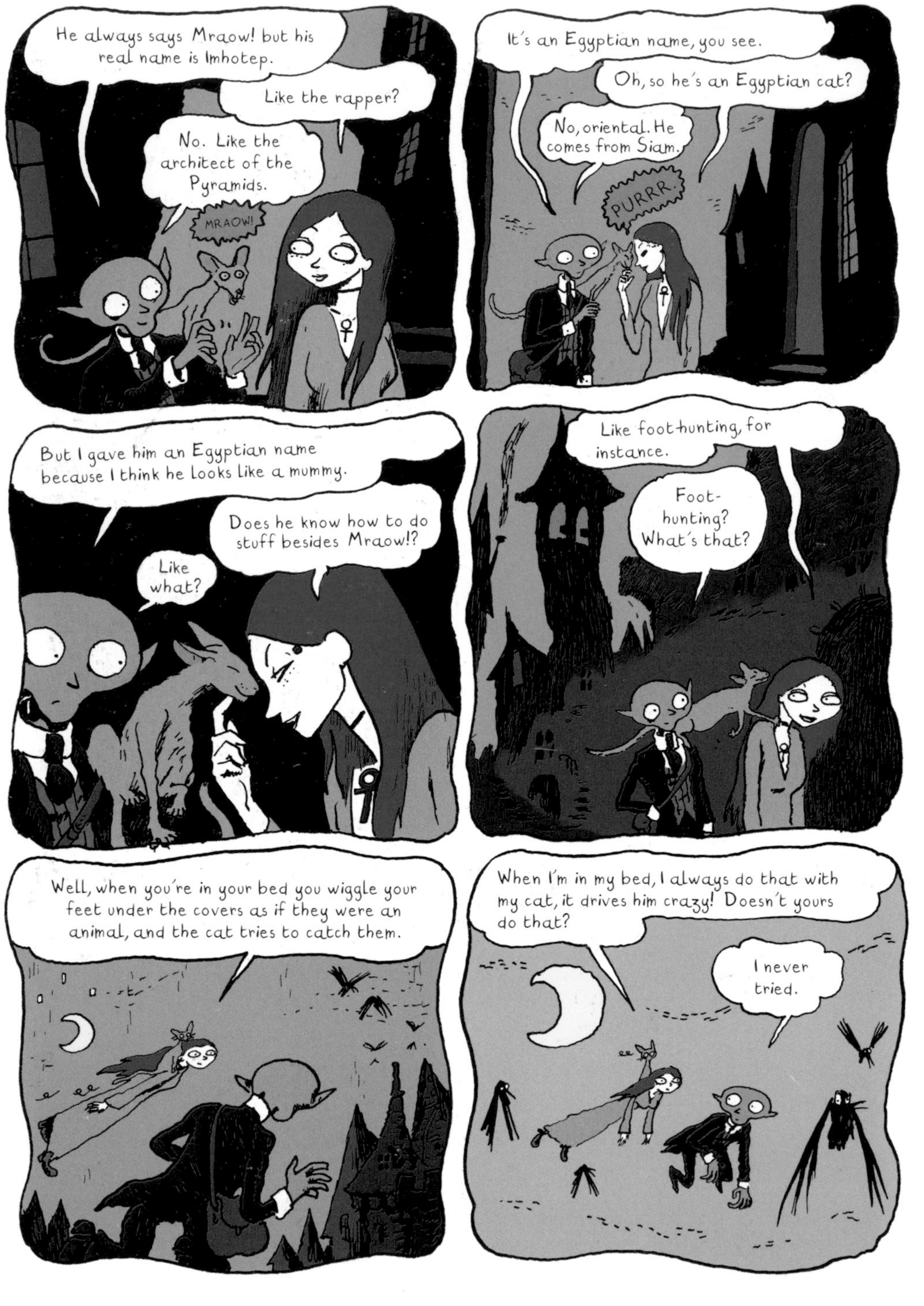
He always says Mraow! but his real name is Imhotep.
Like the rapper?
No. Like the architect of the Pyramids.
MRAOW!
It's an Egyptian name, you see.
Oh, so he's an Egyptian cat?
No, oriental. He comes from Siam.
PURRR.
But I gave him an Egyptian name because I think he looks like a mummy.
Does he know how to do stuff besides Mraow!?
Like what?
Like foot-hunting, for instance.
Foot-hunting? What's that?
Well, when you're in your bed you wiggle your feet under the covers as if they were an animal, and the cat tries to catch them.
When I'm in my bed, I always do that with my cat, it drives him crazy! Doesn't yours do that?
I never tried.

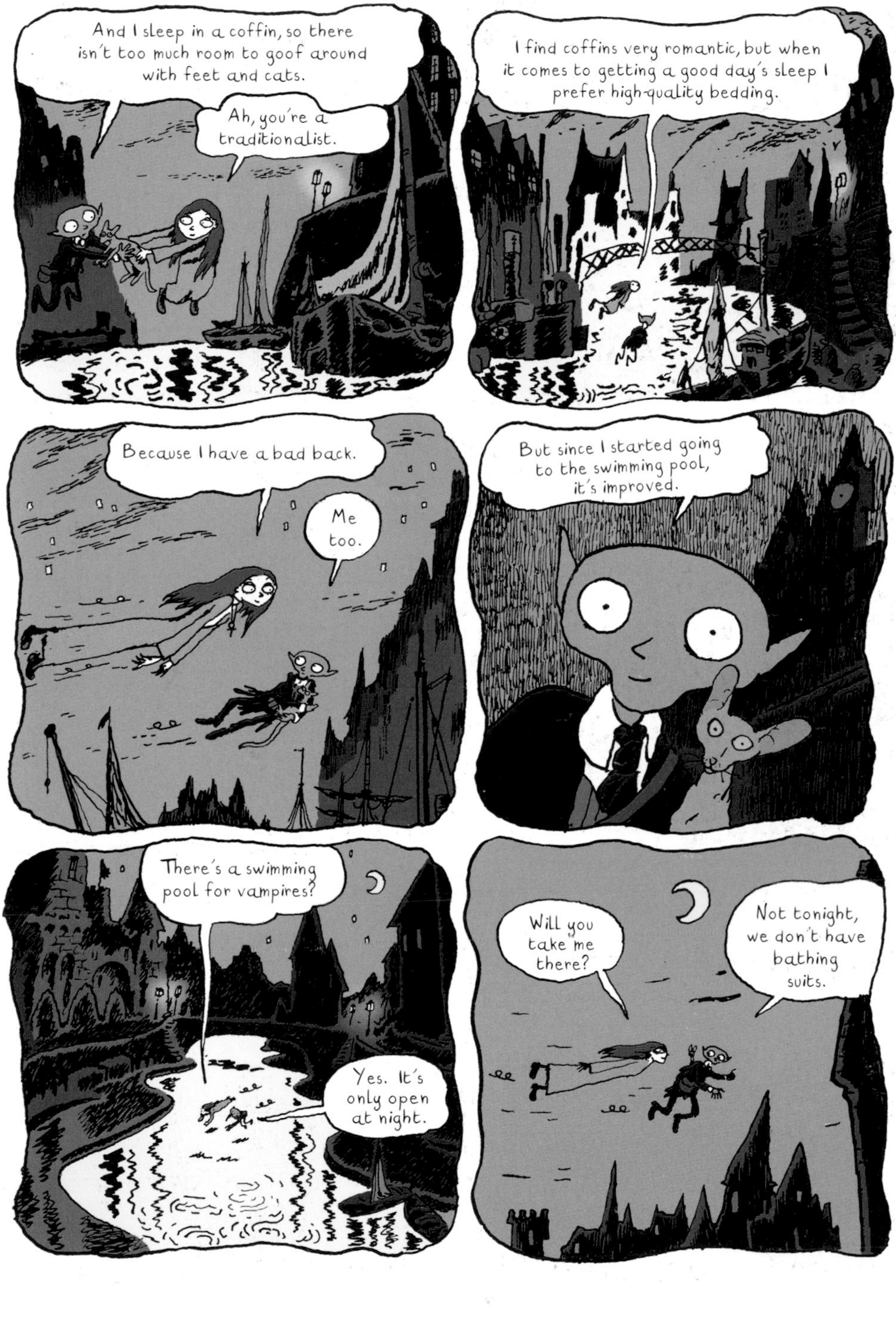

And I sleep in a coffin, so there isn't too much room to goof around with feet and cats.
Ah, you're a traditionalist.
I find coffins very romantic, but when it comes to getting a good day's sleep I prefer high-quality bedding.
Because I have a bad back.
Me too.
But since I started going to the swimming pool, it's improved.
There's a swimming pool for vampires?
Yes. It's only open at night.
Will you take me there?
Not tonight, we don't have bathing suits.

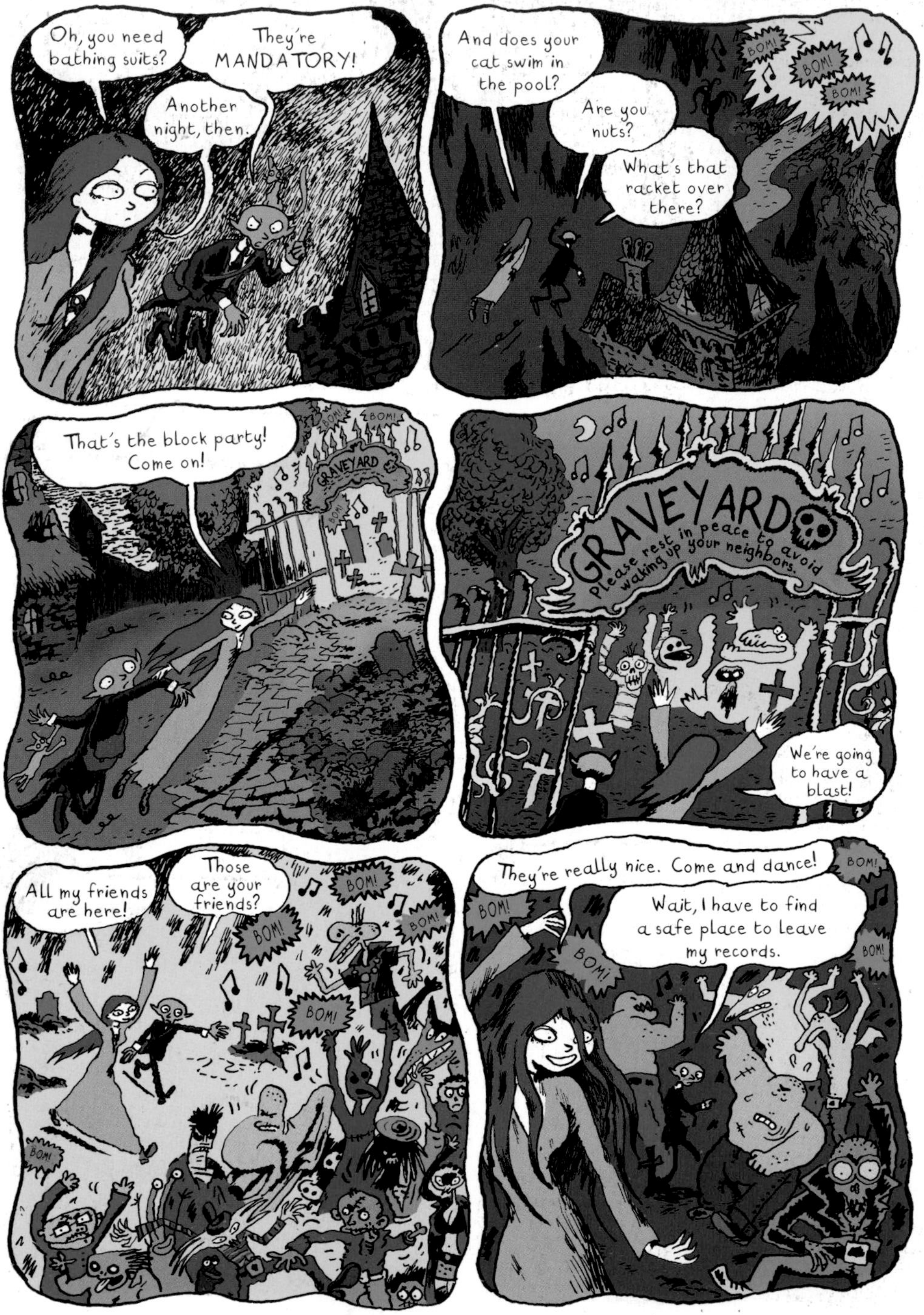
Oh, you need bathing suits?
They're MANDATORY!
Another night, then.
And does your cat swim in the pool?
Are you nuts?
What's that racket over there?
BOM!
BOM!
BOM!
That's the block party! Come on!
GRAVEYARD
Please rest in peace to avoid waking up your neighbors.
We're going to have a blast!
All my friends are here!
Those are your friends?
BOM!
They're really nice. Come and dance!
Wait, I have to find a safe place to leave my records.
BOM!

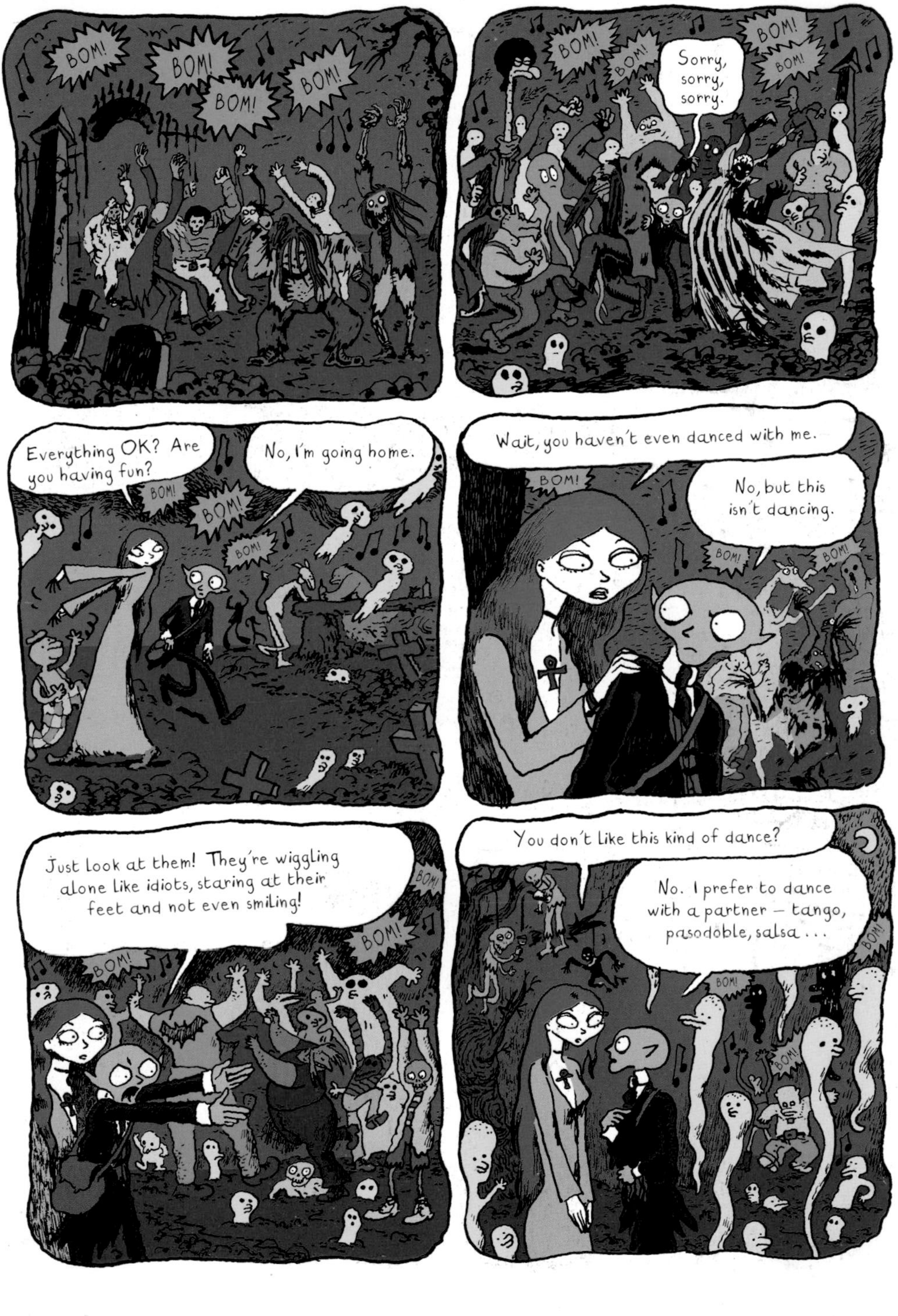
BOM!
BOM!
BOM!
BOM!
BOM!
BOM!
BOM!
BOM!
Sorry, sorry, sorry.
Everything OK? Are you having fun?
No, I'm going home.
BOM!
BOM!
BOM!
Wait, you haven't even danced with me.
No, but this isn't dancing.
BOM!
BOM!
BOM!
Just look at them! They're wiggling alone like idiots, staring at their feet and not even smiling!
BOM!
BOM!
BOM!
You don't like this kind of dance?
No. I prefer to dance with a partner – tango, pasodoble, salsa . . .
BOM!
BOM!
BOM!

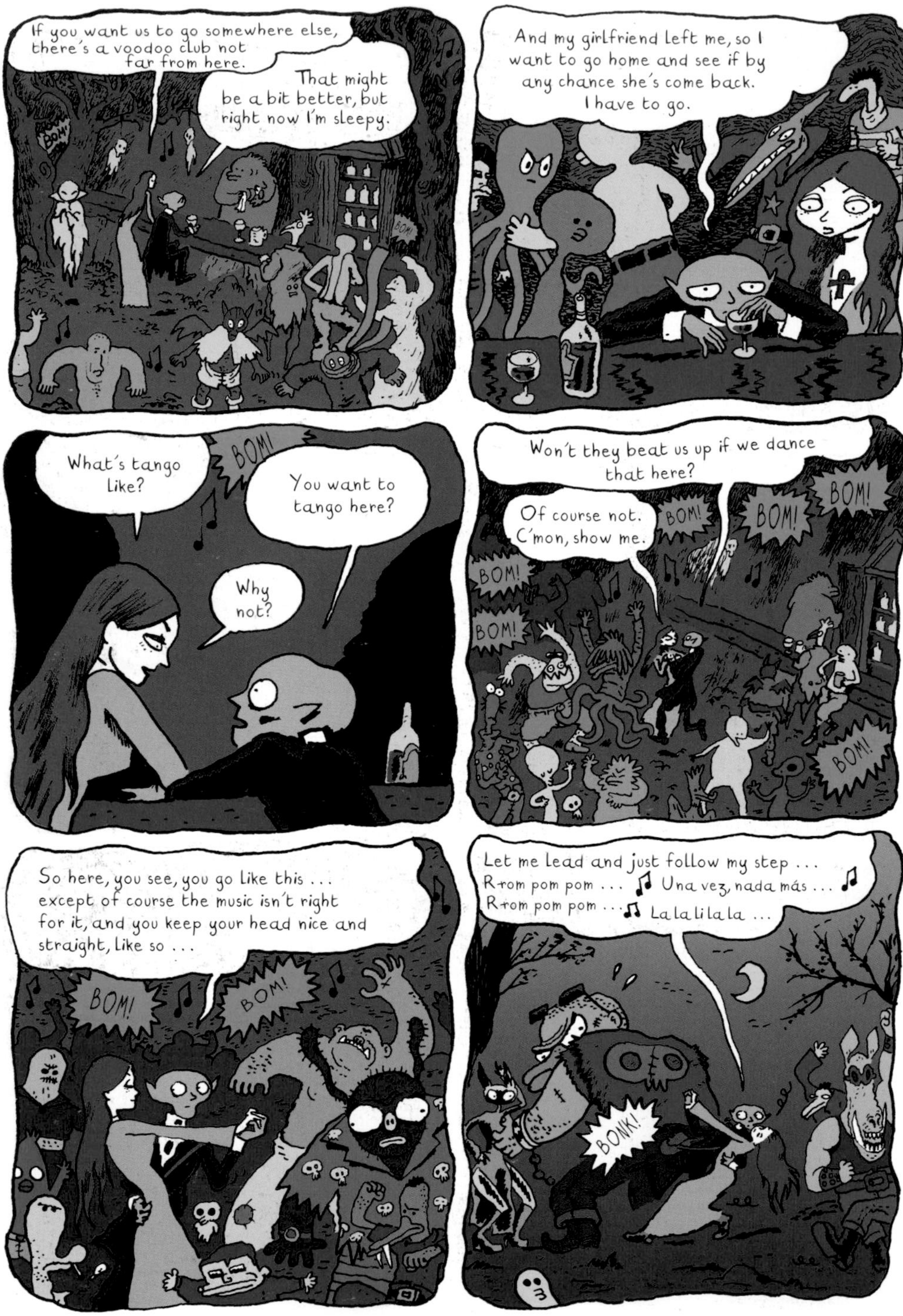
If you want us to go somewhere else, there's a voodoo club not far from here.
That might be a bit better, but right now I'm sleepy.
BOM!
BOM!
And my girlfriend left me, so I want to go home and see if by any chance she's come back. I have to go.
What's tango like?
BOM!
You want to tango here?
Why not?
Won't they beat us up if we dance that here?
Of course not. C'mon, show me.
BOM!
BOM!
BOM!
BOM!
BOM!
BOM!
So here, you see, you go like this . . . except of course the music isn't right for it, and you keep your head nice and straight, like so . . .
BOM!
BOM!
Let me lead and just follow my step . . . R-rom pom pom . . . Una vez, nada más . . . R-rom pom pom . . . Lalalilala . . .
BONK!

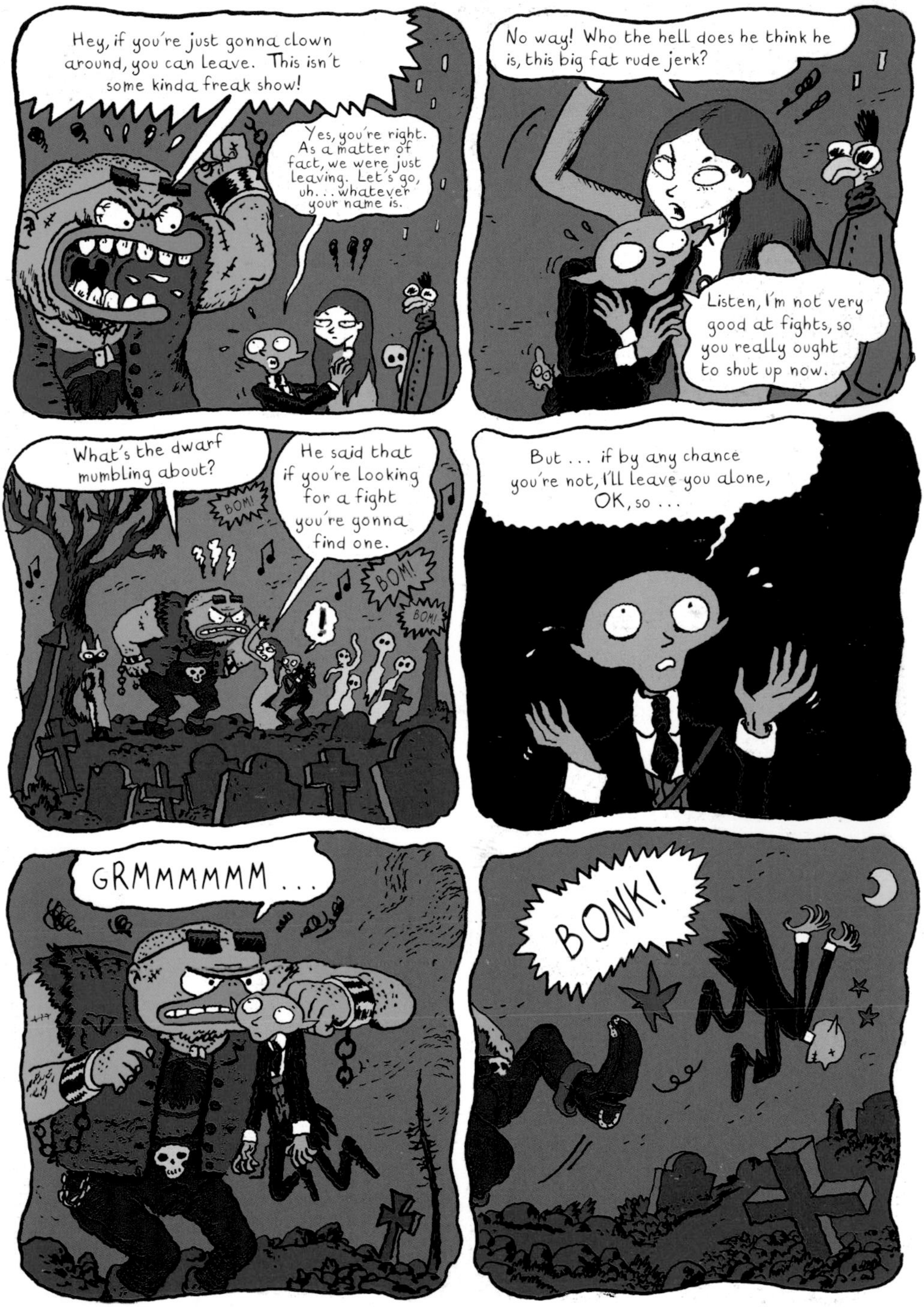
Hey, if you're just gonna clown around, you can leave. This isn't some kinda freak show!
Yes, you're right. As a matter of fact, we were just leaving. Let's go, uh... whatever your name is.
No way! Who the hell does he think he is, this big fat rude jerk?
Listen, I'm not very good at fights, so you really ought to shut up now.
What's the dwarf mumbling about?
He said that if you're looking for a fight you're gonna find one.
BOM!
BOM!
BOM!
But ... if by any chance you're not, I'll leave you alone, OK, so ...
GRMMMMMM ...
BONK!

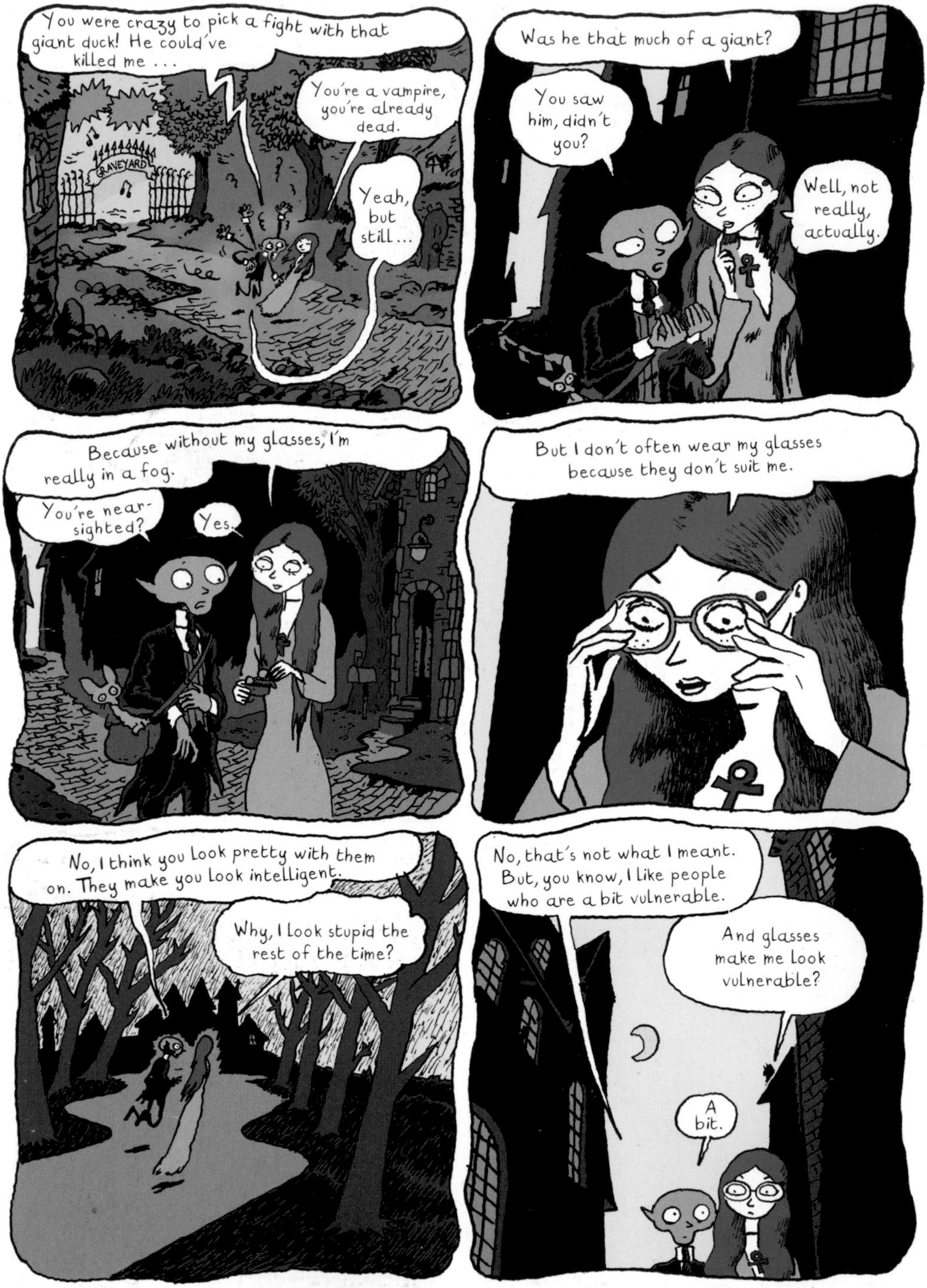
You were crazy to pick a fight with that giant duck! He could've killed me . . .
You're a vampire, you're already dead.
Yeah, but still . . .
GRAVEYARD
Was he that much of a giant?
You saw him, didn't you?
Well, not really, actually.
Because without my glasses, I'm really in a fog.
You're near-sighted?
Yes.
But I don't often wear my glasses because they don't suit me.
No, I think you look pretty with them on. They make you look intelligent.
Why, I look stupid the rest of the time?
No, that's not what I meant. But, you know, I like people who are a bit vulnerable.
And glasses make me look vulnerable?
A bit.

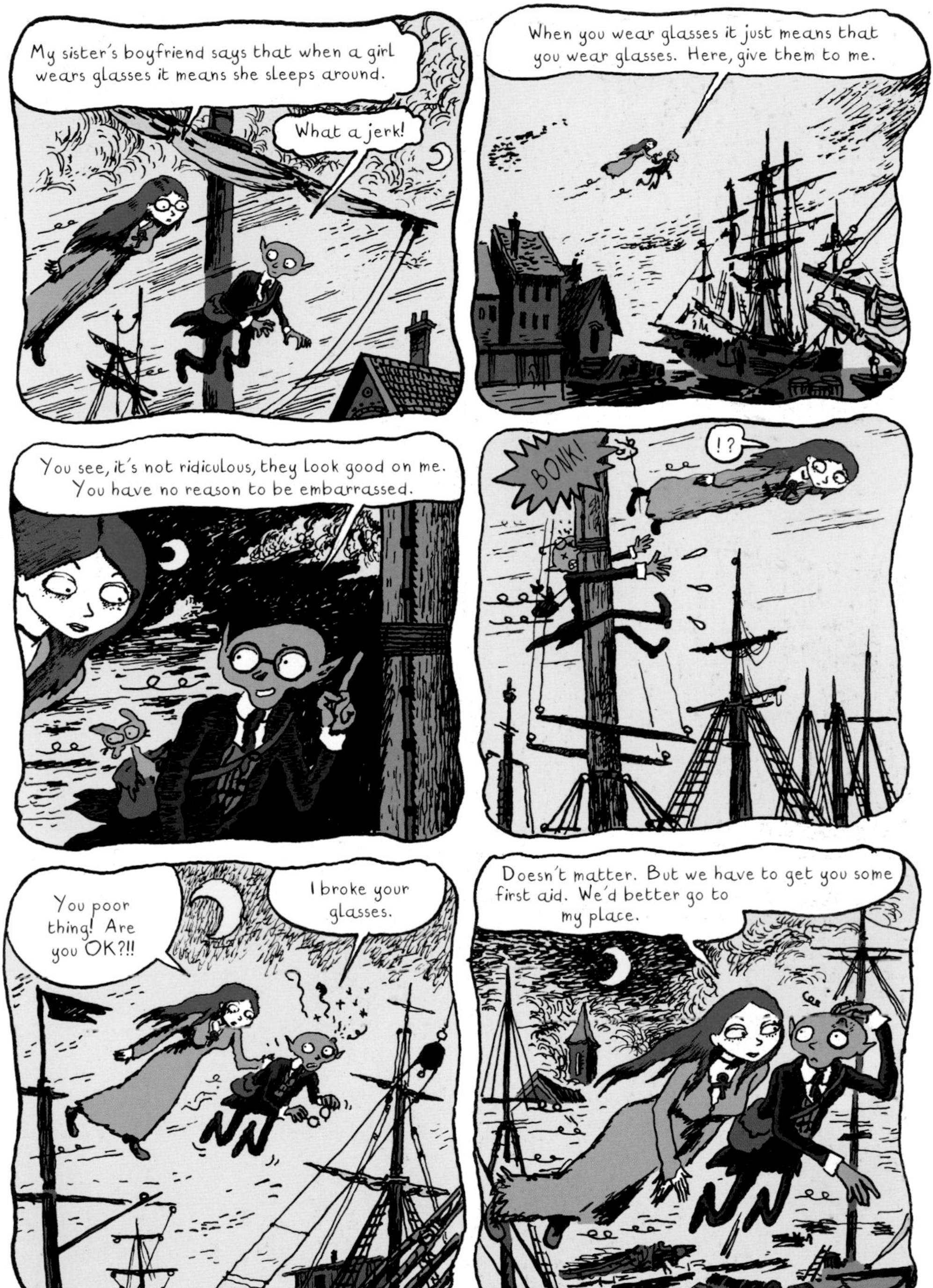
My sister's boyfriend says that when a girl wears glasses it means she sleeps around.
What a jerk!
When you wear glasses it just means that you wear glasses. Here, give them to me.
You see, it's not ridiculous, they look good on me. You have no reason to be embarrassed.
BONK!
!?
You poor thing! Are you OK?!!
I broke your glasses.
Doesn't matter. But we have to get you some first aid. We'd better go to my place.

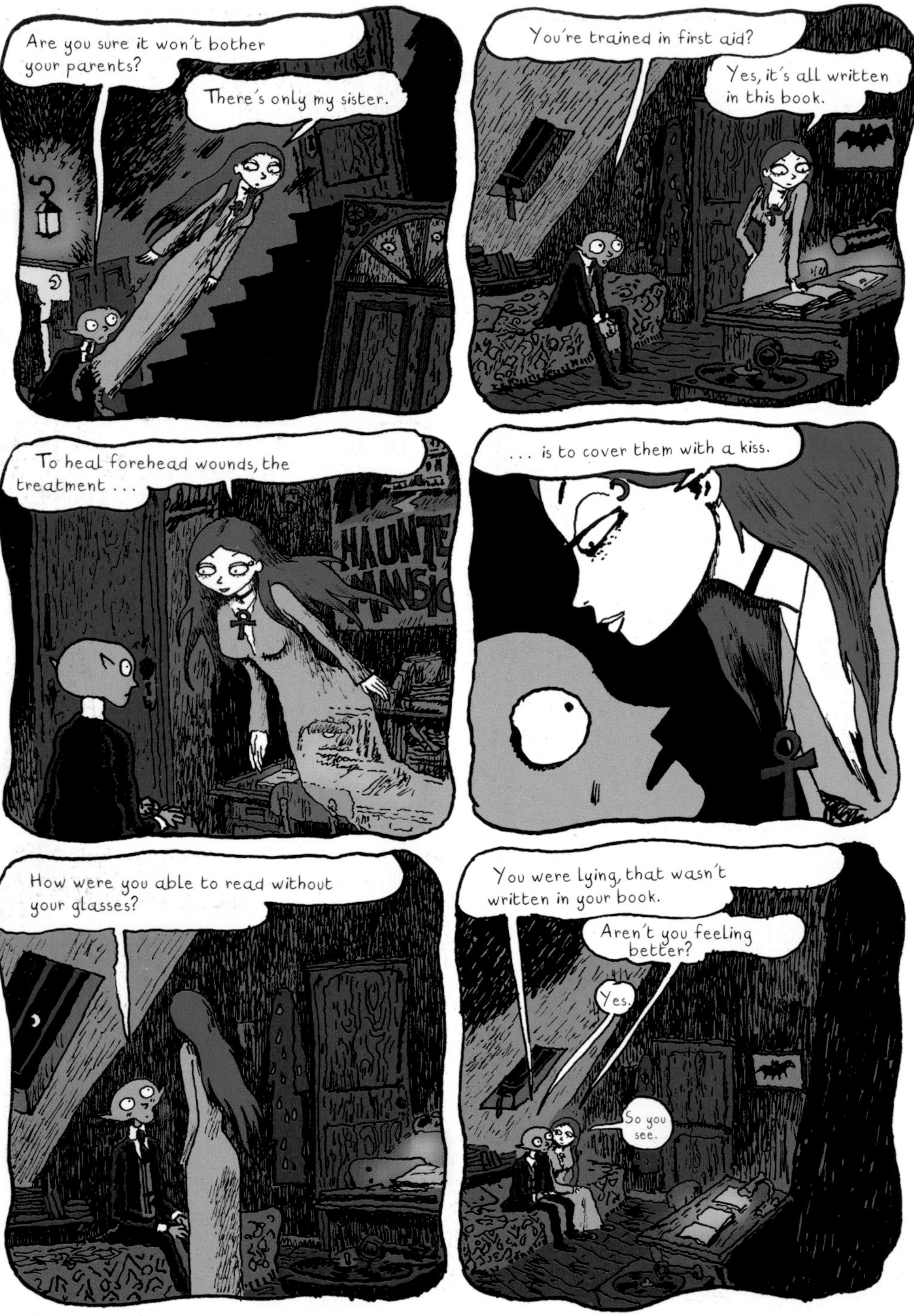
Are you sure it won't bother your parents?
There's only my sister.
You're trained in first aid?
Yes, it's all written in this book.
To heal forehead wounds, the treatment . . .
HAUNTE
MANSIO
. . . is to cover them with a kiss.
How were you able to read without your glasses?
You were lying, that wasn't written in your book.
Aren't you feeling better?
Yes.
So you see.

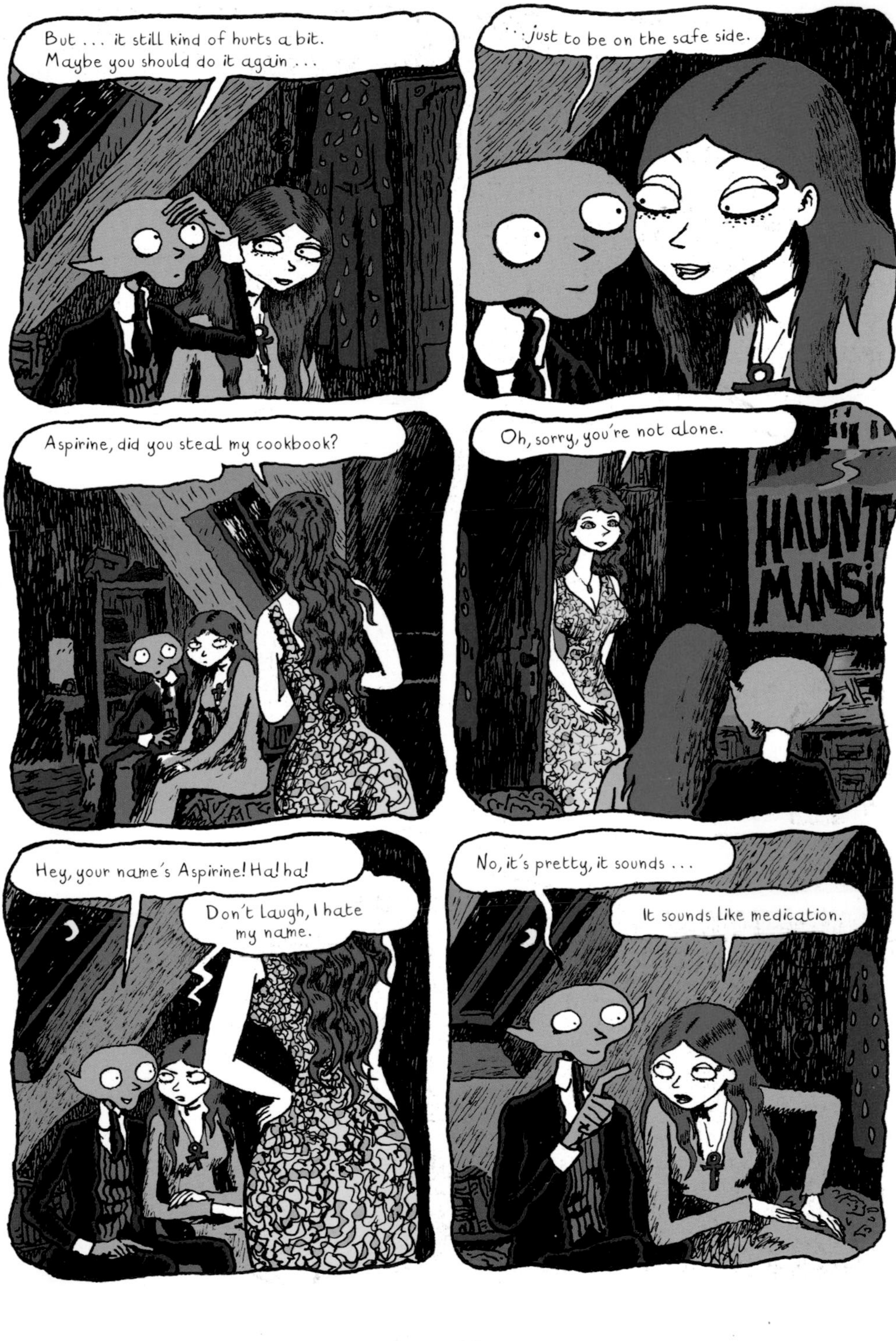
But . . . it still kind of hurts a bit. Maybe you should do it again . . .
. . . just to be on the safe side.
Aspirine, did you steal my cookbook?
Oh, sorry, you're not alone.
HAUNT
MANSI
Hey, your name's Aspirine! Ha! ha!
Don't laugh, I hate my name.
No, it's pretty, it sounds . . .
It sounds like medication.

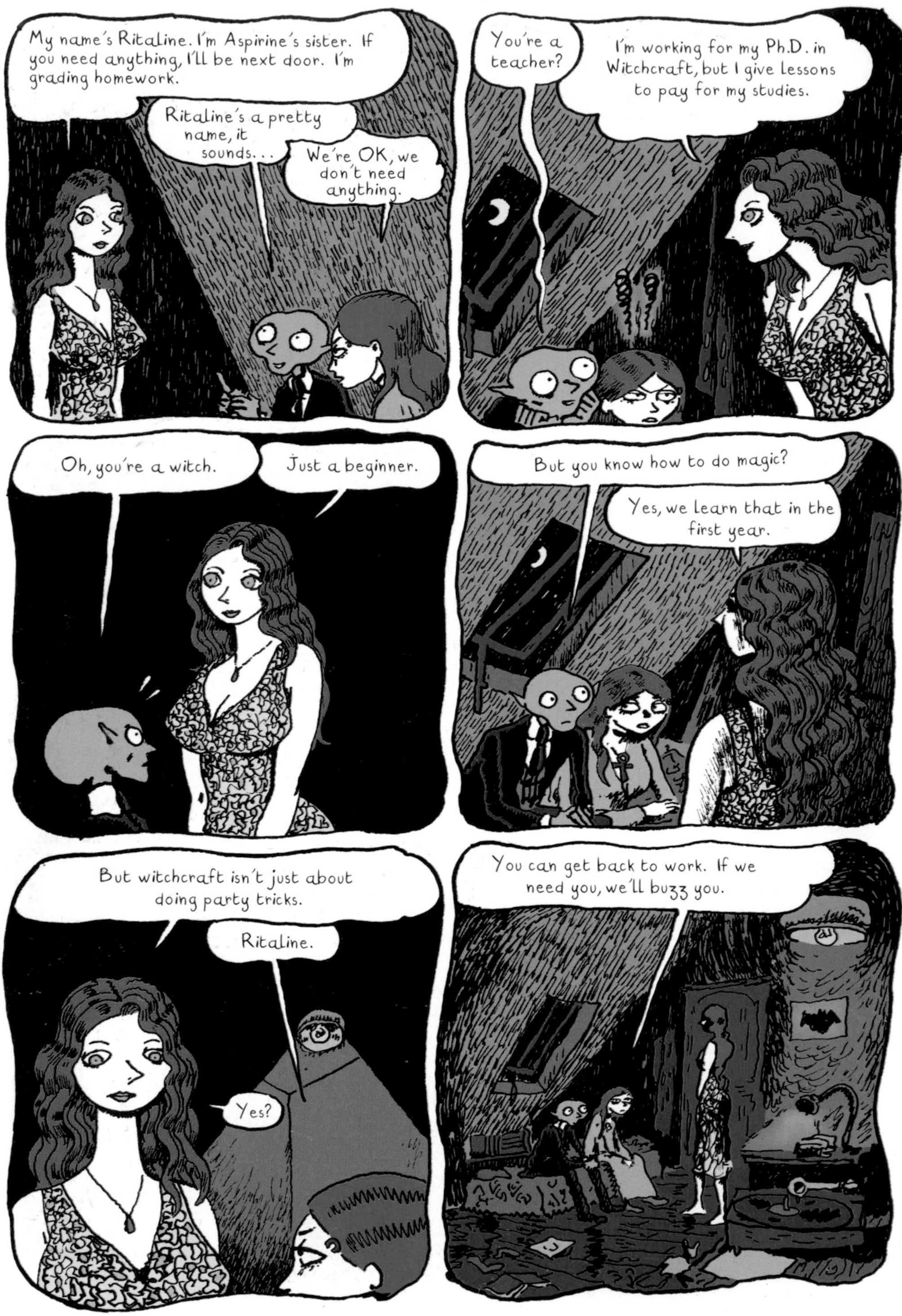

My name's Ritaline. I'm Aspirine's sister. If you need anything, I'll be next door. I'm grading homework.
Ritaline's a pretty name, it sounds...
We're OK, we don't need anything.
You're a teacher?
I'm working for my Ph.D. in Witchcraft, but I give lessons to pay for my studies.
Oh, you're a witch.
Just a beginner.
But you know how to do magic?
Yes, we learn that in the first year.
But witchcraft isn't just about doing party tricks.
Ritaline.
Yes?
You can get back to work. If we need you, we'll buzz you.

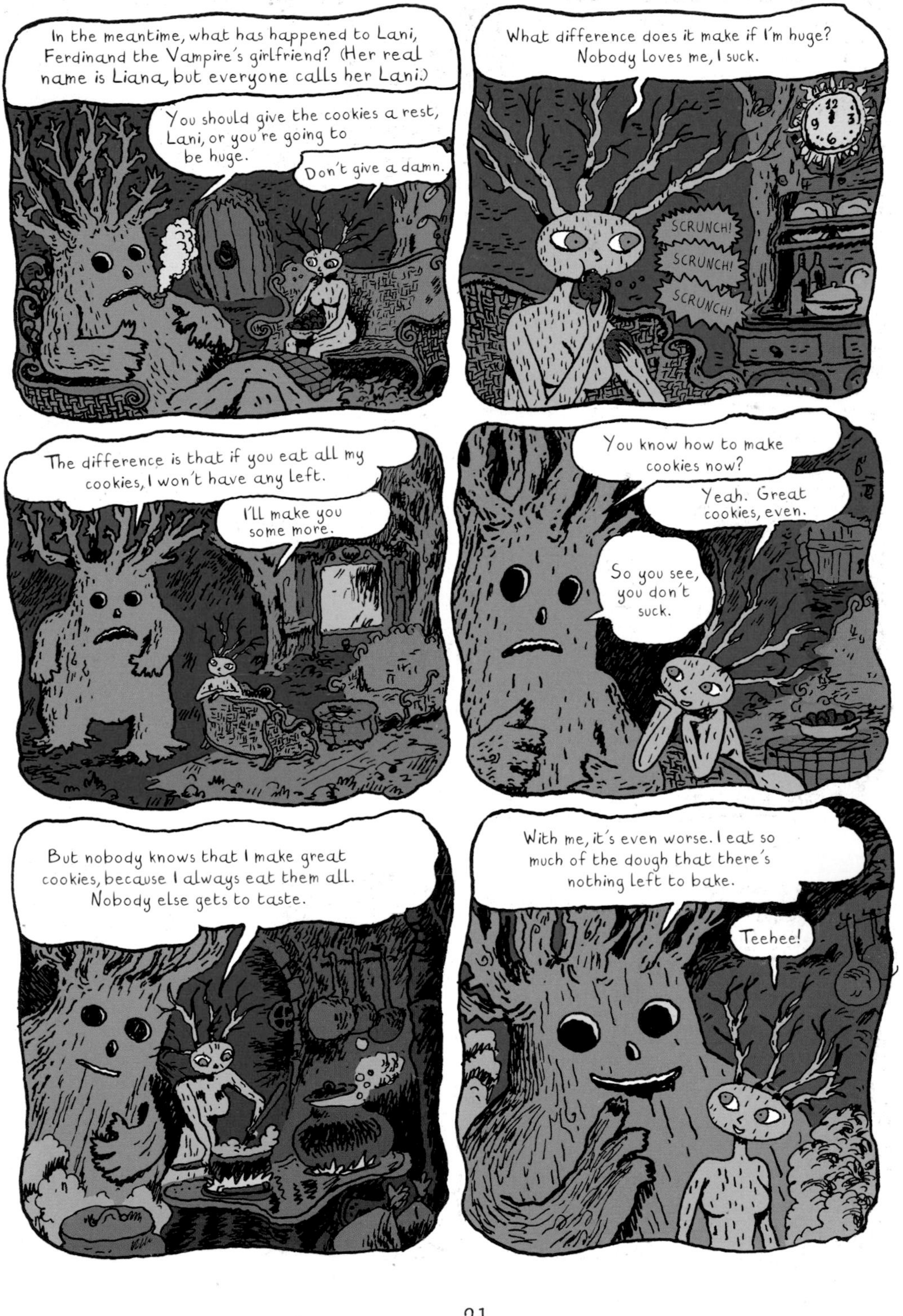
In the meantime, what has happened to Lani, Ferdinand the Vampire's girlfriend? (Her real name is Liana, but everyone calls her Lani.)
You should give the cookies a rest, Lani, or you're going to be huge.
Don't give a damn.
What difference does it make if I'm huge? Nobody loves me, I suck.
SCRUNCH!
SCRUNCH!
SCRUNCH!
The difference is that if you eat all my cookies, I won't have any left.
I'll make you some more.
You know how to make cookies now?
Yeah. Great cookies, even.
So you see, you don't suck.
But nobody knows that I make great cookies, because I always eat them all. Nobody else gets to taste.
With me, it's even worse. I eat so much of the dough that there's nothing left to bake.
Teehee!

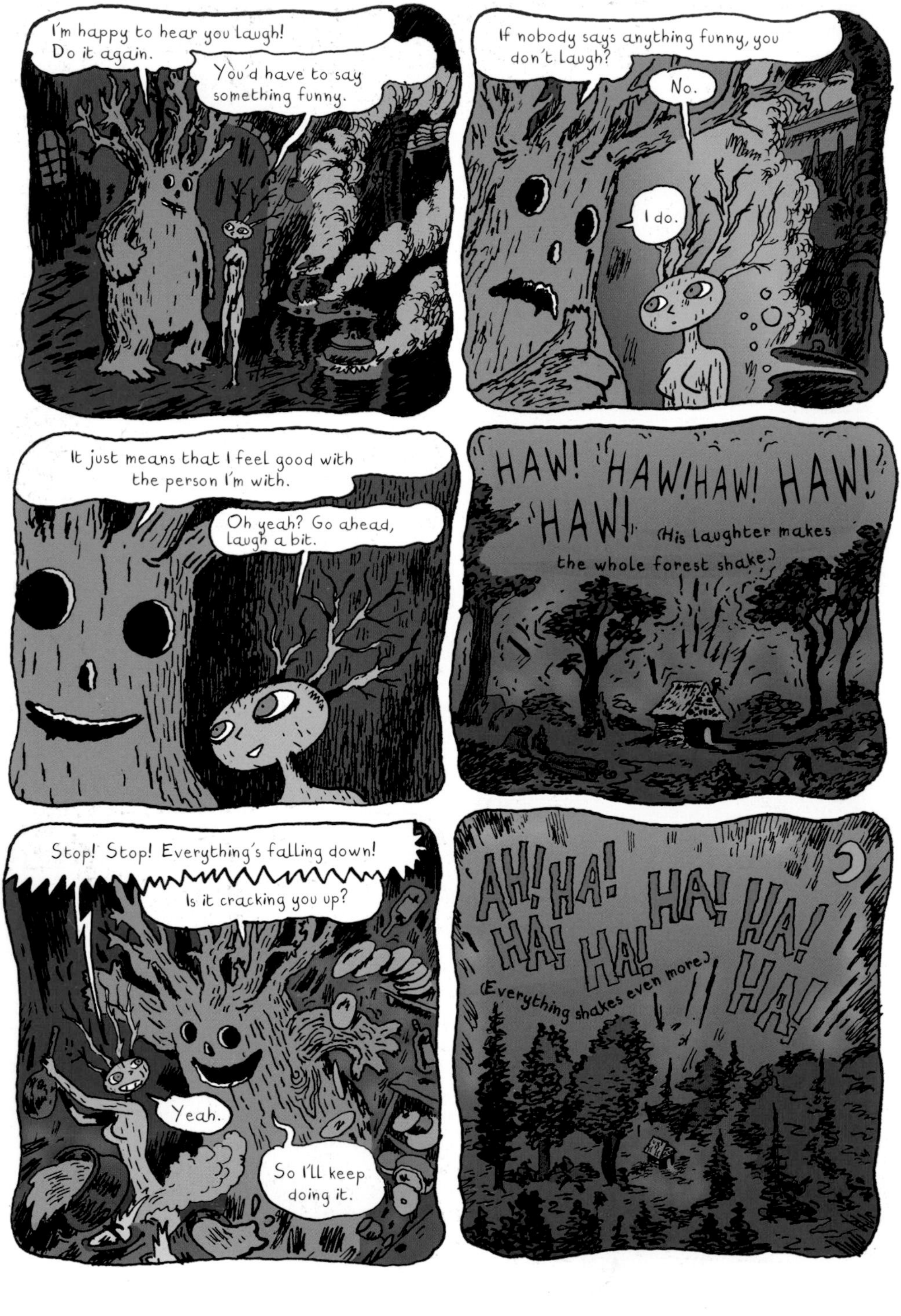
I'm happy to hear you laugh! Do it again.
You'd have to say something funny.
If nobody says anything funny, you don't laugh?
No.
I do.
It just means that I feel good with the person I'm with.
Oh yeah? Go ahead, laugh a bit.
HAW! HAW! HAW! HAW! HAW!
(His laughter makes the whole forest shake.)
Stop! Stop! Everything's falling down!
Is it cracking you up?
Yeah.
So I'll keep doing it.
AH! HA! HA! HA! HA! HA! HA! HA!
(Everything shakes even more.)

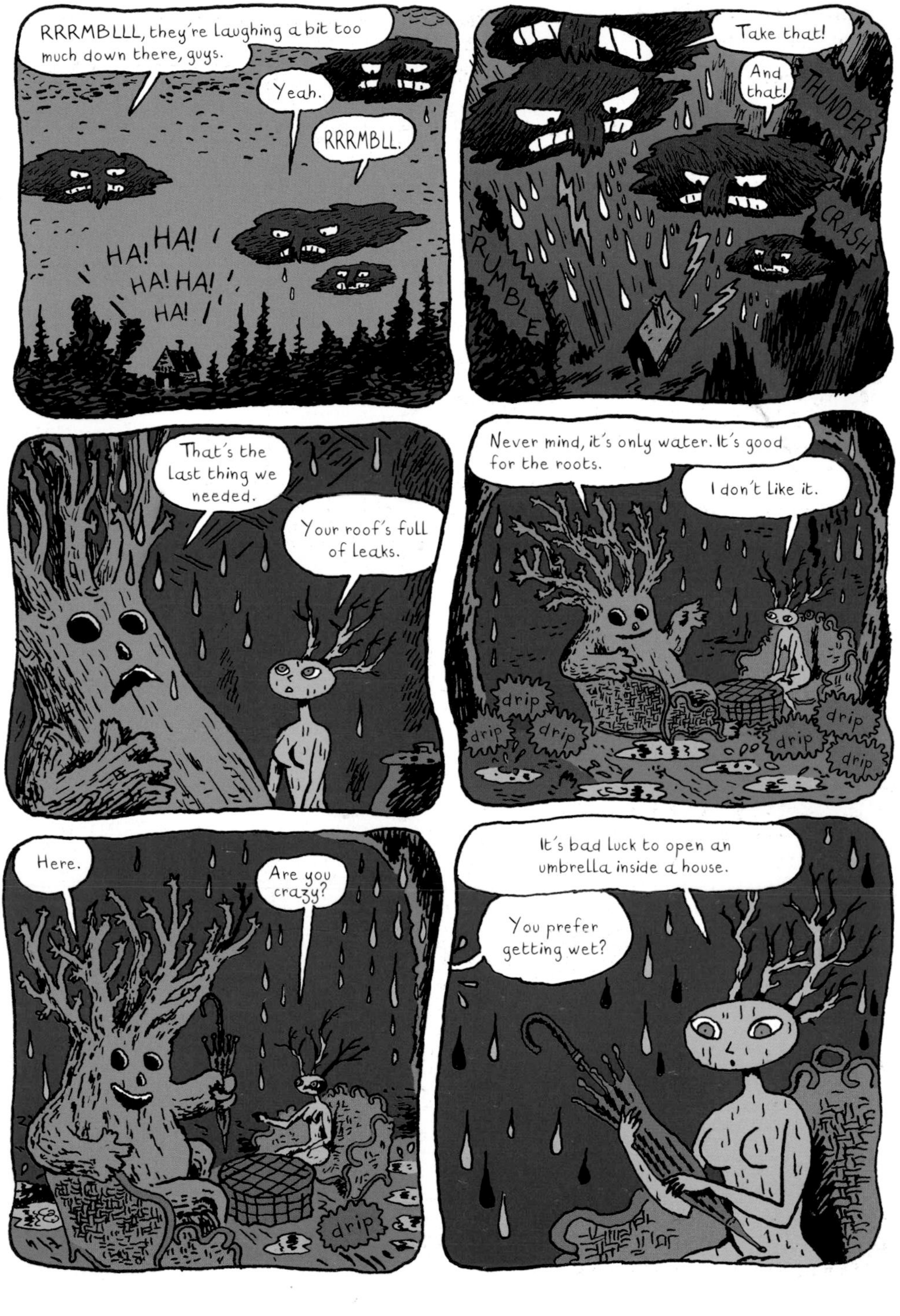
RRRMBLLL, they're laughing a bit too much down there, guys.
Yeah.
RRRMBLL.
HA! HA! HA! HA! HA!
Take that!
And that!
THUNDER
CRASH
RUMBLE
That's the last thing we needed.
Your roof's full of leaks.
Never mind, it's only water. It's good for the roots.
I don't like it.
drip drip drip drip drip drip
Here.
Are you crazy?
drip
It's bad luck to open an umbrella inside a house.
You prefer getting wet?

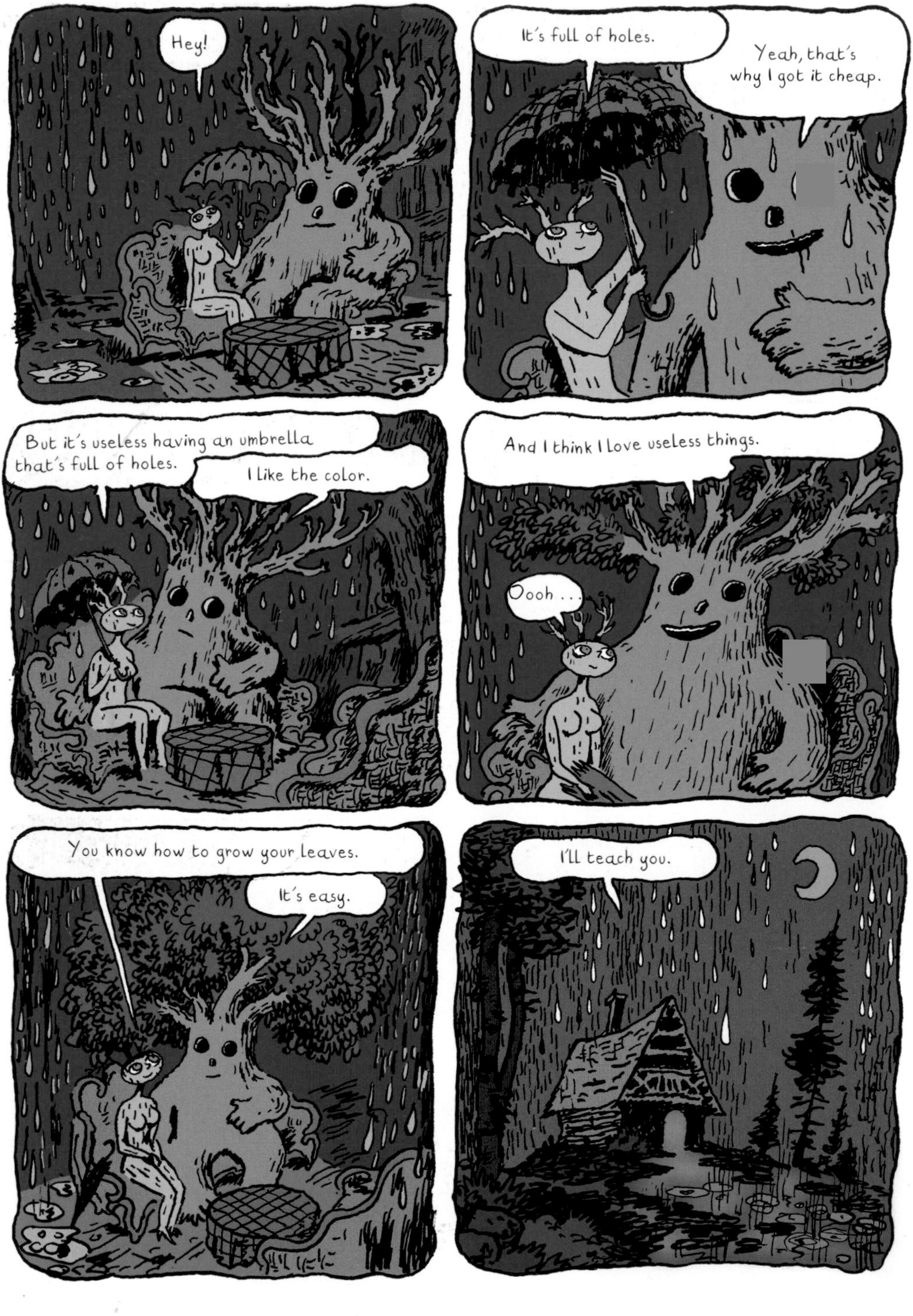
Hey!
It's full of holes.
Yeah, that's why I got it cheap.
But it's useless having an umbrella that's full of holes.
I like the color.
And I think I love useless things.
Oooh...
You know how to grow your leaves.
It's easy.
I'll teach you.

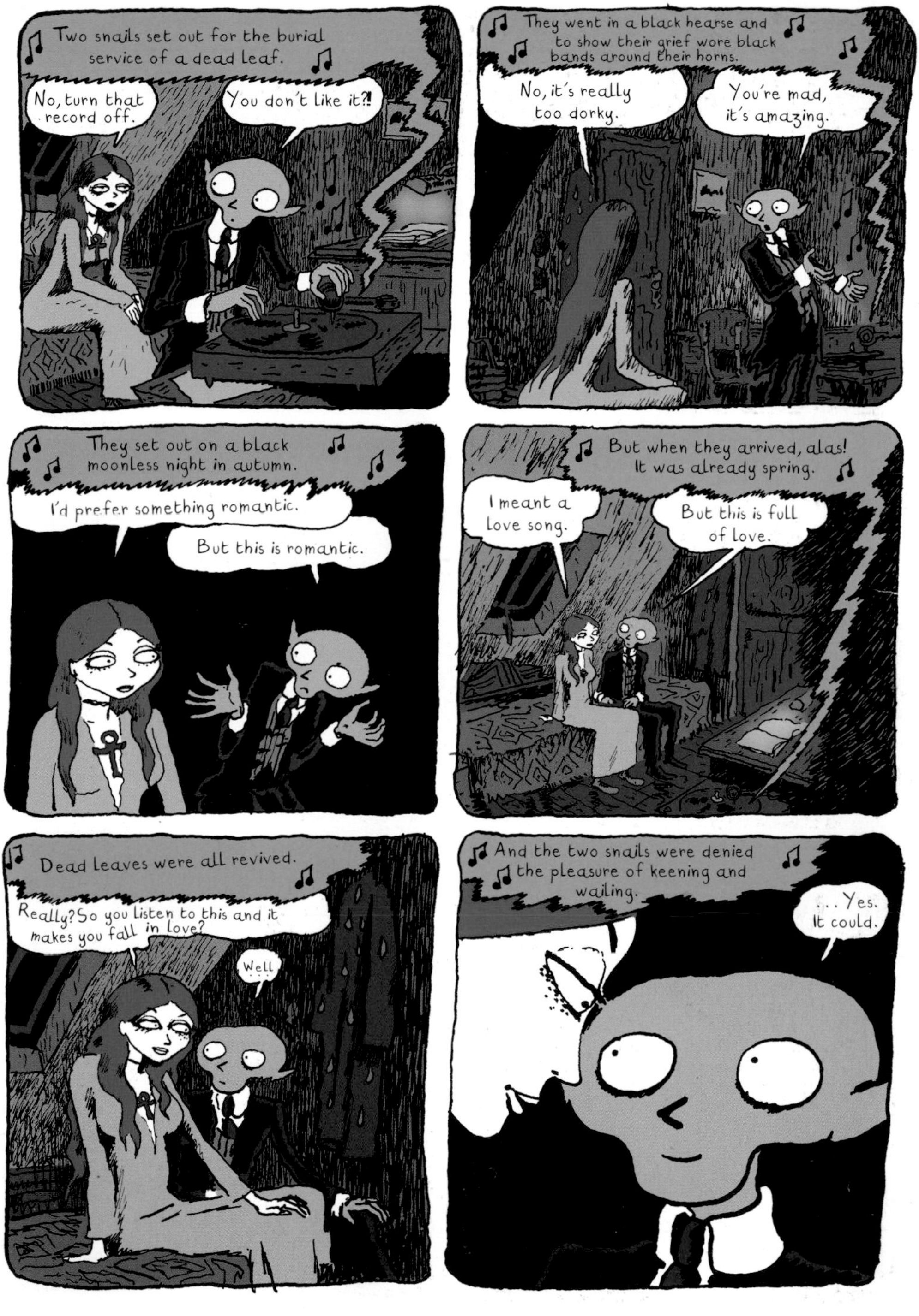
Two snails set out for the burial service of a dead leaf.
No, turn that record off.
You don't like it?!
They went in a black hearse and to show their grief wore black bands around their horns.
No, it's really too dorky.
You're mad, it's amazing.
They set out on a black moonless night in autumn.
I'd prefer something romantic.
But this is romantic.
But when they arrived, alas! It was already spring.
I meant a love song.
But this is full of love.
Dead leaves were all revived.
Really? So you listen to this and it makes you fall in love?
Well . . .
And the two snails were denied the pleasure of keening and wailing.
. . . Yes. It could.

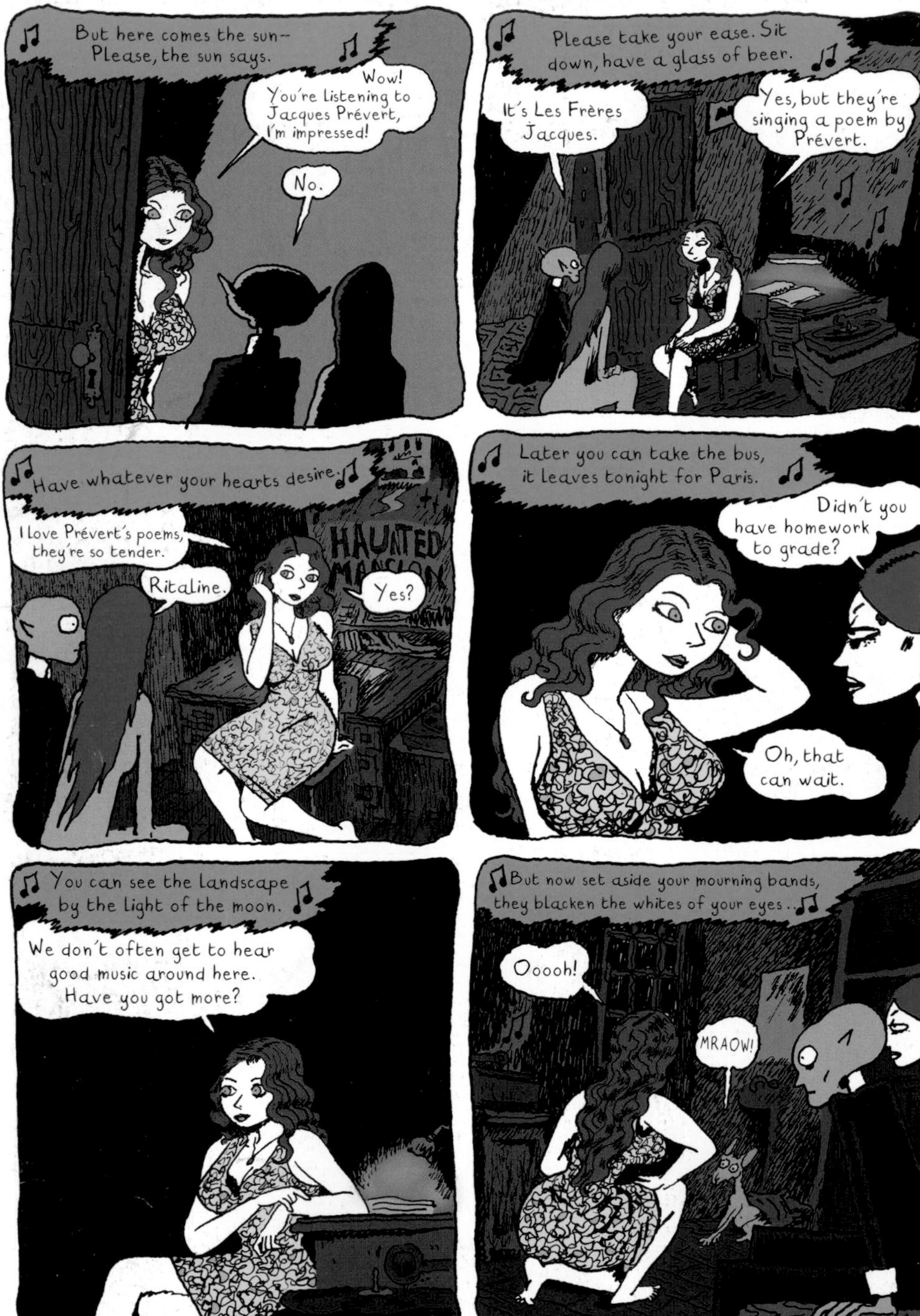
But here comes the sun-- Please, the sun says.
Wow! You're listening to Jacques Prévert, I'm impressed!
No.
Please take your ease. Sit down, have a glass of beer.
It's Les Frères Jacques.
Yes, but they're singing a poem by Prévert.
Have whatever your hearts desire.
I love Prévert's poems, they're so tender.
Ritaline.
Yes?
HAUNTED MANSION
Later you can take the bus, it leaves tonight for Paris.
Didn't you have homework to grade?
Oh, that can wait.
You can see the landscape by the light of the moon.
We don't often get to hear good music around here. Have you got more?
But now set aside your mourning bands, they blacken the whites of your eyes..
Ooooh!
MRAOW!

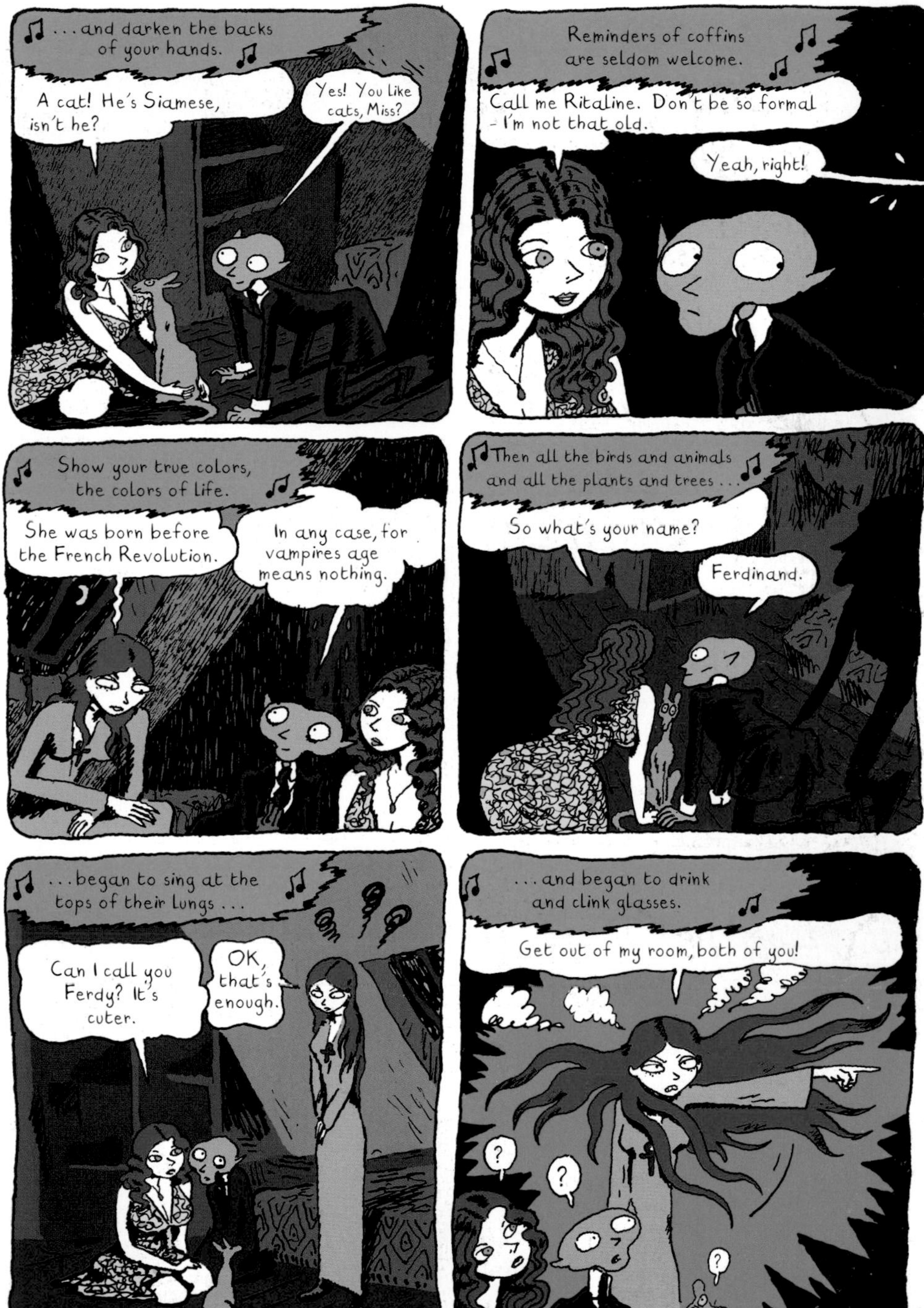
...and darken the backs of your hands.
A cat! He's Siamese, isn't he?
Yes! You like cats, Miss?
Reminders of coffins are seldom welcome.
Call me Ritaline. Don't be so formal - I'm not that old.
Yeah, right!
Show your true colors, the colors of life.
She was born before the French Revolution.
In any case, for vampires age means nothing.
Then all the birds and animals and all the plants and trees...
So what's your name?
Ferdinand.
...began to sing at the tops of their lungs...
Can I call you Ferdy? It's cuter.
OK, that's enough.
...and began to drink and clink glasses.
Get out of my room, both of you!
?
?
?

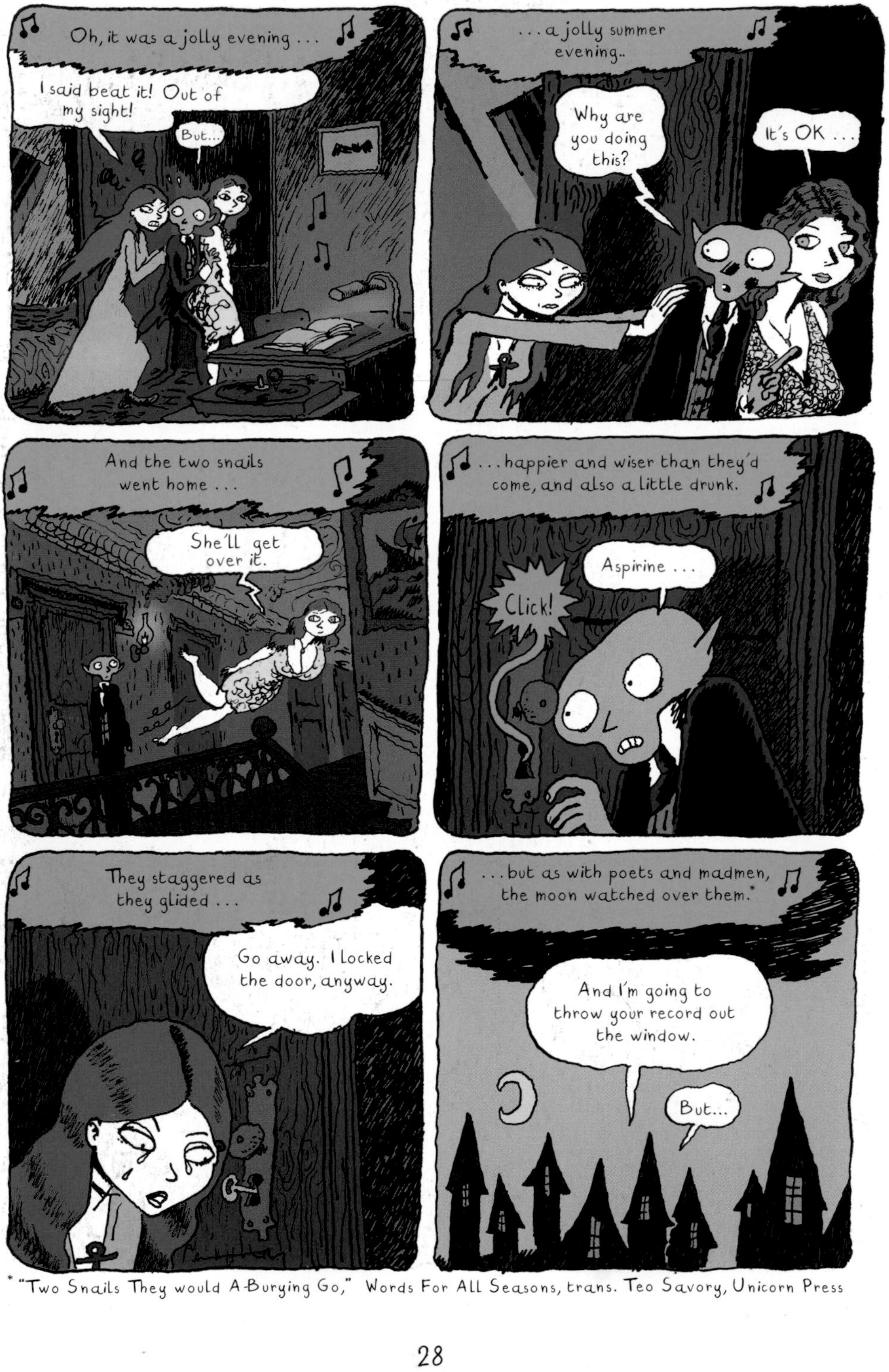
Oh, it was a jolly evening . . .
I said beat it! Out of my sight!
But...
. . . a jolly summer evening..
Why are you doing this?
It's OK . . .
And the two snails went home . . .
She'll get over it.
. . . happier and wiser than they'd come, and also a little drunk.
Click!
Aspirine . . .
They staggered as they glided . . .
Go away. I locked the door, anyway.
. . . but as with poets and madmen, the moon watched over them.*
And I'm going to throw your record out the window.
But...

* "Two Snails They would A-Burying Go," Words For All Seasons, trans. Teo Savory, Unicorn Press

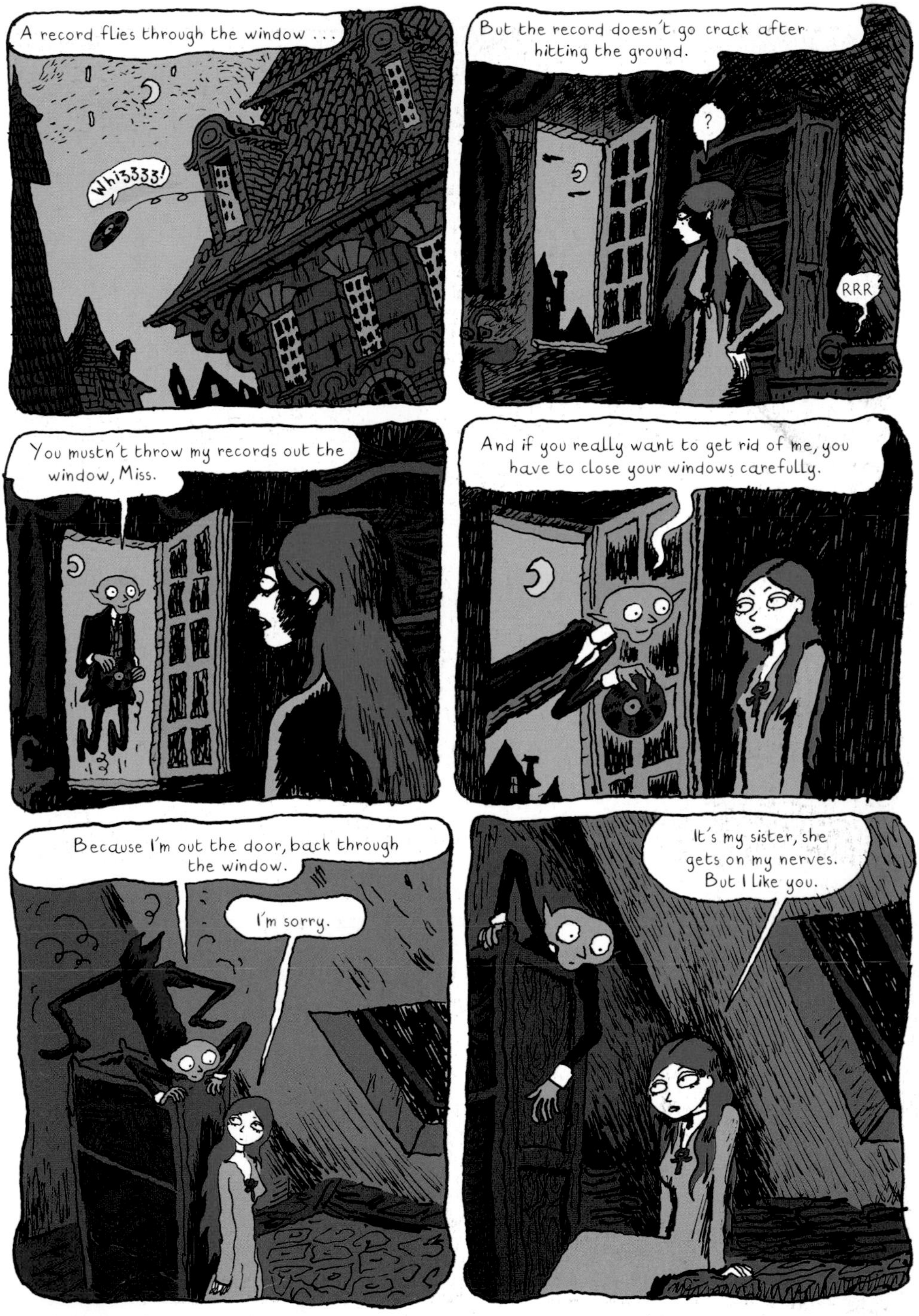
A record flies through the window . . .
Whizzzz!
But the record doesn't go crack after hitting the ground.
?
RRR
You mustn't throw my records out the window, Miss.
And if you really want to get rid of me, you have to close your windows carefully.
Because I'm out the door, back through the window.
I'm sorry.
It's my sister, she gets on my nerves. But I like you.

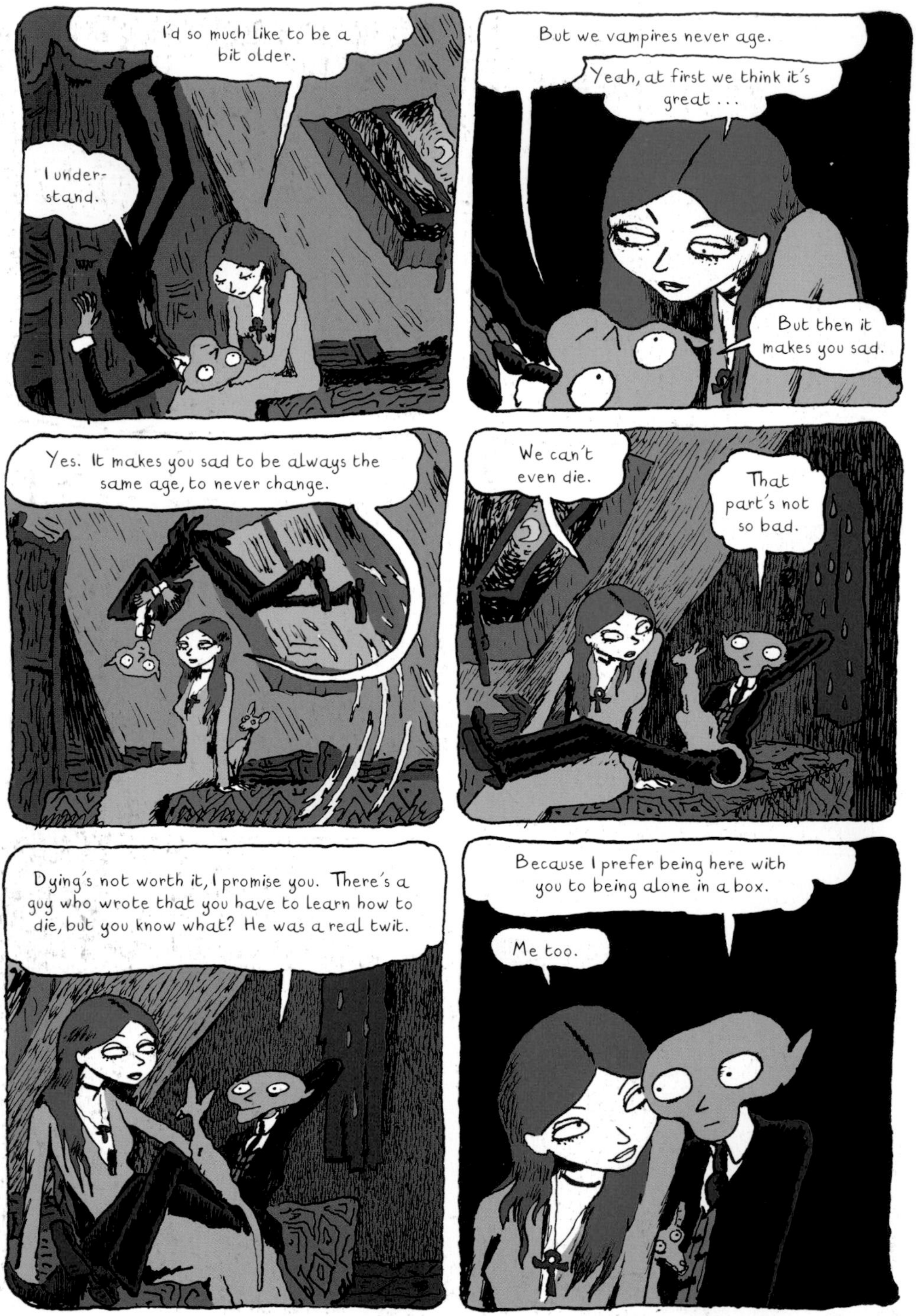
I'd so much like to be a bit older.
I under-stand.
But we vampires never age.
Yeah, at first we think it's great . . .
But then it makes you sad.
Yes. It makes you sad to be always the same age, to never change.
We can't even die.
That part's not so bad.
Dying's not worth it, I promise you. There's a guy who wrote that you have to learn how to die, but you know what? He was a real twit.
Because I prefer being here with you to being alone in a box.
Me too.

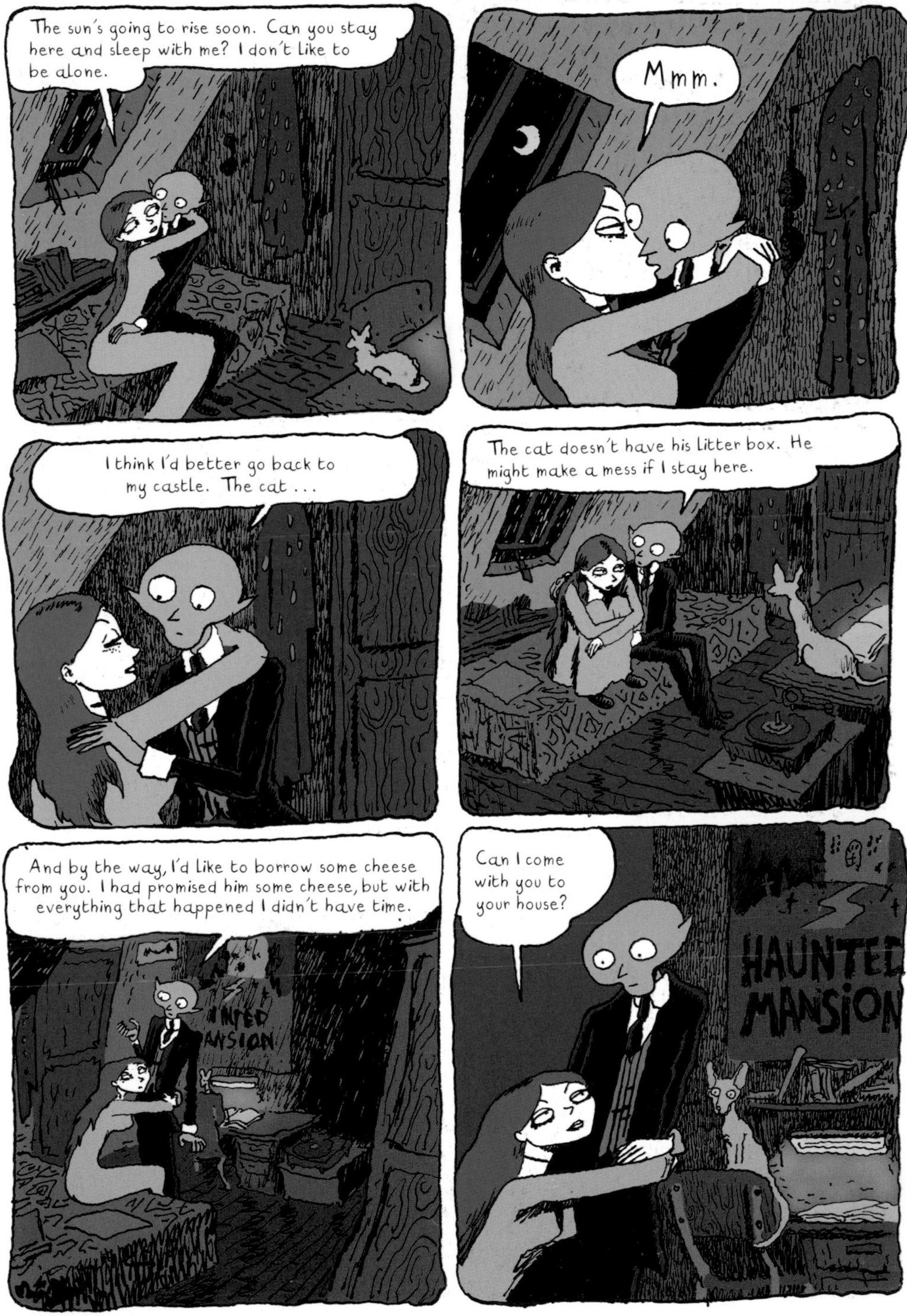
The sun's going to rise soon. Can you stay here and sleep with me? I don't like to be alone.
Mmm.
I think I'd better go back to my castle. The cat . . .
The cat doesn't have his litter box. He might make a mess if I stay here.
And by the way, I'd like to borrow some cheese from you. I had promised him some cheese, but with everything that happened I didn't have time.
Can I come with you to your house?

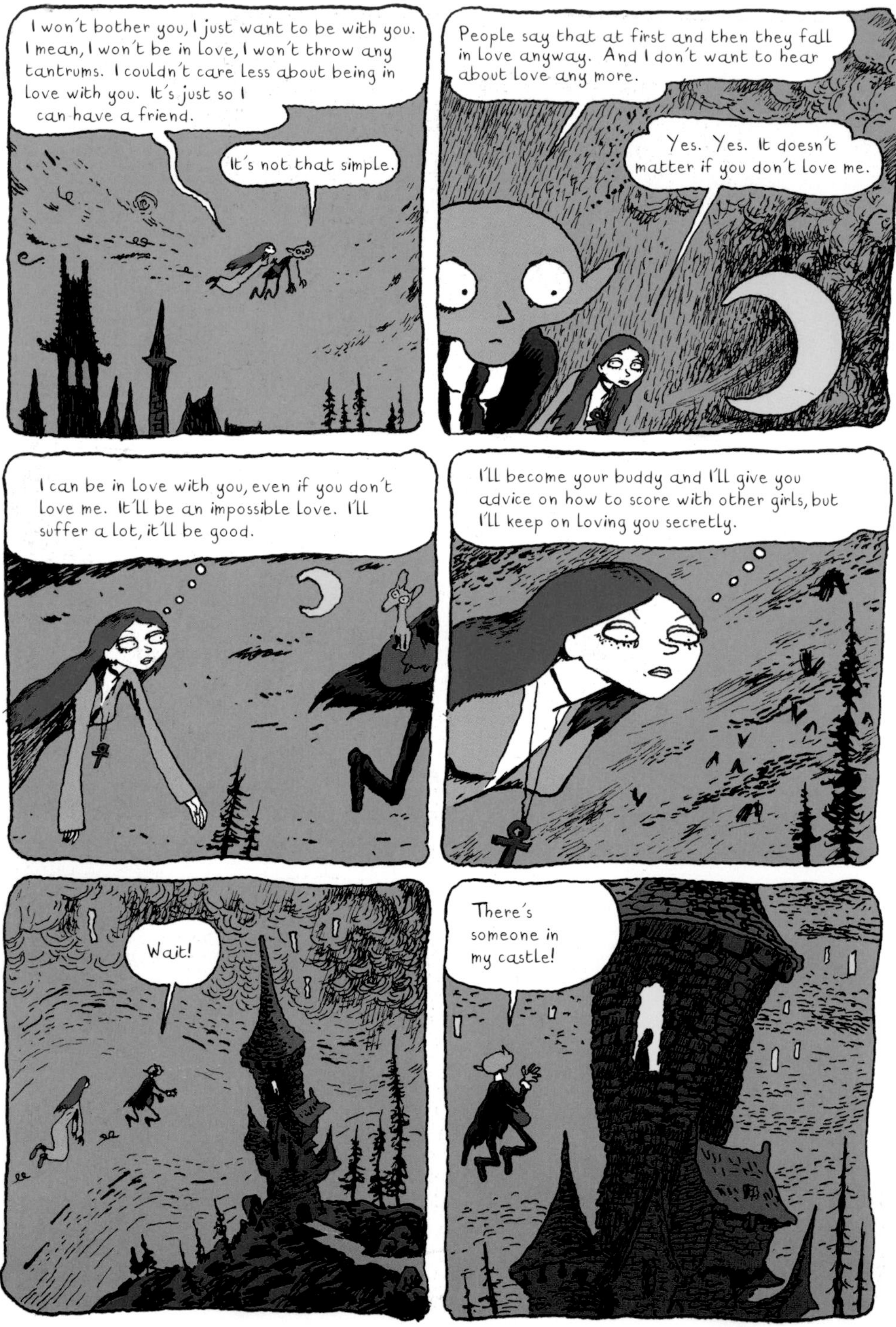
I won't bother you, I just want to be with you. I mean, I won't be in love, I won't throw any tantrums. I couldn't care less about being in love with you. It's just so I can have a friend.
It's not that simple.
People say that at first and then they fall in love anyway. And I don't want to hear about love any more.
Yes. Yes. It doesn't matter if you don't love me.
I can be in love with you, even if you don't love me. It'll be an impossible love. I'll suffer a lot, it'll be good.
I'll become your buddy and I'll give you advice on how to score with other girls, but I'll keep on loving you secretly.
Wait!
There's someone in my castle!

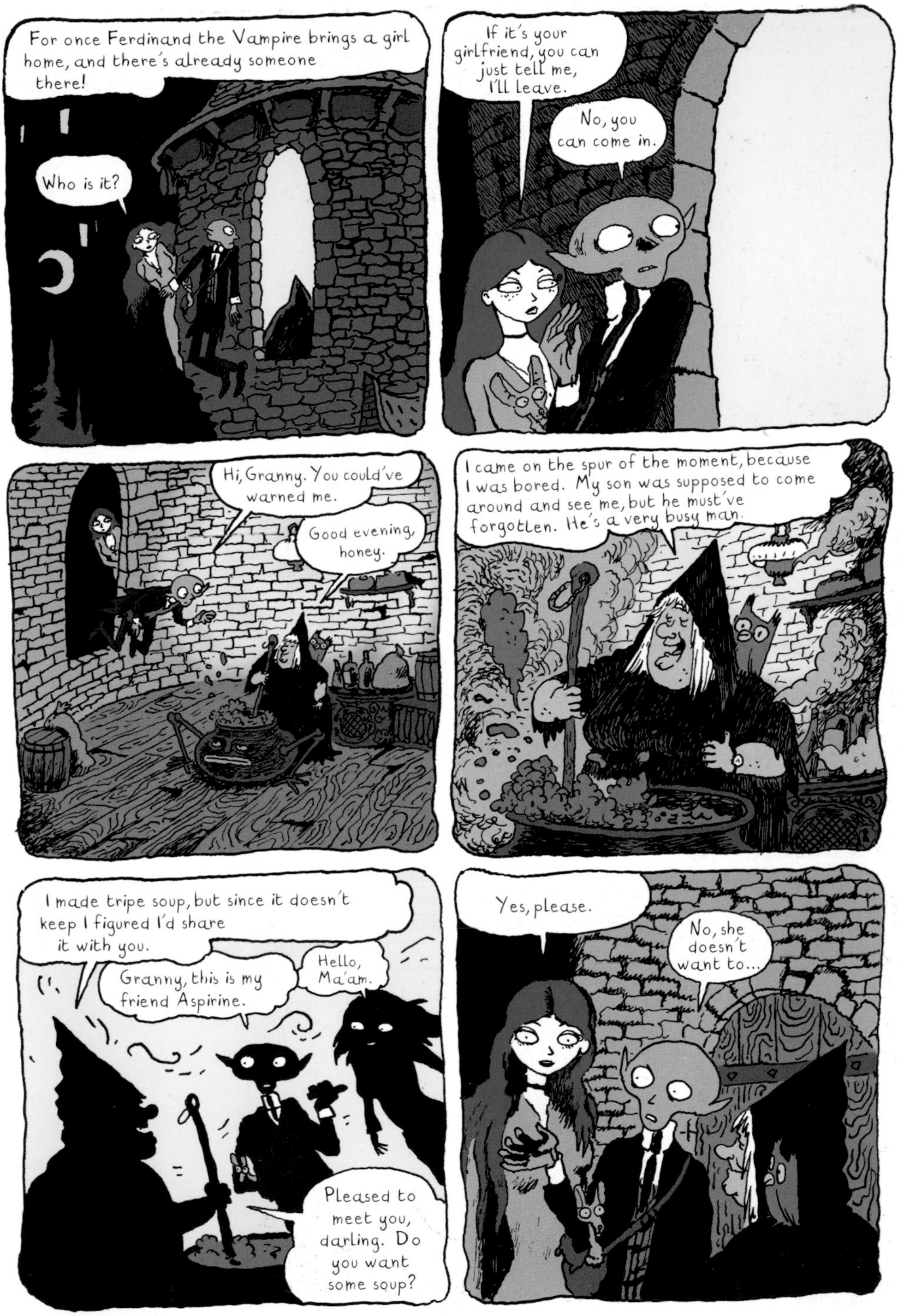
For once Ferdinand the Vampire brings a girl home, and there's already someone there!
Who is it?
If it's your girlfriend, you can just tell me, I'll leave.
No, you can come in.
Hi, Granny. You could've warned me.
Good evening, honey.
I came on the spur of the moment, because I was bored. My son was supposed to come around and see me, but he must've forgotten. He's a very busy man.
I made tripe soup, but since it doesn't keep I figured I'd share it with you.
Granny, this is my friend Aspirine.
Hello, Ma'am.
Pleased to meet you, darling. Do you want some soup?
Yes, please.
No, she doesn't want to...

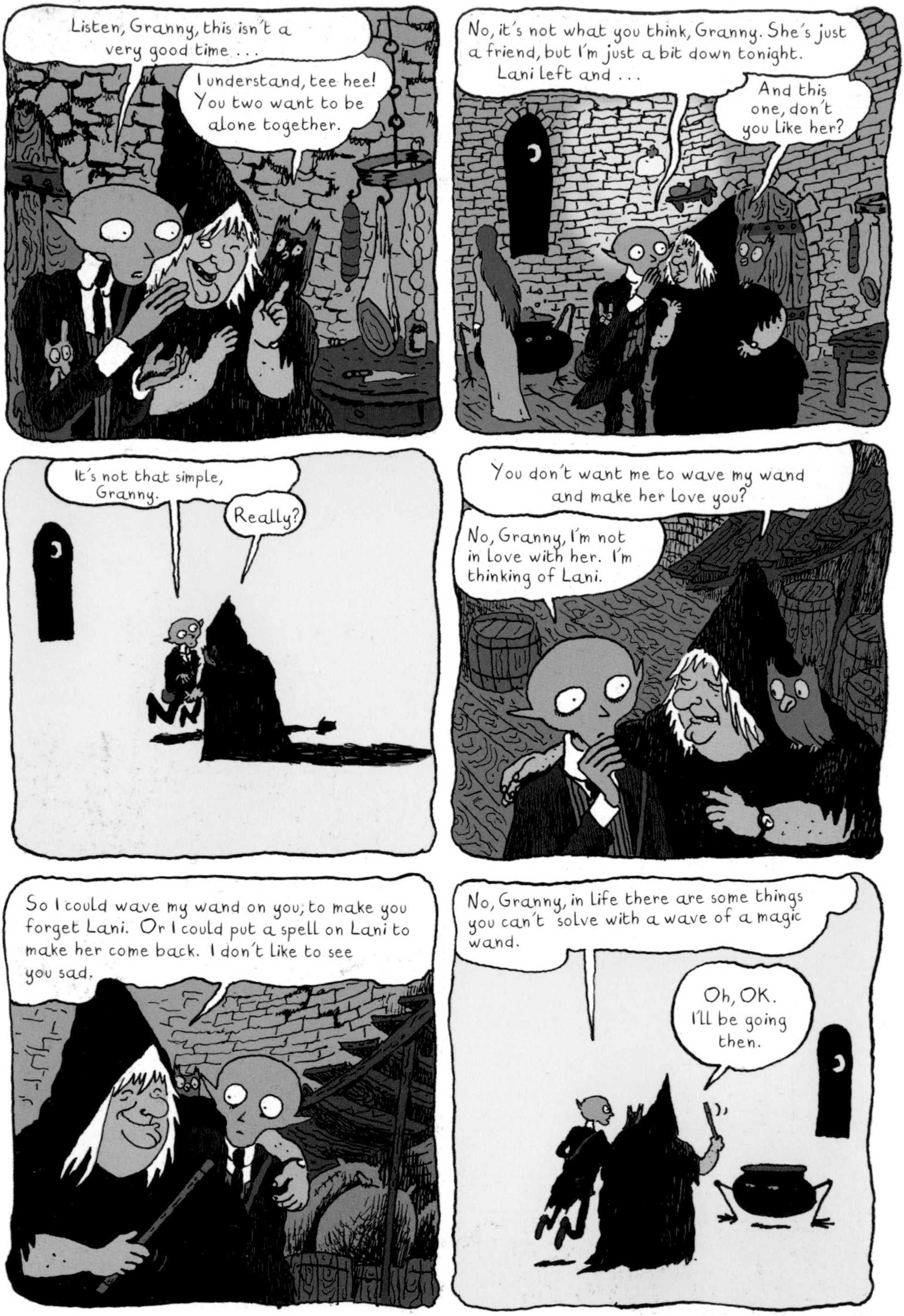

Listen, Granny, this isn't a very good time . . .
I understand, tee hee! You two want to be alone together.
No, it's not what you think, Granny. She's just a friend, but I'm just a bit down tonight. Lani left and . . .
And this one, don't you like her?
It's not that simple, Granny.
Really?
You don't want me to wave my wand and make her love you?
No, Granny, I'm not in love with her. I'm thinking of Lani.
So I could wave my wand on you, to make you forget Lani. Or I could put a spell on Lani to make her come back. I don't like to see you sad.
No, Granny, in life there are some things you can't solve with a wave of a magic wand.
Oh, OK. I'll be going then.

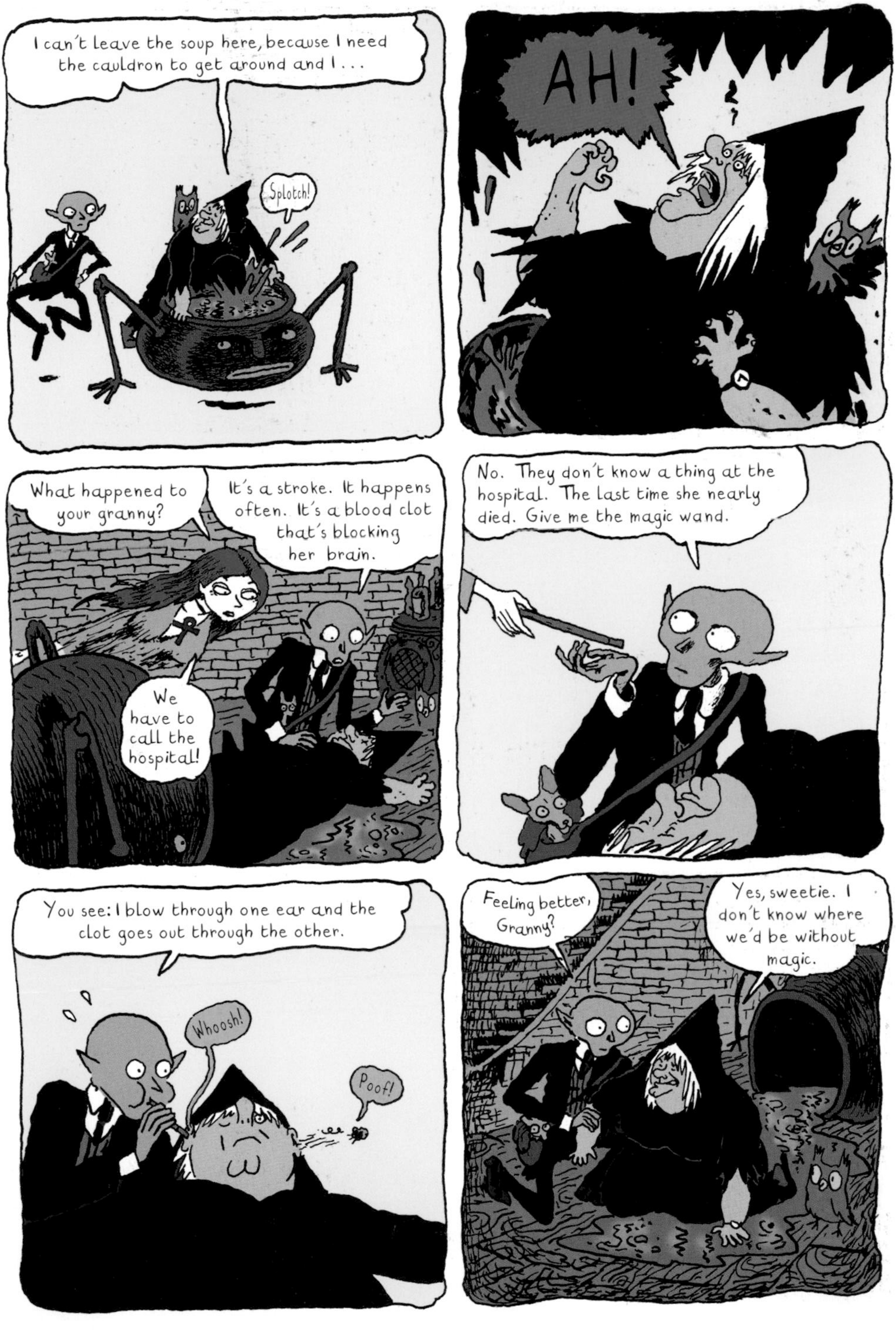
I can't leave the soup here, because I need the cauldron to get around and I...
Splotch!
AH!
What happened to your granny?
It's a stroke. It happens often. It's a blood clot that's blocking her brain.
We have to call the hospital!
No. They don't know a thing at the hospital. The last time she nearly died. Give me the magic wand.
You see: I blow through one ear and the clot goes out through the other.
Whoosh!
Poof!
Feeling better, Granny?
Yes, sweetie. I don't know where we'd be without magic.

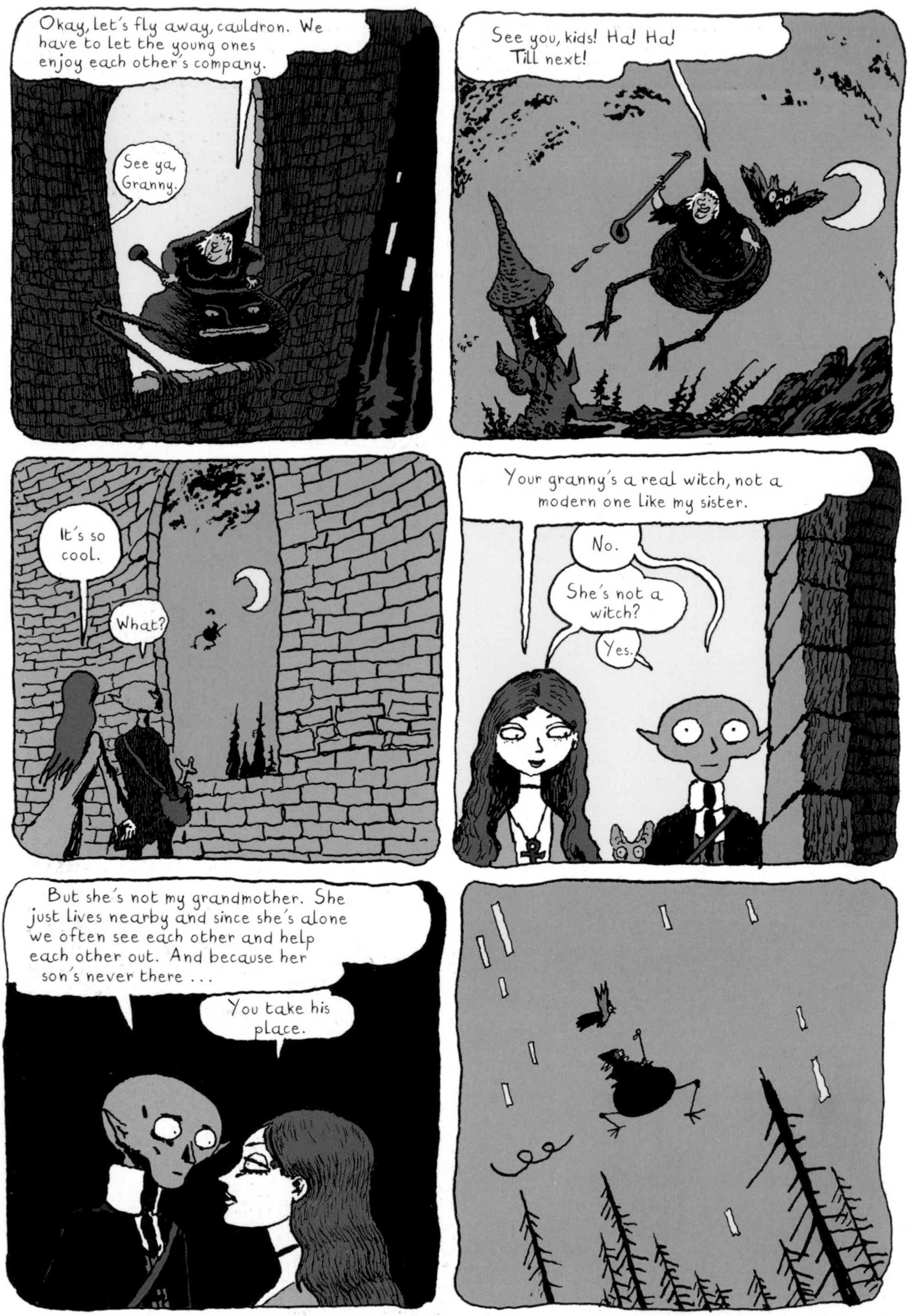
Okay, let's fly away, cauldron. We have to let the young ones enjoy each other's company.
See ya, Granny.
See you, kids! Ha! Ha! Till next!
It's so cool.
What?
Your granny's a real witch, not a modern one like my sister.
No.
She's not a witch?
Yes.
But she's not my grandmother. She just lives nearby and since she's alone we often see each other and help each other out. And because her son's never there . . .
You take his place.

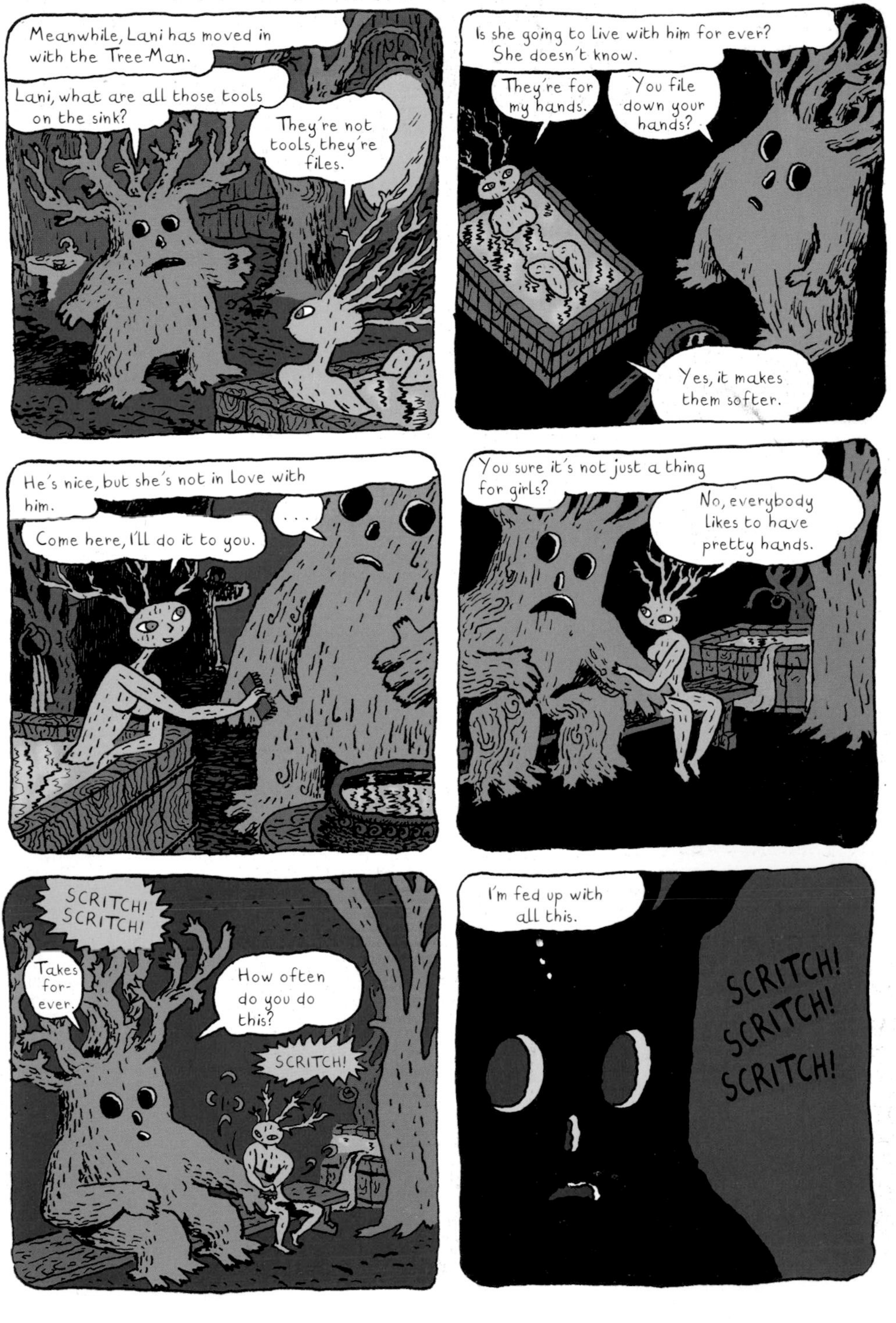
Meanwhile, Lani has moved in with the Tree-Man.
Lani, what are all those tools on the sink?
They're not tools, they're files.
Is she going to live with him for ever? She doesn't know.
They're for my hands.
You file down your hands?
Yes, it makes them softer.
He's nice, but she's not in love with him.
Come here, I'll do it to you.
. . .
You sure it's not just a thing for girls?
No, everybody likes to have pretty hands.
SCRITCH! SCRITCH!
Takes for-ever.
How often do you do this?
SCRITCH!
I'm fed up with all this.
SCRITCH! SCRITCH! SCRITCH!

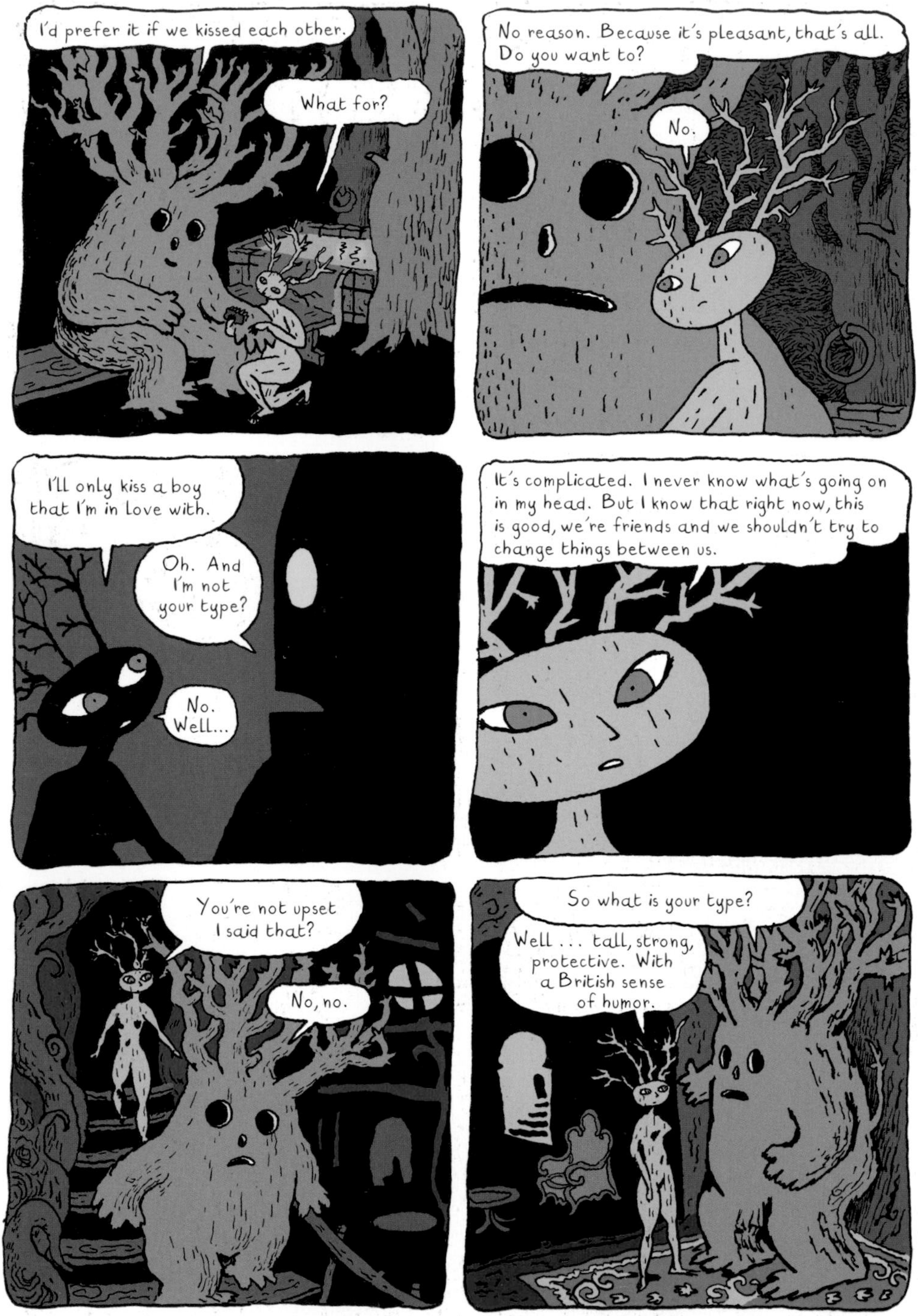
I'd prefer it if we kissed each other.
What for?
No reason. Because it's pleasant, that's all. Do you want to?
No.
I'll only kiss a boy that I'm in love with.
Oh. And I'm not your type?
No. Well...
It's complicated. I never know what's going on in my head. But I know that right now, this is good, we're friends and we shouldn't try to change things between us.
You're not upset I said that?
No, no.
So what is your type?
Well . . . tall, strong, protective. With a British sense of humor.

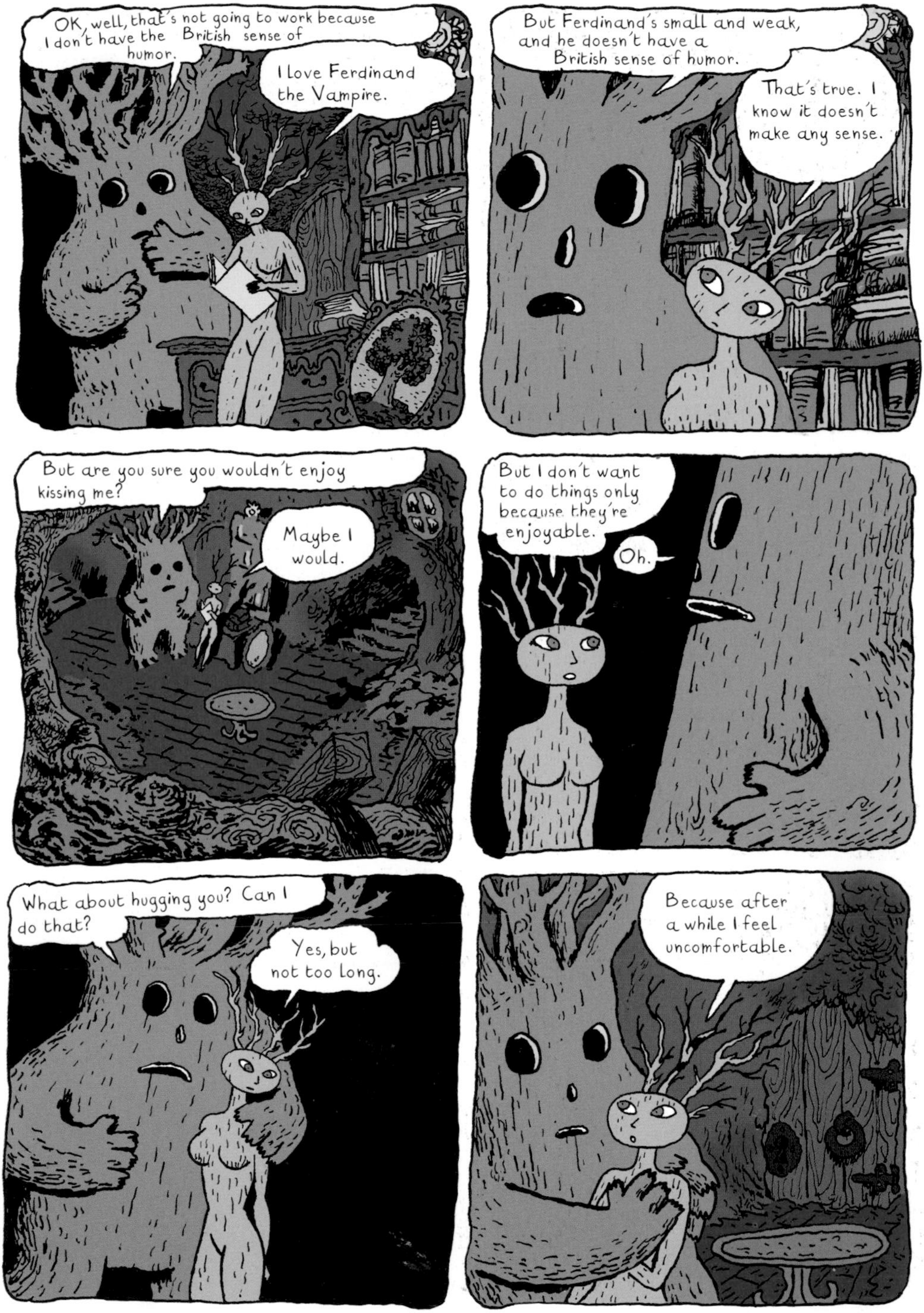
OK, well, that's not going to work because I don't have the British sense of humor.
I love Ferdinand the Vampire.
But Ferdinand's small and weak, and he doesn't have a British sense of humor.
That's true. I know it doesn't make any sense.
But are you sure you wouldn't enjoy kissing me?
Maybe I would.
But I don't want to do things only because they're enjoyable.
Oh.
What about hugging you? Can I do that?
Yes, but not too long.
Because after a while I feel uncomfortable.

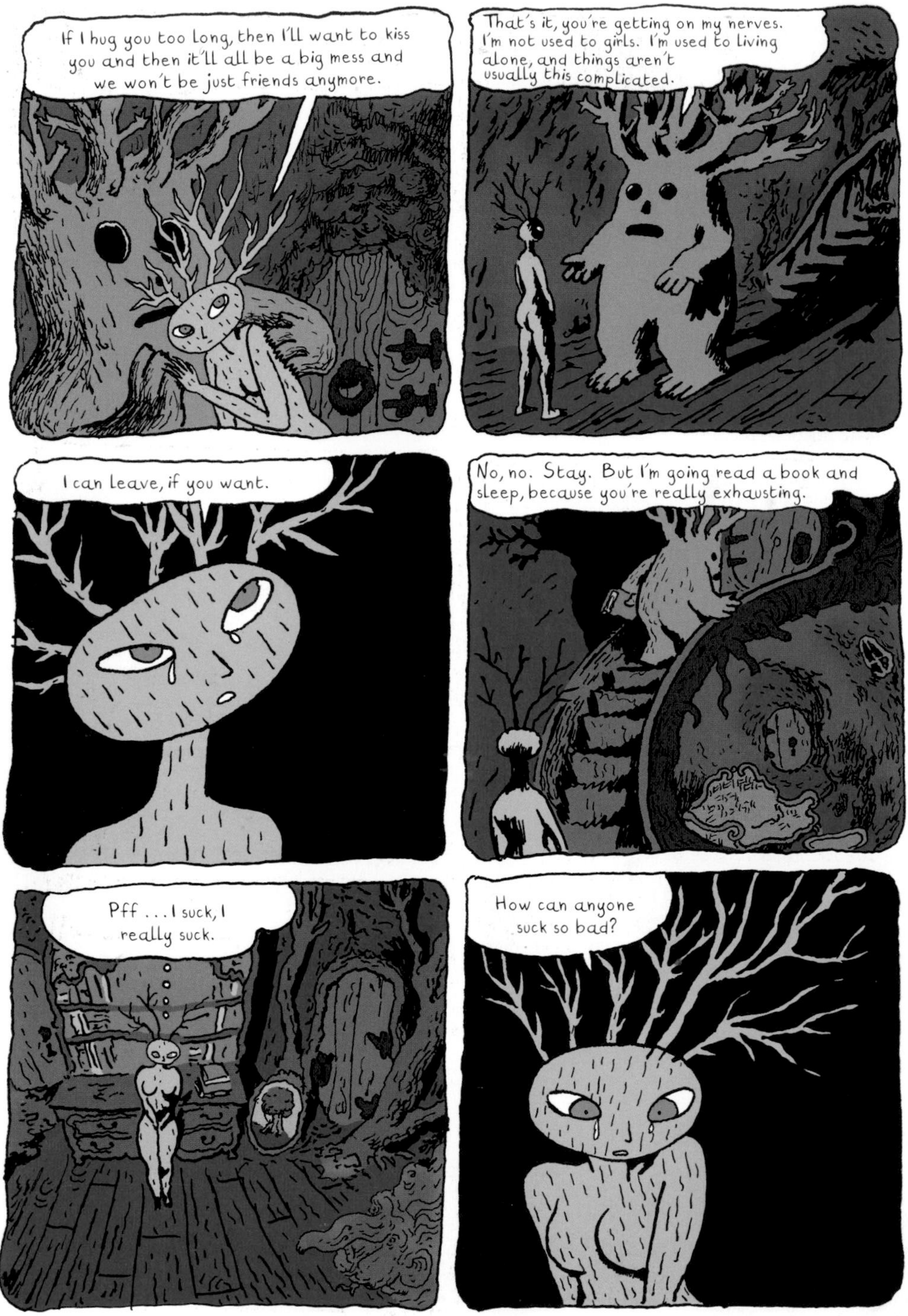
If I hug you too long, then I'll want to kiss you and then it'll all be a big mess and we won't be just friends anymore.
That's it, you're getting on my nerves. I'm not used to girls. I'm used to living alone, and things aren't usually this complicated.
I can leave, if you want.
No, no. Stay. But I'm going read a book and sleep, because you're really exhausting.
Pff . . . I suck, I really suck.
How can anyone suck so bad?

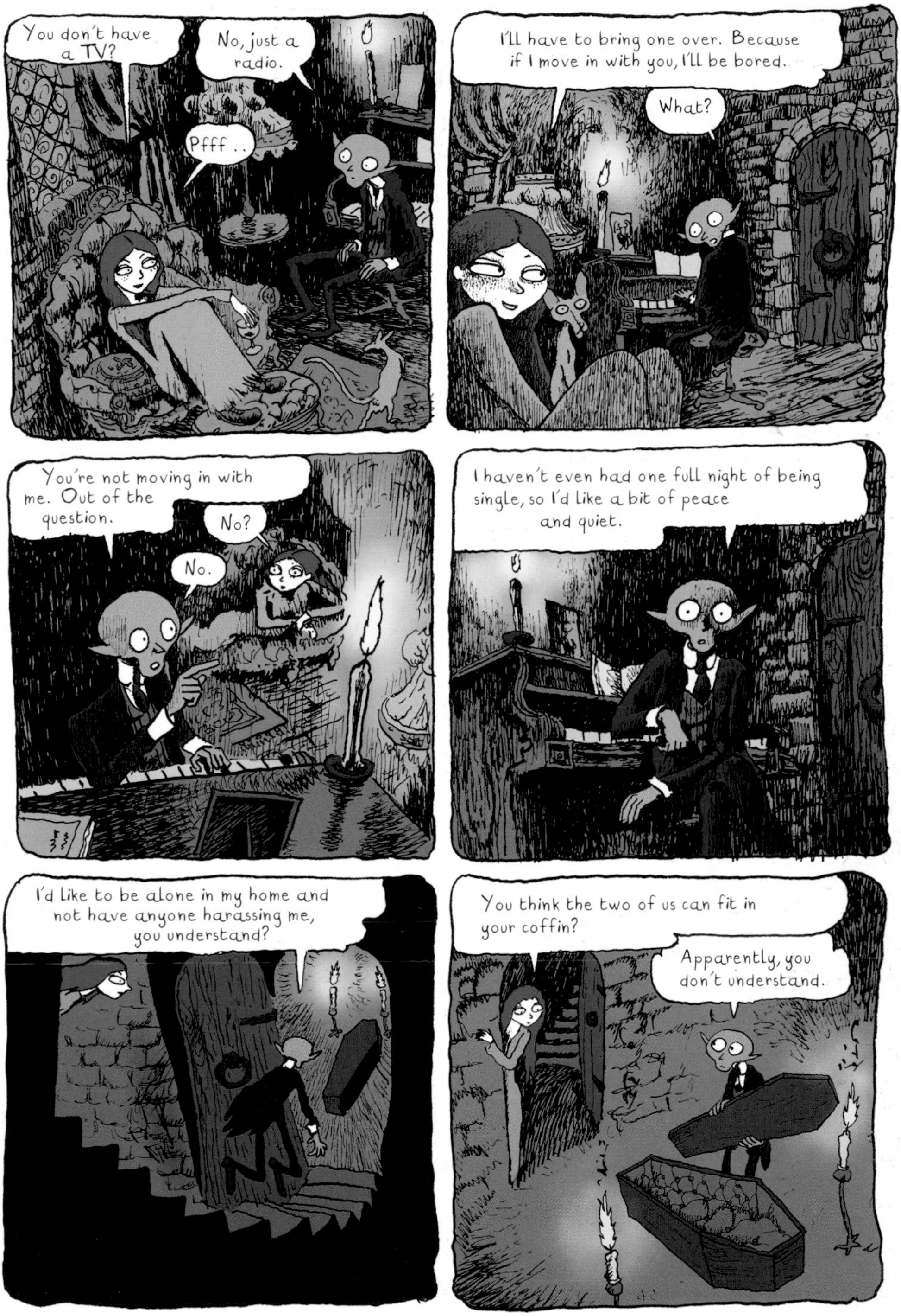
You don't have a TV?
No, just a radio.
Pfff..
I'll have to bring one over. Because if I move in with you, I'll be bored.
What?
You're not moving in with me. Out of the question.
No?
No.
I haven't even had one full night of being single, so I'd like a bit of peace and quiet.
I'd like to be alone in my home and not have anyone harassing me, you understand?
You think the two of us can fit in your coffin?
Apparently, you don't understand.

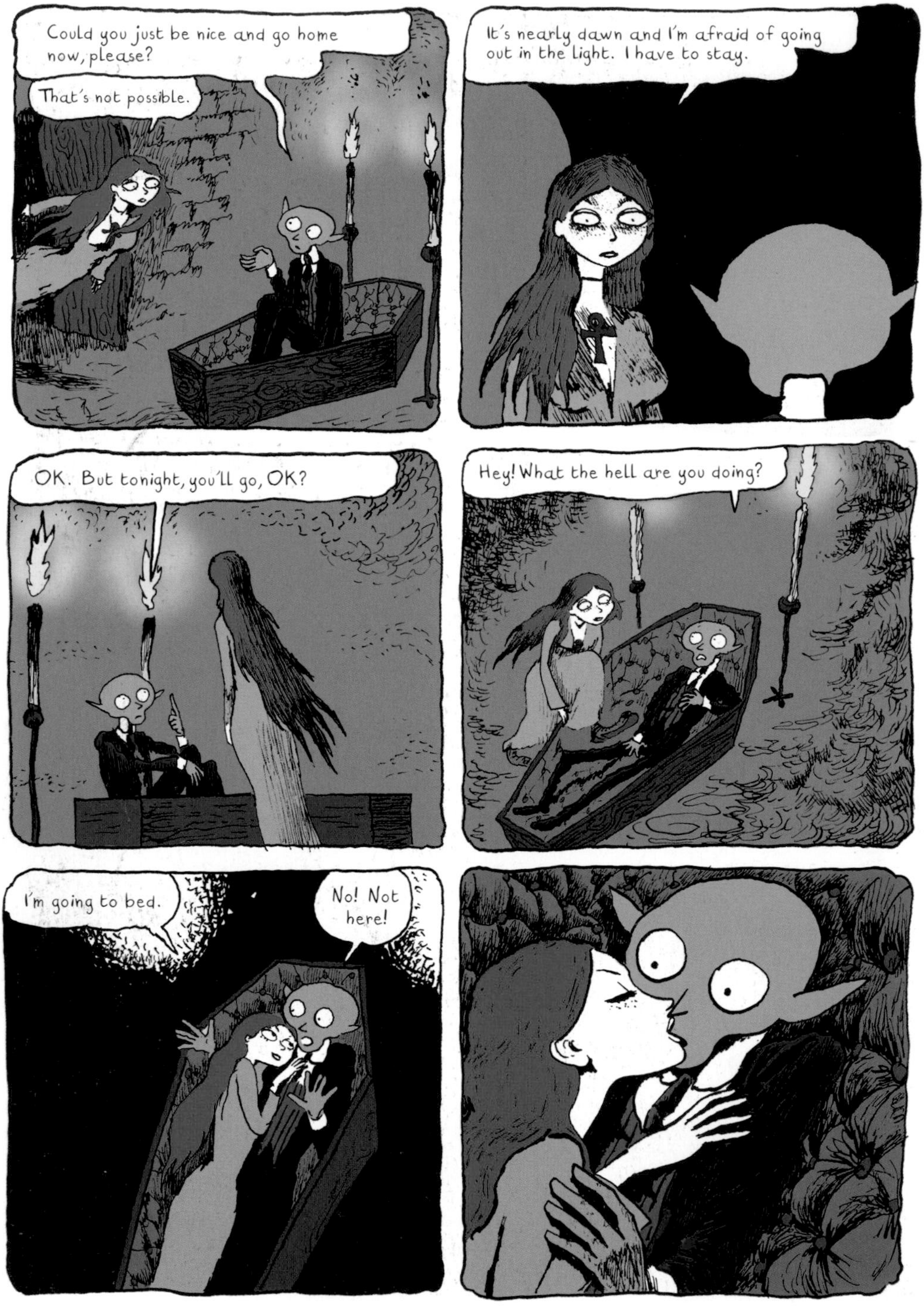
Could you just be nice and go home now, please?
That's not possible.
It's nearly dawn and I'm afraid of going out in the light. I have to stay.
OK. But tonight, you'll go, OK?
Hey! What the hell are you doing?
I'm going to bed.
No! Not here!

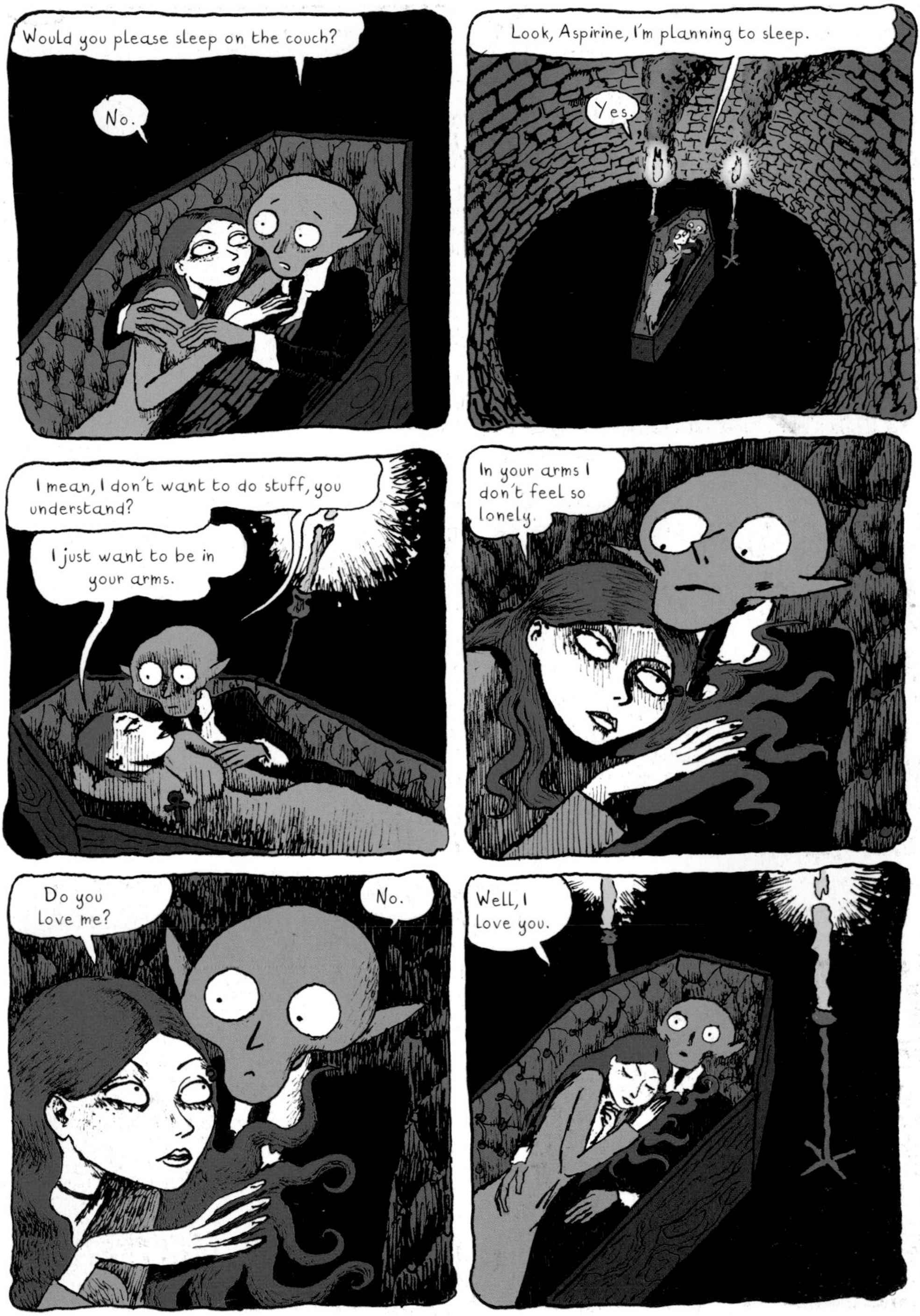

Would you please sleep on the couch?
No.
Look, Aspirine, I'm planning to sleep.
Yes.
I mean, I don't want to do stuff, you understand?
I just want to be in your arms.
In your arms I don't feel so lonely.
Do you love me?
No.
Well, I love you.

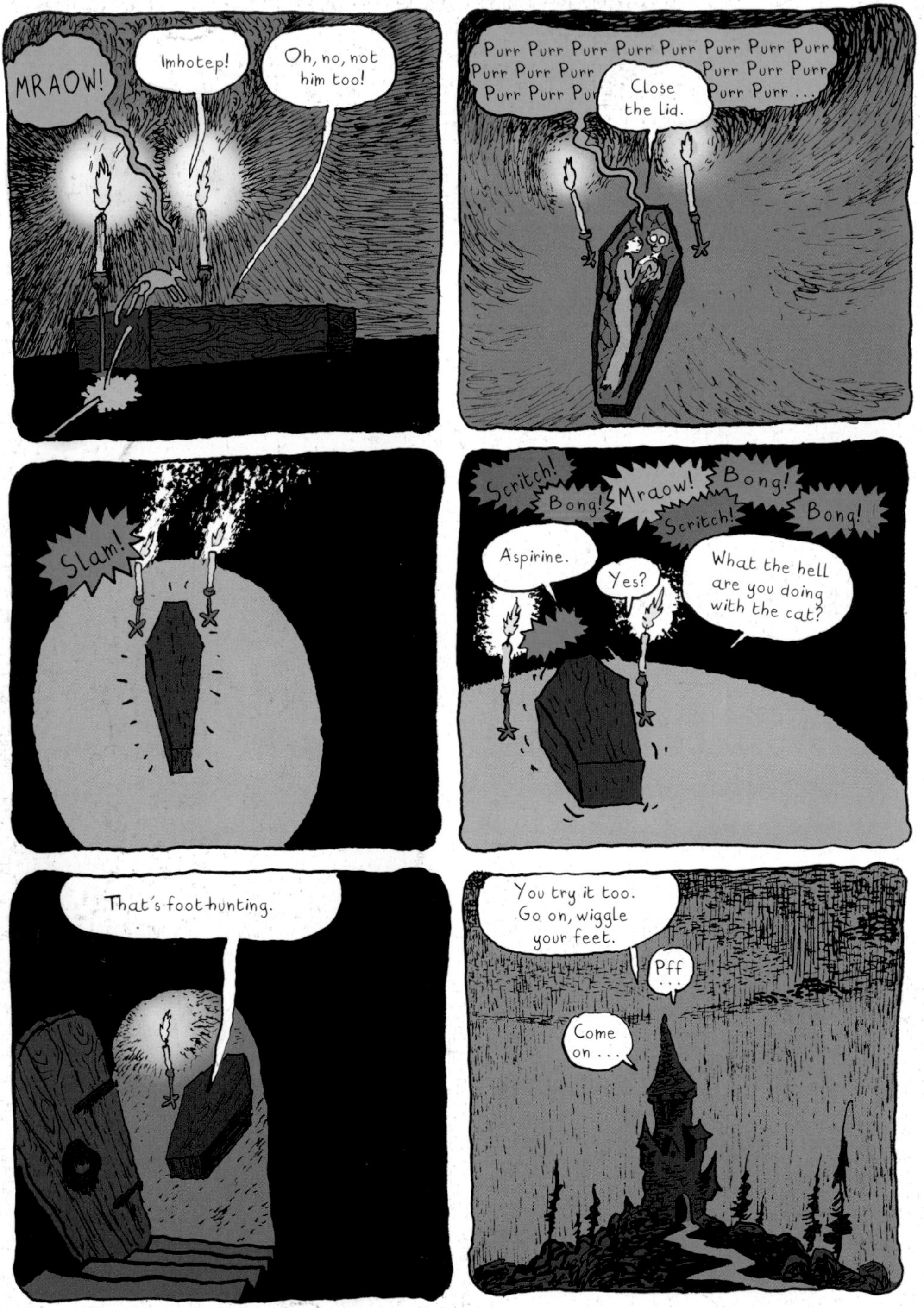
MRAOW!
Imhotep!
Oh, no, not him too!
Purr Purr Purr Purr Purr Purr Purr Purr Purr Purr Purr Purr Purr Purr Purr Purr Pur Purr Purr . . .
Close the lid.
Slam!
Scritch!
Bong!
Mraow!
Bong!
Scritch!
Bong!
Aspirine.
Yes?
What the hell are you doing with the cat?
That's foot-hunting.
You try it too. Go on, wiggle your feet.
Pff . . .
Come on . . .

Joann Sfar, February 9, 2001

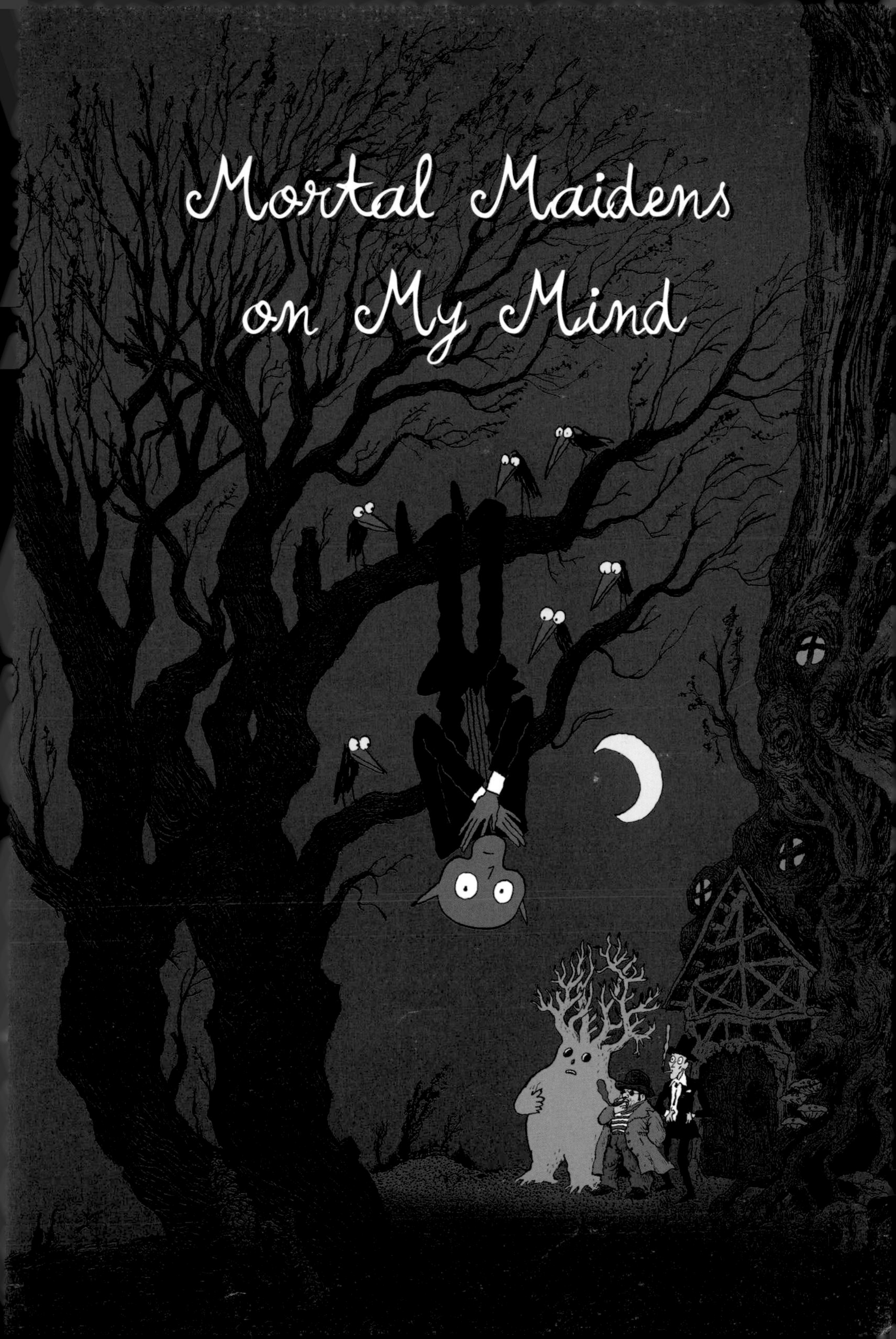
Mortal Maidens
on My Mind

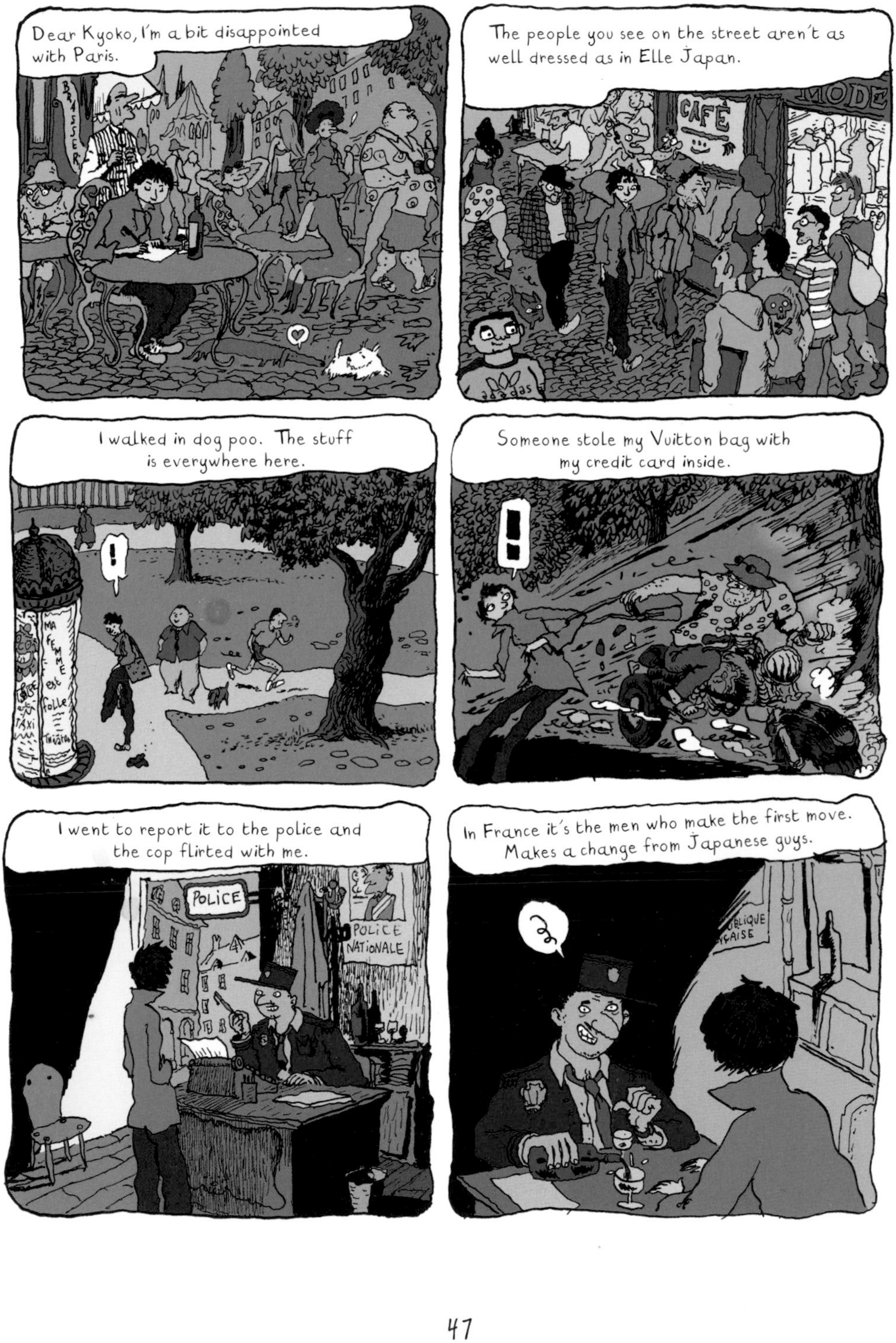
Dear Kyoko, I'm a bit disappointed with Paris.
The people you see on the street aren't as well dressed as in Elle Japan.
CAFÉ
MODE
I walked in dog poo. The stuff is everywhere here.
MA FEMME est folle
TAXI
Someone stole my Vuitton bag with my credit card inside.
I went to report it to the police and the cop flirted with me.
POLICE
POLICE NATIONALE
In France it's the men who make the first move. Makes a change from Japanese guys.

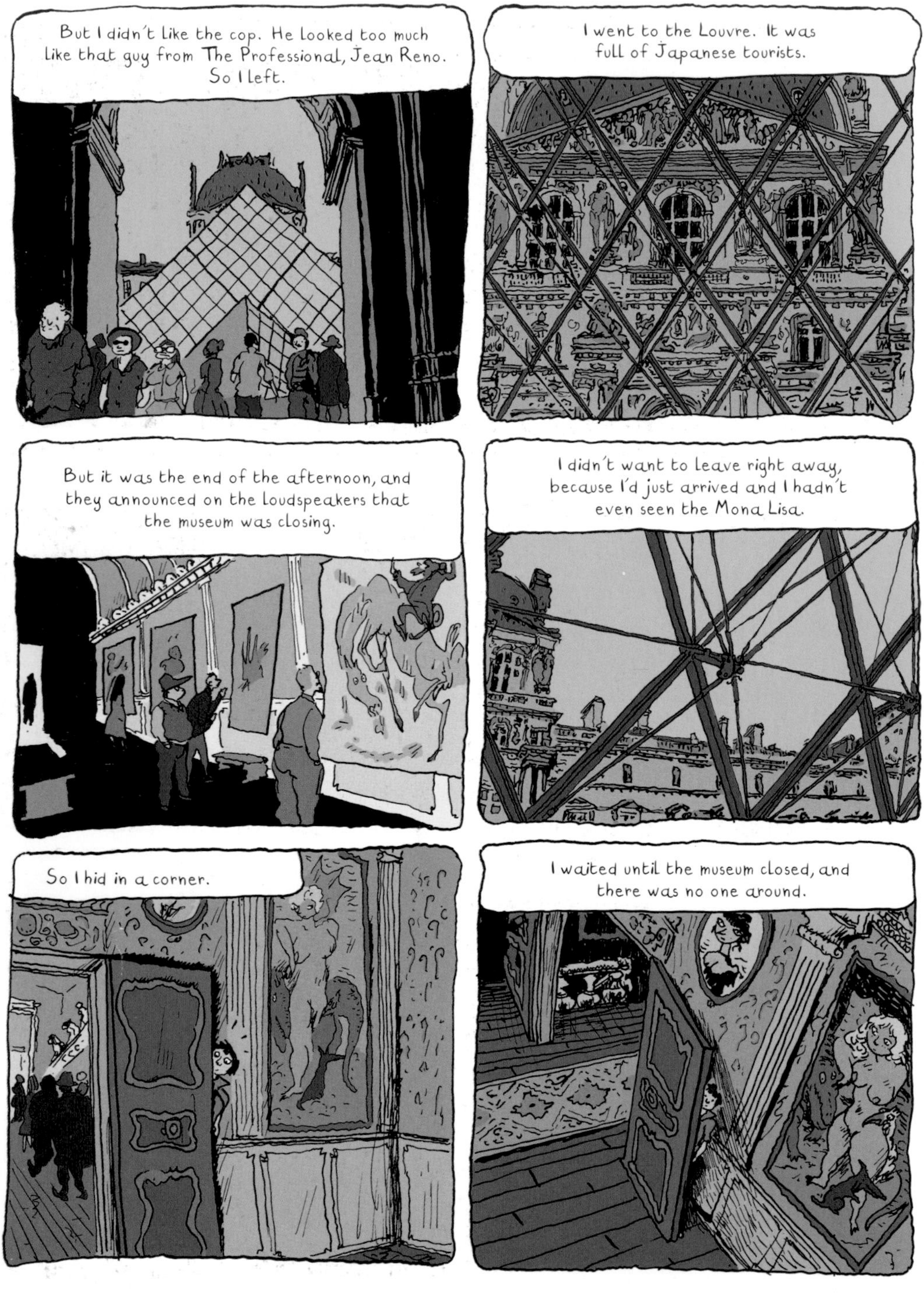

But I didn't like the cop. He looked too much like that guy from The Professional, Jean Reno. So I left.
I went to the Louvre. It was full of Japanese tourists.
But it was the end of the afternoon, and they announced on the loudspeakers that the museum was closing.
I didn't want to leave right away, because I'd just arrived and I hadn't even seen the Mona Lisa.
So I hid in a corner.
I waited until the museum closed, and there was no one around.

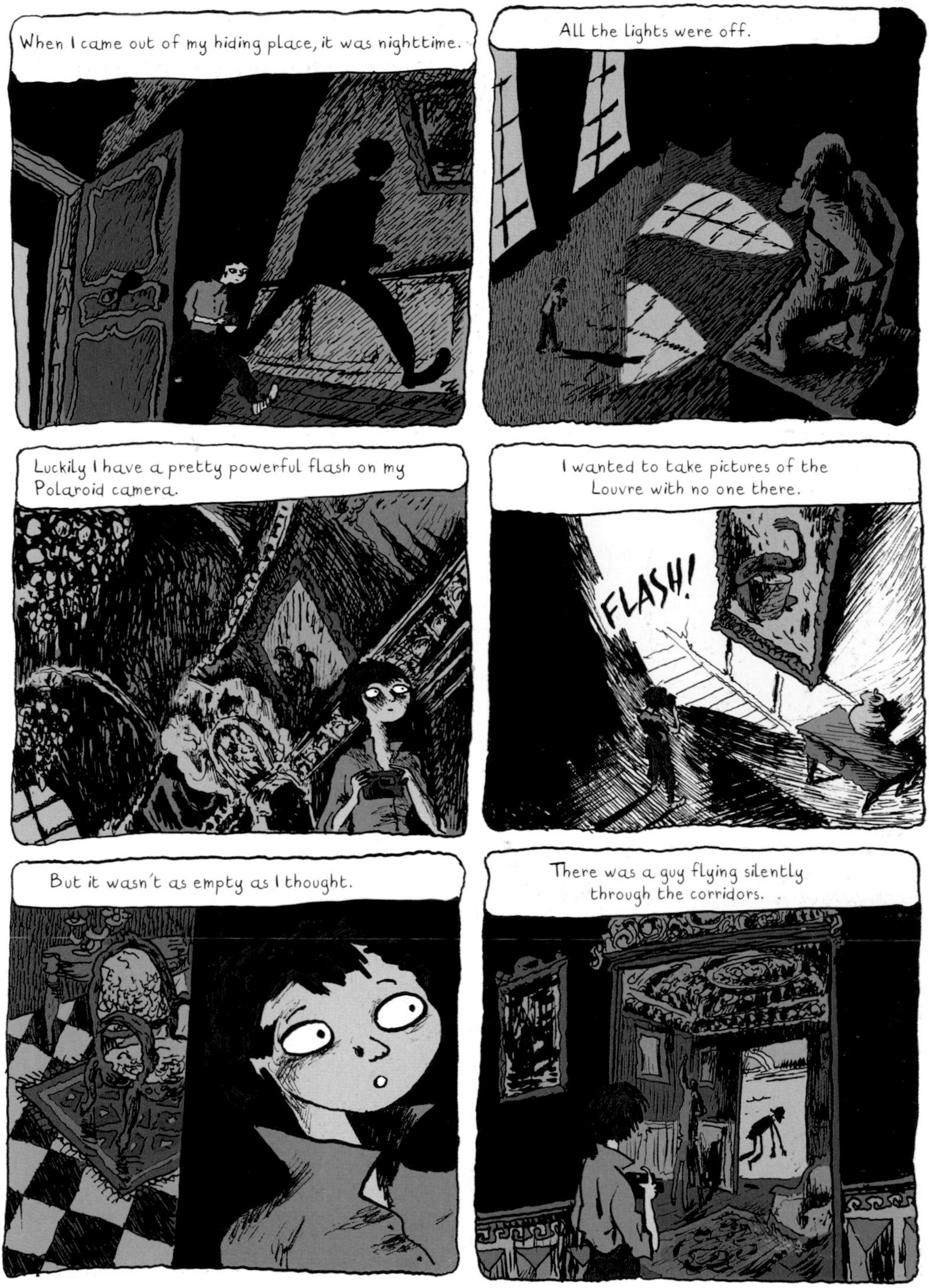
When I came out of my hiding place, it was nighttime.
All the lights were off.
Luckily I have a pretty powerful flash on my Polaroid camera.
I wanted to take pictures of the Louvre with no one there.
FLASH!
But it wasn't as empty as I thought.
There was a guy flying silently through the corridors.

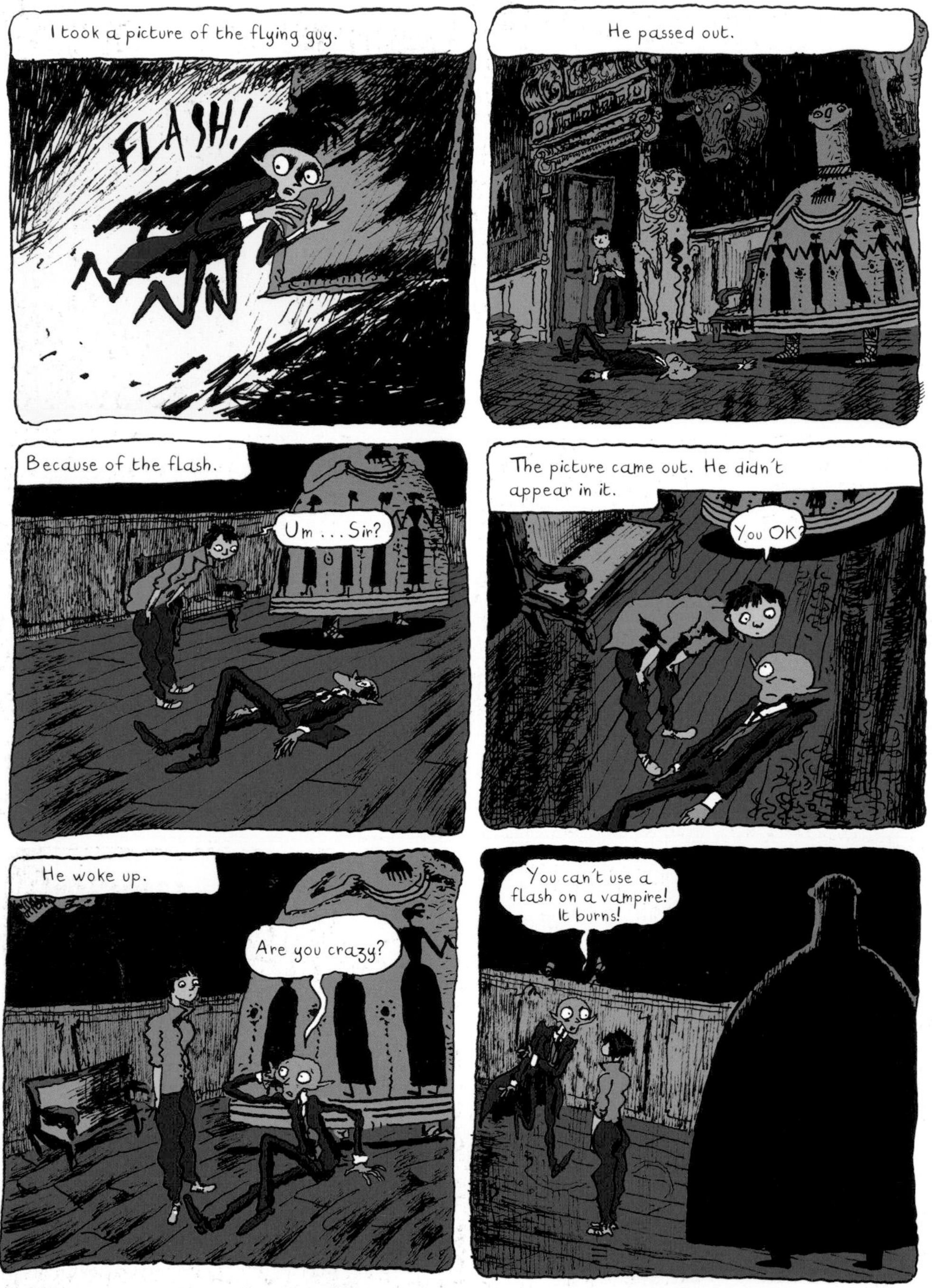
I took a picture of the flying guy.
FLASH!
He passed out.
Because of the flash.
Um . . . Sir?
The picture came out. He didn't appear in it.
You OK?
He woke up.
Are you crazy?
You can't use a flash on a vampire! It burns!

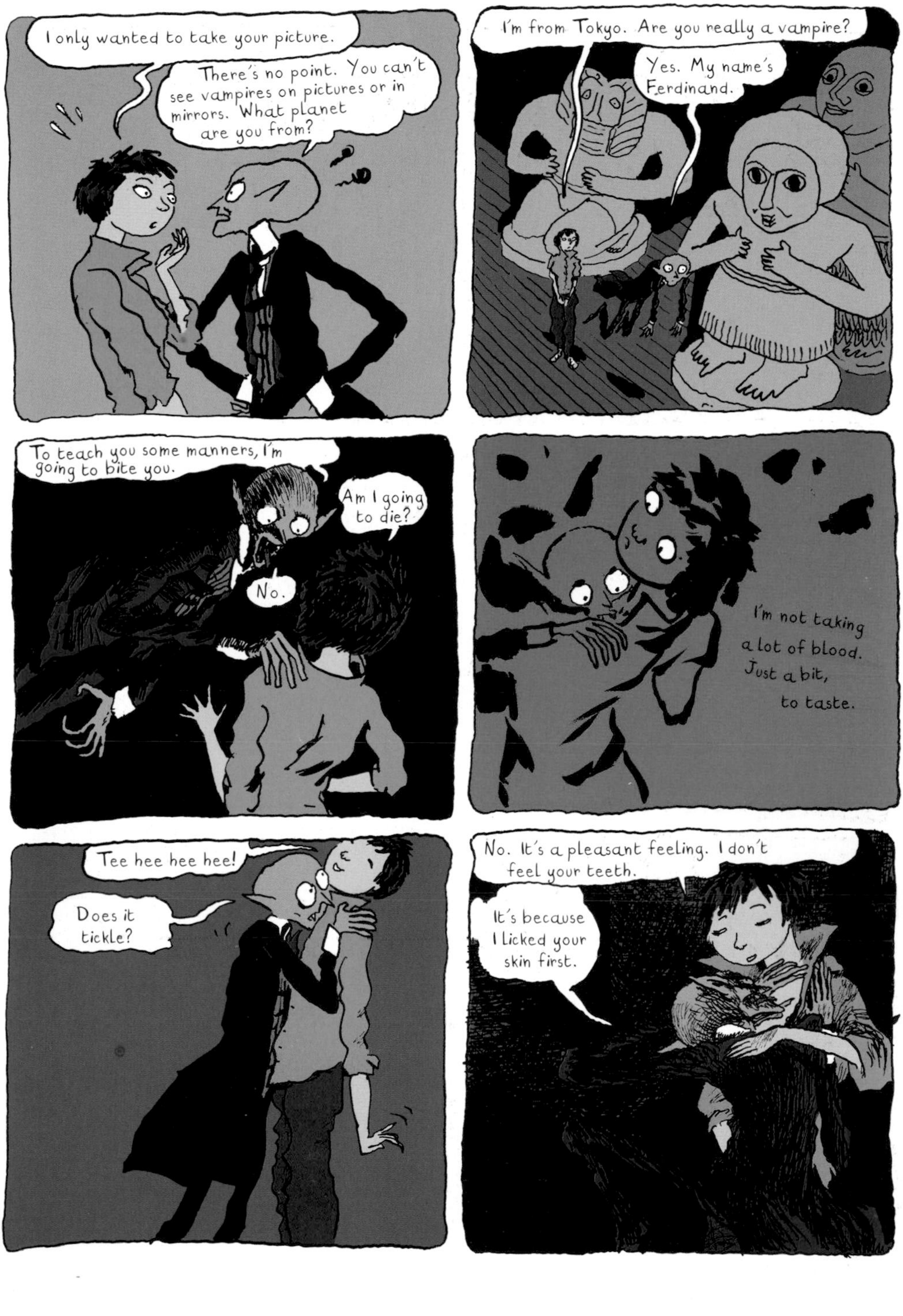
I only wanted to take your picture.
There's no point. You can't see vampires on pictures or in mirrors. What planet are you from?
I'm from Tokyo. Are you really a vampire?
Yes. My name's Ferdinand.
To teach you some manners, I'm going to bite you.
Am I going to die?
No.
I'm not taking a lot of blood. Just a bit, to taste.
Tee hee hee hee!
Does it tickle?
No. It's a pleasant feeling. I don't feel your teeth.
It's because I licked your skin first.

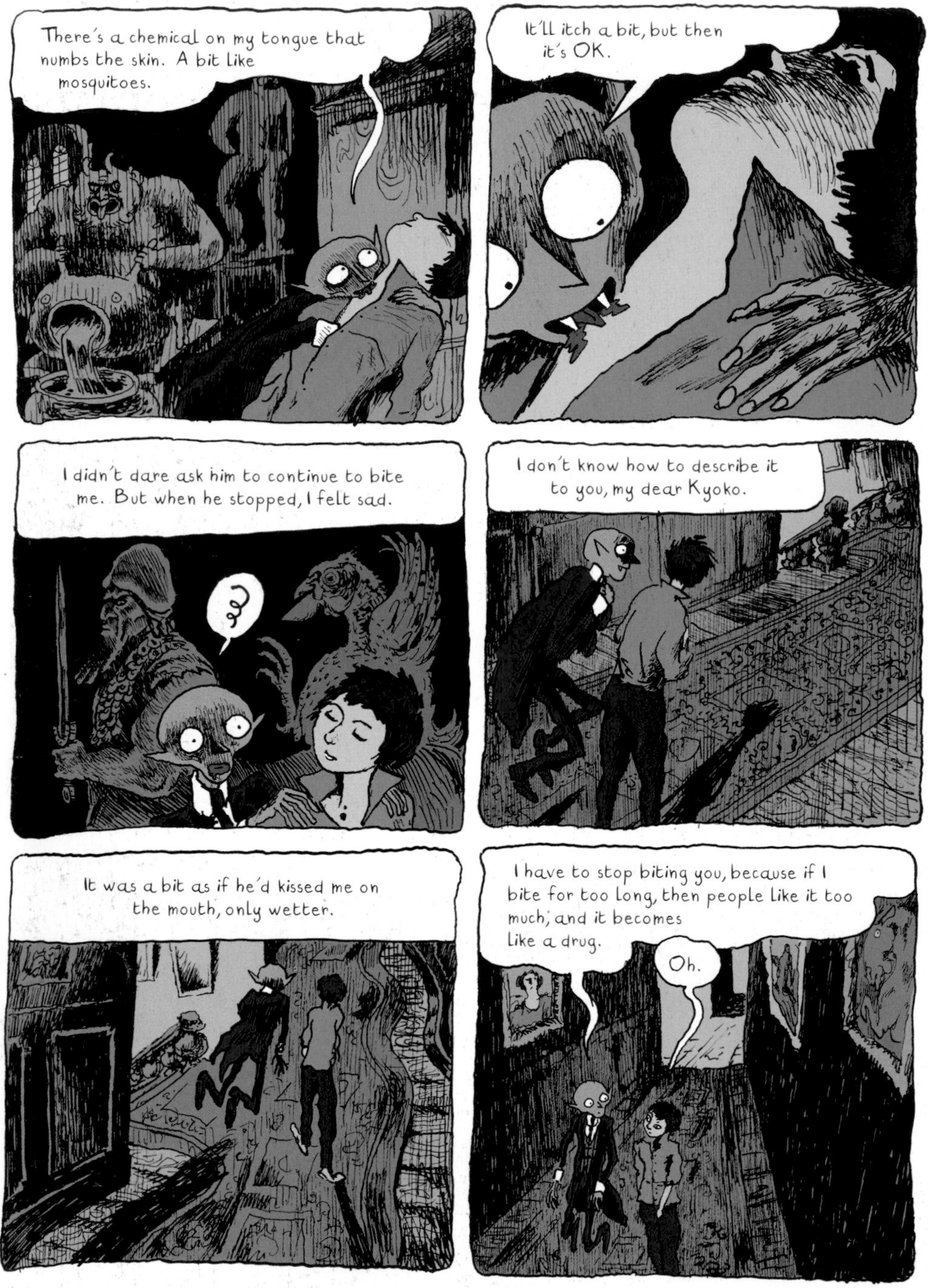
There's a chemical on my tongue that numbs the skin. A bit like mosquitoes.
It'll itch a bit, but then it's OK.
I didn't dare ask him to continue to bite me. But when he stopped, I felt sad.
?
I don't know how to describe it to you, my dear Kyoko.
It was a bit as if he'd kissed me on the mouth, only wetter.
I have to stop biting you, because if I bite for too long, then people like it too much, and it becomes like a drug.
Oh.

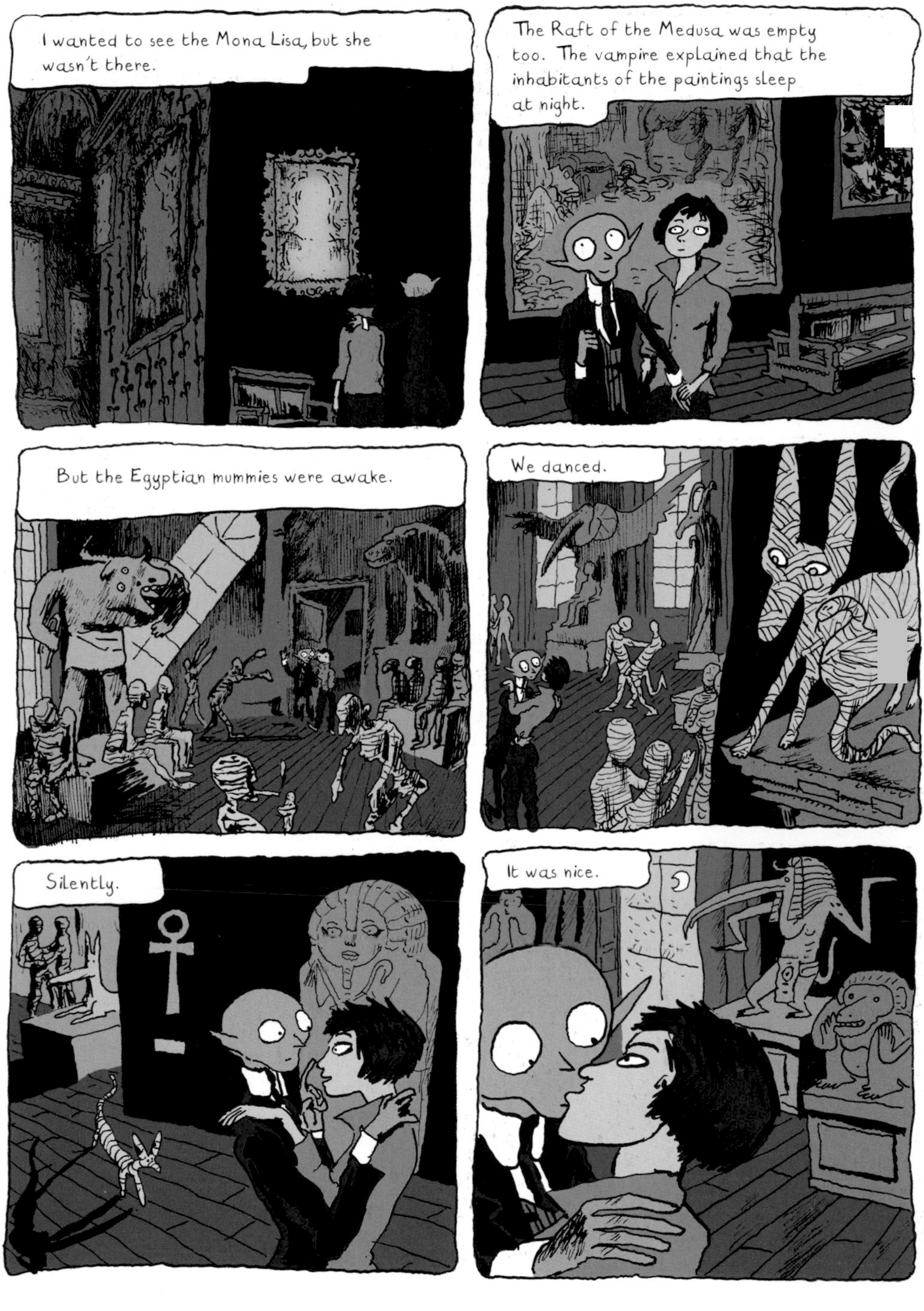

I wanted to see the Mona Lisa, but she wasn't there.
The Raft of the Medusa was empty too. The vampire explained that the inhabitants of the paintings sleep at night.
But the Egyptian mummies were awake.
We danced.
Silently.
It was nice.

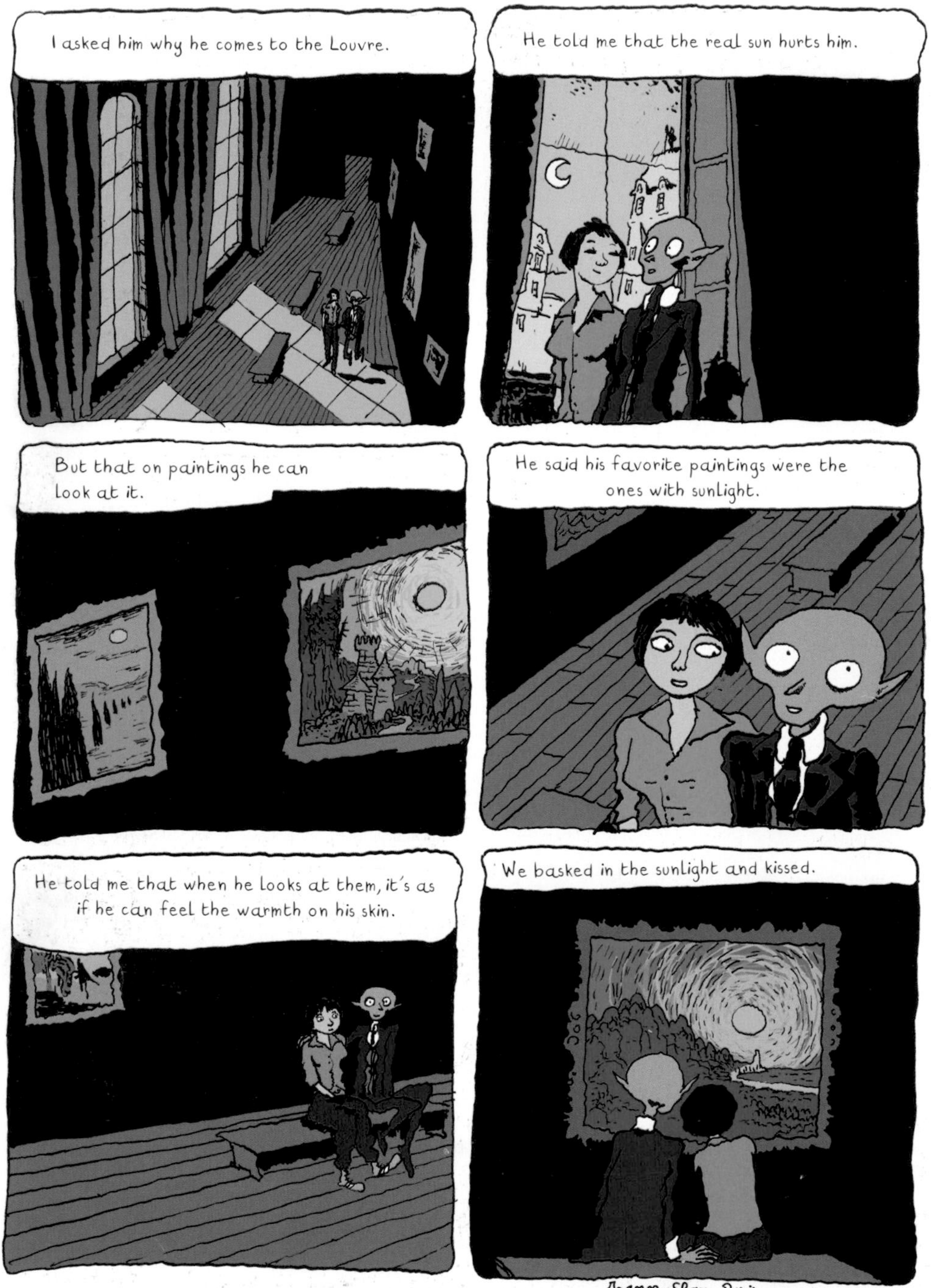
I asked him why he comes to the Louvre.
He told me that the real sun hurts him.
But that on paintings he can look at it.
He said his favorite paintings were the ones with sunlight.
He told me that when he looks at them, it's as if he can feel the warmth on his skin.
We basked in the sunlight and kissed.
Joann Sfar, Paris

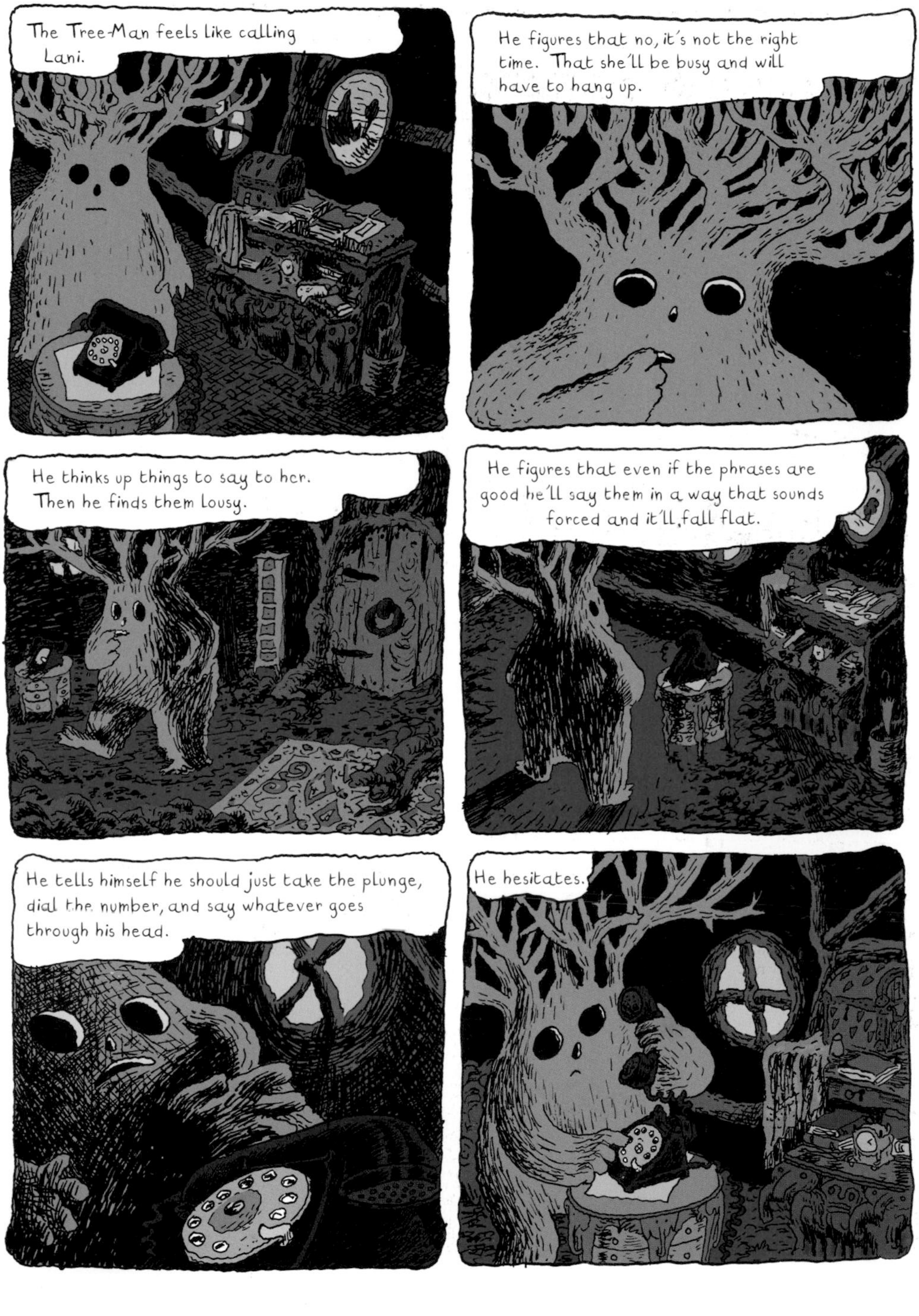
The Tree-Man feels like calling Lani.
He figures that no, it's not the right time. That she'll be busy and will have to hang up.
He thinks up things to say to her. Then he finds them lousy.
He figures that even if the phrases are good he'll say them in a way that sounds forced and it'll fall flat.
He tells himself he should just take the plunge, dial the number, and say whatever goes through his head.
He hesitates.

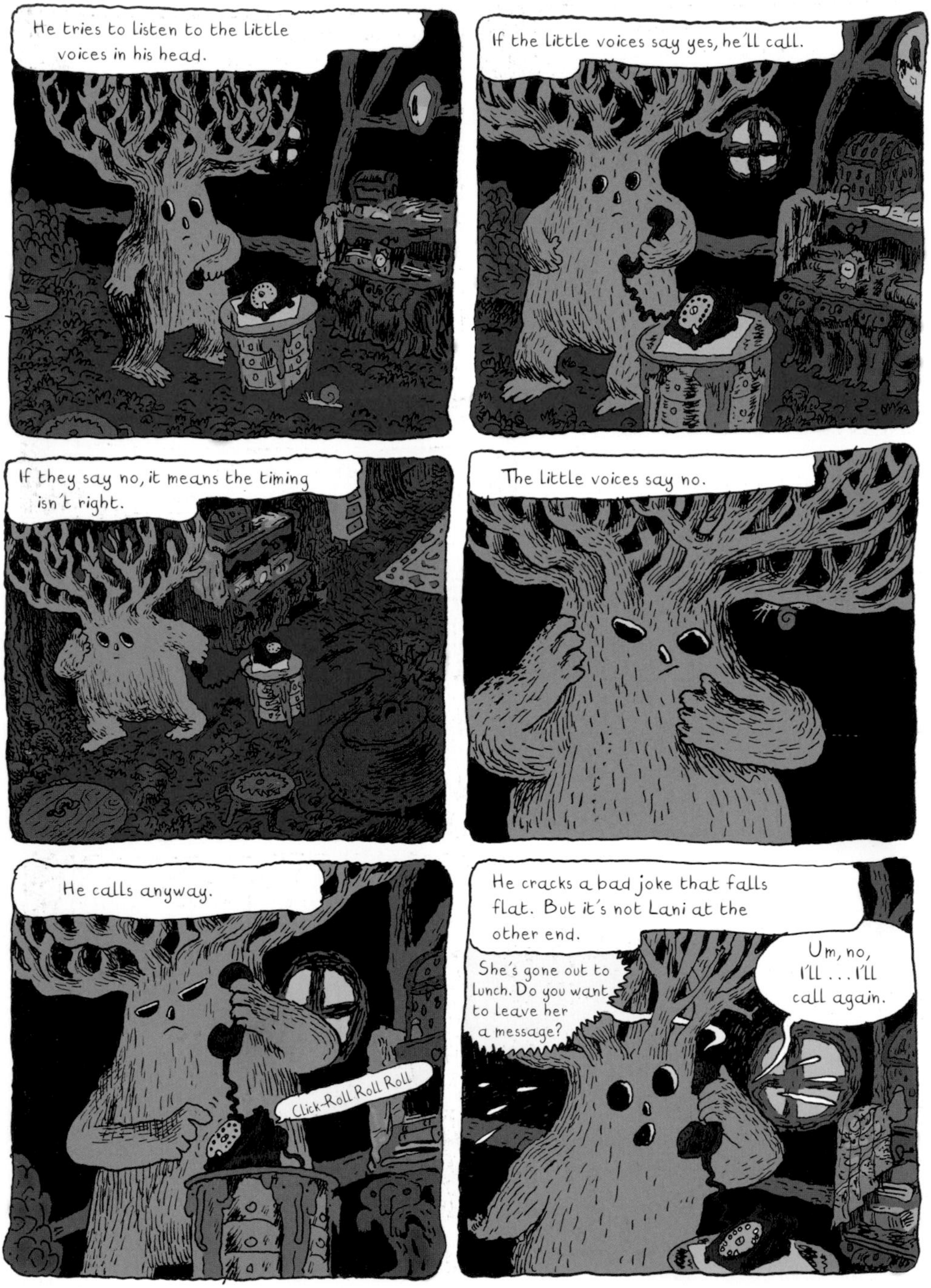
He tries to listen to the little voices in his head.
If the little voices say yes, he'll call.
If they say no, it means the timing isn't right.
The little voices say no.
He calls anyway.
Click-Roll Roll Roll
He cracks a bad joke that falls flat. But it's not Lani at the other end.
She's gone out to lunch. Do you want to leave her a message?
Um, no, I'll . . . I'll call again.

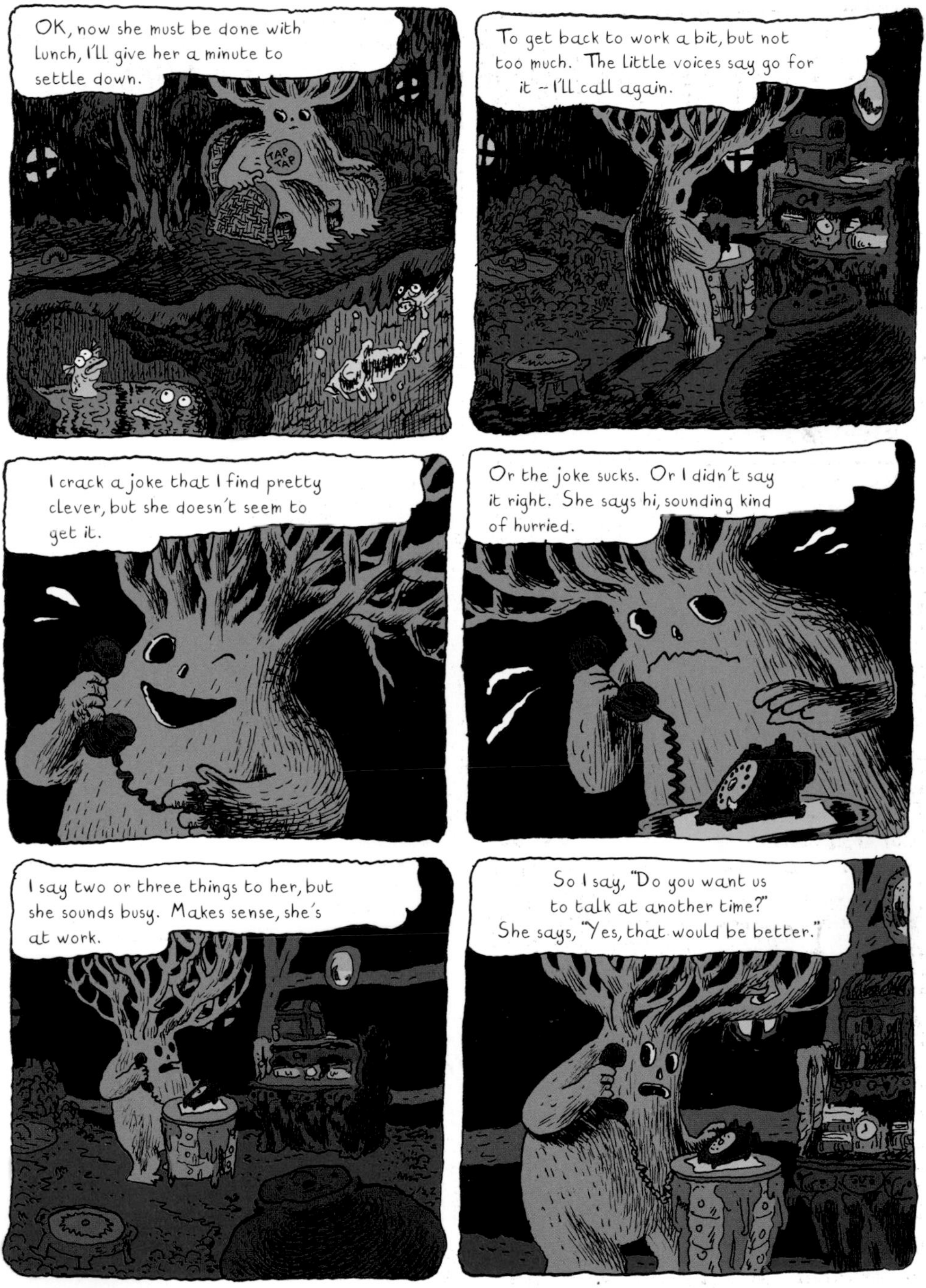
OK, now she must be done with lunch, I'll give her a minute to settle down.
TAP TAP
To get back to work a bit, but not too much. The little voices say go for it – I'll call again.
I crack a joke that I find pretty clever, but she doesn't seem to get it.
Or the joke sucks. Or I didn't say it right. She says hi, sounding kind of hurried.
I say two or three things to her, but she sounds busy. Makes sense, she's at work.
So I say, "Do you want us to talk at another time?" She says, "Yes, that would be better."

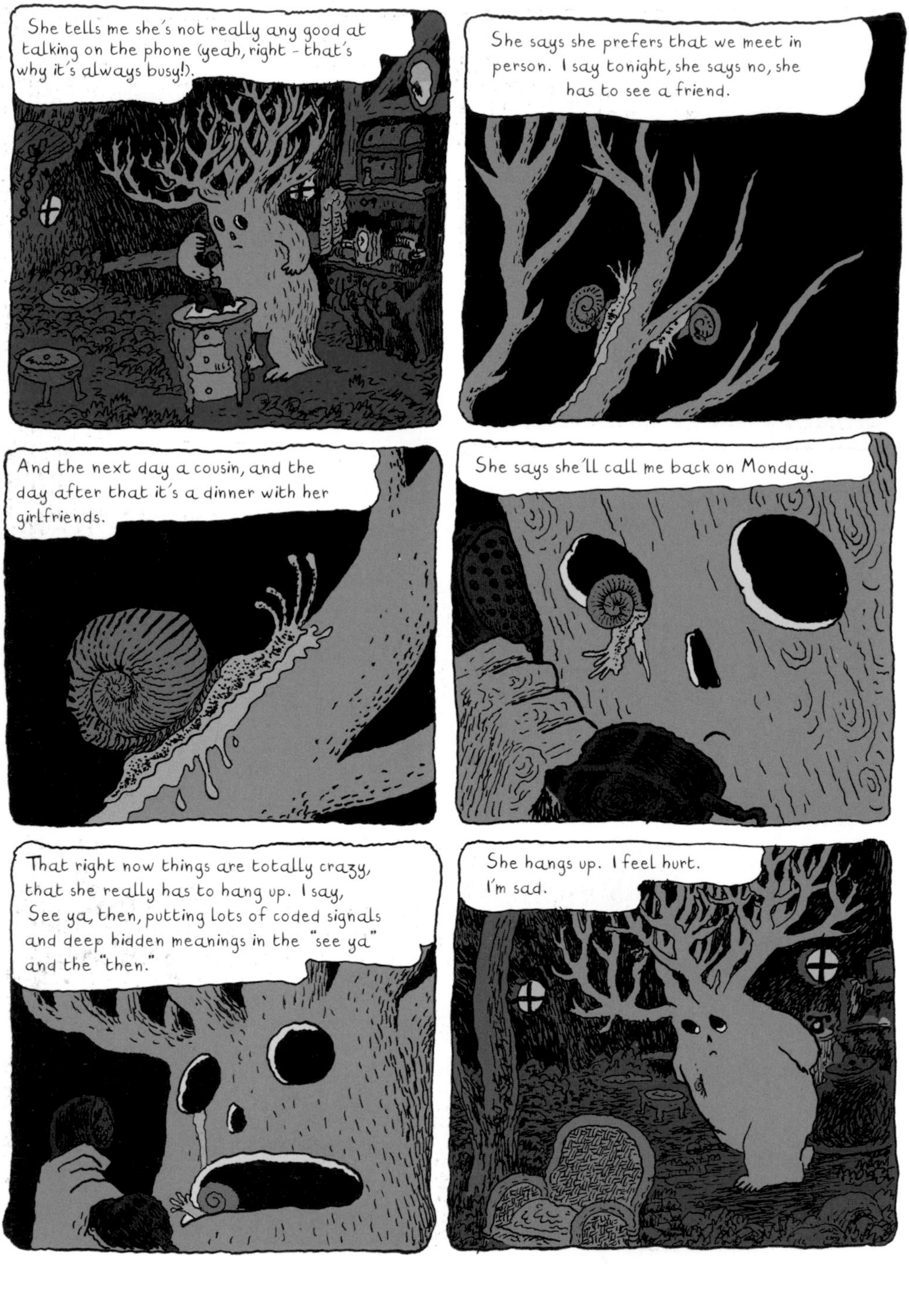
She tells me she's not really any good at talking on the phone (yeah, right - that's why it's always busy!).
She says she prefers that we meet in person. I say tonight, she says no, she has to see a friend.
And the next day a cousin, and the day after that it's a dinner with her girlfriends.
She says she'll call me back on Monday.
That right now things are totally crazy, that she really has to hang up. I say, See ya, then, putting lots of coded signals and deep hidden meanings in the "see ya" and the "then."
She hangs up. I feel hurt. I'm sad.

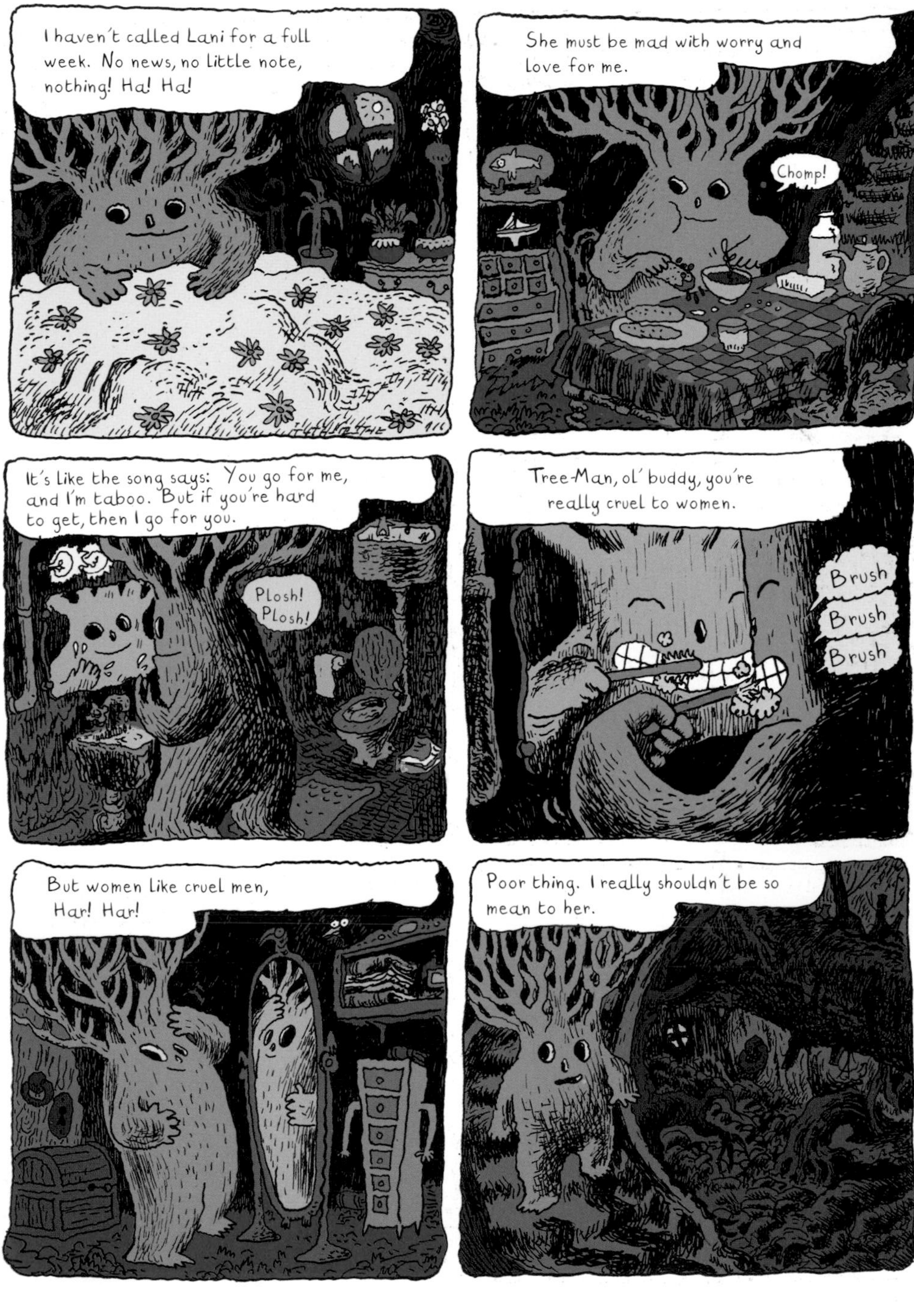
I haven't called Lani for a full week. No news, no little note, nothing! Ha! Ha!
She must be mad with worry and love for me.
Chomp!
It's like the song says: You go for me, and I'm taboo. But if you're hard to get, then I go for you.
Plosh! Plosh!
Tree-Man, ol' buddy, you're really cruel to women.
Brush
Brush
Brush
But women like cruel men, Har! Har!
Poor thing. I really shouldn't be so mean to her.

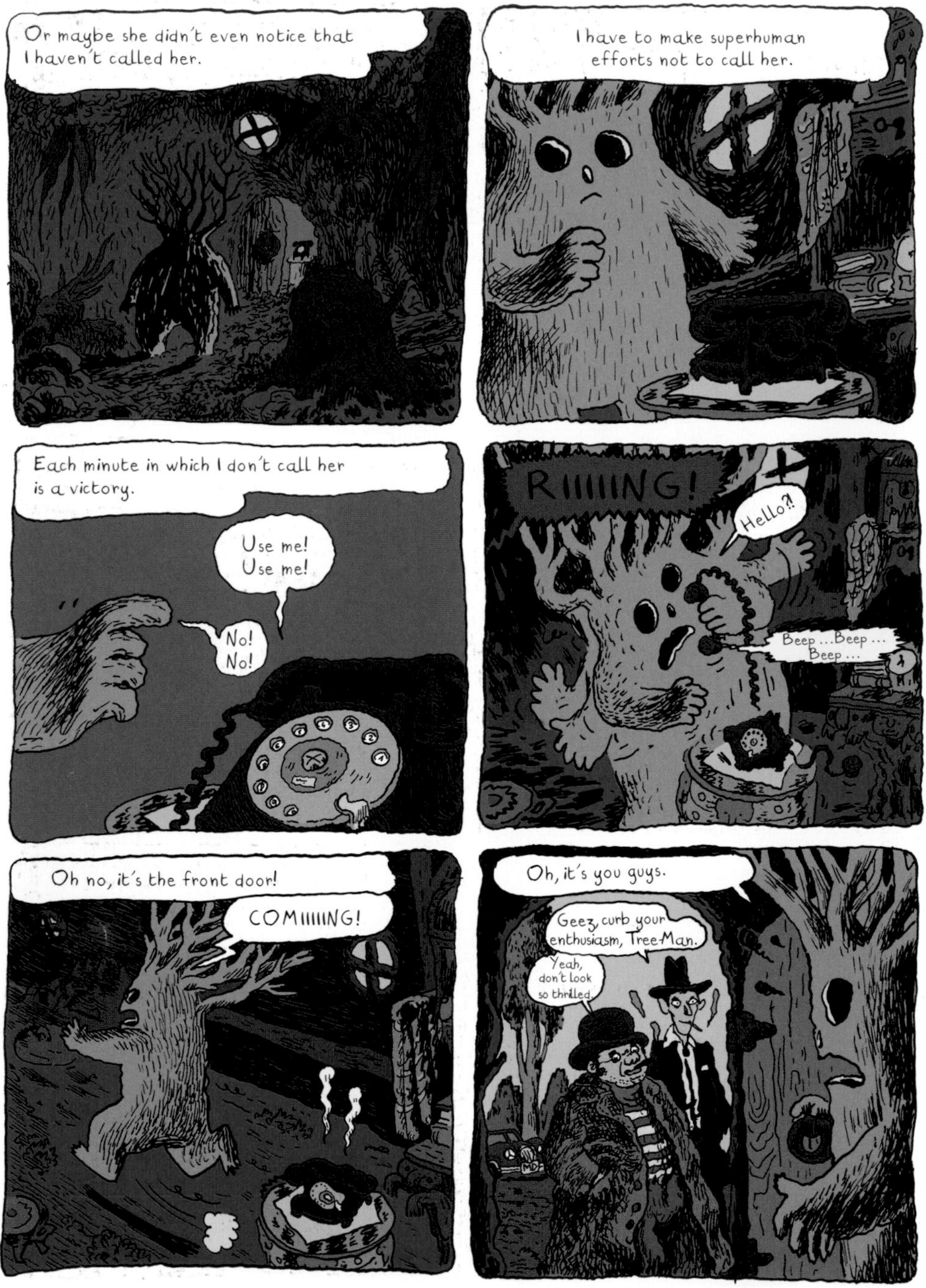
Or maybe she didn't even notice that I haven't called her.
I have to make superhuman efforts not to call her.
Each minute in which I don't call her is a victory.
Use me! Use me!
No! No!
RIIIIING!
Hello?!
Beep ... Beep ... Beep ...
Oh no, it's the front door!
COMIIIIING!
Oh, it's you guys.
Geez, curb your enthusiasm, Tree-Man.
Yeah, don't look so thrilled.

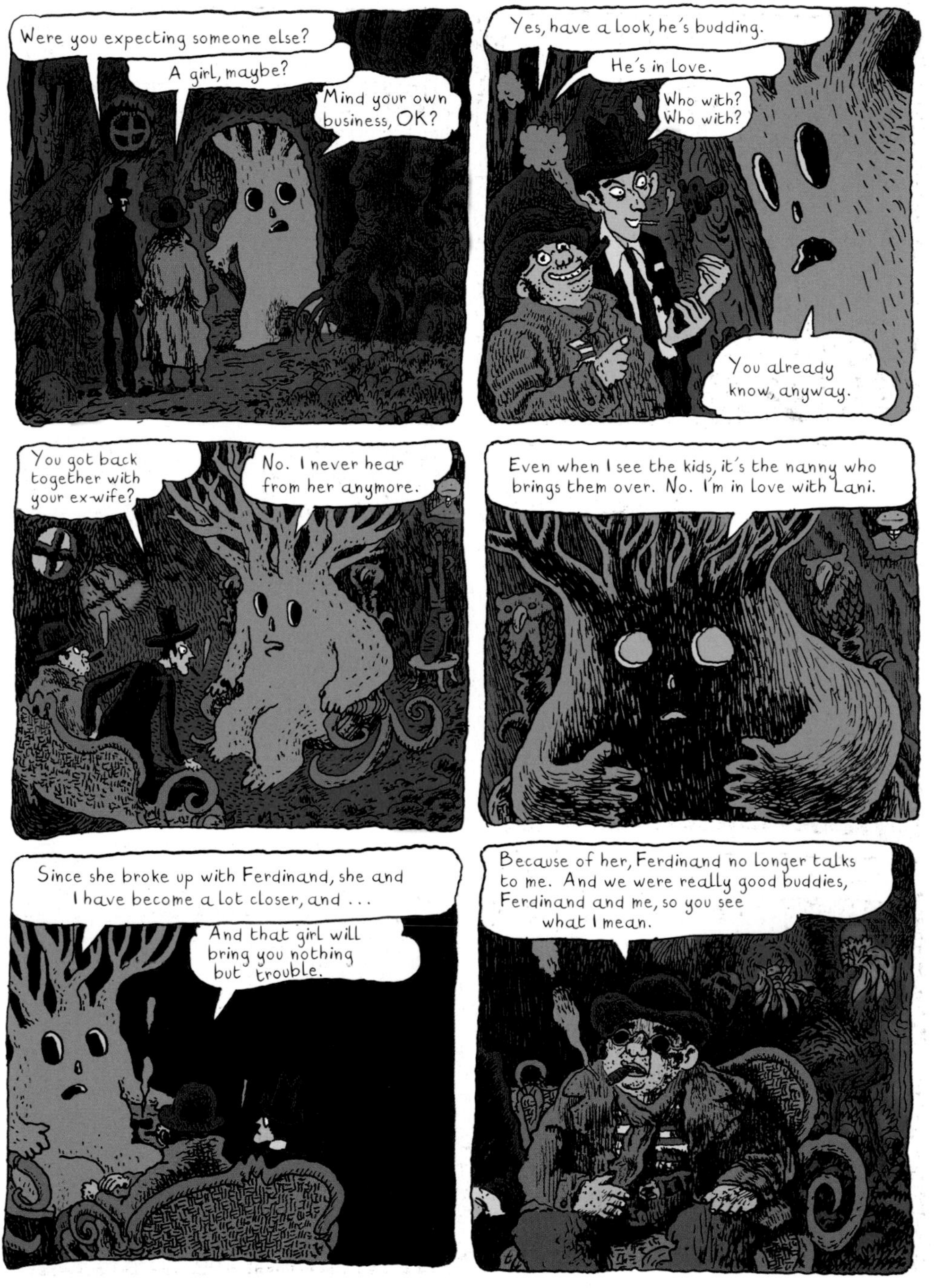
Were you expecting someone else?
A girl, maybe?
Mind your own business, OK?
Yes, have a look, he's budding.
He's in love.
Who with? Who with?
You already know, anyway.
You got back together with your ex-wife?
No. I never hear from her anymore.
Even when I see the kids, it's the nanny who brings them over. No. I'm in love with Lani.
Since she broke up with Ferdinand, she and I have become a lot closer, and . . .
And that girl will bring you nothing but trouble.
Because of her, Ferdinand no longer talks to me. And we were really good buddies, Ferdinand and me, so you see what I mean.

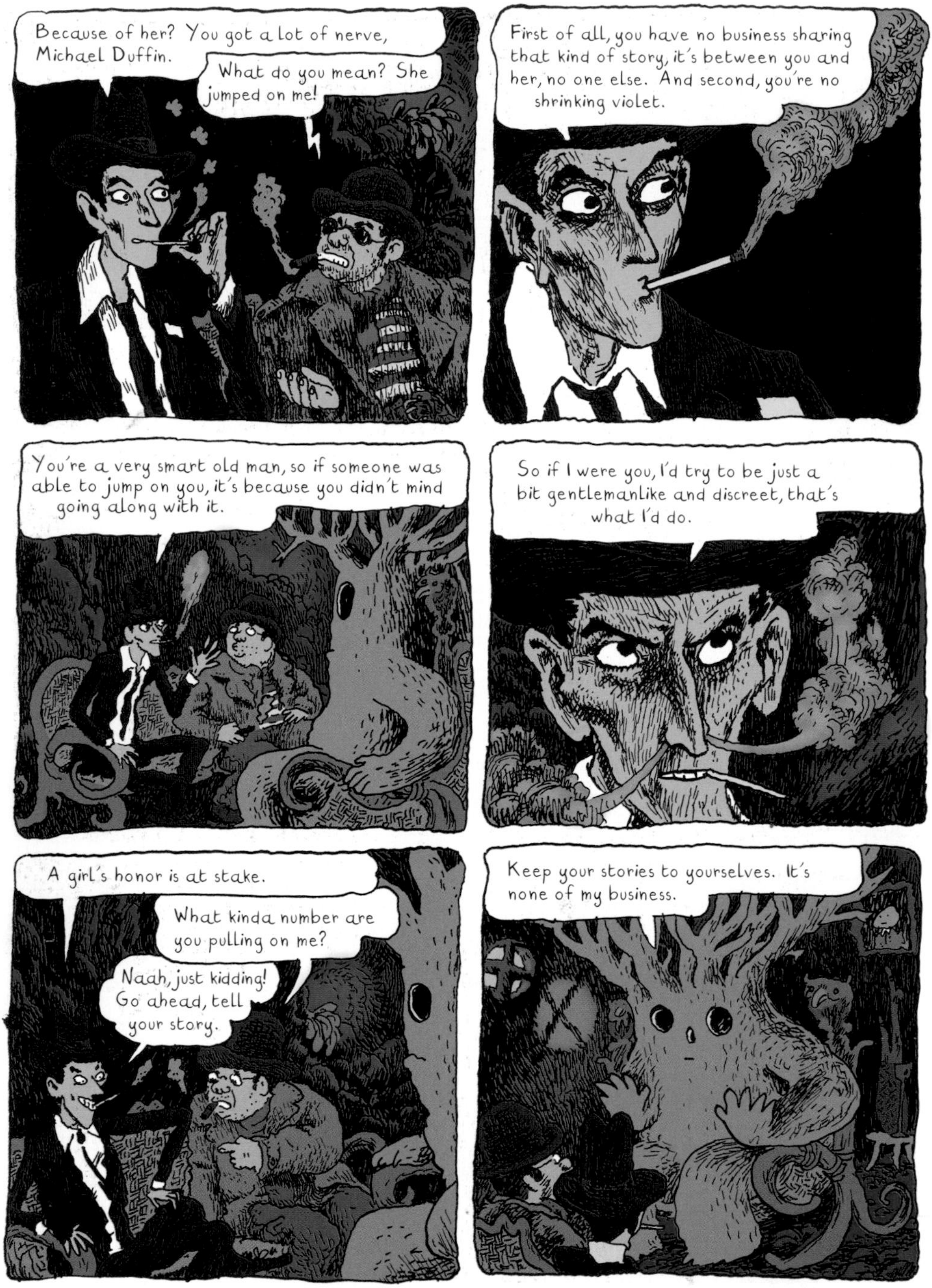

Because of her? You got a lot of nerve, Michael Duffin.
What do you mean? She jumped on me!
First of all, you have no business sharing that kind of story, it's between you and her, no one else. And second, you're no shrinking violet.
You're a very smart old man, so if someone was able to jump on you, it's because you didn't mind going along with it.
So if I were you, I'd try to be just a bit gentlemanlike and discreet, that's what I'd do.
A girl's honor is at stake.
What kinda number are you pulling on me?
Naah, just kidding! Go ahead, tell your story.
Keep your stories to yourselves. It's none of my business.

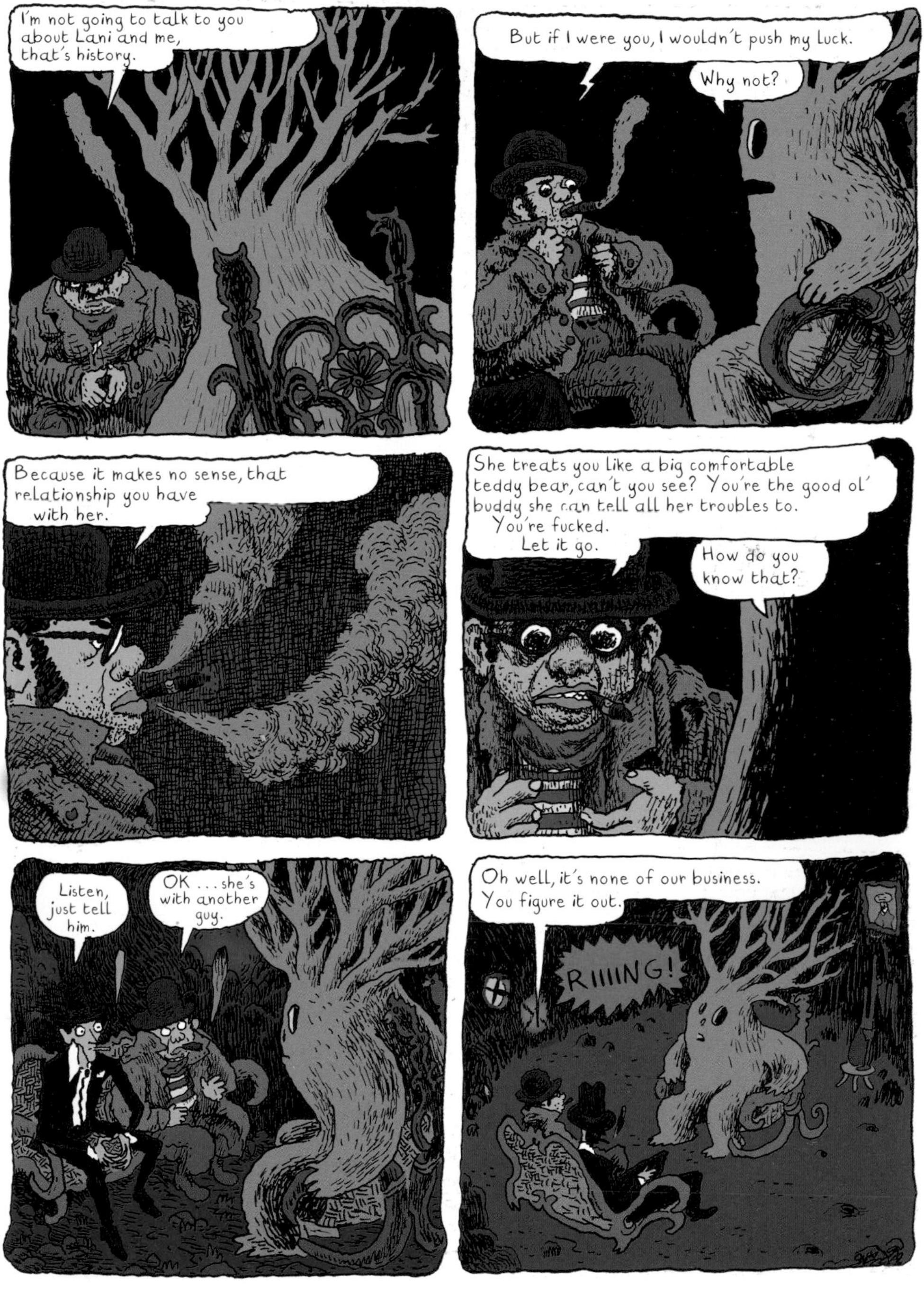
I'm not going to talk to you about Lani and me, that's history.
But if I were you, I wouldn't push my luck.
Why not?
Because it makes no sense, that relationship you have with her.
She treats you like a big comfortable teddy bear, can't you see? You're the good ol' buddy she can tell all her troubles to. You're fucked. Let it go.
How do you know that?
Listen, just tell him.
OK ... she's with another guy.
Oh well, it's none of our business. You figure it out.
RIIIING!

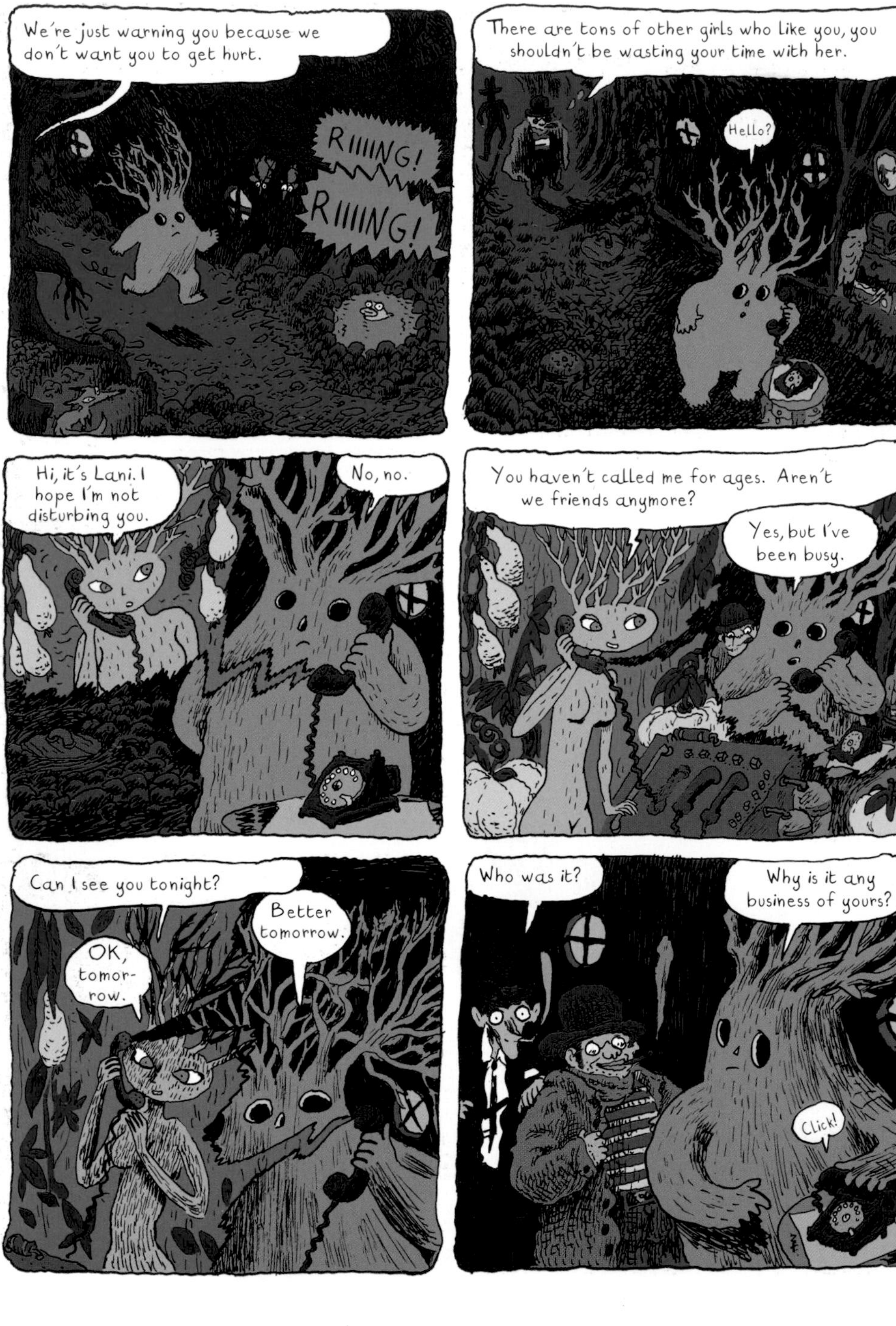
We're just warning you because we don't want you to get hurt.
RIIIING!
RIIIING!
There are tons of other girls who like you, you shouldn't be wasting your time with her.
Hello?
Hi, it's Lani. I hope I'm not disturbing you.
No, no.
You haven't called me for ages. Aren't we friends anymore?
Yes, but I've been busy.
Can I see you tonight?
Better tomorrow.
OK, tomorrow.
Who was it?
Why is it any business of yours?
Click!

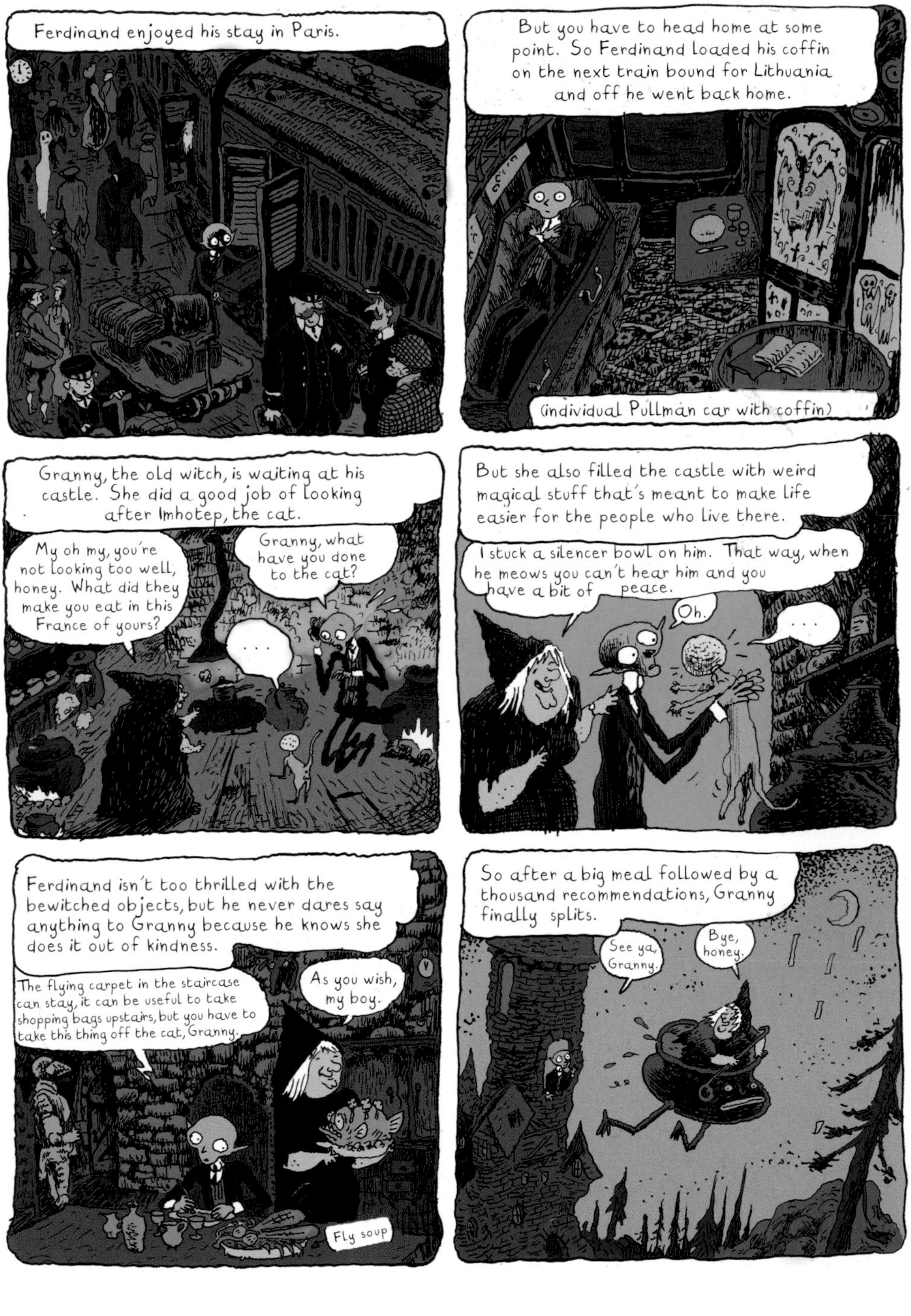
Ferdinand enjoyed his stay in Paris.
But you have to head home at some point. So Ferdinand loaded his coffin on the next train bound for Lithuania and off he went back home.
(individual Pullman car with coffin)
Granny, the old witch, is waiting at his castle. She did a good job of looking after Imhotep, the cat.
My oh my, you're not looking too well, honey. What did they make you eat in this France of yours?
Granny, what have you done to the cat?
...
But she also filled the castle with weird magical stuff that's meant to make life easier for the people who live there.
I stuck a silencer bowl on him. That way, when he meows you can't hear him and you have a bit of peace.
Oh.
...
Ferdinand isn't too thrilled with the bewitched objects, but he never dares say anything to Granny because he knows she does it out of kindness.
The flying carpet in the staircase can stay, it can be useful to take shopping bags upstairs, but you have to take this thing off the cat, Granny.
As you wish, my boy.
Fly soup
So after a big meal followed by a thousand recommendations, Granny finally splits.
See ya, Granny.
Bye, honey.

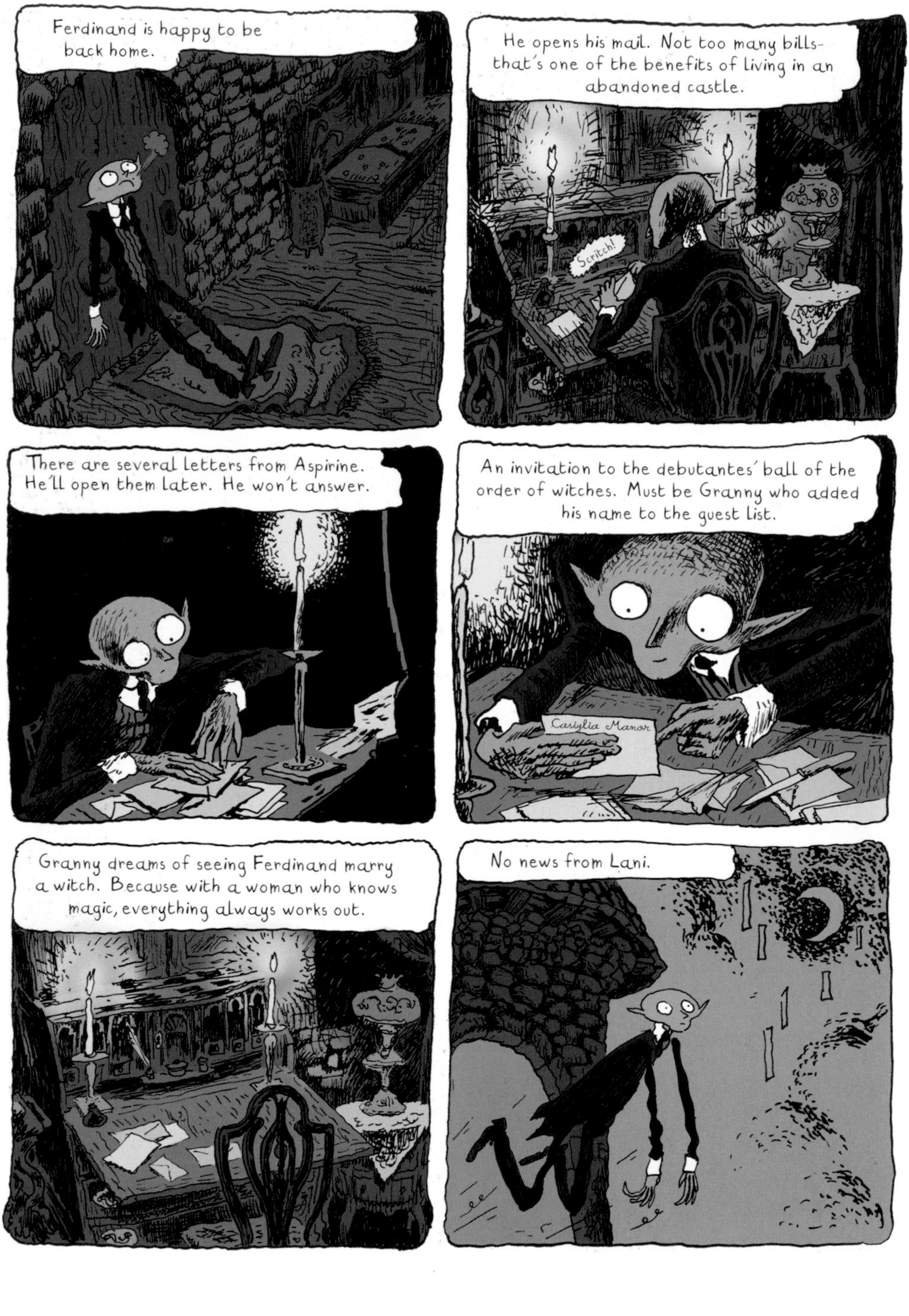
Ferdinand is happy to be back home.
He opens his mail. Not too many bills-that's one of the benefits of living in an abandoned castle.
Scritch!
There are several letters from Aspirine. He'll open them later. He won't answer.
An invitation to the debutantes' ball of the order of witches. Must be Granny who added his name to the guest list.
Casiglia Manor
Granny dreams of seeing Ferdinand marry a witch. Because with a woman who knows magic, everything always works out.
No news from Lani.

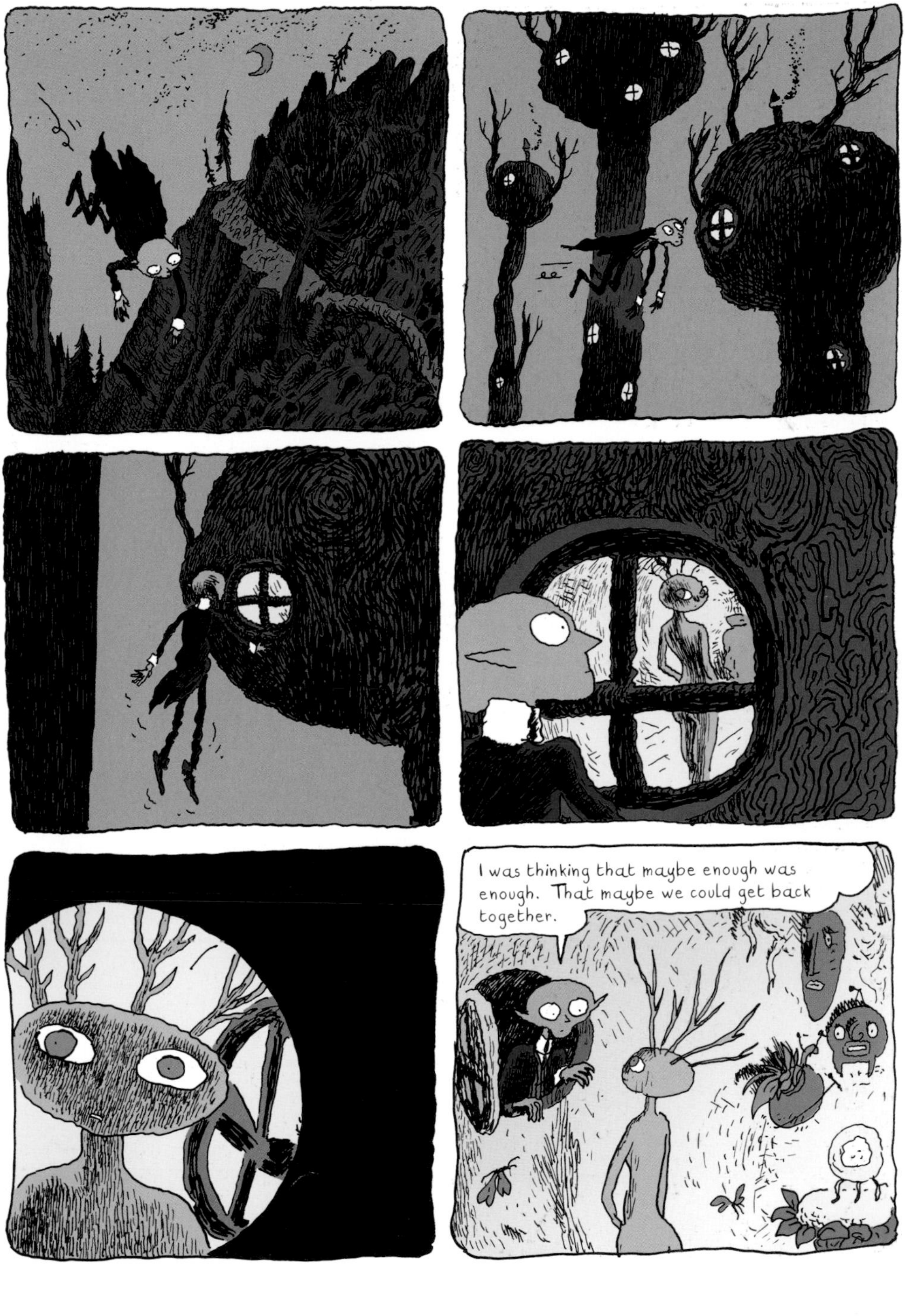
I was thinking that maybe enough was enough. That maybe we could get back together.

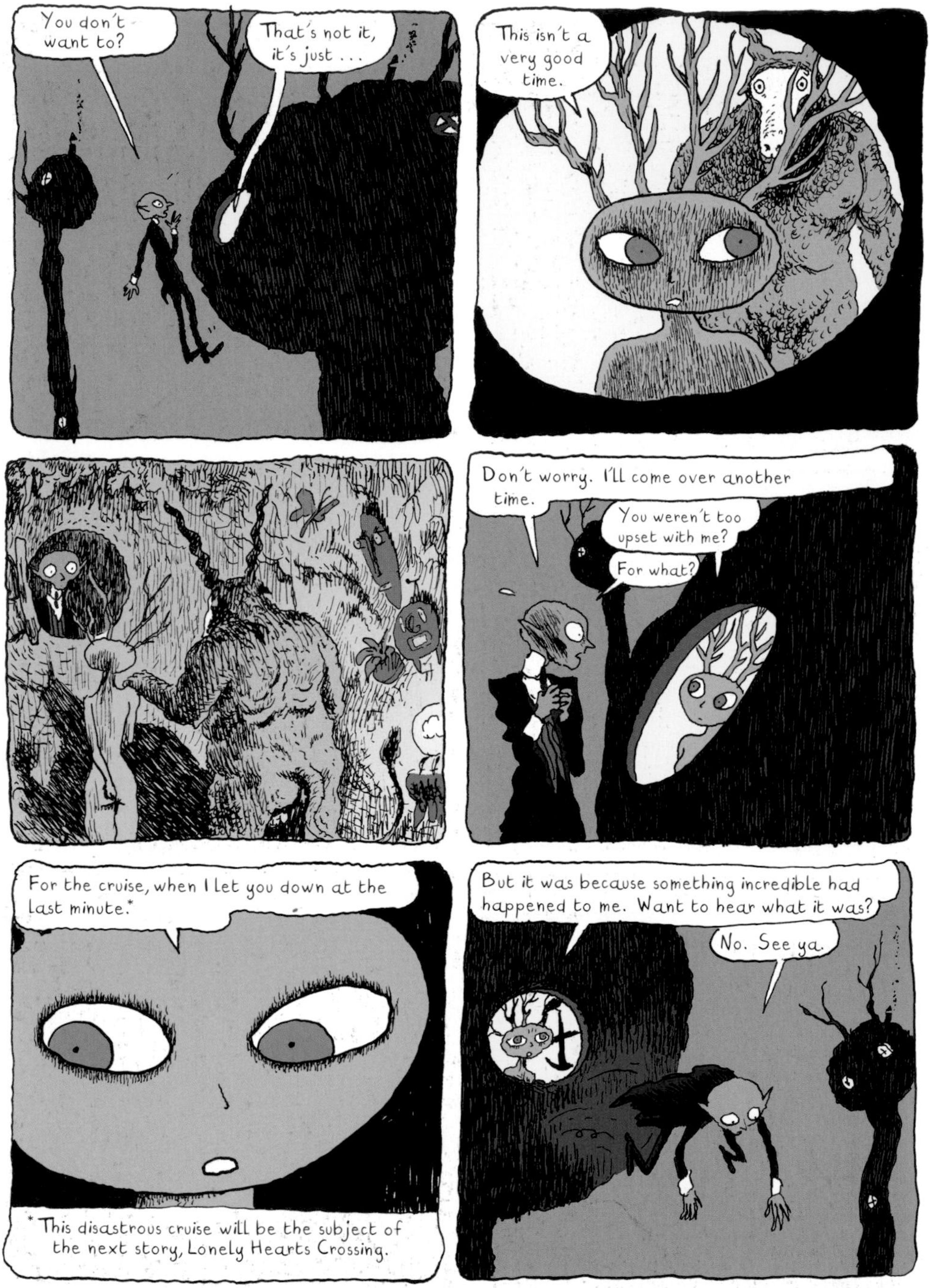
You don't want to?
That's not it, it's just . . .
This isn't a very good time.
Don't worry. I'll come over another time.
You weren't too upset with me?
For what?
For the cruise, when I let you down at the last minute.*
* This disastrous cruise will be the subject of the next story, Lonely Hearts Crossing.
But it was because something incredible had happened to me. Want to hear what it was?
No. See ya.

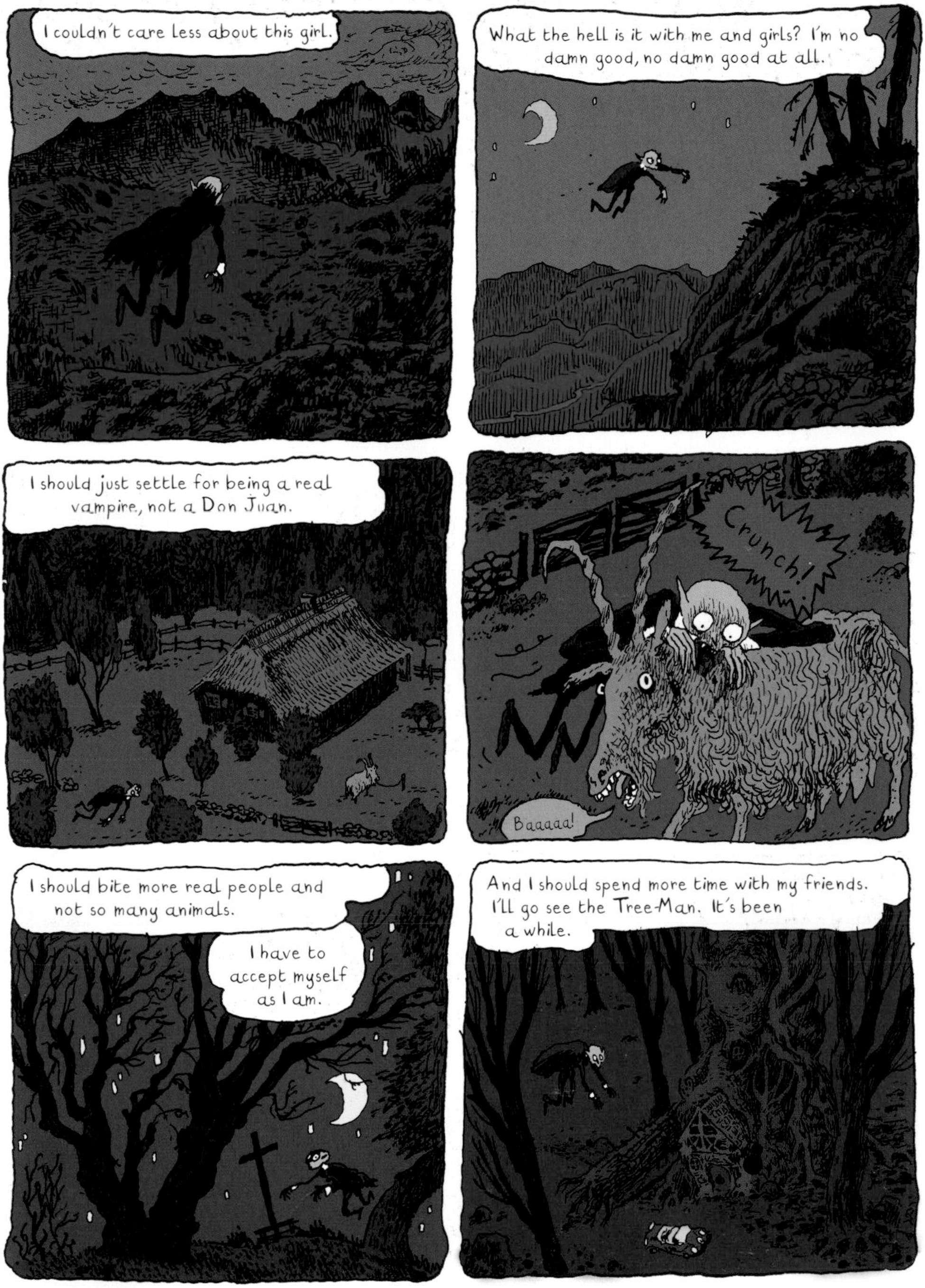
I couldn't care less about this girl.
What the hell is it with me and girls? I'm no damn good, no damn good at all.
I should just settle for being a real vampire, not a Don Juan.
Crunch!
Baaaaa!
I should bite more real people and not so many animals.
I have to accept myself as I am.
And I should spend more time with my friends. I'll go see the Tree-Man. It's been a while.

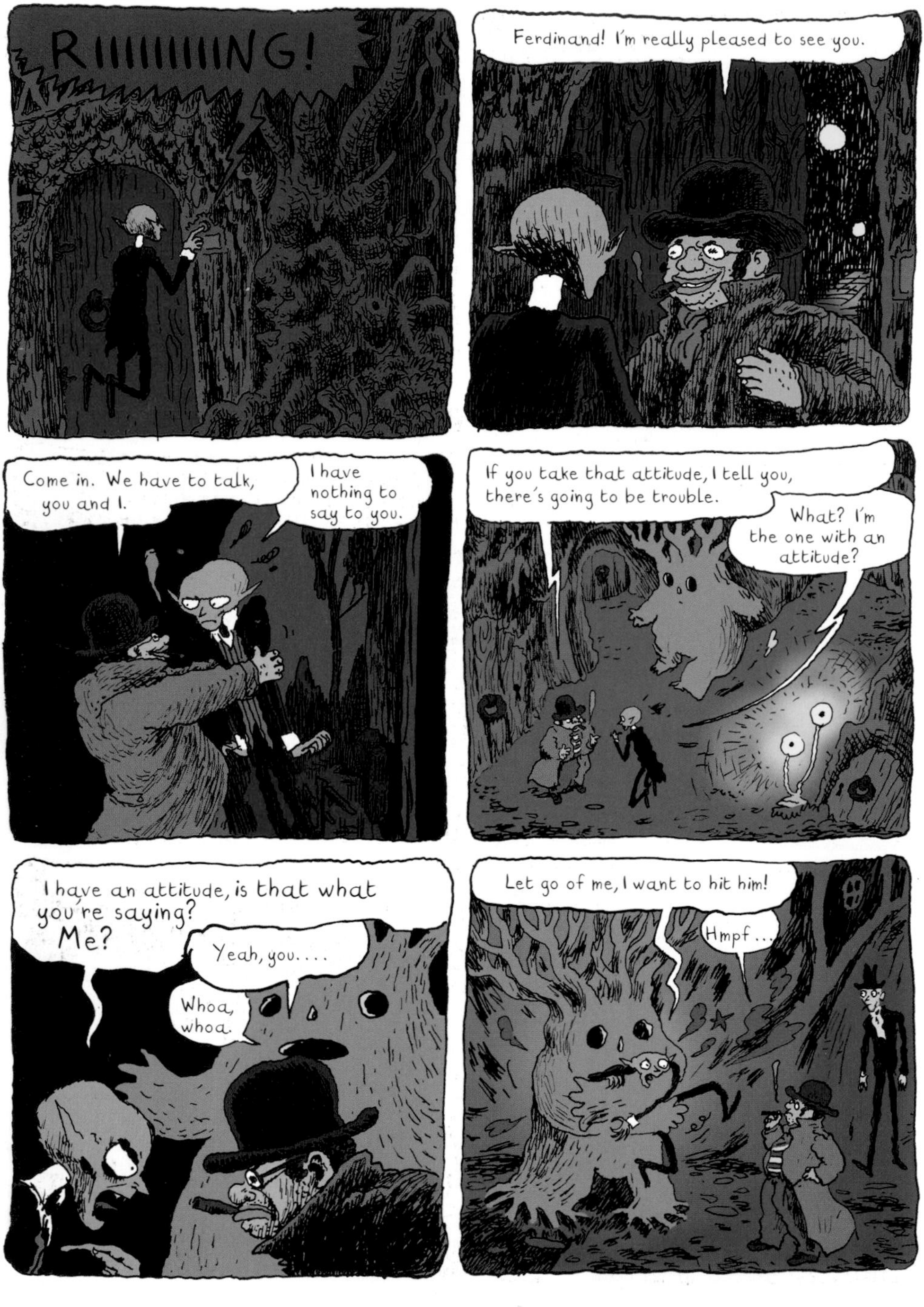
RIIIIIIIIING!
Ferdinand! I'm really pleased to see you.
Come in. We have to talk, you and I.
I have nothing to say to you.
If you take that attitude, I tell you, there's going to be trouble.
What? I'm the one with an attitude?
I have an attitude, is that what you're saying? Me?
Yeah, you....
Whoa, whoa.
Let go of me, I want to hit him!
Hmpf...

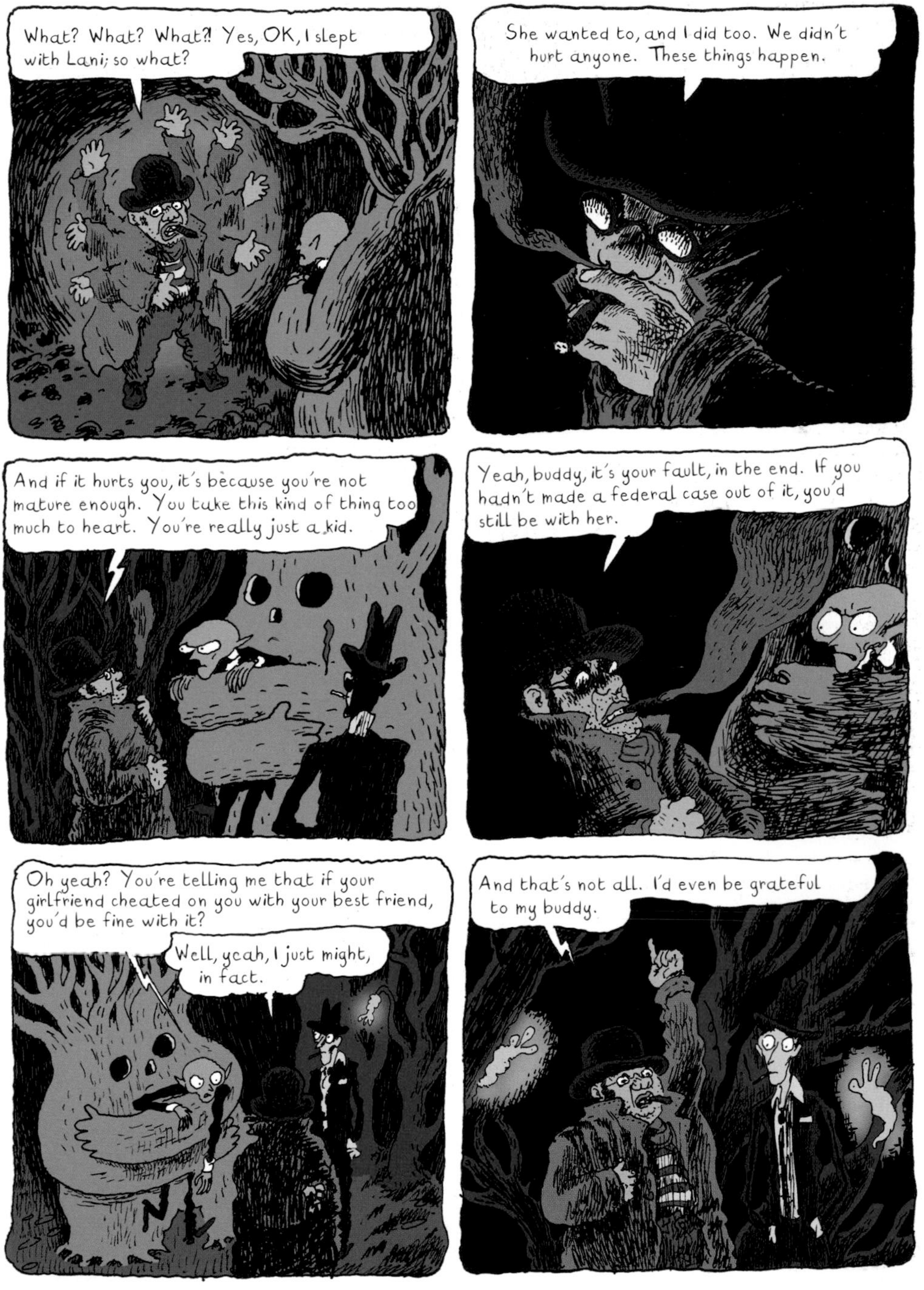
What? What? What?! Yes, OK, I slept with Lani; so what?
She wanted to, and I did too. We didn't hurt anyone. These things happen.
And if it hurts you, it's because you're not mature enough. You take this kind of thing too much to heart. You're really just a kid.
Yeah, buddy, it's your fault, in the end. If you hadn't made a federal case out of it, you'd still be with her.
Oh yeah? You're telling me that if your girlfriend cheated on you with your best friend, you'd be fine with it?
Well, yeah, I just might, in fact.
And that's not all. I'd even be grateful to my buddy.

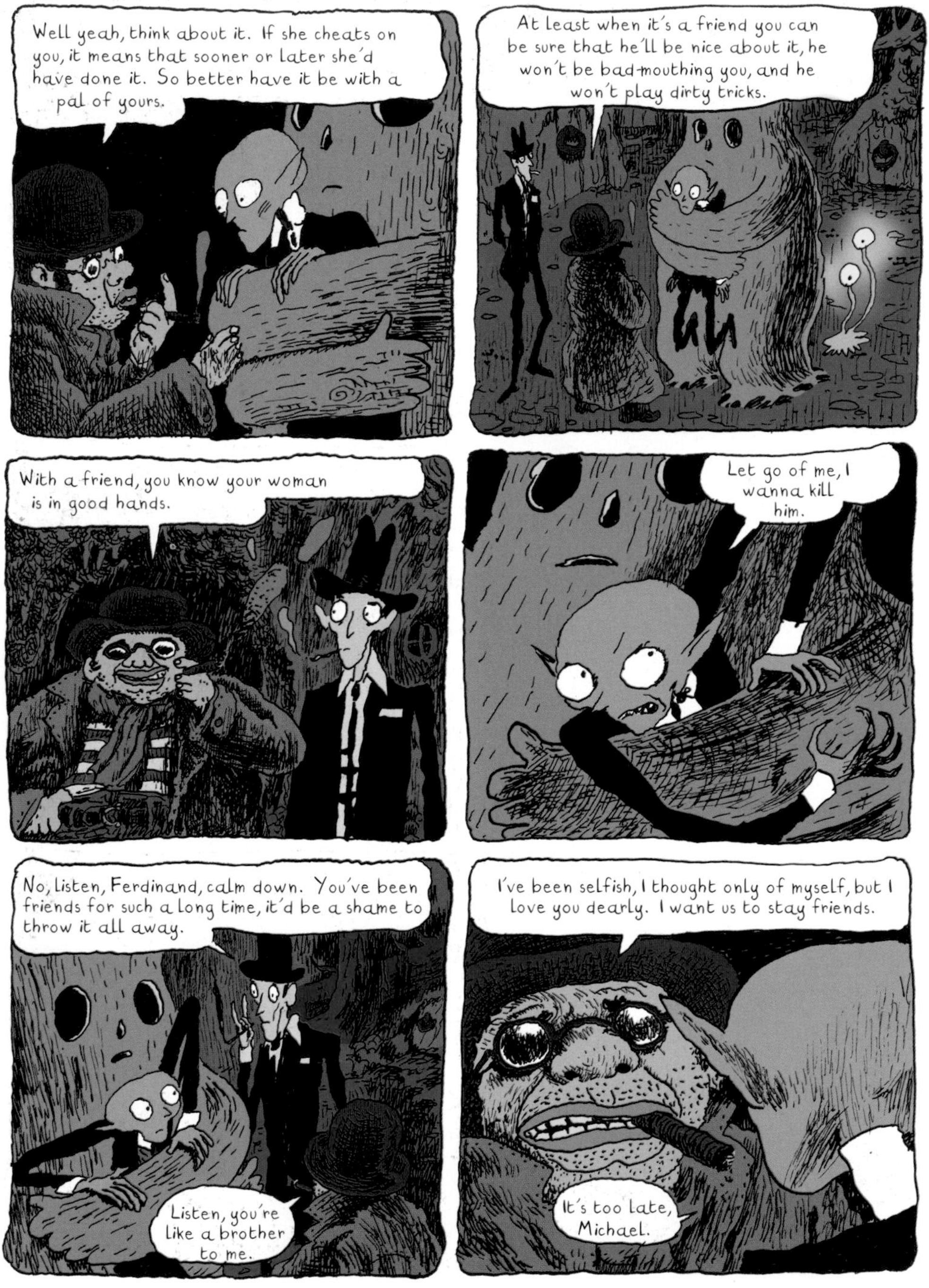
Well yeah, think about it. If she cheats on you, it means that sooner or later she'd have done it. So better have it be with a pal of yours.
At least when it's a friend you can be sure that he'll be nice about it, he won't be bad-mouthing you, and he won't play dirty tricks.
With a friend, you know your woman is in good hands.
Let go of me, I wanna kill him.
No, listen, Ferdinand, calm down. You've been friends for such a long time, it'd be a shame to throw it all away.
Listen, you're like a brother to me.
I've been selfish, I thought only of myself, but I love you dearly. I want us to stay friends.
It's too late, Michael.

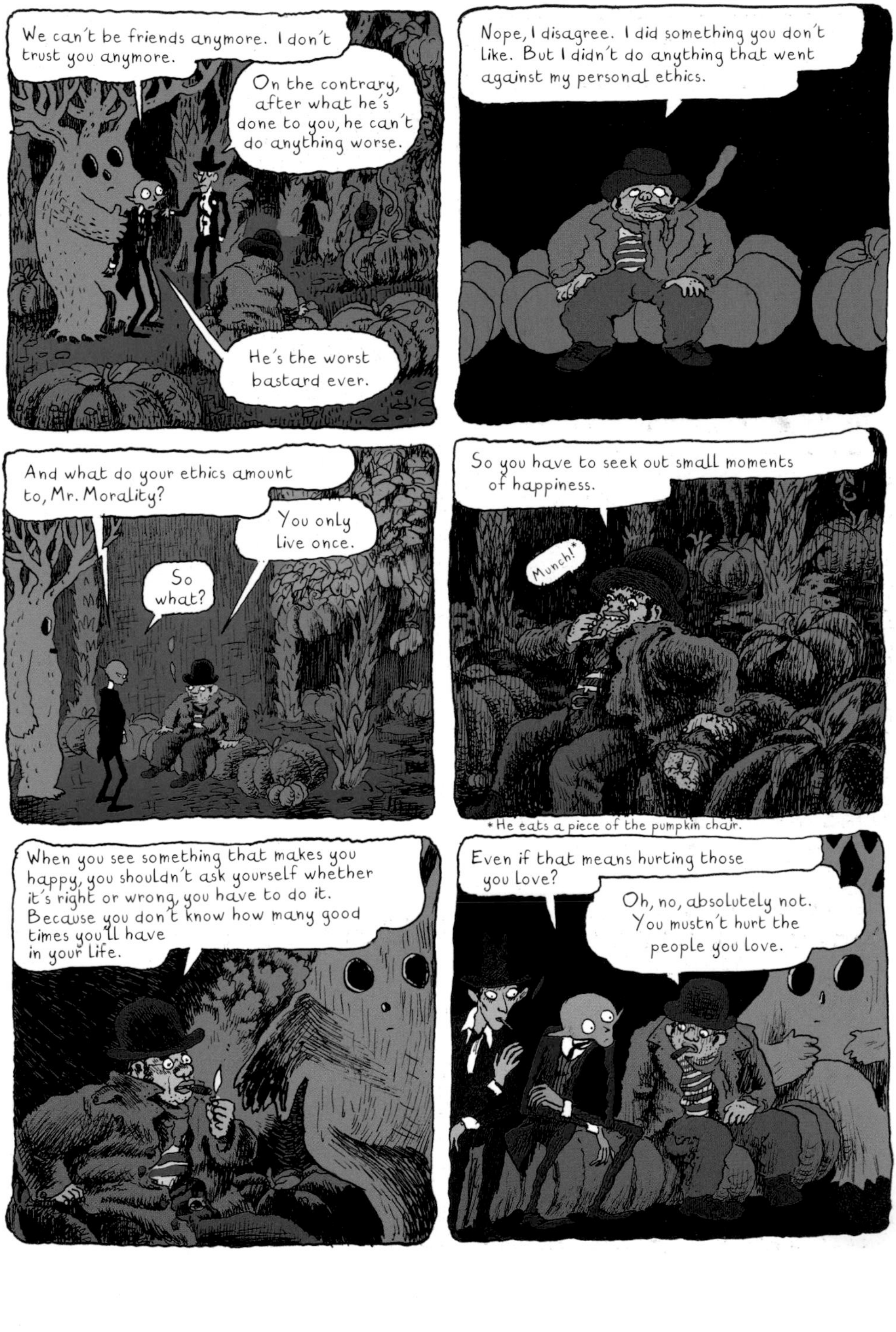
We can't be friends anymore. I don't trust you anymore.
On the contrary, after what he's done to you, he can't do anything worse.
He's the worst bastard ever.
Nope, I disagree. I did something you don't like. But I didn't do anything that went against my personal ethics.
And what do your ethics amount to, Mr. Morality?
You only live once.
So what?
So you have to seek out small moments of happiness.
Munch!*
*He eats a piece of the pumpkin chair.
When you see something that makes you happy, you shouldn't ask yourself whether it's right or wrong, you have to do it. Because you don't know how many good times you'll have in your life.
Even if that means hurting those you love?
Oh, no, absolutely not. You mustn't hurt the people you love.

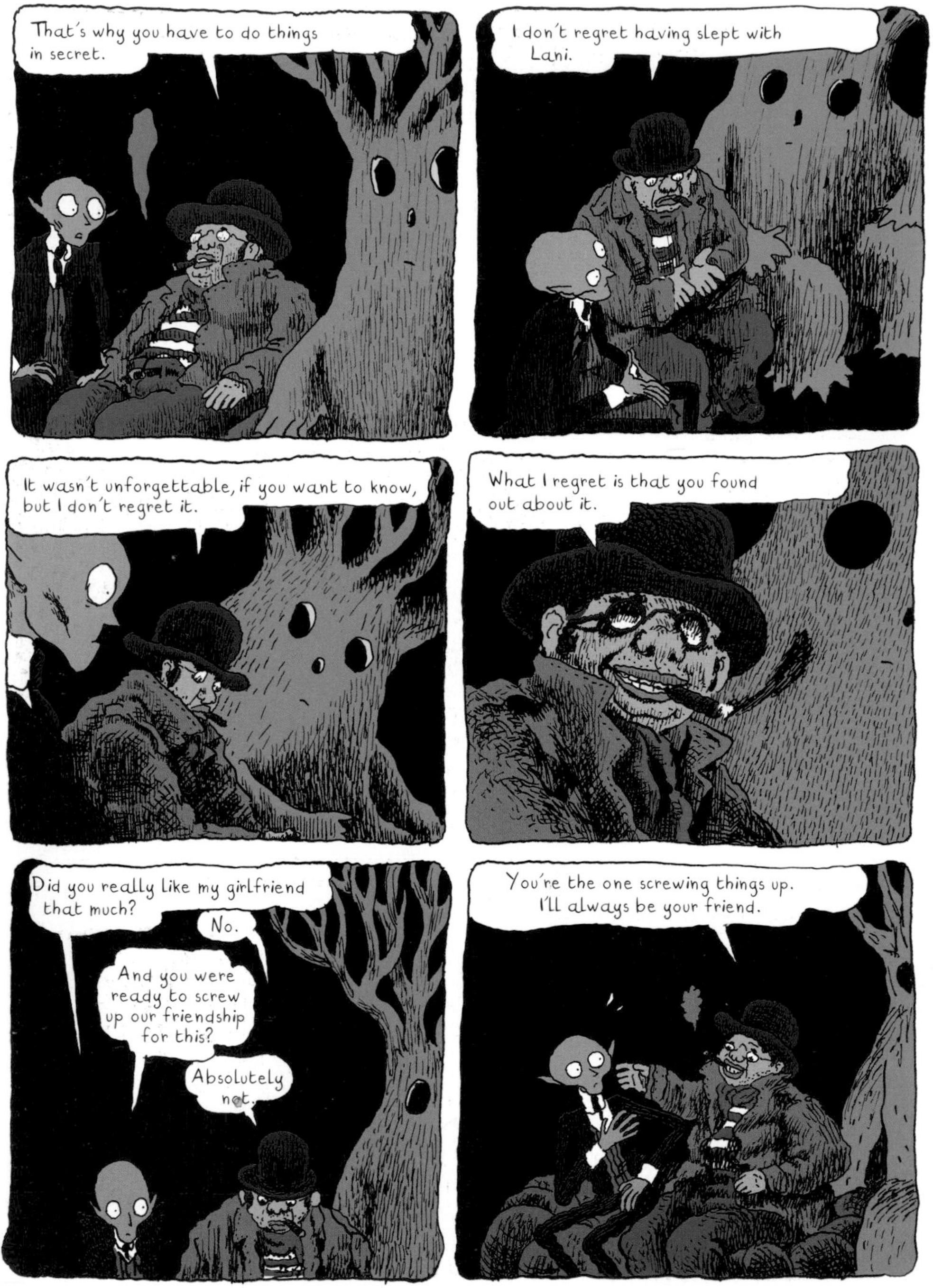
That's why you have to do things in secret.
I don't regret having slept with Lani.
It wasn't unforgettable, if you want to know, but I don't regret it.
What I regret is that you found out about it.
Did you really like my girlfriend that much?
No.
And you were ready to screw up our friendship for this?
Absolutely not.
You're the one screwing things up. I'll always be your friend.

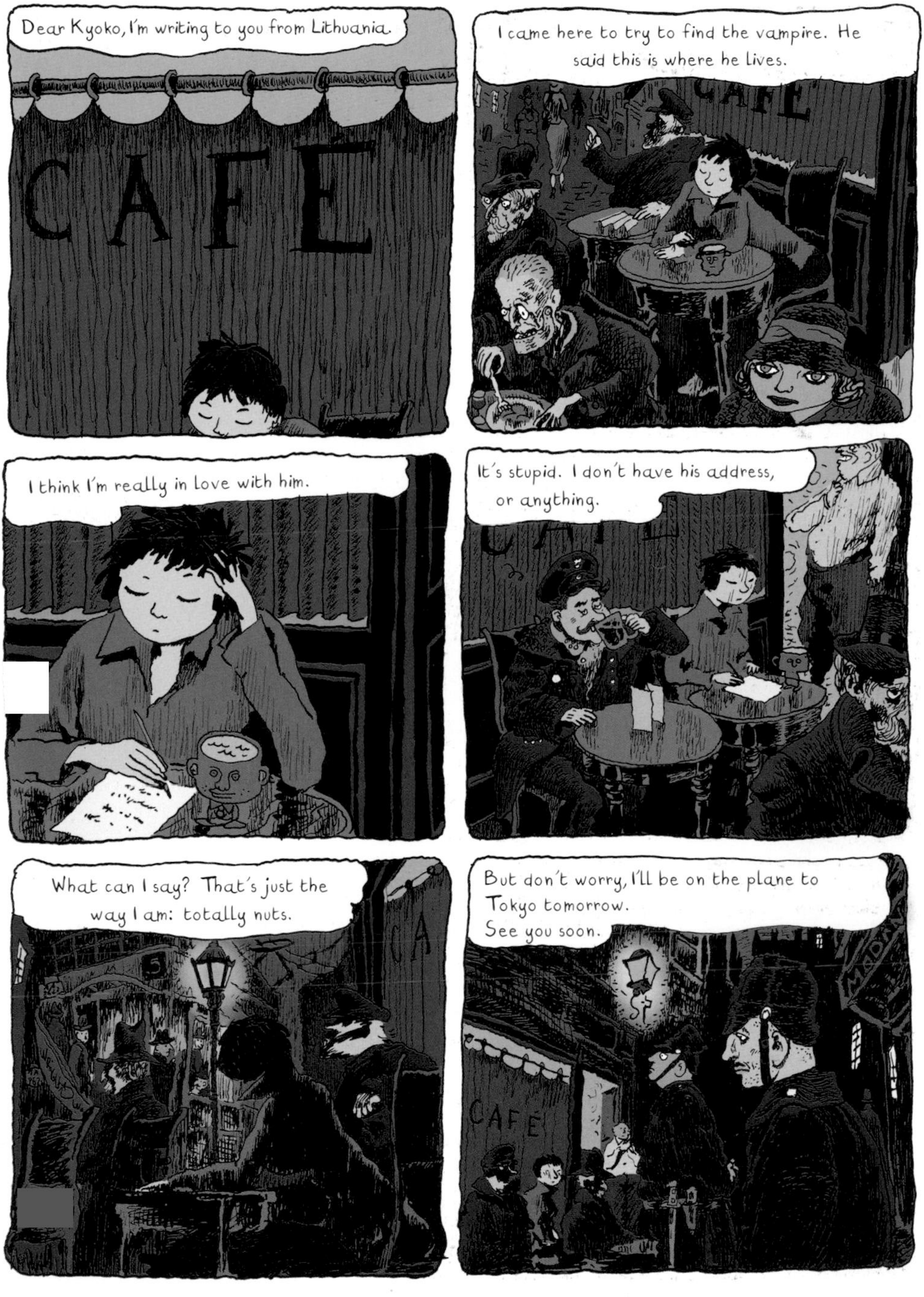
Dear Kyoko, I'm writing to you from Lithuania.
CAFÉ
I came here to try to find the vampire. He said this is where he lives.
I think I'm really in love with him.
It's stupid. I don't have his address, or anything.
What can I say? That's just the way I am: totally nuts.
But don't worry, I'll be on the plane to Tokyo tomorrow. See you soon.
CAFÉ

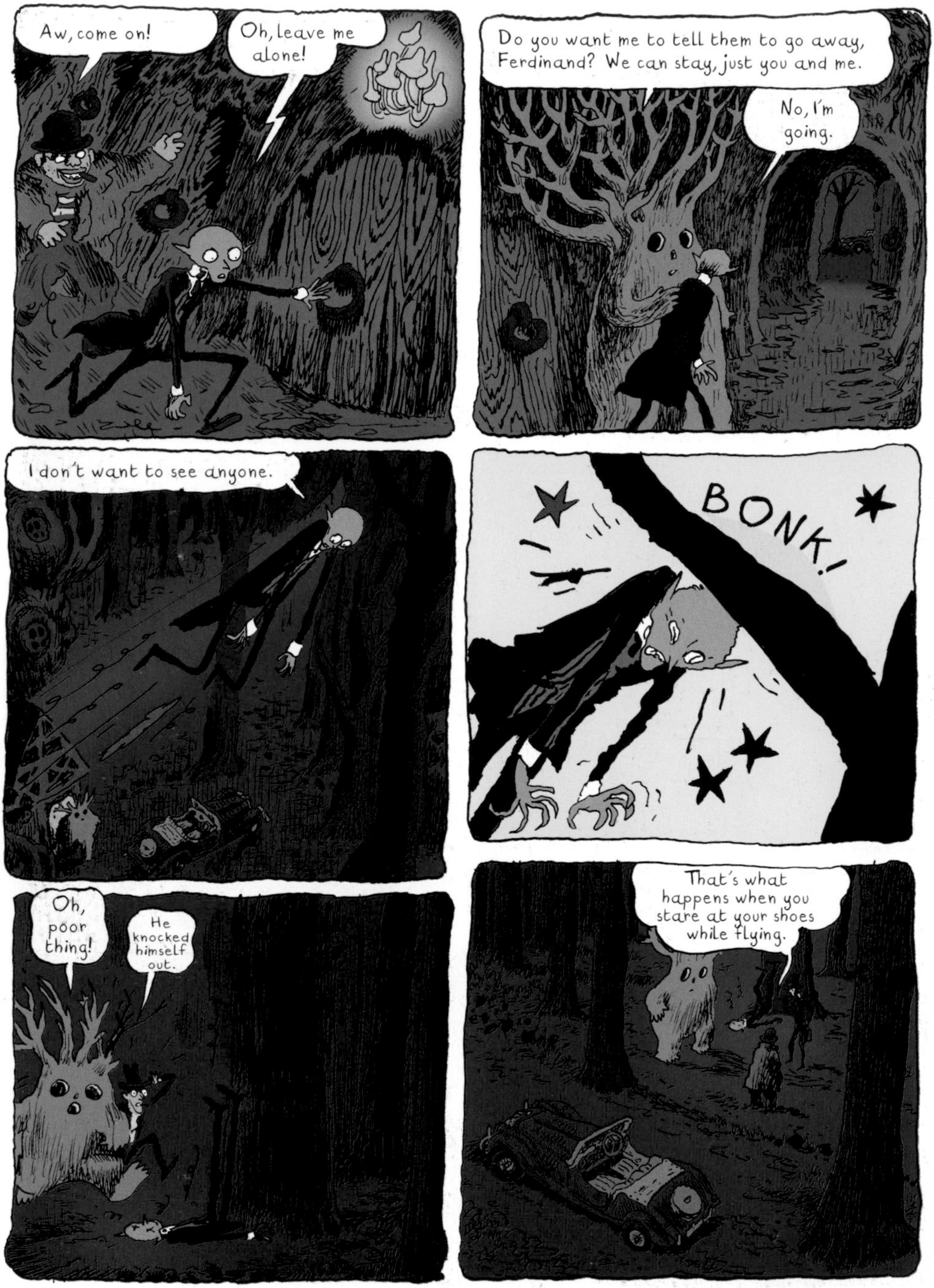
Aw, come on!
Oh, leave me alone!
Do you want me to tell them to go away, Ferdinand? We can stay, just you and me.
No, I'm going.
I don't want to see anyone.
BONK!
Oh, poor thing!
He knocked himself out.
That's what happens when you stare at your shoes while flying.

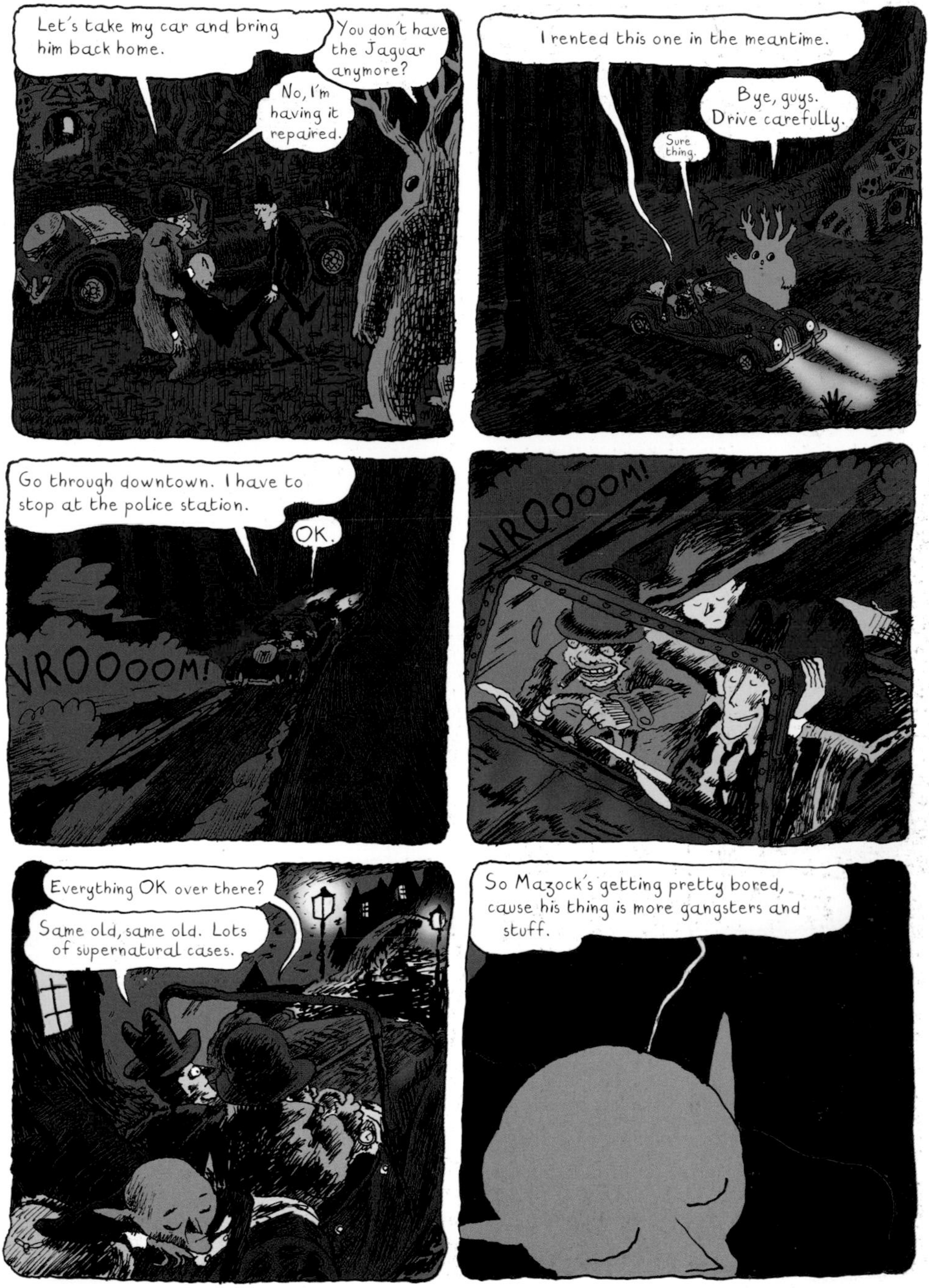
Let's take my car and bring him back home.
You don't have the Jaguar anymore?
No, I'm having it repaired.
I rented this one in the meantime.
Sure thing.
Bye, guys. Drive carefully.
Go through downtown. I have to stop at the police station.
OK.
VROOOOM!
VROOOOM!
Everything OK over there?
Same old, same old. Lots of supernatural cases.
So Mazock's getting pretty bored, cause his thing is more gangsters and stuff.

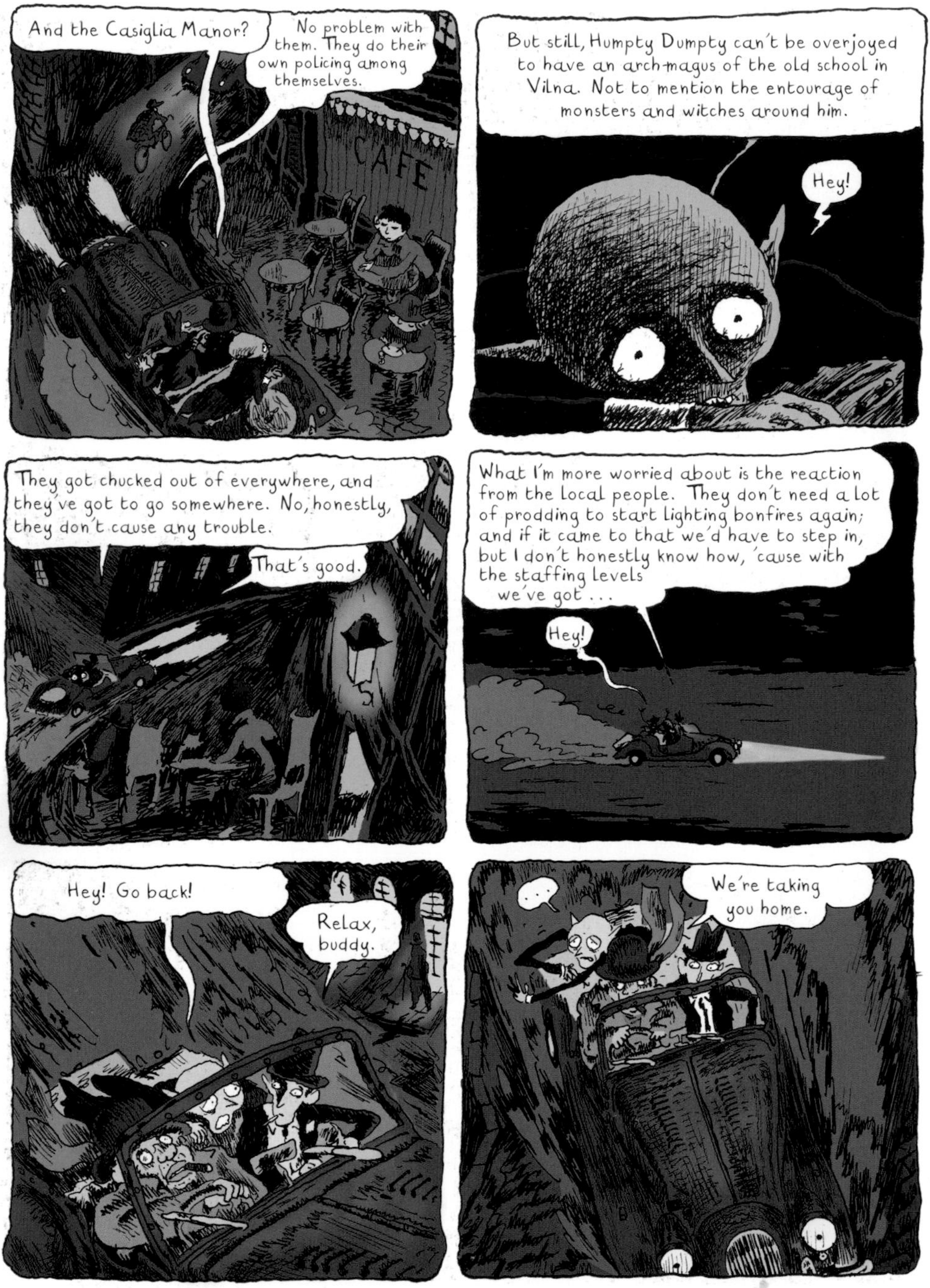
And the Casiglia Manor?
No problem with them. They do their own policing among themselves.
CAFE
But still, Humpty Dumpty can't be overjoyed to have an arch-magus of the old school in Vilna. Not to mention the entourage of monsters and witches around him.
Hey!
They got chucked out of everywhere, and they've got to go somewhere. No, honestly, they don't cause any trouble.
That's good.
What I'm more worried about is the reaction from the local people. They don't need a lot of prodding to start lighting bonfires again; and if it came to that we'd have to step in, but I don't honestly know how, 'cause with the staffing levels we've got . . .
Hey!
Hey! Go back!
Relax, buddy.
. . .
We're taking you home.

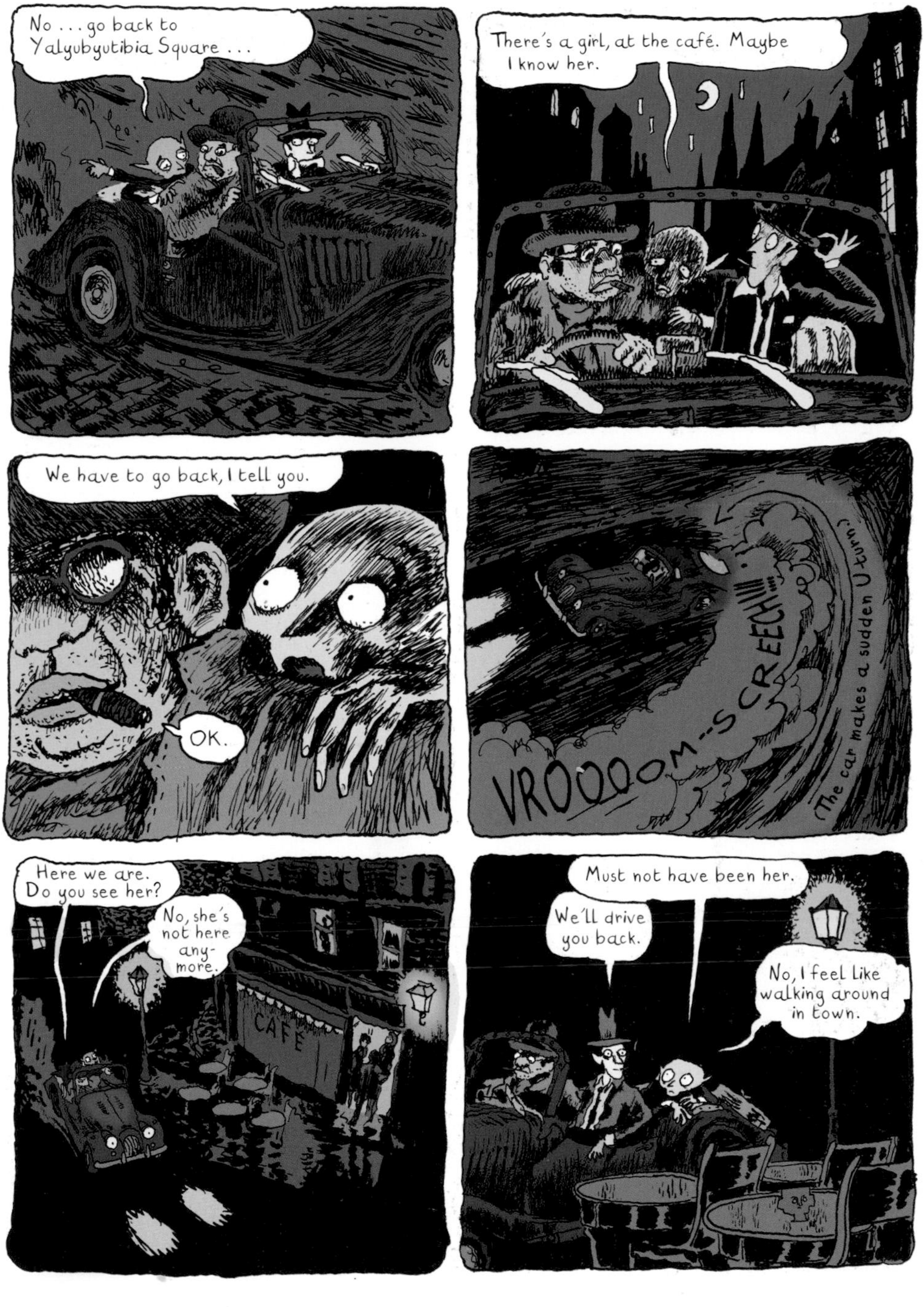
No . . . go back to Yalyubyutibia Square . . .
There's a girl, at the café. Maybe I know her.
We have to go back, I tell you.
OK.
VROOOOOM-SCREEEECH!!!!!!
(The car makes a sudden U-turn.)
Here we are. Do you see her?
No, she's not here any-more.
CAFÉ
Must not have been her.
We'll drive you back.
No, I feel like walking around in town.

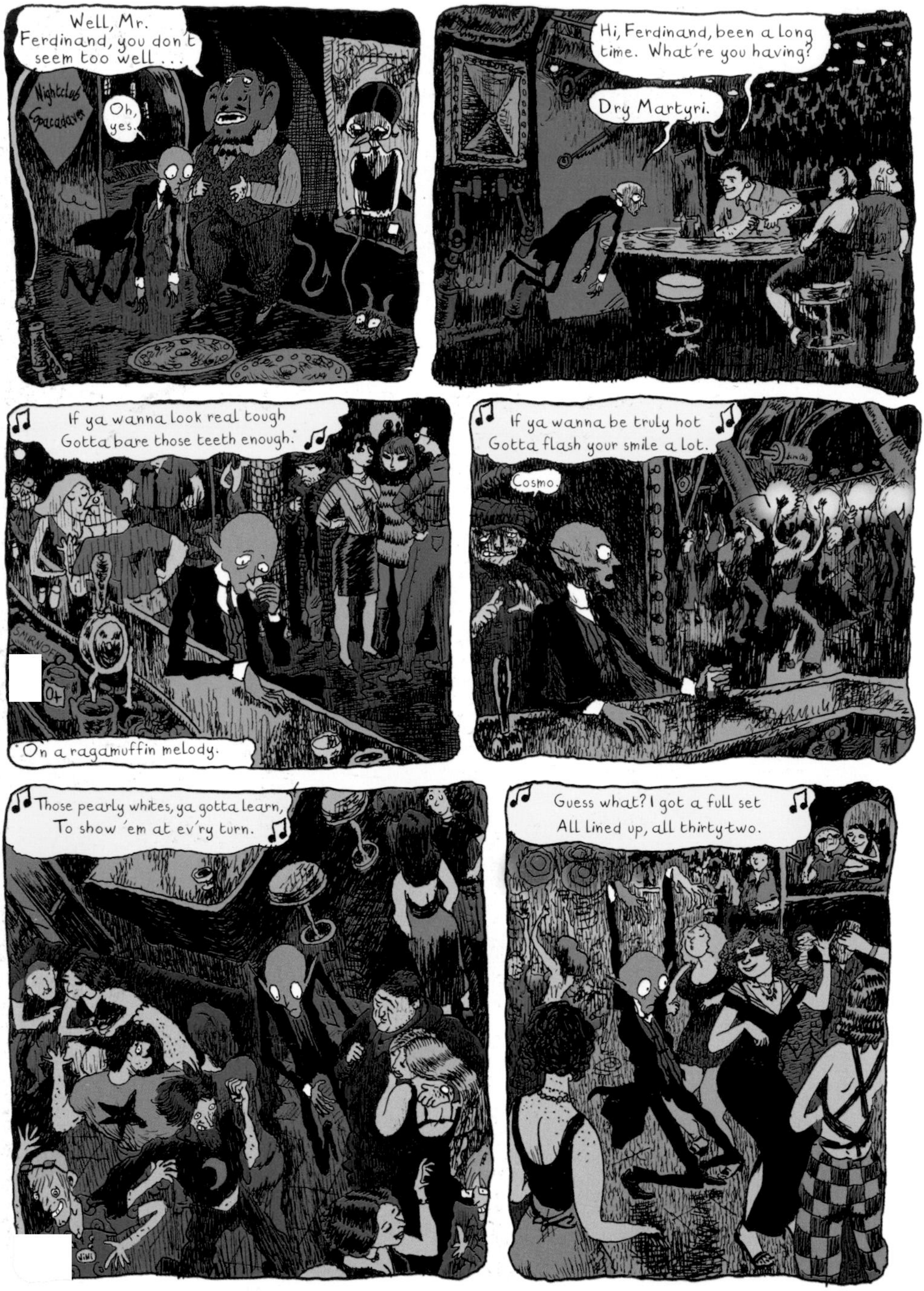
Well, Mr. Ferdinand, you don't seem too well . . .
Nightclub Copacadaver
Oh, yes.
Hi, Ferdinand, been a long time. What're you having?
Dry Martyri.
If ya wanna look real tough
Gotta bare those teeth enough.
On a ragamuffin melody.
If ya wanna be truly hot
Gotta flash your smile a lot.
Cosmo.
Those pearly whites, ya gotta learn,
To show 'em at ev'ry turn.
Guess what? I got a full set
All lined up, all thirty-two.

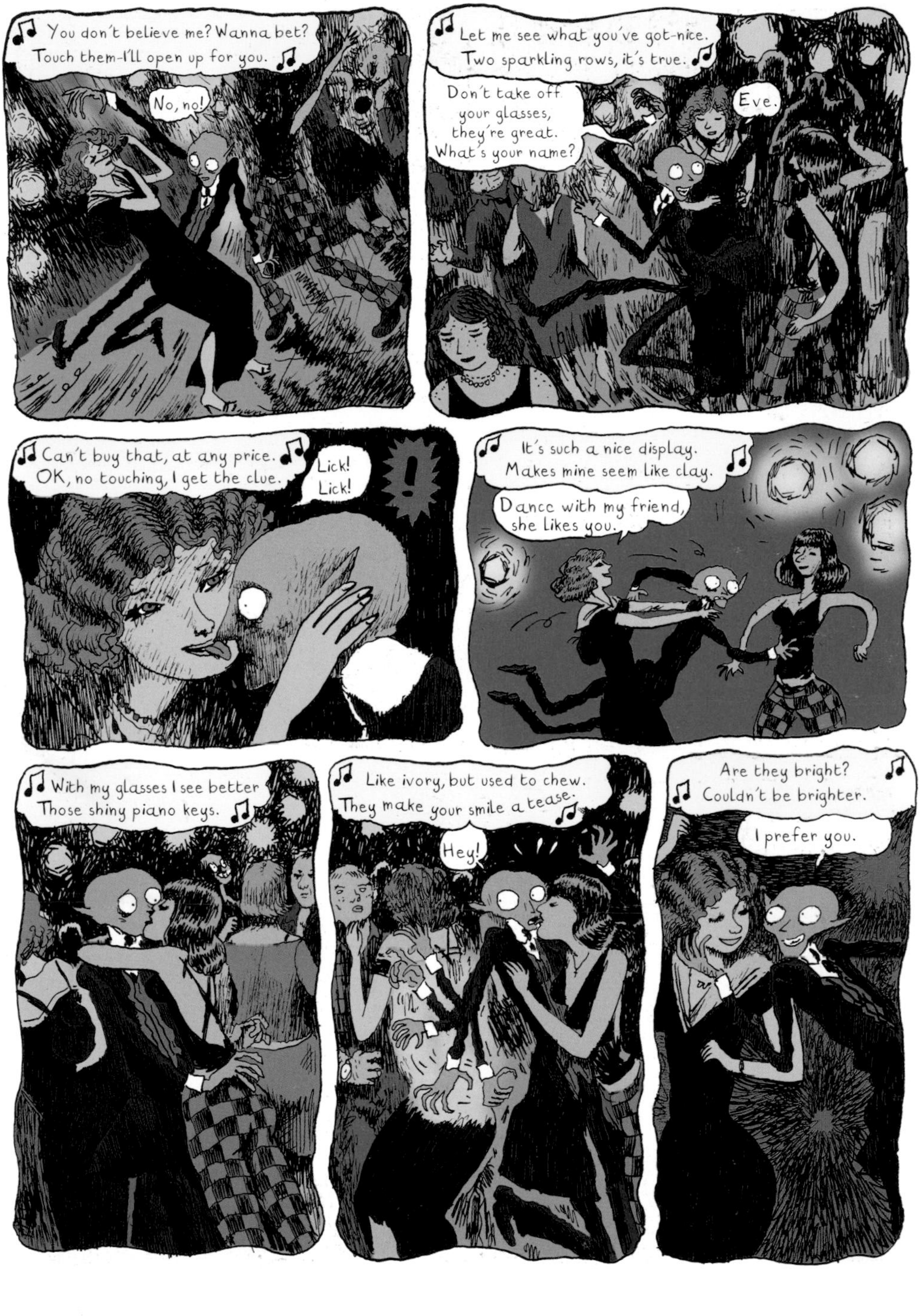
You don't believe me? Wanna bet? Touch them-I'll open up for you.
No, no!
Let me see what you've got-nice. Two sparkling rows, it's true.
Don't take off your glasses, they're great. What's your name?
Eve.
Can't buy that, at any price. OK, no touching, I get the clue.
Lick! Lick!
!
It's such a nice display. Makes mine seem like clay.
Dance with my friend, she likes you.
With my glasses I see better Those shiny piano keys.
Like ivory, but used to chew. They make your smile a tease.
Hey!
Are they bright? Couldn't be brighter.
I prefer you.

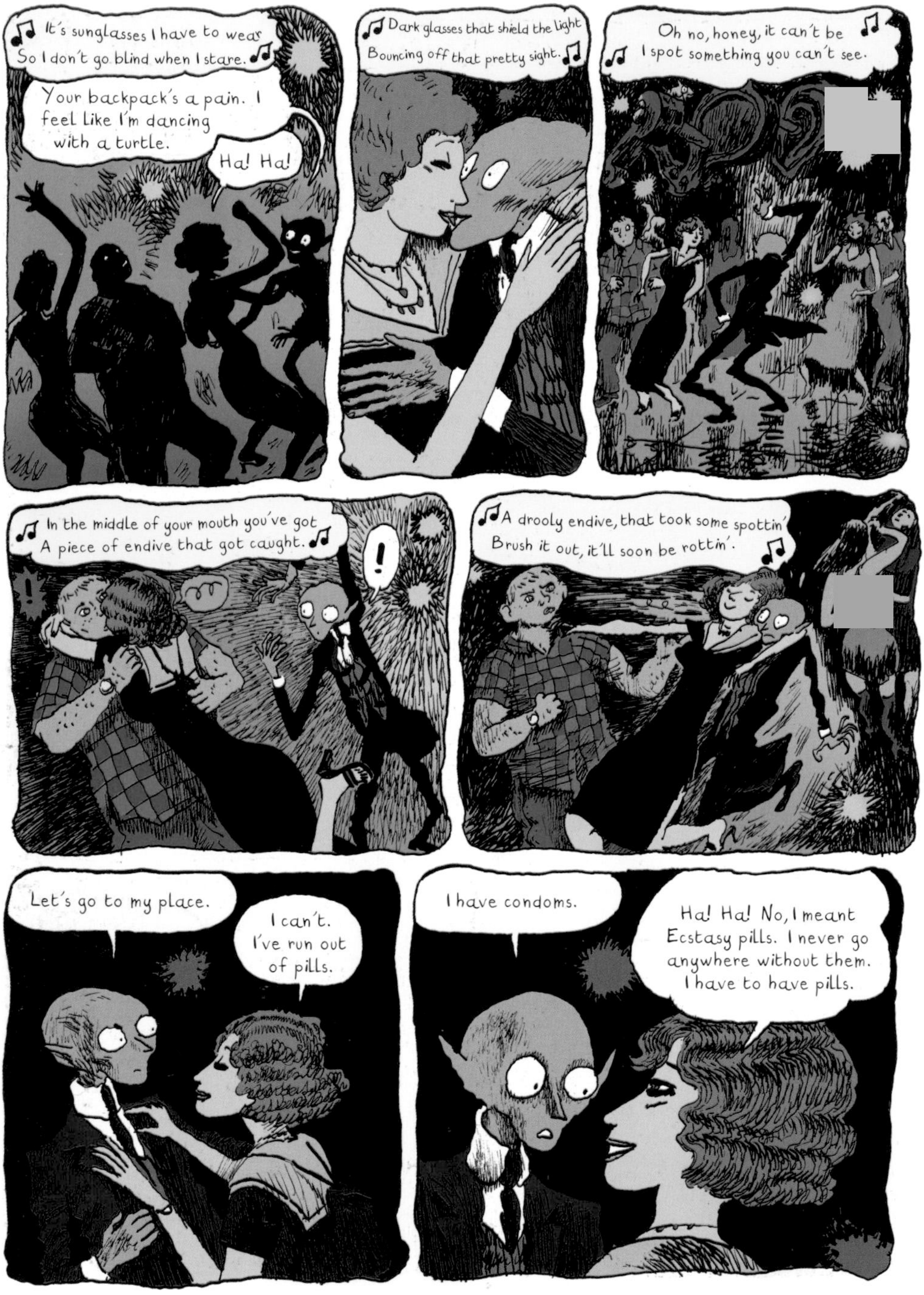
It's sunglasses I have to wear
So I don't go blind when I stare.
Your backpack's a pain. I feel like I'm dancing with a turtle.
Ha! Ha!
Dark glasses that shield the light
Bouncing off that pretty sight.
Oh no, honey, it can't be
I spot something you can't see.
In the middle of your mouth you've got
A piece of endive that got caught.
!
A drooly endive, that took some spottin'
Brush it out, it'll soon be rottin'.
Let's go to my place.
I can't. I've run out of pills.
I have condoms.
Ha! Ha! No, I meant Ecstasy pills. I never go anywhere without them. I have to have pills.

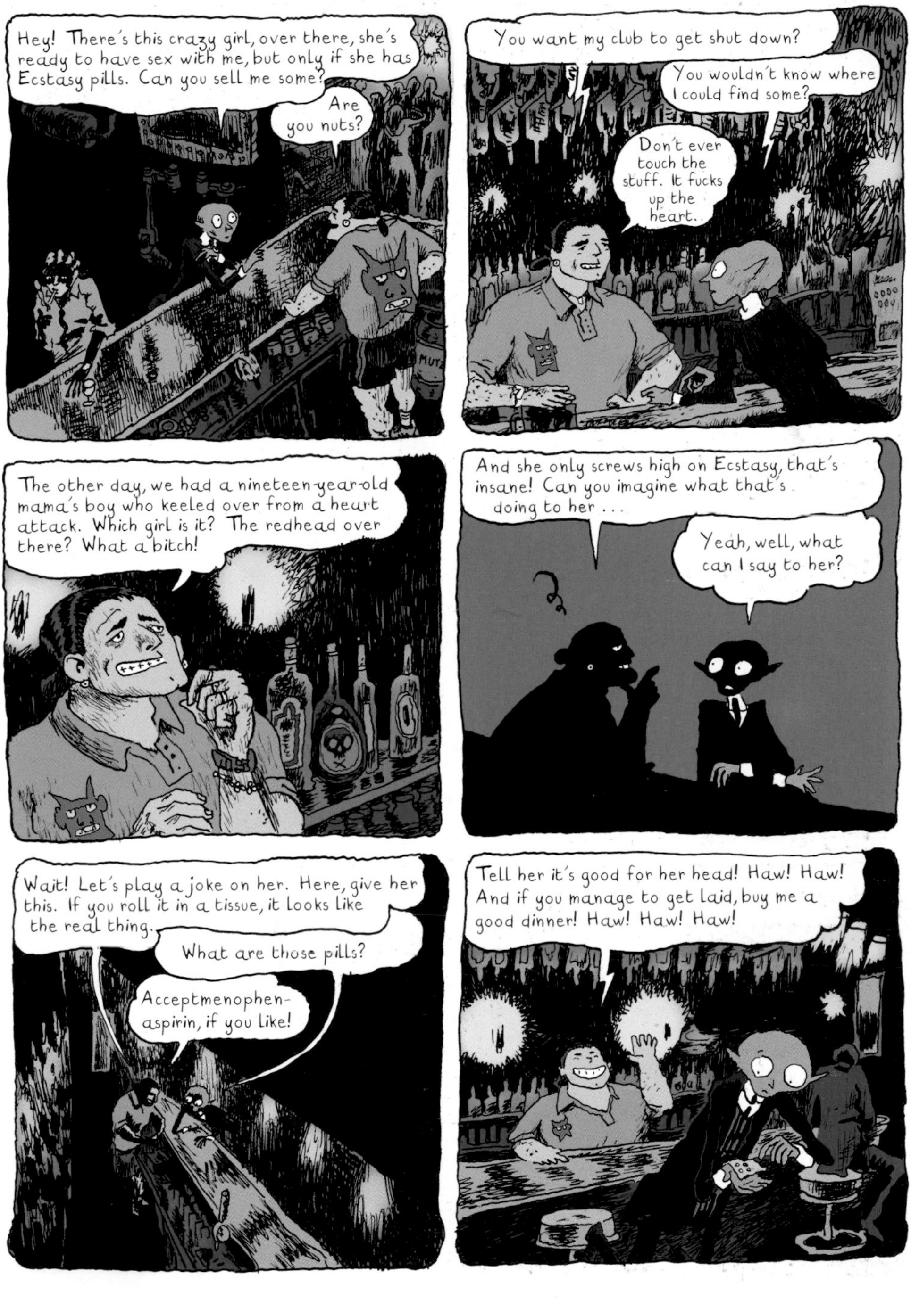
Hey! There's this crazy girl, over there, she's ready to have sex with me, but only if she has Ecstasy pills. Can you sell me some?
Are you nuts?
You want my club to get shut down?
You wouldn't know where I could find some?
Don't ever touch the stuff. It fucks up the heart.
The other day, we had a nineteen-year-old mama's boy who keeled over from a heart attack. Which girl is it? The redhead over there? What a bitch!
And she only screws high on Ecstasy, that's insane! Can you imagine what that's doing to her . . .
Yeah, well, what can I say to her?
Wait! Let's play a joke on her. Here, give her this. If you roll it in a tissue, it looks like the real thing.
What are those pills?
Acceptmenophen-aspirin, if you like!
Tell her it's good for her head! Haw! Haw! And if you manage to get laid, buy me a good dinner! Haw! Haw! Haw!

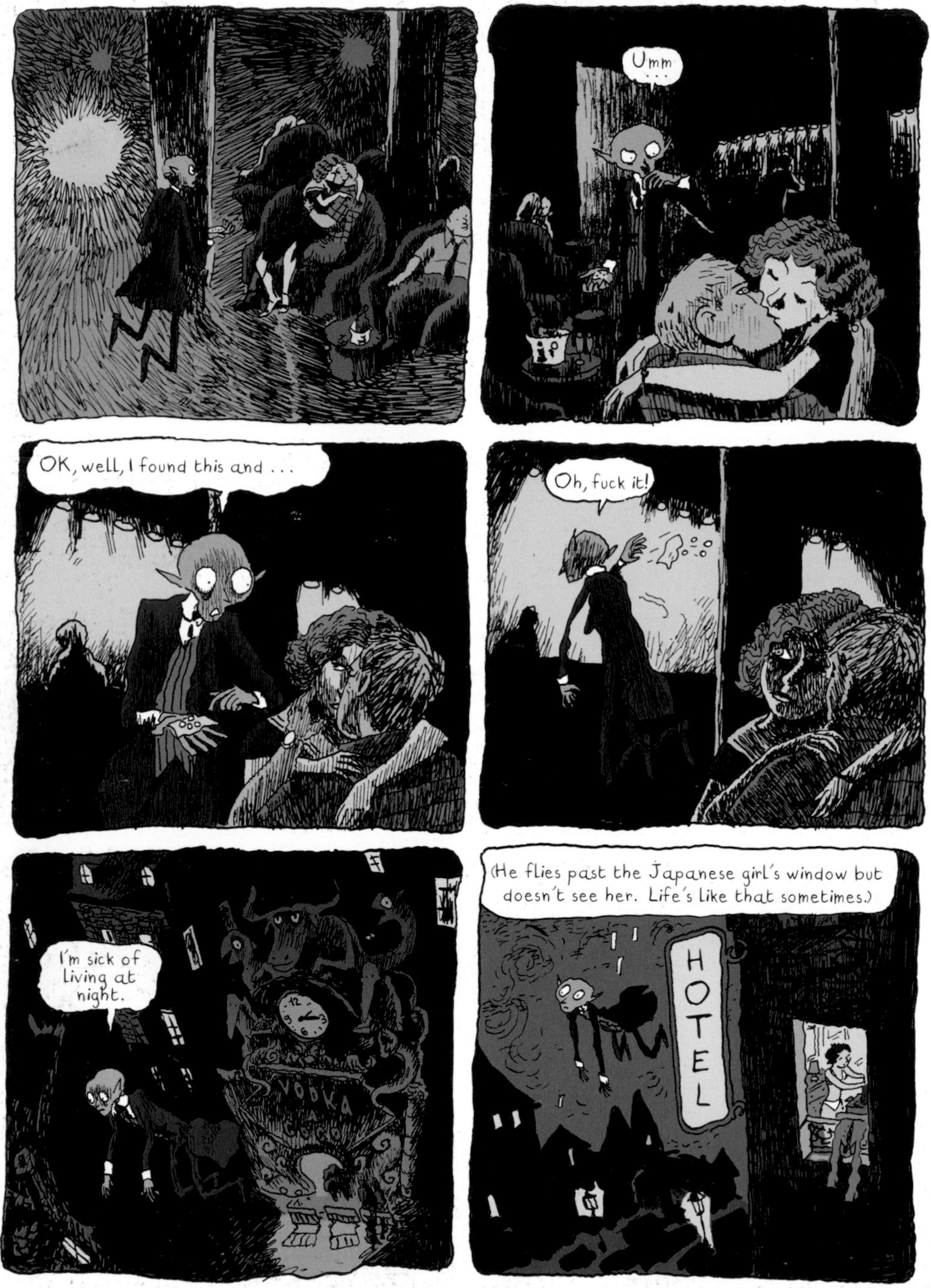
Umm ...
OK, well, I found this and ...
Oh, fuck it!
I'm sick of living at night.
VODKA
(He flies past the Japanese girl's window but doesn't see her. Life's like that sometimes.)
HOTEL

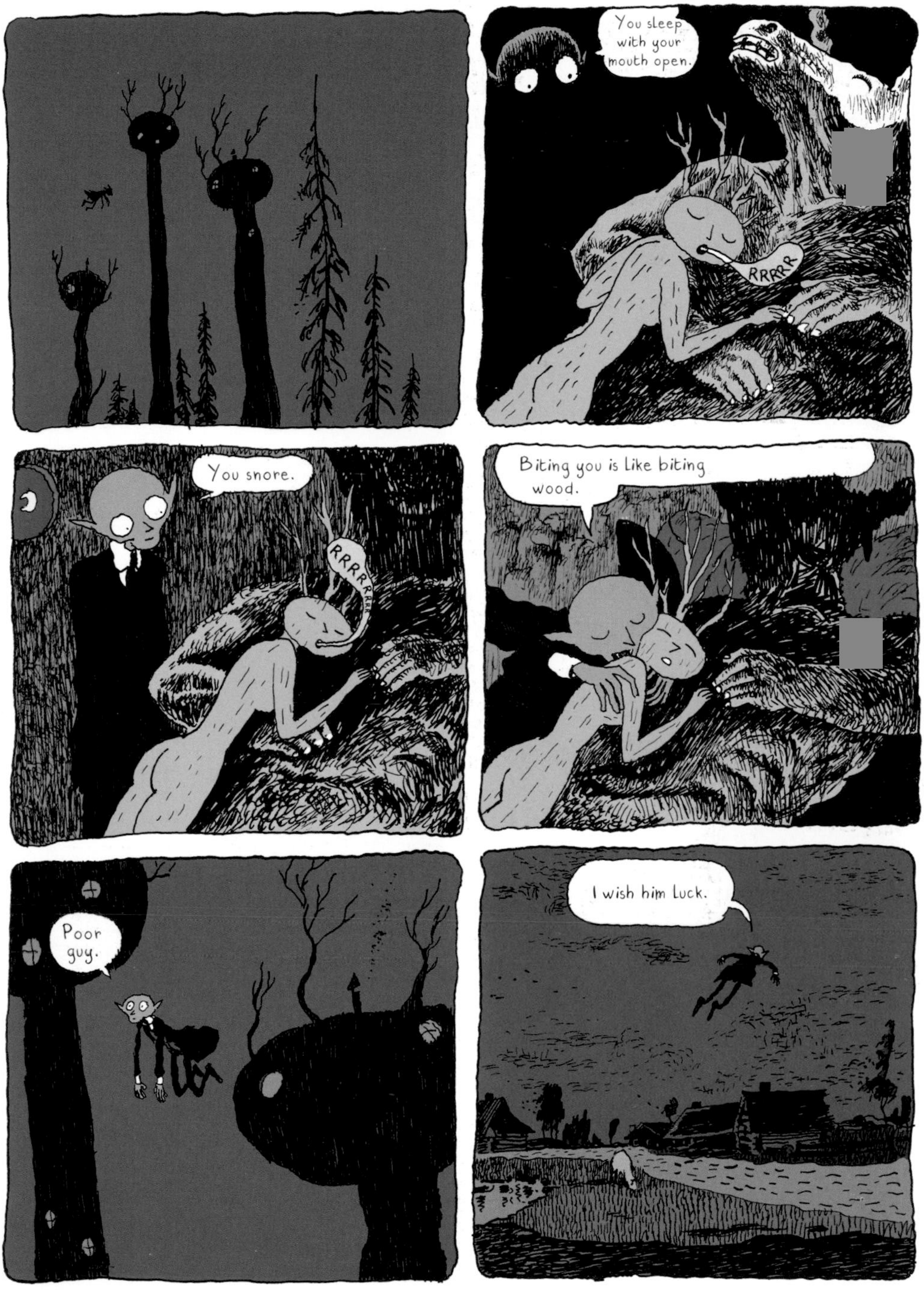

You sleep with your mouth open.
RRRRR
You snore.
RRRRRRRRR
Biting you is like biting wood.
Poor guy.
I wish him luck.

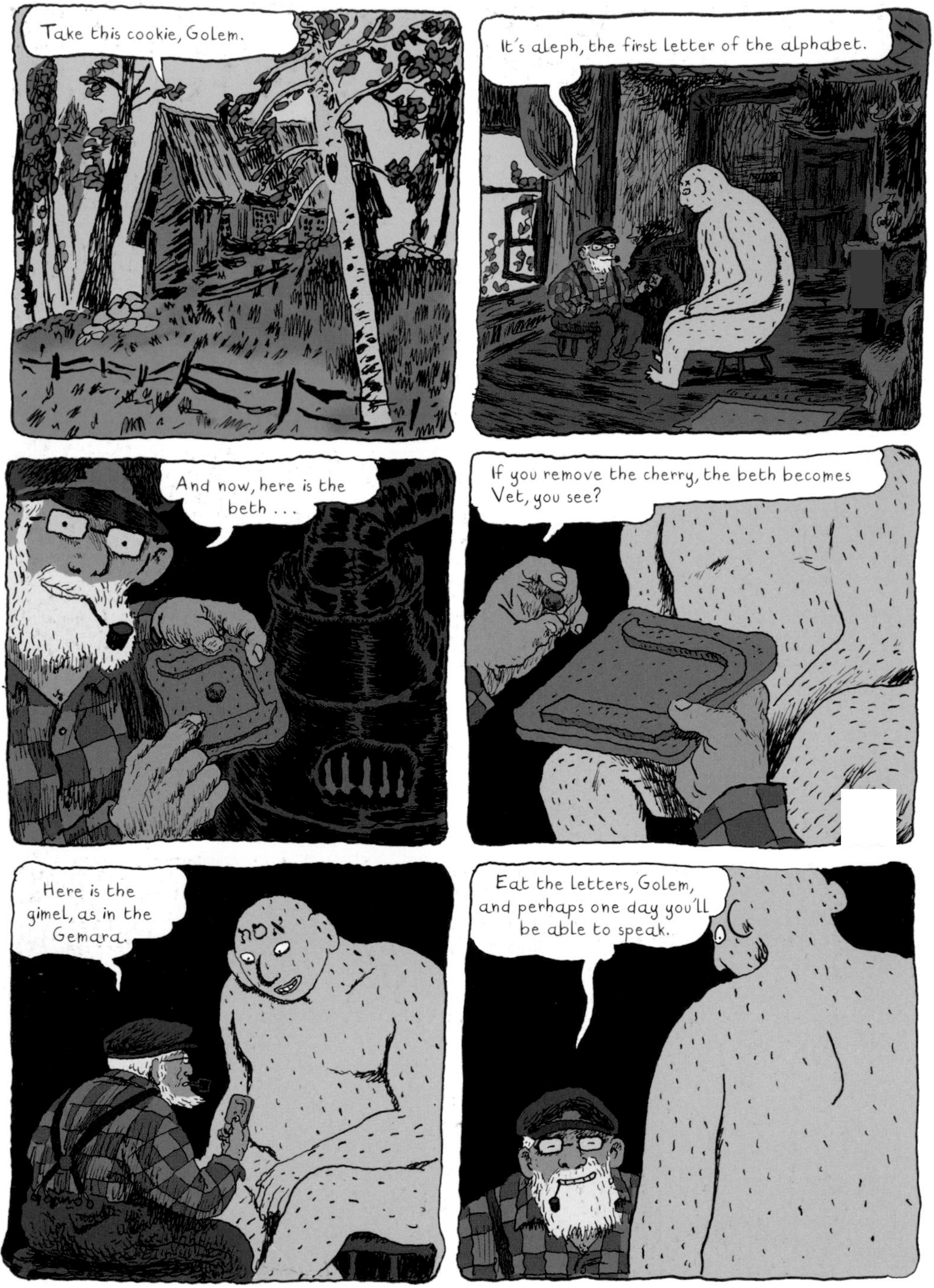
Take this cookie, Golem.
It's aleph, the first letter of the alphabet.
And now, here is the beth . . .
If you remove the cherry, the beth becomes Vet, you see?
Here is the gimel, as in the Gemara.
Eat the letters, Golem, and perhaps one day you'll be able to speak.

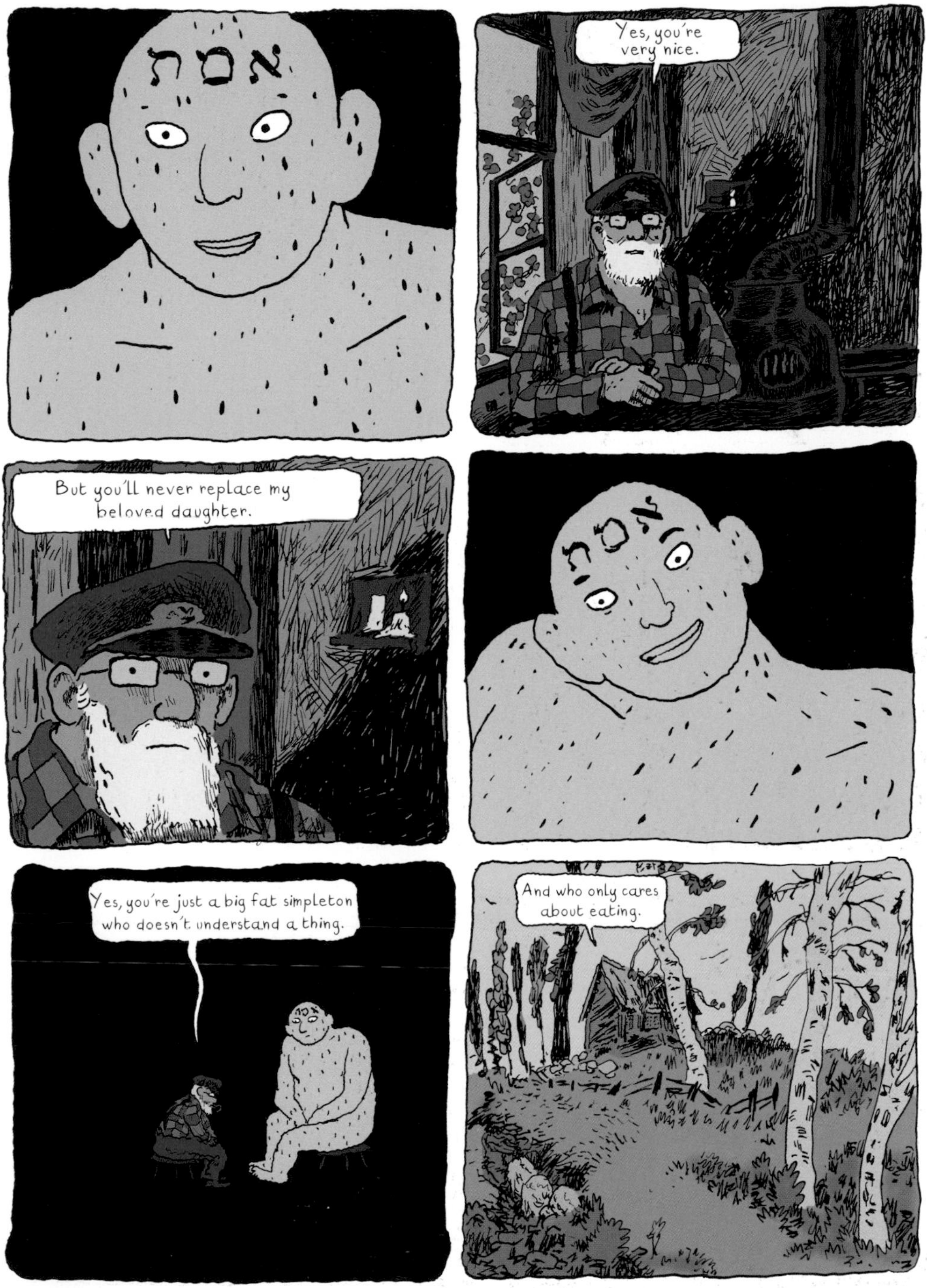
אמת
Yes, you're very nice.
But you'll never replace my beloved daughter.
Yes, you're just a big fat simpleton who doesn't understand a thing.
And who only cares about eating.

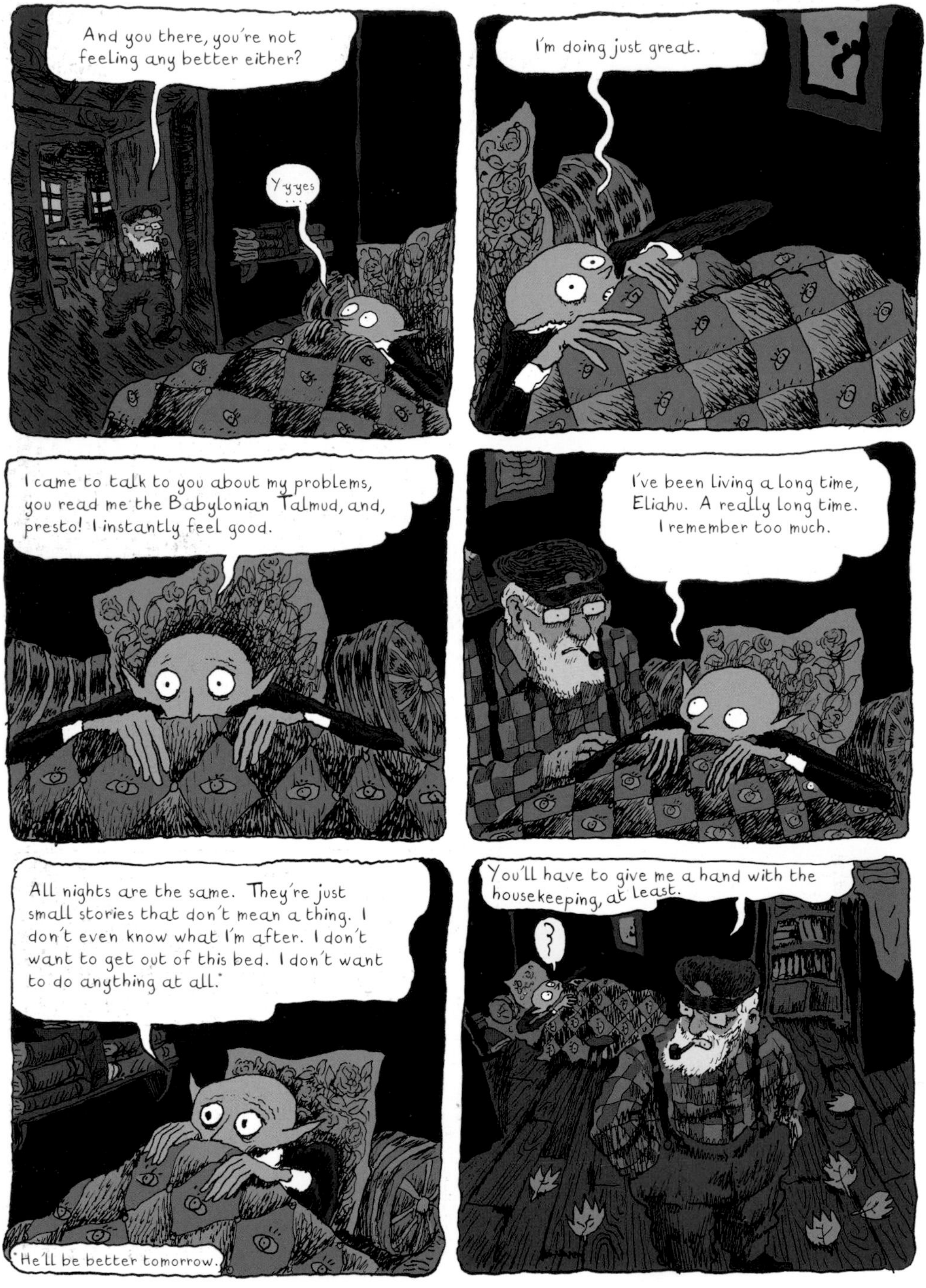
And you there, you're not feeling any better either?
Y-y-yes...
I'm doing just great.
I came to talk to you about my problems, you read me the Babylonian Talmud, and, presto! I instantly feel good.
I've been living a long time, Eliahu. A really long time. I remember too much.
All nights are the same. They're just small stories that don't mean a thing. I don't even know what I'm after. I don't want to get out of this bed. I don't want to do anything at all.*
*He'll be better tomorrow.
You'll have to give me a hand with the housekeeping, at least.
?

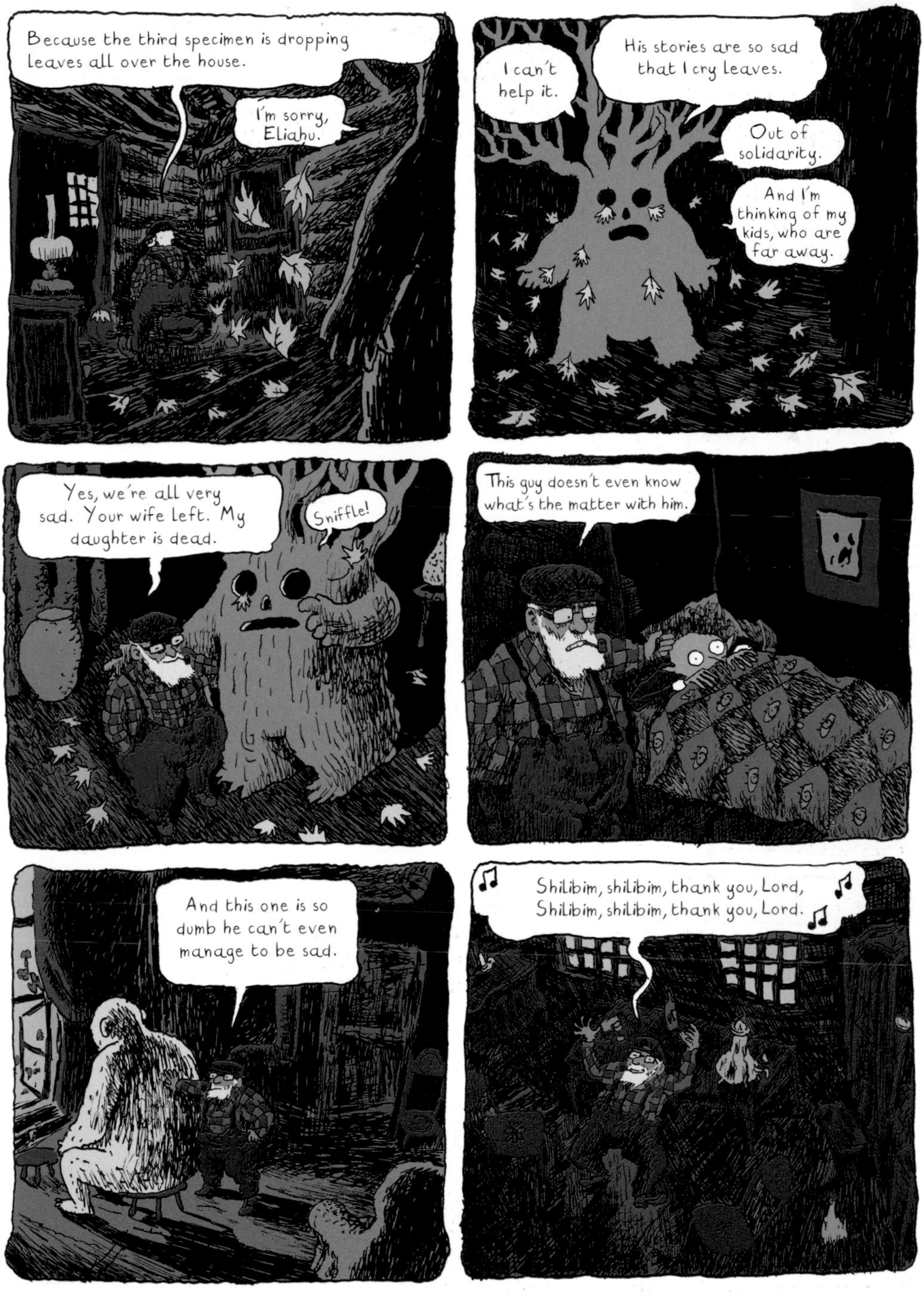
Because the third specimen is dropping leaves all over the house.
I'm sorry, Eliahu.
I can't help it.
His stories are so sad that I cry leaves.
Out of solidarity.
And I'm thinking of my kids, who are far away.
Yes, we're all very sad. Your wife left. My daughter is dead.
Sniffle!
This guy doesn't even know what's the matter with him.
And this one is so dumb he can't even manage to be sad.
Shilibim, shilibim, thank you, Lord,
Shilibim, shilibim, thank you, Lord.

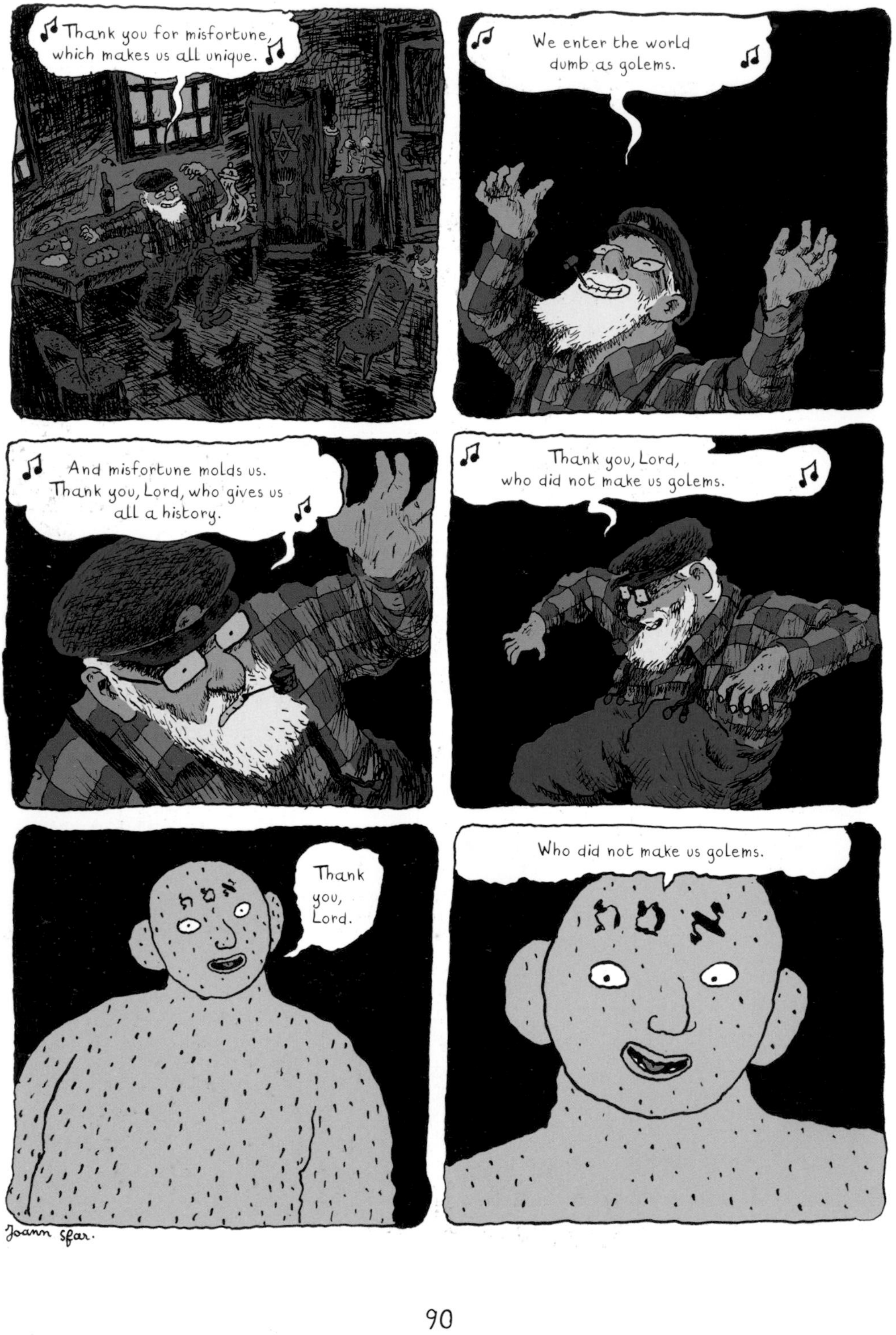
Thank you for misfortune, which makes us all unique.
We enter the world dumb as golems.
And misfortune molds us. Thank you, Lord, who gives us all a history.
Thank you, Lord, who did not make us golems.
אמת
Thank you, Lord.
Who did not make us golems.
אמת
Joann Sfar.

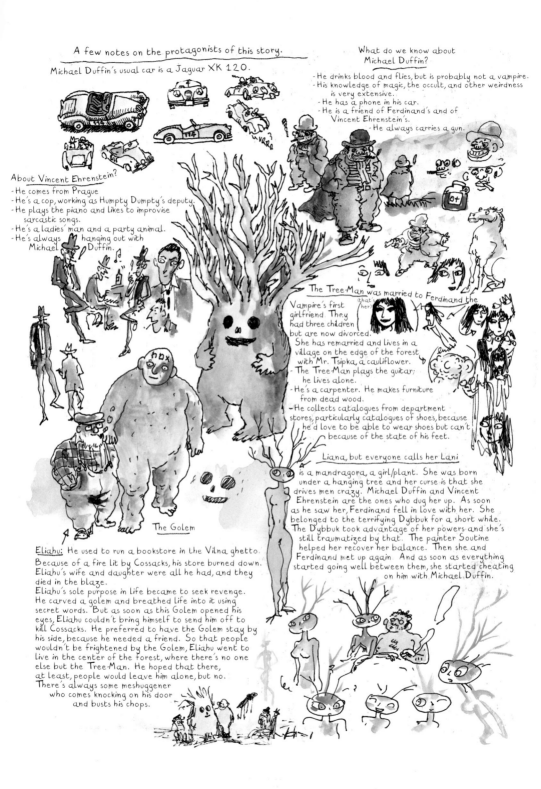

A few notes on the protagonists of this story.

Michael Duffin's usual car is a Jaguar XK 120.

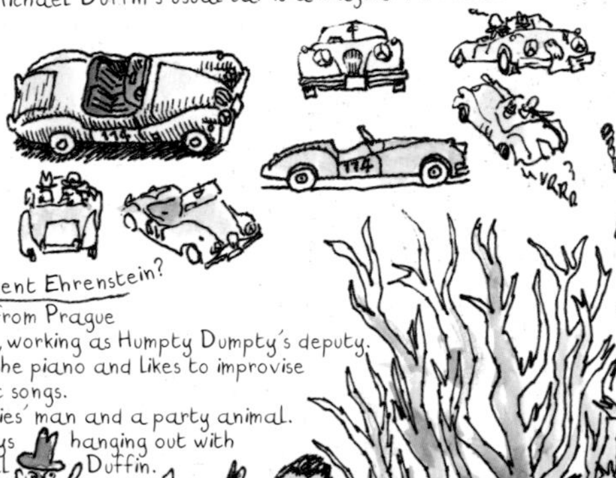

What do we know about Michael Duffin?

- He drinks blood and flies, but is probably not a vampire.
- His knowledge of magic, the occult, and other weirdness is very extensive.
- He has a phone in his car.
- He is a friend of Ferdinand's and of Vincent Ehrenstein's.
- He always carries a gun.

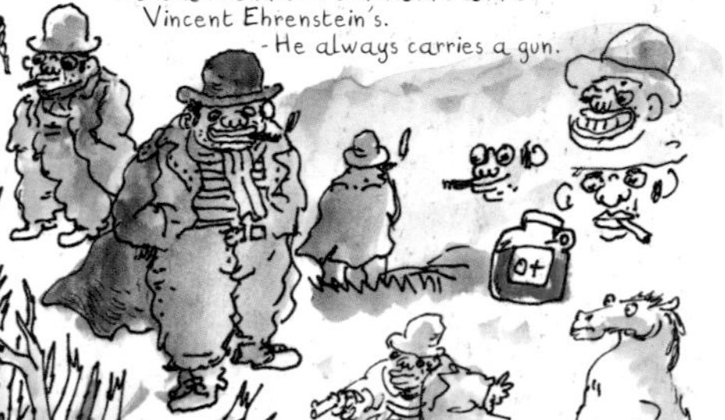

About Vincent Ehrenstein?

- He comes from Prague
- He's a cop, working as Humpty Dumpty's deputy.
- He plays the piano and likes to improvise sarcastic songs.
- He's a ladies' man and a party animal.
- He's always hanging out with Michael Duffin.

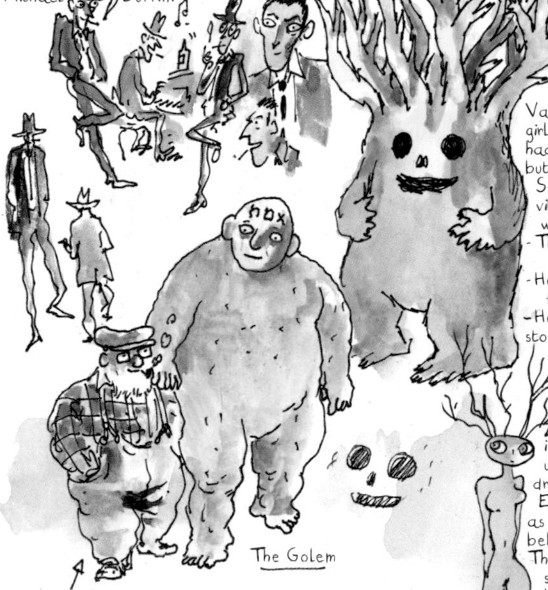

The Golem

The Tree-Man was married to Ferdinand the Vampire's first girlfriend (that's her). They had three children but are now divorced. She has remarried and lives in a village on the edge of the forest with Mr. Tsipka, a cauliflower.

- The Tree-Man plays the guitar; he lives alone.
- He's a carpenter. He makes furniture from dead wood.
- He collects catalogues from department stores, particularly catalogues of shoes, because he'd love to be able to wear shoes but can't because of the state of his feet.

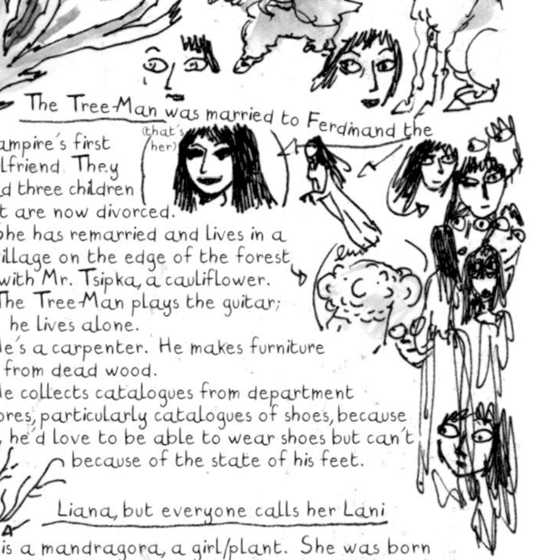

Liana, but everyone calls her Lani is a mandragora, a girl/plant. She was born under a hanging tree and her curse is that she drives men crazy. Michael Duffin and Vincent Ehrenstein are the ones who dug her up. As soon as he saw her, Ferdinand fell in love with her. She belonged to the terrifying Dybbuk for a short while. The Dybbuk took advantage of her powers and she's still traumatized by that. The painter Soutine helped her recover her balance. Then she and Ferdinand met up again. And as soon as everything started going well between them, she started cheating on him with Michael Duffin.

Eliahu: He used to run a bookstore in the Vilna ghetto. Because of a fire lit by Cossacks, his store burned down. Eliahu's wife and daughter were all he had, and they died in the blaze.
Eliahu's sole purpose in life became to seek revenge. He carved a golem and breathed life into it using secret words. But as soon as this Golem opened his eyes, Eliahu couldn't bring himself to send him off to kill Cossacks. He preferred to have the Golem stay by his side, because he needed a friend. So that people wouldn't be frightened by the Golem, Eliahu went to live in the center of the forest, where there's no one else but the Tree-Man. He hoped that there, at least, people would leave him alone, but no. There's always some meshuggener who comes knocking on his door and busts his chops.

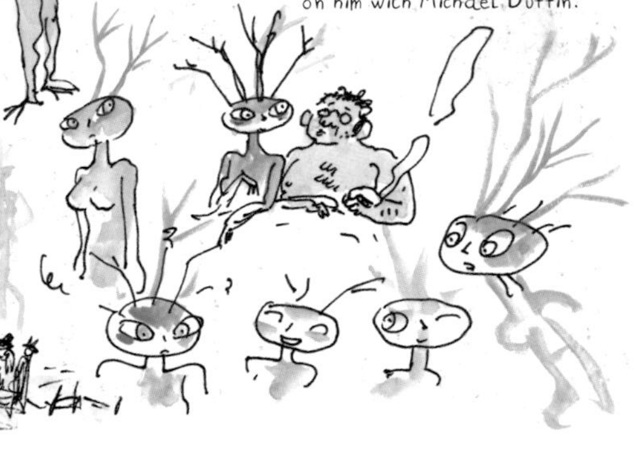

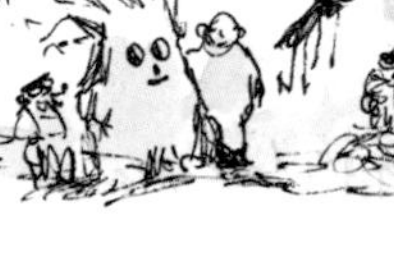

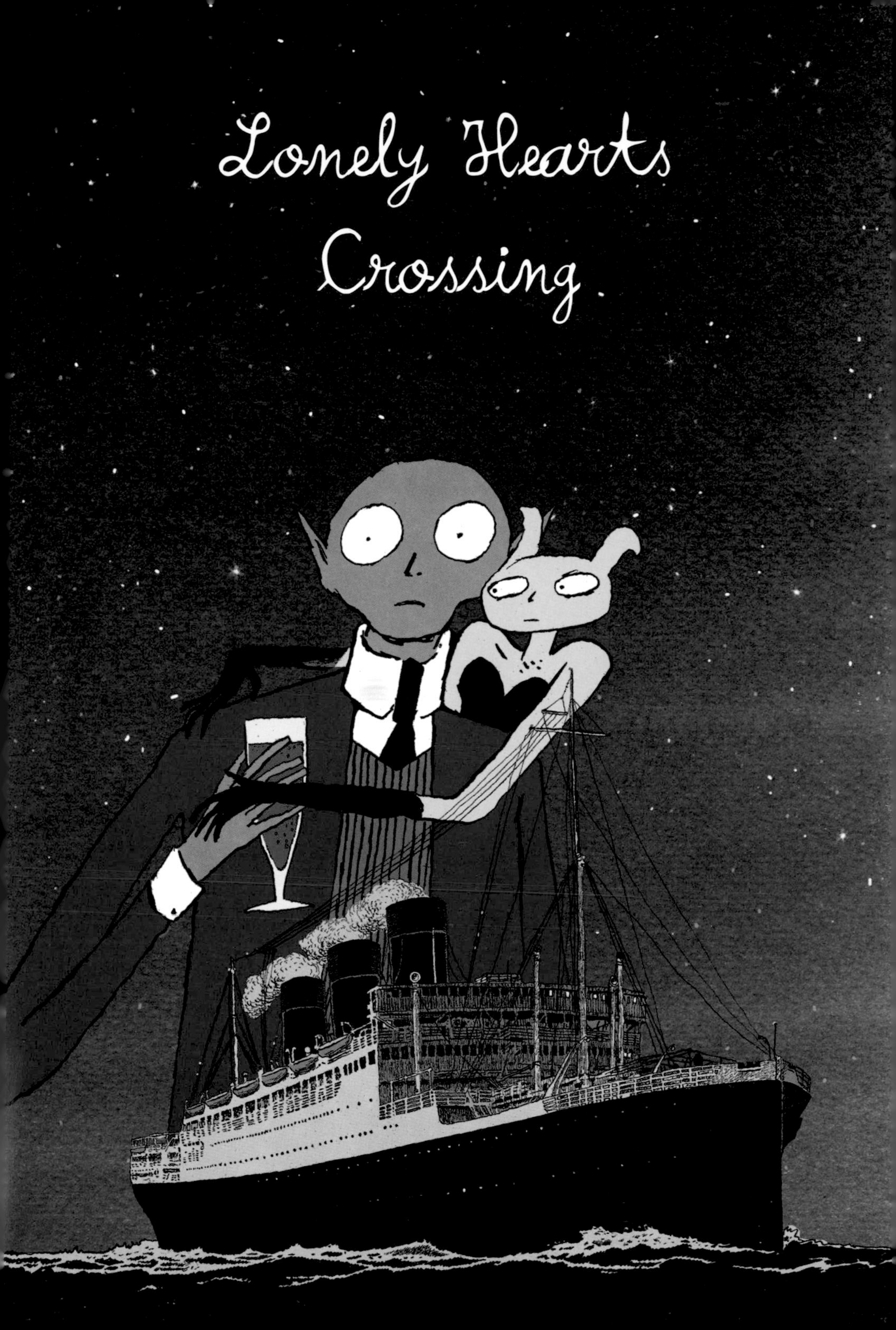
Lonely Hearts
Crossing

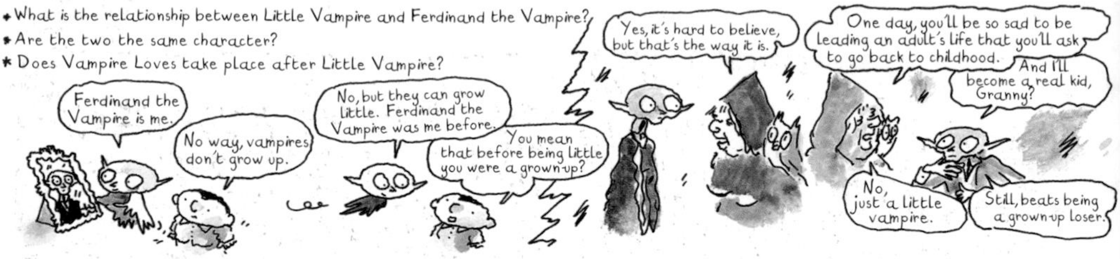

* What is the relationship between Little Vampire and Ferdinand the Vampire?
* Are the two the same character?
* Does Vampire Loves take place after Little Vampire?
Ferdinand the Vampire is me.
No way, vampires don't grow up.
No, but they can grow little. Ferdinand the Vampire was me before.
You mean that before being little you were a grown-up?
Yes, it's hard to believe, but that's the way it is.
One day, you'll be so sad to be leading an adult's life that you'll ask to go back to childhood.
And I'll become a real kid, Granny?
No, just a little vampire.
Still, beats being a grown-up loser.

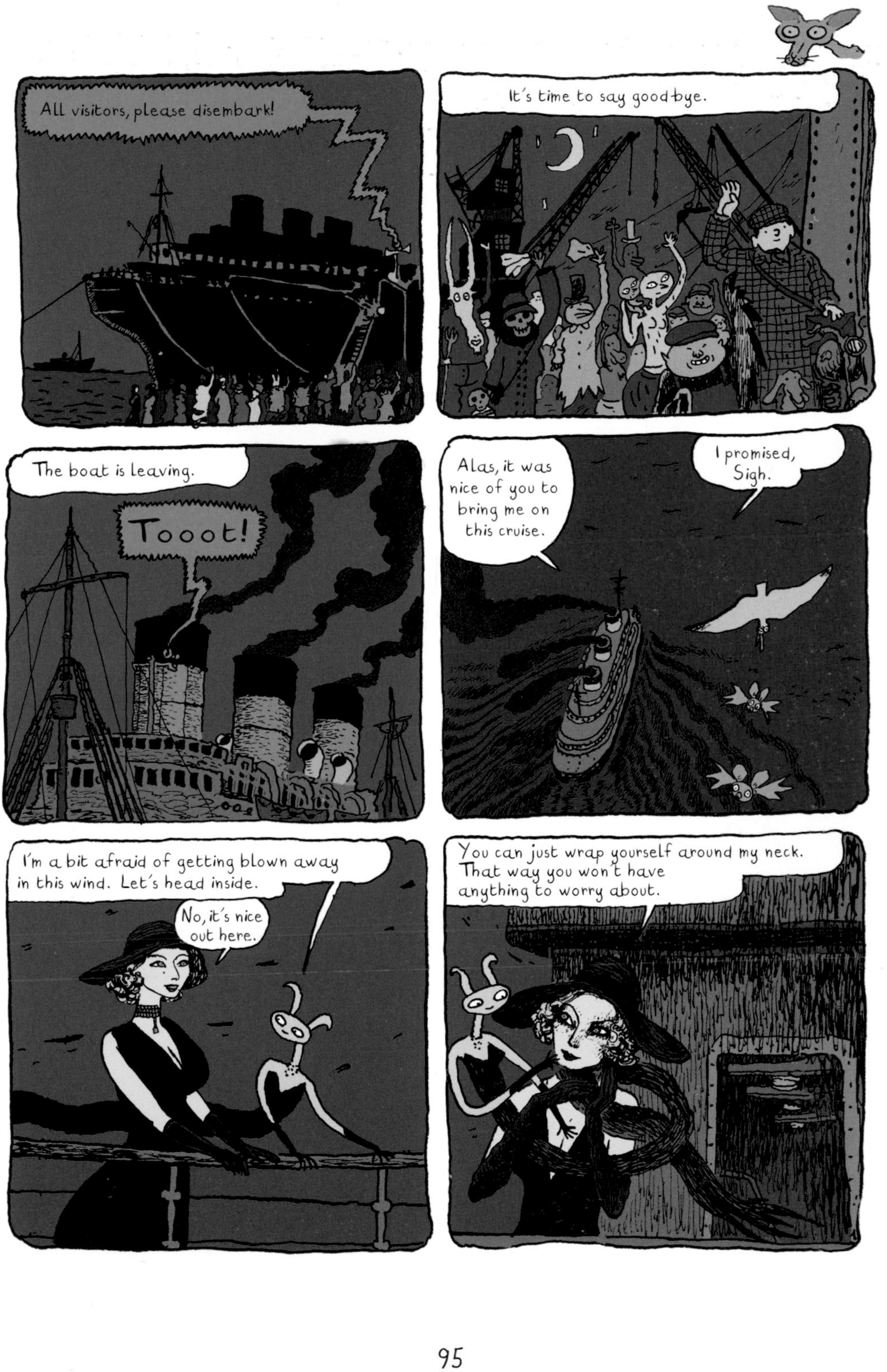
All visitors, please disembark!
It's time to say goodbye.
The boat is leaving.
Tooot!
Alas, it was nice of you to bring me on this cruise.
I promised, Sigh.
I'm a bit afraid of getting blown away in this wind. Let's head inside.
No, it's nice out here.
You can just wrap yourself around my neck. That way you won't have anything to worry about.

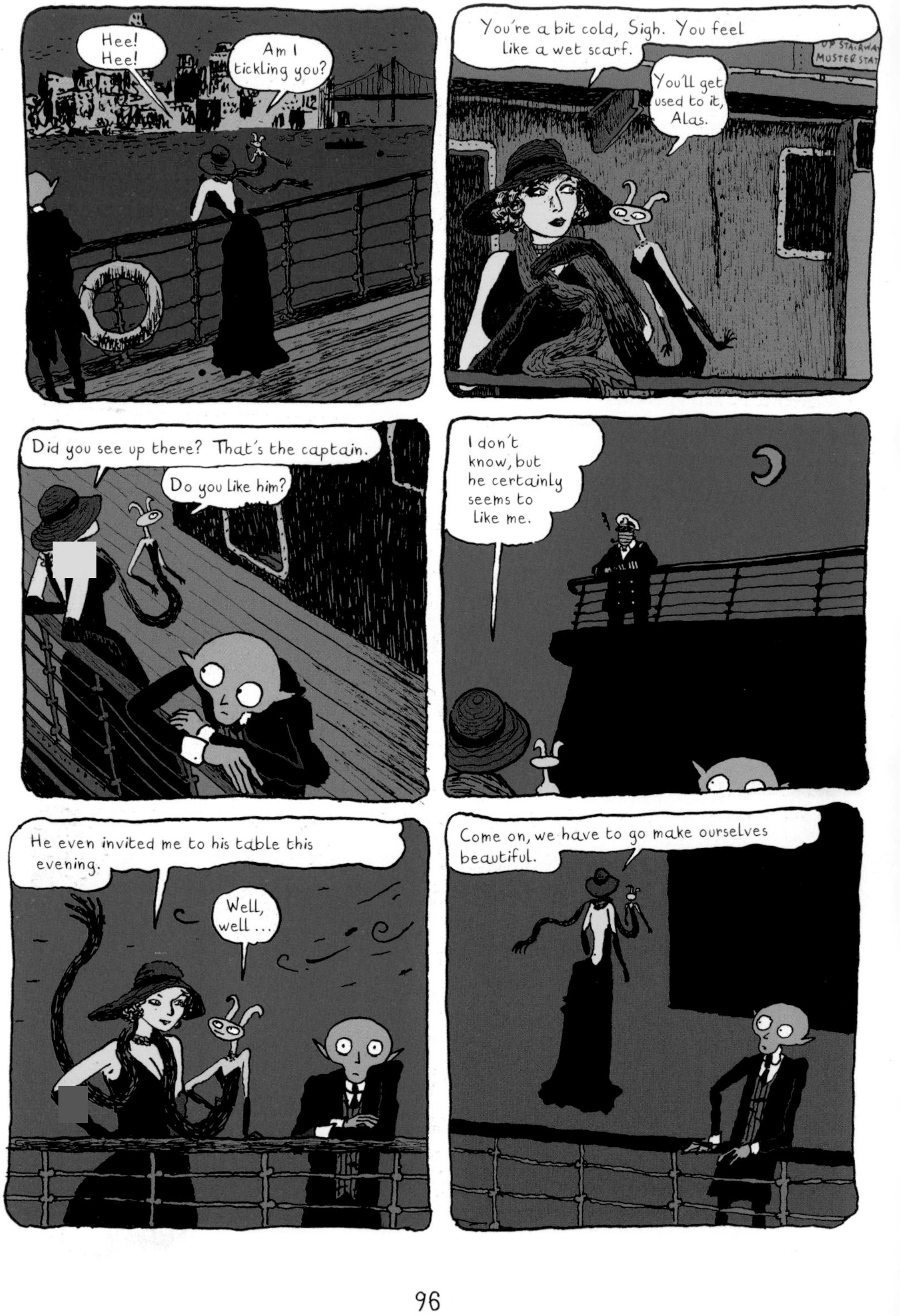
Hee! Hee!
Am I tickling you?
You're a bit cold, Sigh. You feel like a wet scarf.
You'll get used to it, Alas.
Did you see up there? That's the captain.
Do you like him?
I don't know, but he certainly seems to like me.
He even invited me to his table this evening.
Well, well...
Come on, we have to go make ourselves beautiful.

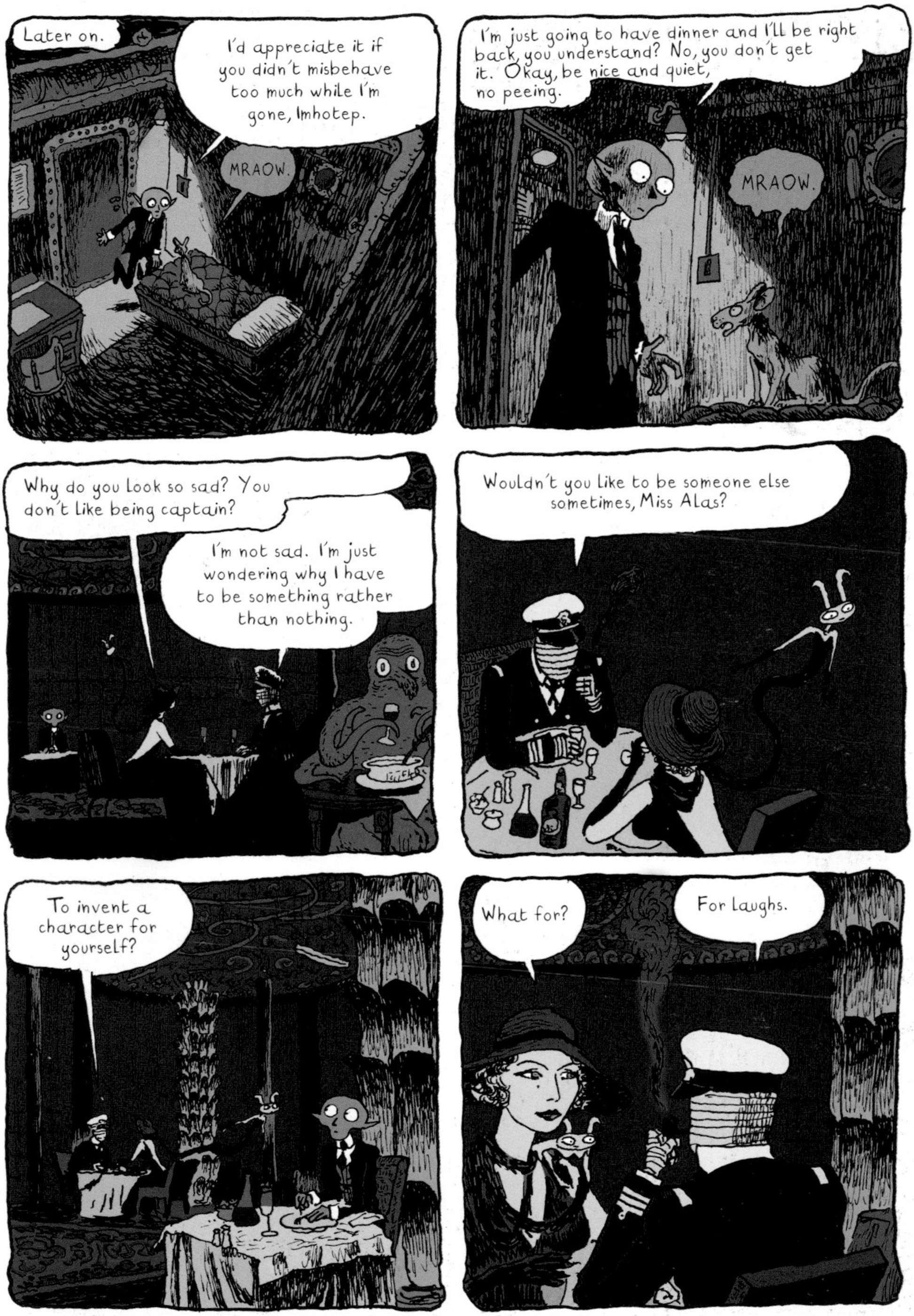
Later on.
I'd appreciate it if you didn't misbehave too much while I'm gone, Imhotep.
MRAOW.
I'm just going to have dinner and I'll be right back, you understand? No, you don't get it. Okay, be nice and quiet, no peeing.
MRAOW.
Why do you look so sad? You don't like being captain?
I'm not sad. I'm just wondering why I have to be something rather than nothing.
Wouldn't you like to be someone else sometimes, Miss Alas?
To invent a character for yourself?
What for?
For laughs.

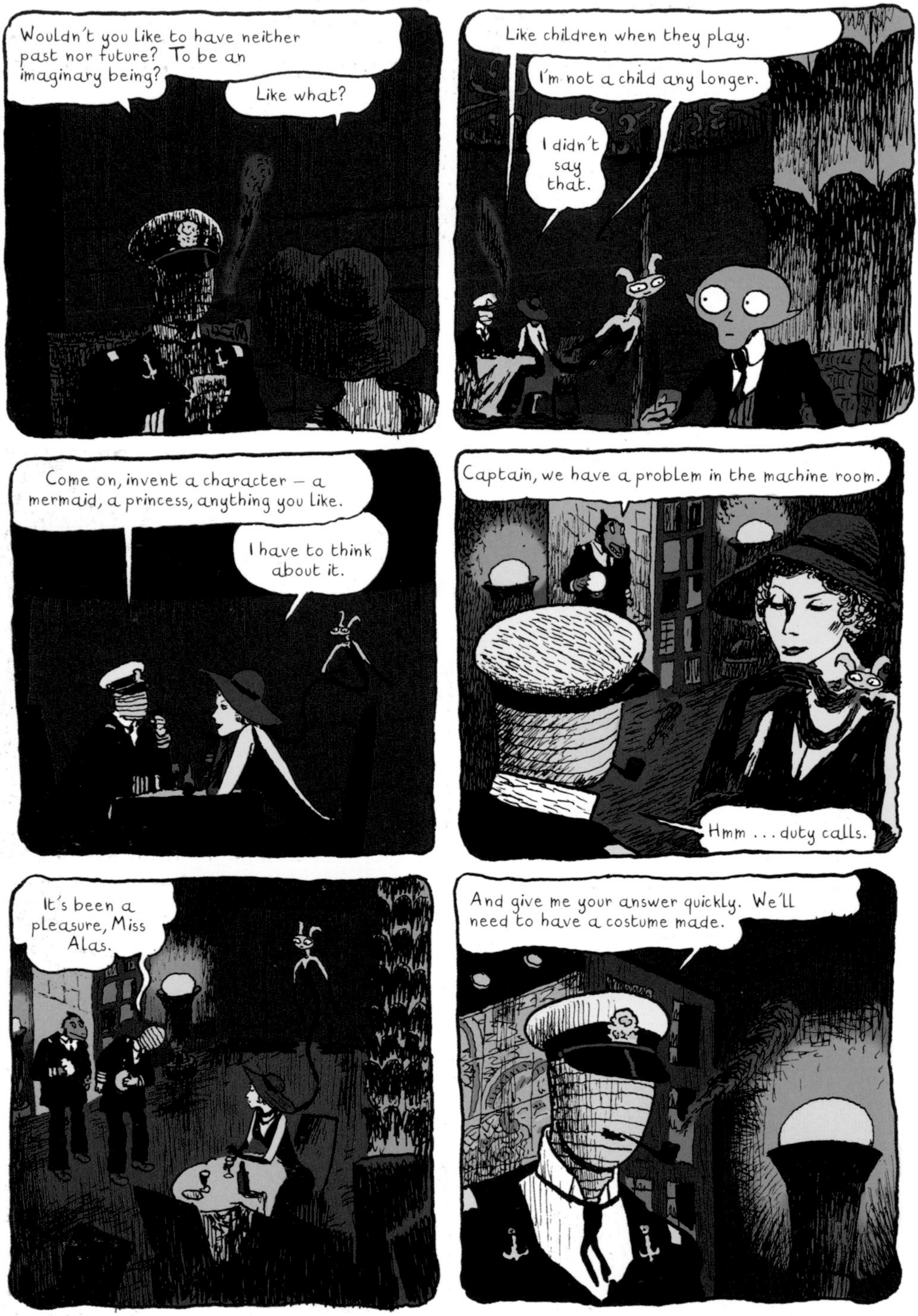
Wouldn't you like to have neither past nor future? To be an imaginary being?
Like what?
Like children when they play.
I'm not a child any longer.
I didn't say that.
Come on, invent a character – a mermaid, a princess, anything you like.
I have to think about it.
Captain, we have a problem in the machine room.
Hmm . . . duty calls.
It's been a pleasure, Miss Alas.
And give me your answer quickly. We'll need to have a costume made.

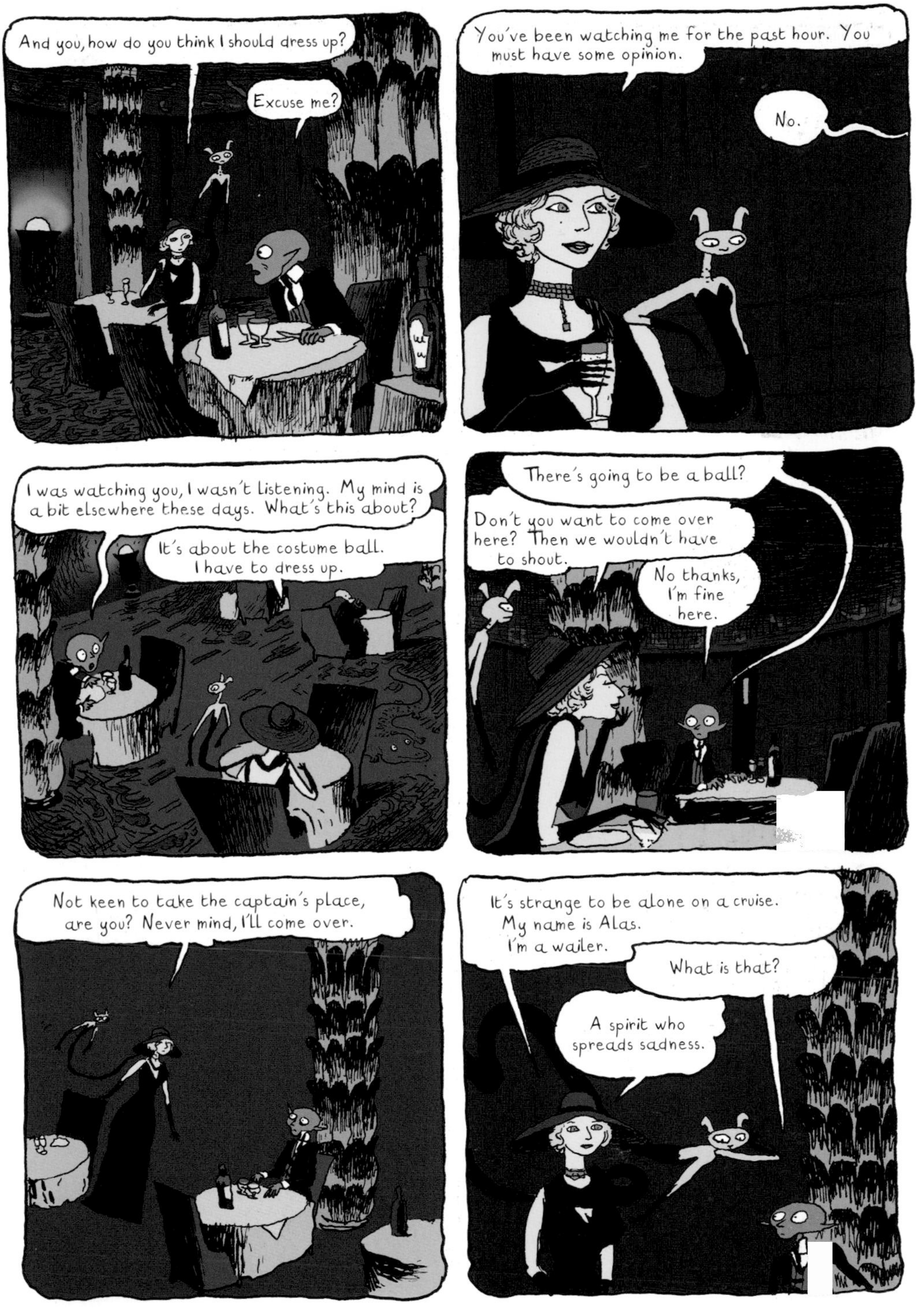
And you, how do you think I should dress up?
Excuse me?
You've been watching me for the past hour. You must have some opinion.
No.
I was watching you, I wasn't listening. My mind is a bit elsewhere these days. What's this about?
It's about the costume ball. I have to dress up.
There's going to be a ball?
Don't you want to come over here? Then we wouldn't have to shout.
No thanks, I'm fine here.
Not keen to take the captain's place, are you? Never mind, I'll come over.
It's strange to be alone on a cruise. My name is Alas. I'm a wailer.
What is that?
A spirit who spreads sadness.

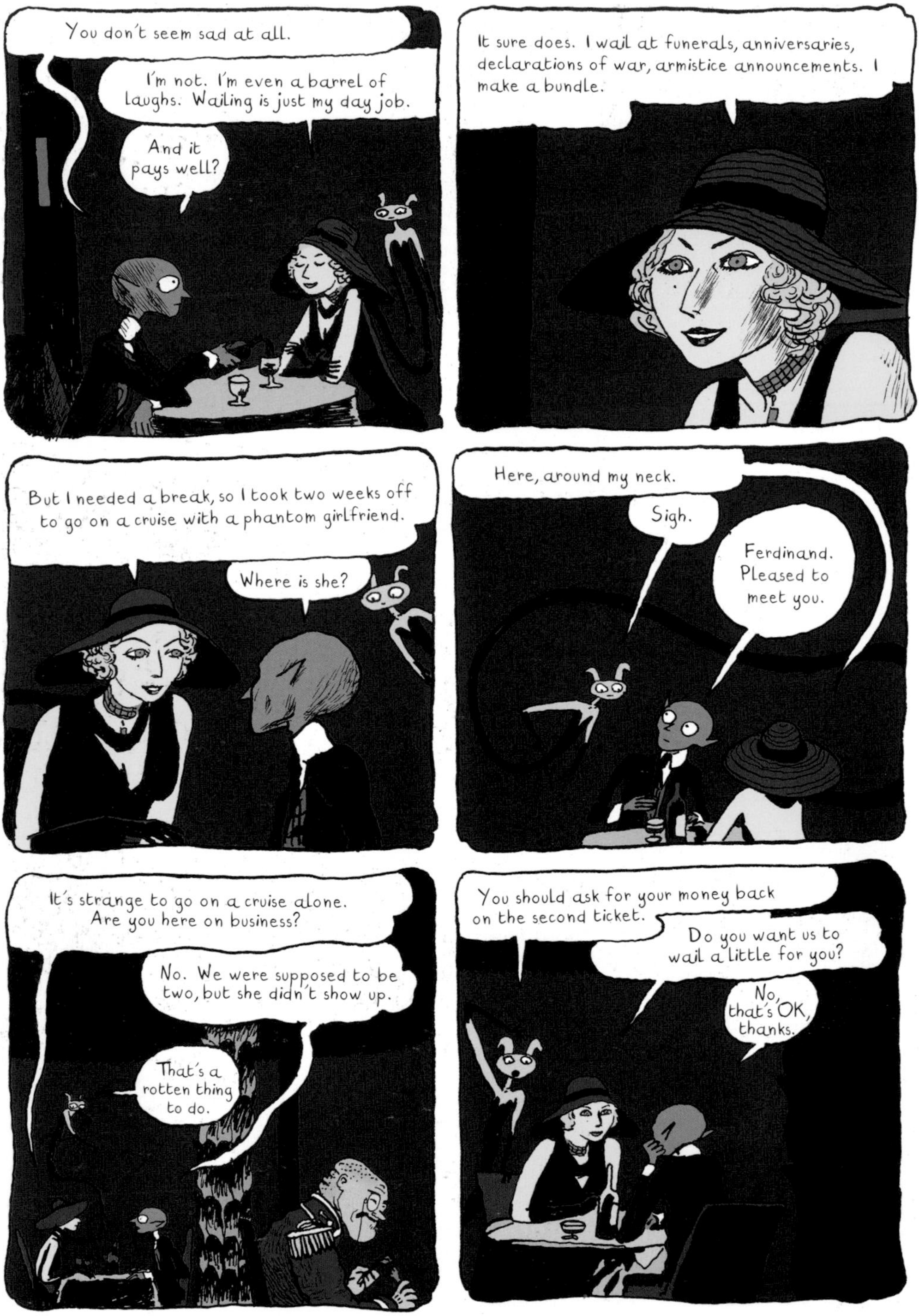
You don't seem sad at all.
I'm not. I'm even a barrel of laughs. Wailing is just my day job.
And it pays well?
It sure does. I wail at funerals, anniversaries, declarations of war, armistice announcements. I make a bundle.
But I needed a break, so I took two weeks off to go on a cruise with a phantom girlfriend.
Where is she?
Here, around my neck.
Sigh.
Ferdinand. Pleased to meet you.
It's strange to go on a cruise alone. Are you here on business?
No. We were supposed to be two, but she didn't show up.
That's a rotten thing to do.
You should ask for your money back on the second ticket.
Do you want us to wail a little for you?
No, that's OK, thanks.

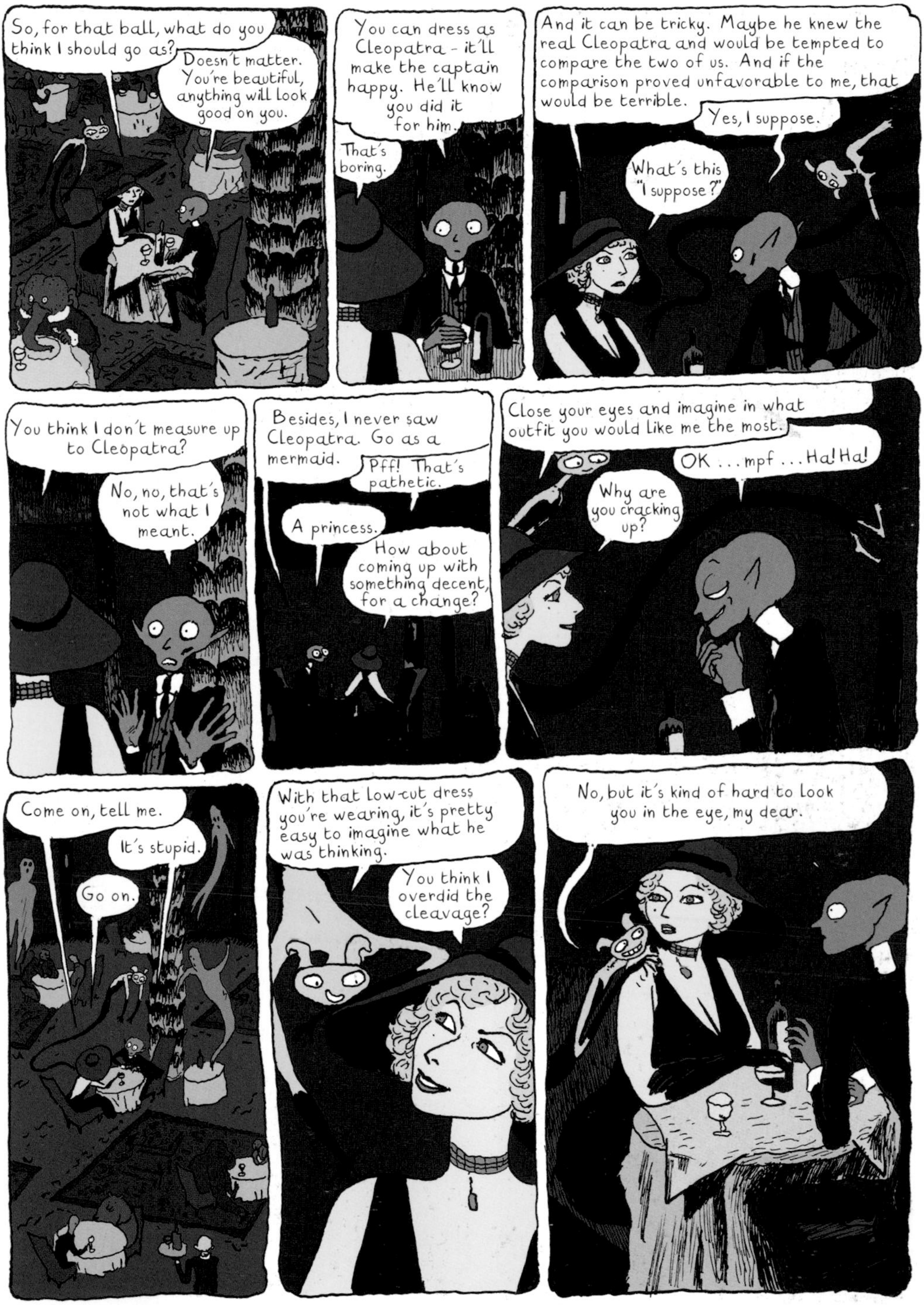
So, for that ball, what do you think I should go as?
Doesn't matter. You're beautiful, anything will look good on you.
You can dress as Cleopatra - it'll make the captain happy. He'll know you did it for him.
That's boring.
And it can be tricky. Maybe he knew the real Cleopatra and would be tempted to compare the two of us. And if the comparison proved unfavorable to me, that would be terrible.
Yes, I suppose.
What's this "I suppose?"
You think I don't measure up to Cleopatra?
No, no, that's not what I meant.
Besides, I never saw Cleopatra. Go as a mermaid.
Pff! That's pathetic.
A princess.
How about coming up with something decent, for a change?
Close your eyes and imagine in what outfit you would like me the most.
OK ... mpf ... Ha! Ha!
Why are you cracking up?
Come on, tell me.
It's stupid.
Go on.
With that low-cut dress you're wearing, it's pretty easy to imagine what he was thinking.
You think I overdid the cleavage?
No, but it's kind of hard to look you in the eye, my dear.

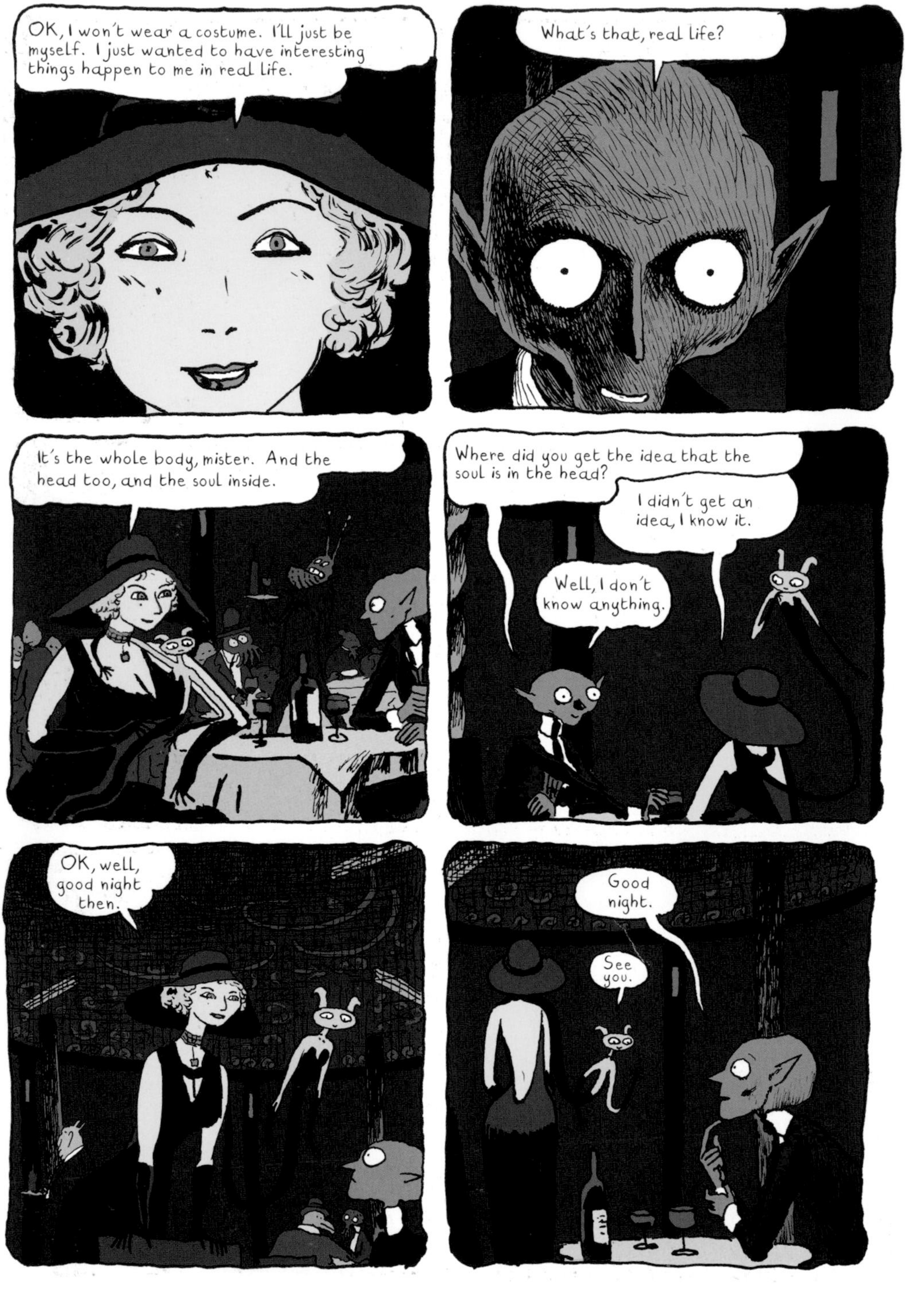
OK, I won't wear a costume. I'll just be myself. I just wanted to have interesting things happen to me in real life.
What's that, real life?
It's the whole body, mister. And the head too, and the soul inside.
Where did you get the idea that the soul is in the head?
I didn't get an idea, I know it.
Well, I don't know anything.
OK, well, good night then.
Good night.
See you.

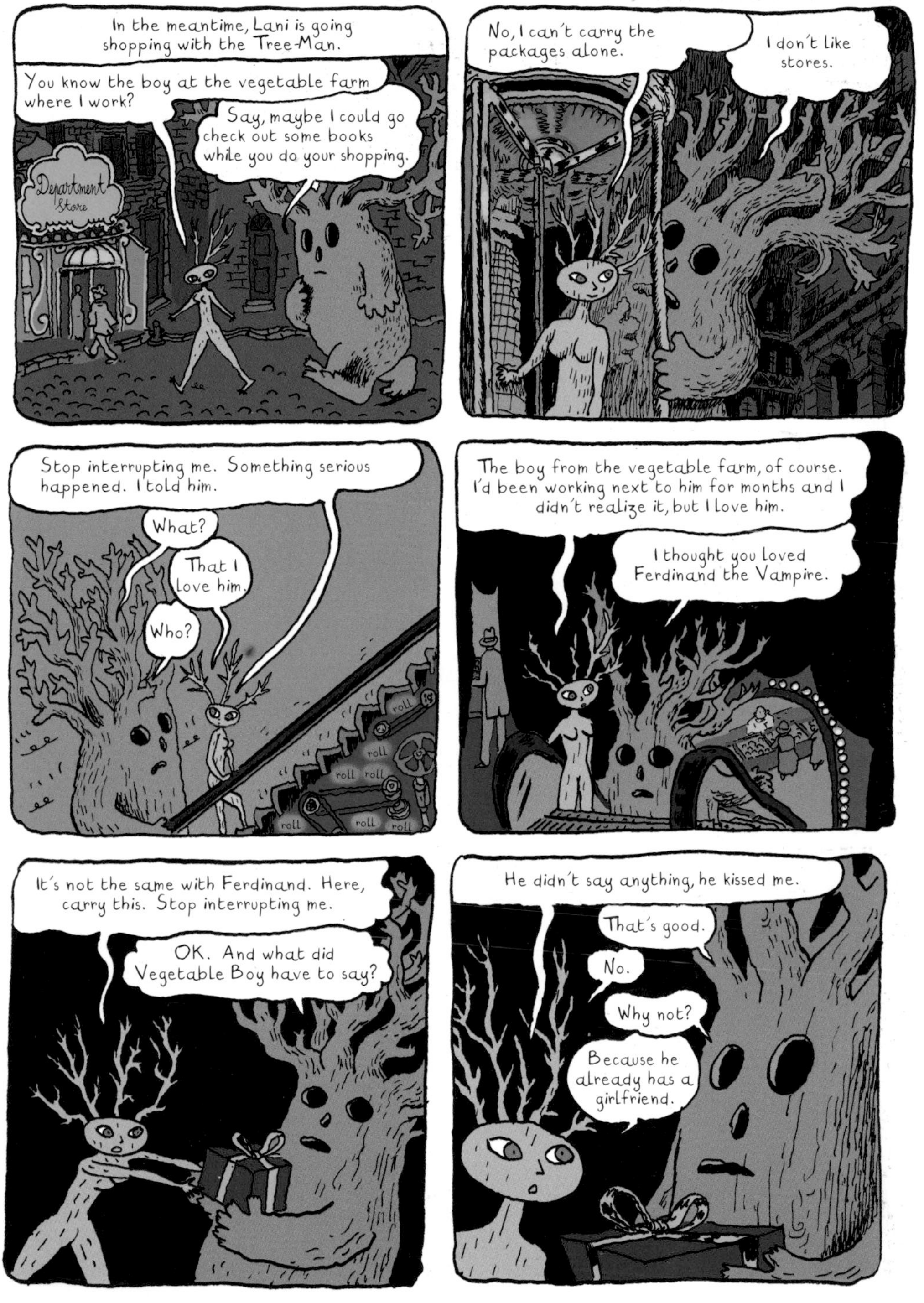
In the meantime, Lani is going shopping with the Tree-Man.
You know the boy at the vegetable farm where I work?
Say, maybe I could go check out some books while you do your shopping.
Department Store
No, I can't carry the packages alone.
I don't like stores.
Stop interrupting me. Something serious happened. I told him.
What?
That I love him.
Who?
roll
roll
roll
roll
roll
roll
roll
The boy from the vegetable farm, of course. I'd been working next to him for months and I didn't realize it, but I love him.
I thought you loved Ferdinand the Vampire.
It's not the same with Ferdinand. Here, carry this. Stop interrupting me.
OK. And what did Vegetable Boy have to say?
He didn't say anything, he kissed me.
That's good.
No.
Why not?
Because he already has a girlfriend.

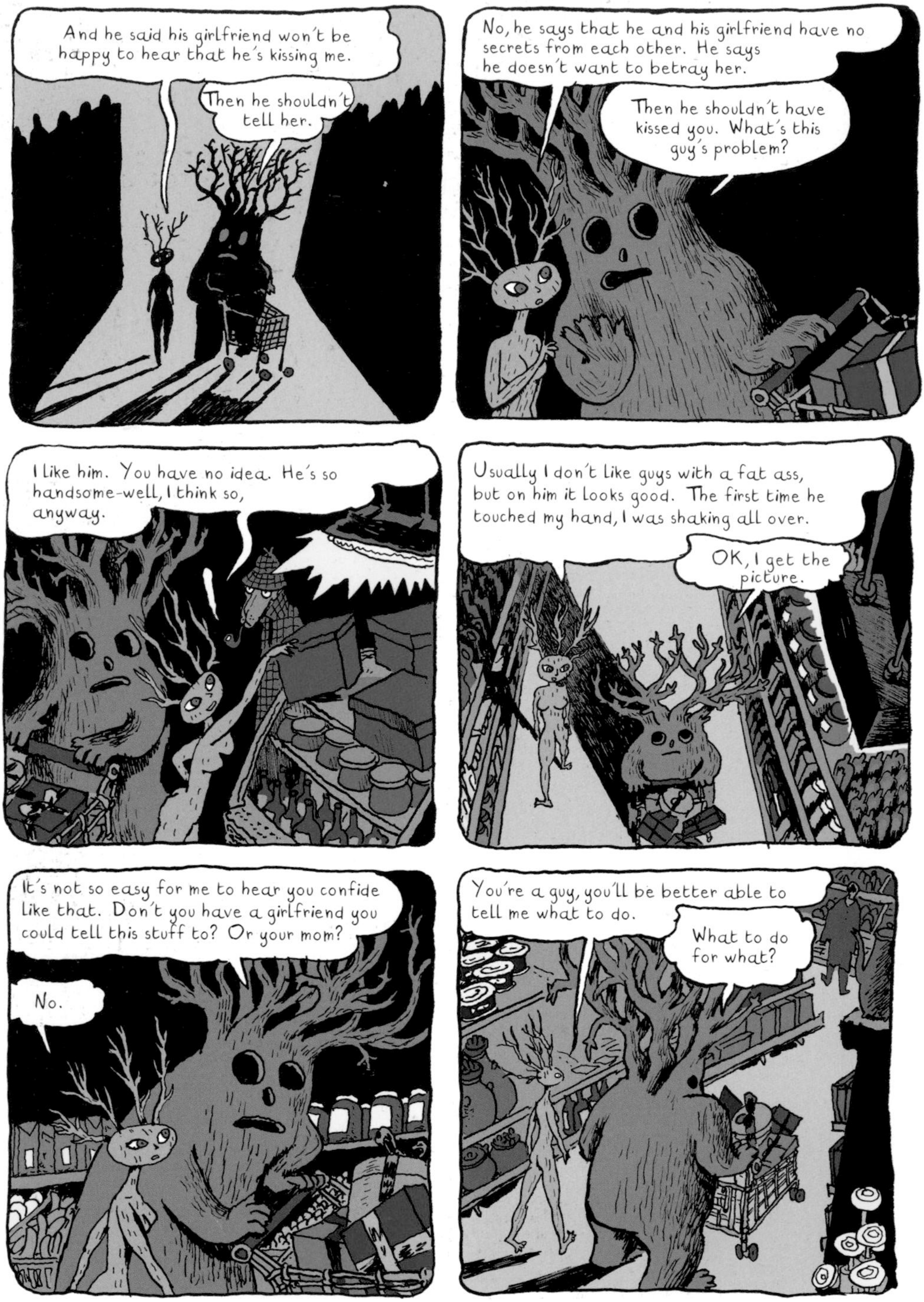

And he said his girlfriend won't be happy to hear that he's kissing me.
Then he shouldn't tell her.
No, he says that he and his girlfriend have no secrets from each other. He says he doesn't want to betray her.
Then he shouldn't have kissed you. What's this guy's problem?
I like him. You have no idea. He's so handsome-well, I think so, anyway.
Usually I don't like guys with a fat ass, but on him it looks good. The first time he touched my hand, I was shaking all over.
OK, I get the picture.
It's not so easy for me to hear you confide like that. Don't you have a girlfriend you could tell this stuff to? Or your mom?
No.
You're a guy, you'll be better able to tell me what to do.
What to do for what?

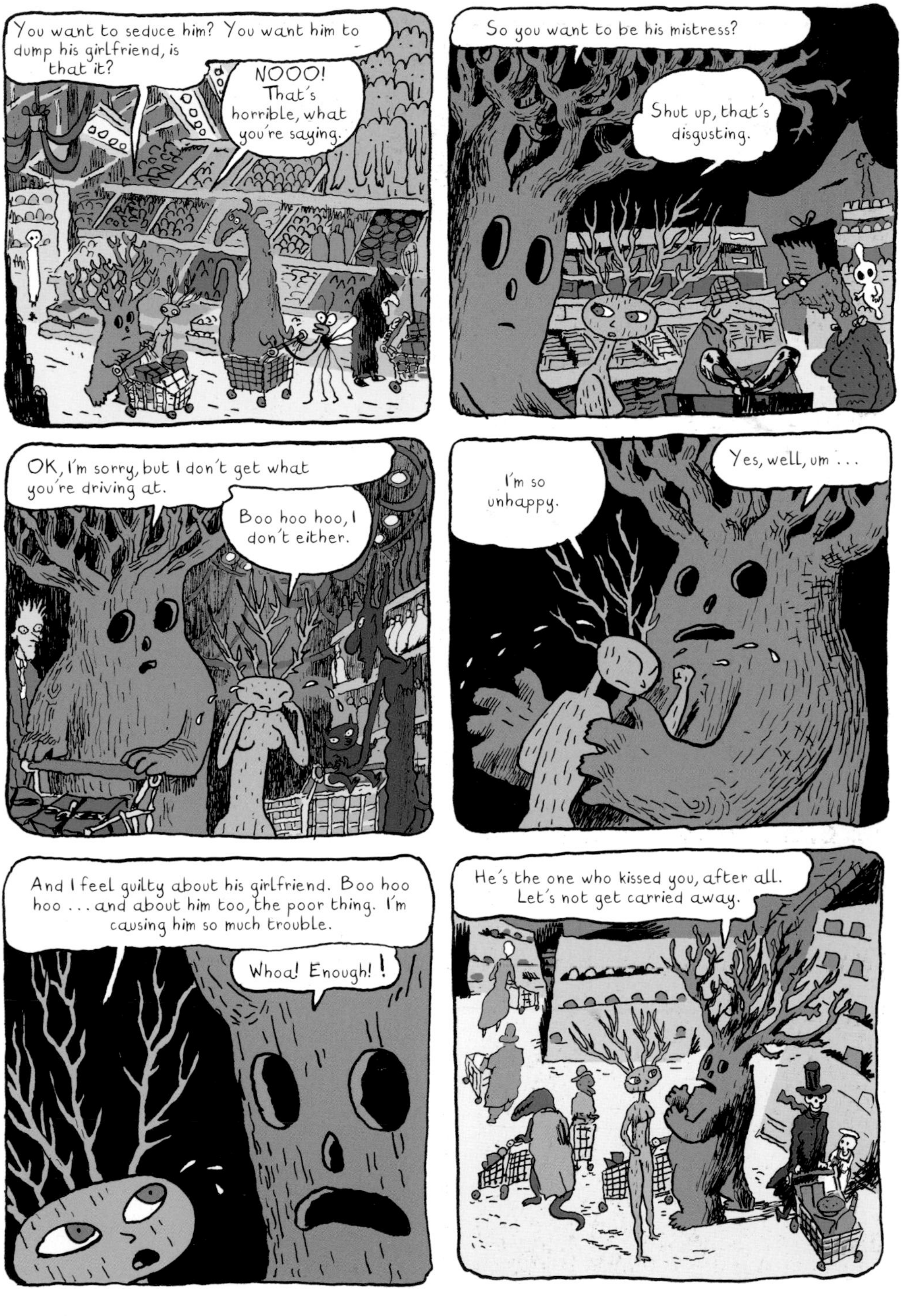
You want to seduce him? You want him to dump his girlfriend, is that it?
NOOO! That's horrible, what you're saying.
So you want to be his mistress?
Shut up, that's disgusting.
OK, I'm sorry, but I don't get what you're driving at.
Boo hoo hoo, I don't either.
I'm so unhappy.
Yes, well, um . . .
And I feel guilty about his girlfriend. Boo hoo hoo . . . and about him too, the poor thing. I'm causing him so much trouble.
Whoa! Enough!!
He's the one who kissed you, after all. Let's not get carried away.

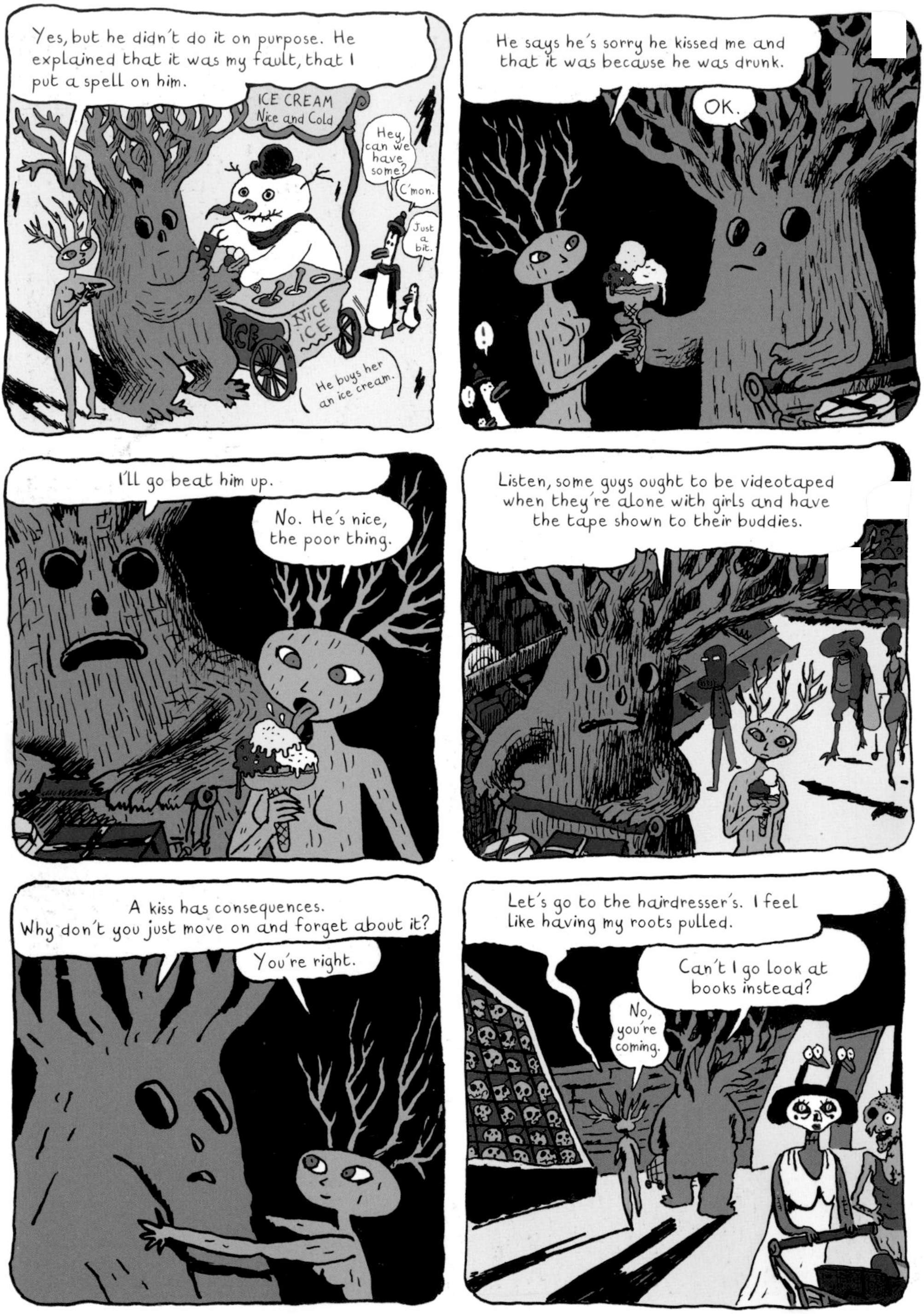
Yes, but he didn't do it on purpose. He explained that it was my fault, that I put a spell on him.
ICE CREAM
Nice and Cold
Hey, can we have some?
C'mon.
Just a bit.
NICE ICE
ICE
He buys her an ice cream.
He says he's sorry he kissed me and that it was because he was drunk.
OK.
I'll go beat him up.
No. He's nice, the poor thing.
Listen, some guys ought to be videotaped when they're alone with girls and have the tape shown to their buddies.
A kiss has consequences.
Why don't you just move on and forget about it?
You're right.
Let's go to the hairdresser's. I feel like having my roots pulled.
Can't I go look at books instead?
No, you're coming.

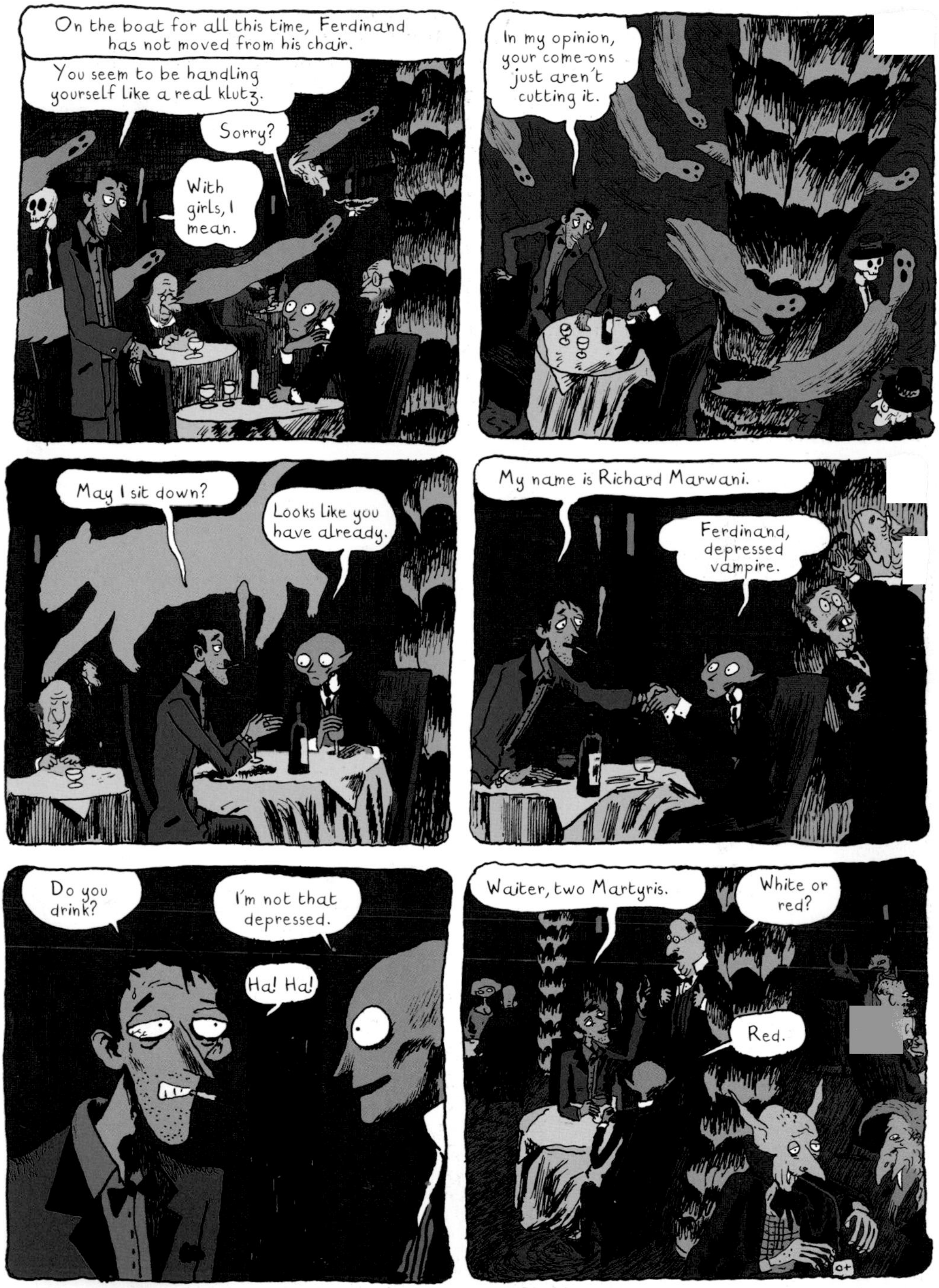
On the boat for all this time, Ferdinand has not moved from his chair.
You seem to be handling yourself like a real klutz.
Sorry?
With girls, I mean.
In my opinion, your come-ons just aren't cutting it.
May I sit down?
Looks like you have already.
My name is Richard Marwani.
Ferdinand, depressed vampire.
Do you drink?
I'm not that depressed.
Ha! Ha!
Waiter, two Martyris.
White or red?
Red.

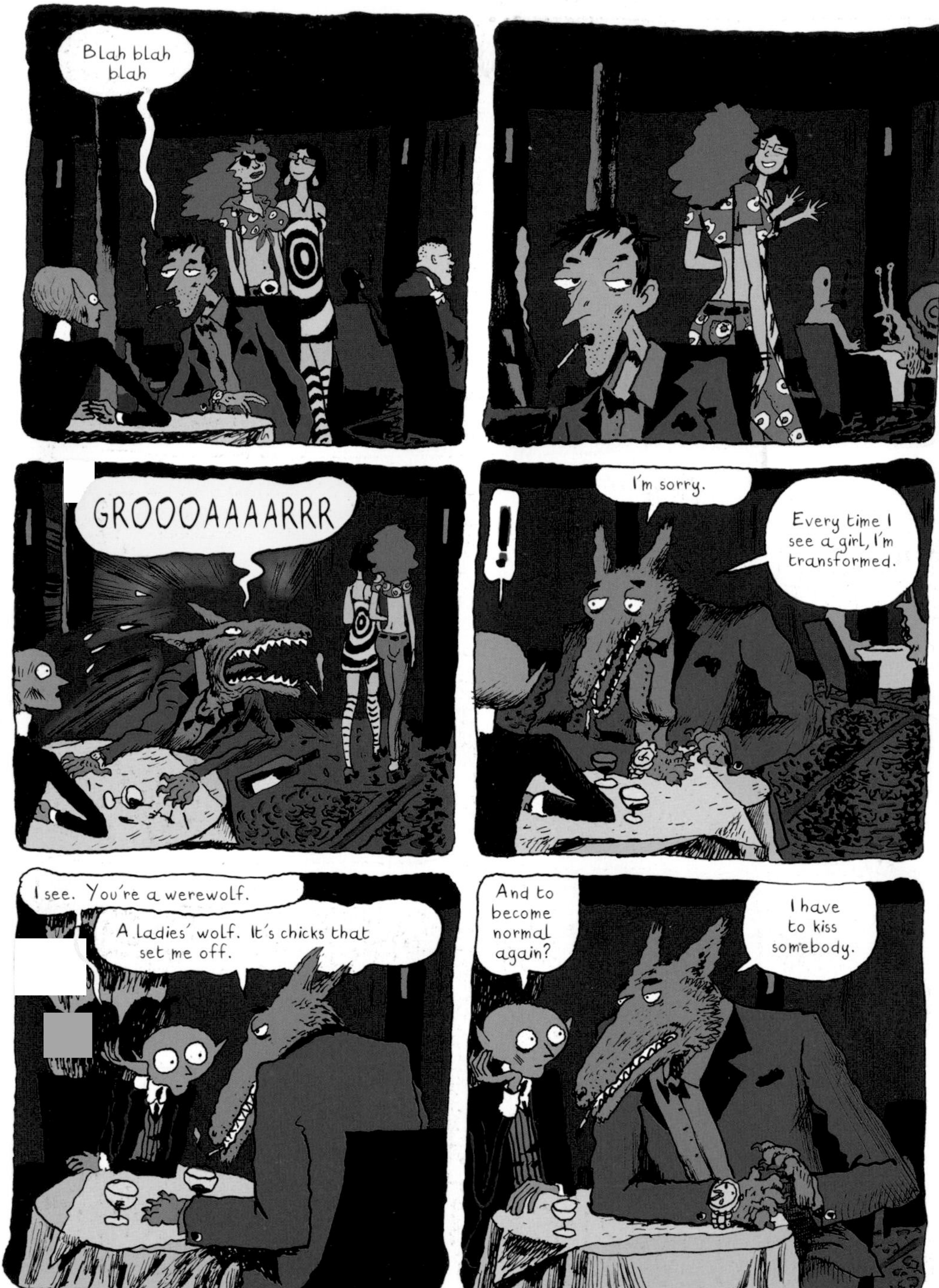
Blah blah blah
GROOOAAAARRR
I'm sorry.
!
Every time I see a girl, I'm transformed.
I see. You're a werewolf.
A ladies' wolf. It's chicks that set me off.
And to become normal again?
I have to kiss somebody.

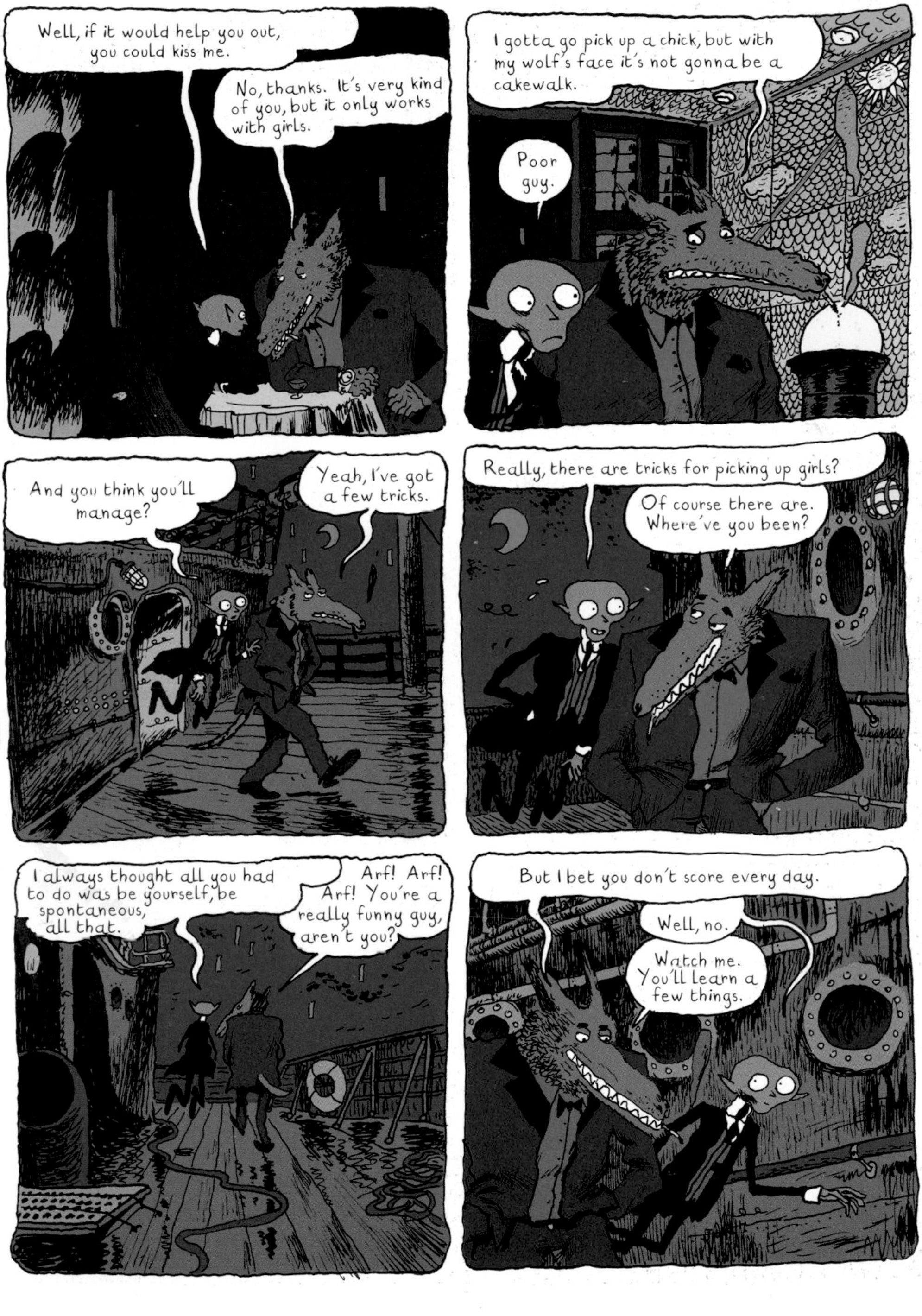
Well, if it would help you out, you could kiss me.
No, thanks. It's very kind of you, but it only works with girls.
I gotta go pick up a chick, but with my wolf's face it's not gonna be a cakewalk.
Poor guy.
And you think you'll manage?
Yeah, I've got a few tricks.
Really, there are tricks for picking up girls?
Of course there are. Where've you been?
I always thought all you had to do was be yourself, be spontaneous, all that.
Arf! Arf! Arf! You're a really funny guy, aren't you?
But I bet you don't score every day.
Well, no.
Watch me. You'll learn a few things.

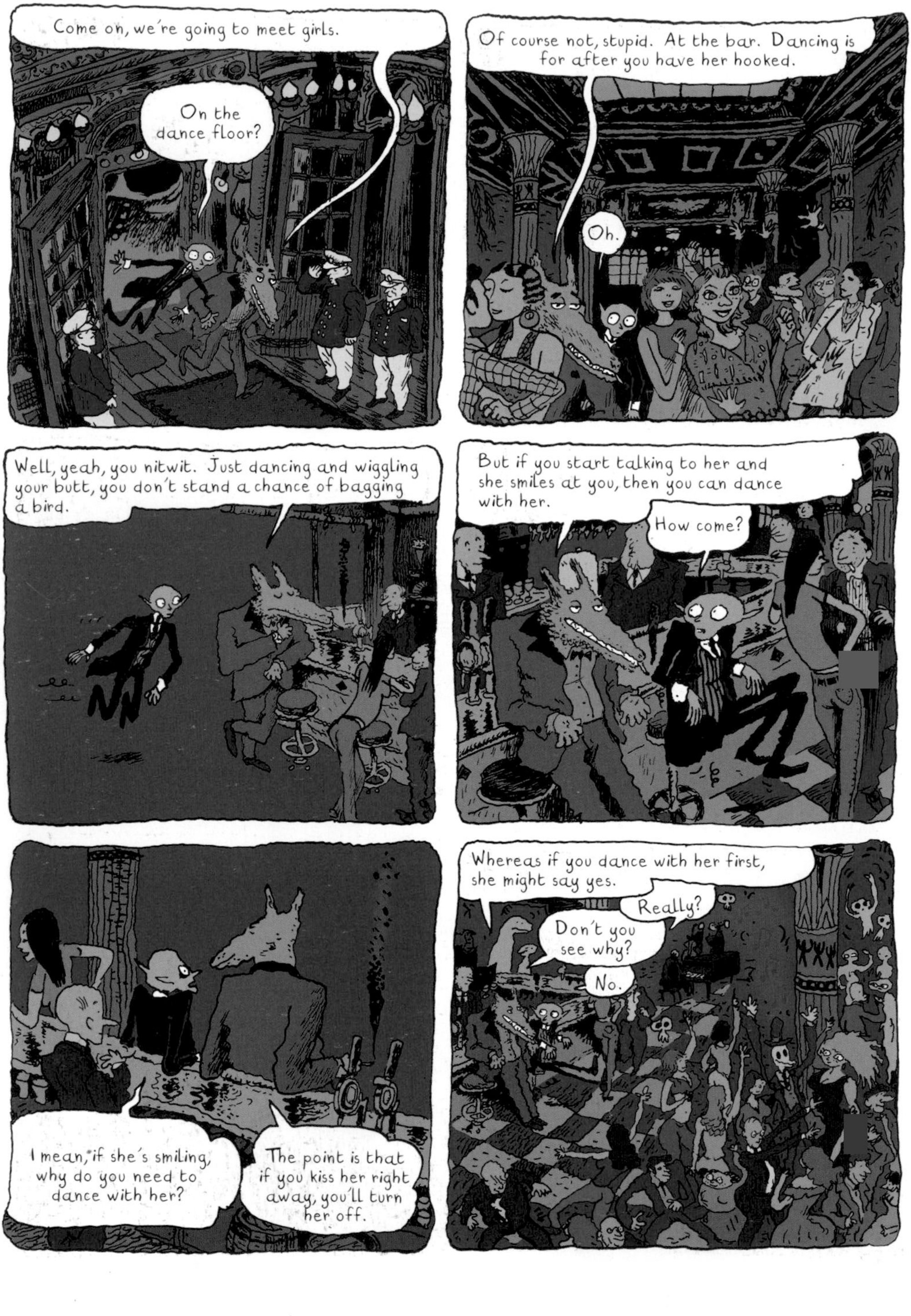
Come on, we're going to meet girls.
On the dance floor?
Of course not, stupid. At the bar. Dancing is for after you have her hooked.
Oh.
Well, yeah, you nitwit. Just dancing and wiggling your butt, you don't stand a chance of bagging a bird.
But if you start talking to her and she smiles at you, then you can dance with her.
How come?
I mean, if she's smiling, why do you need to dance with her?
The point is that if you kiss her right away, you'll turn her off.
Whereas if you dance with her first, she might say yes.
Really?
Don't you see why?
No.

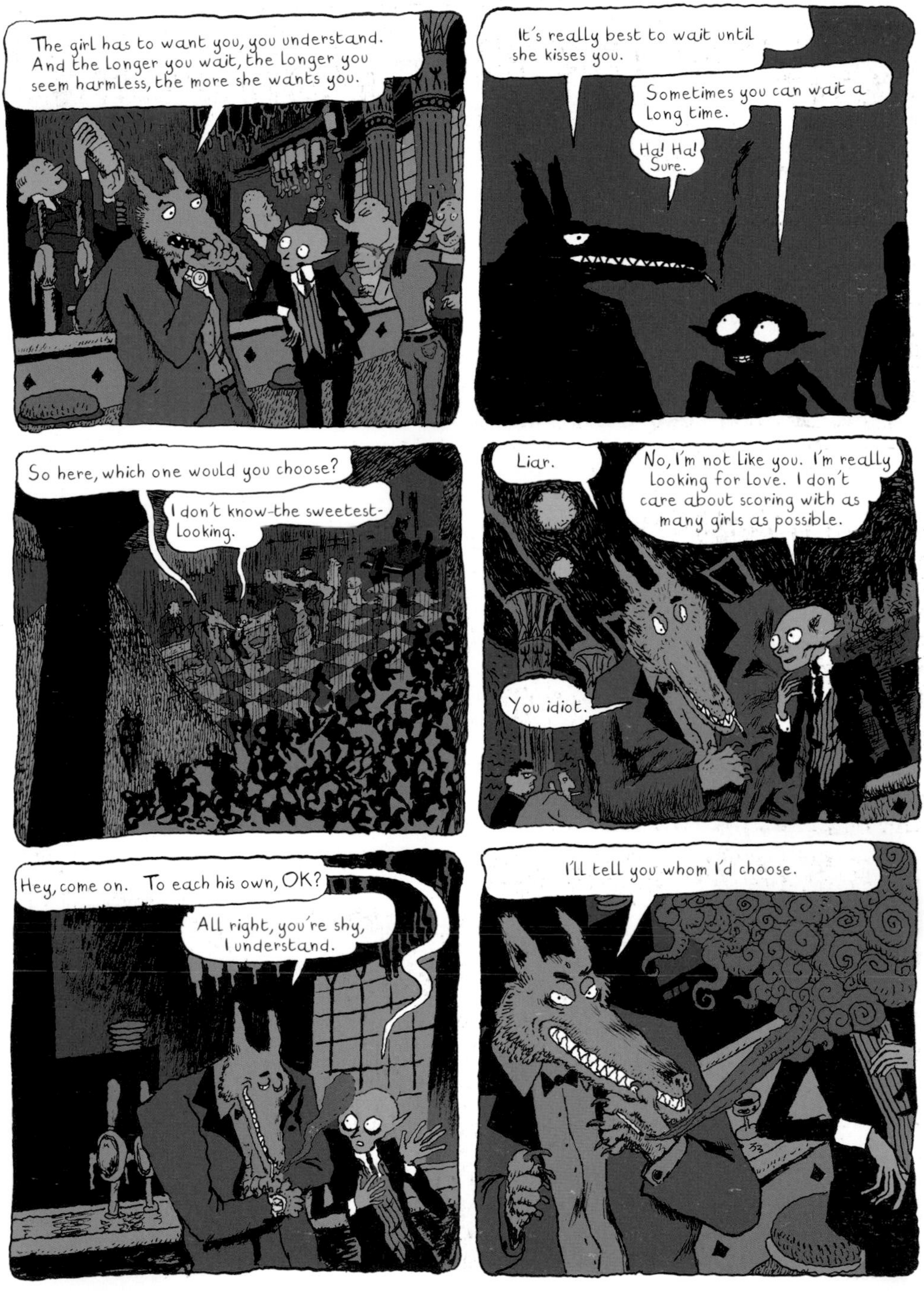
The girl has to want you, you understand. And the longer you wait, the longer you seem harmless, the more she wants you.
It's really best to wait until she kisses you.
Sometimes you can wait a long time.
Ha! Ha! Sure.
So here, which one would you choose?
I don't know-the sweetest-looking.
Liar.
No, I'm not like you. I'm really looking for love. I don't care about scoring with as many girls as possible.
You idiot.
Hey, come on. To each his own, OK?
All right, you're shy, I understand.
I'll tell you whom I'd choose.

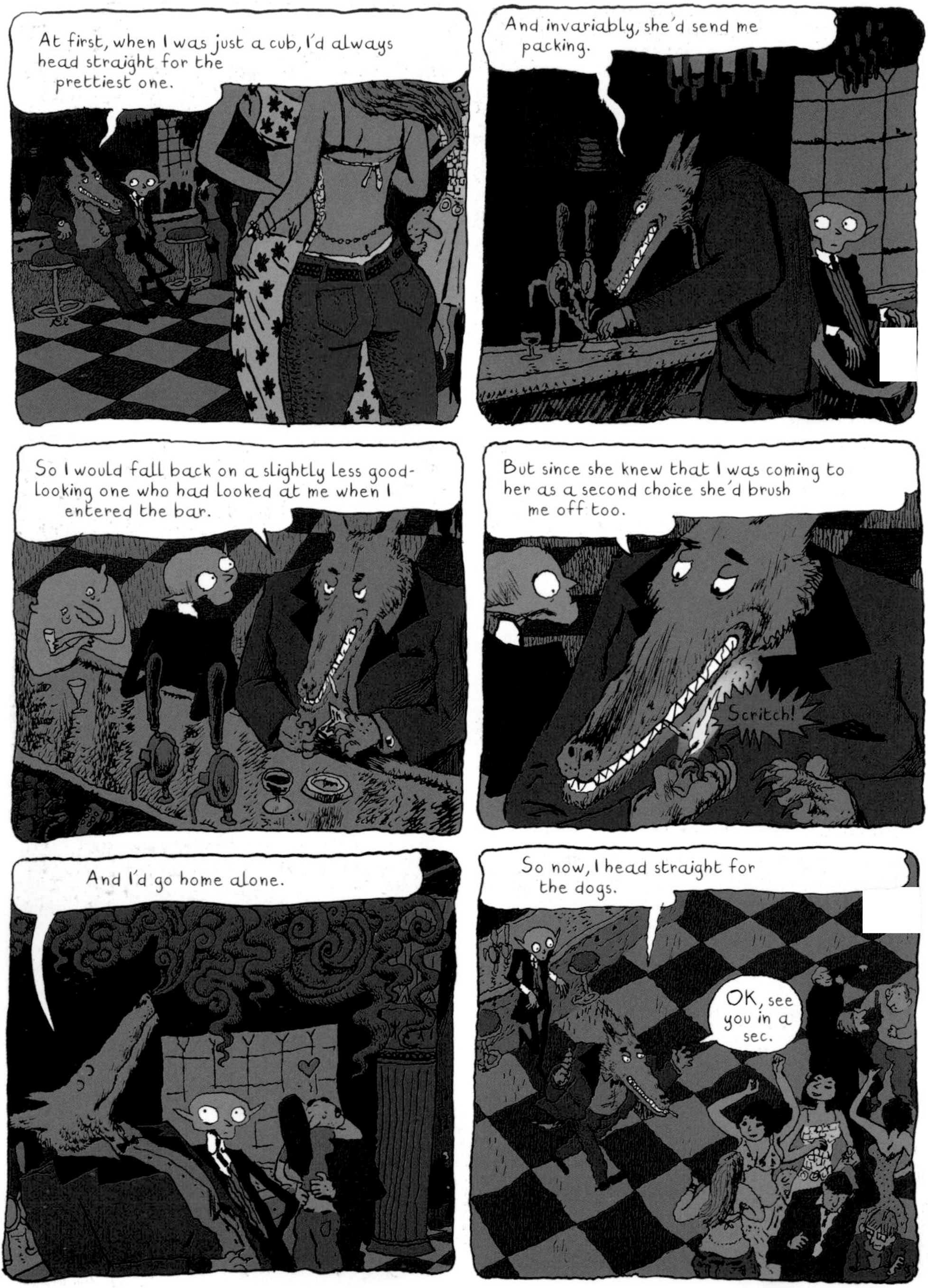
At first, when I was just a cub, I'd always head straight for the prettiest one.
And invariably, she'd send me packing.
So I would fall back on a slightly less good-looking one who had looked at me when I entered the bar.
But since she knew that I was coming to her as a second choice she'd brush me off too.
Scritch!
And I'd go home alone.
So now, I head straight for the dogs.
OK, see you in a sec.

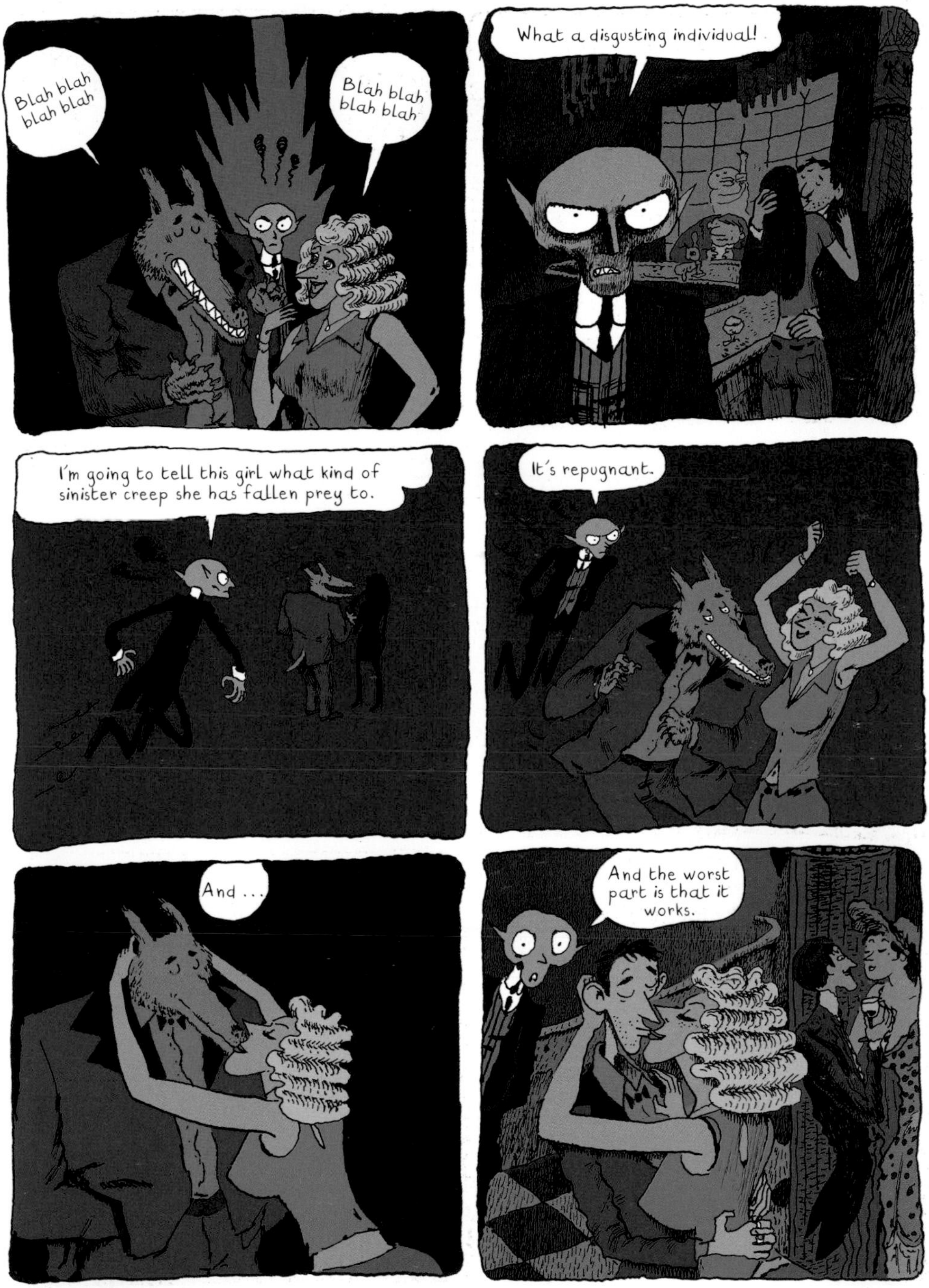

Blah blah blah blah
Blah blah blah blah
What a disgusting individual!
I'm going to tell this girl what kind of sinister creep she has fallen prey to.
It's repugnant.
And ...
And the worst part is that it works.

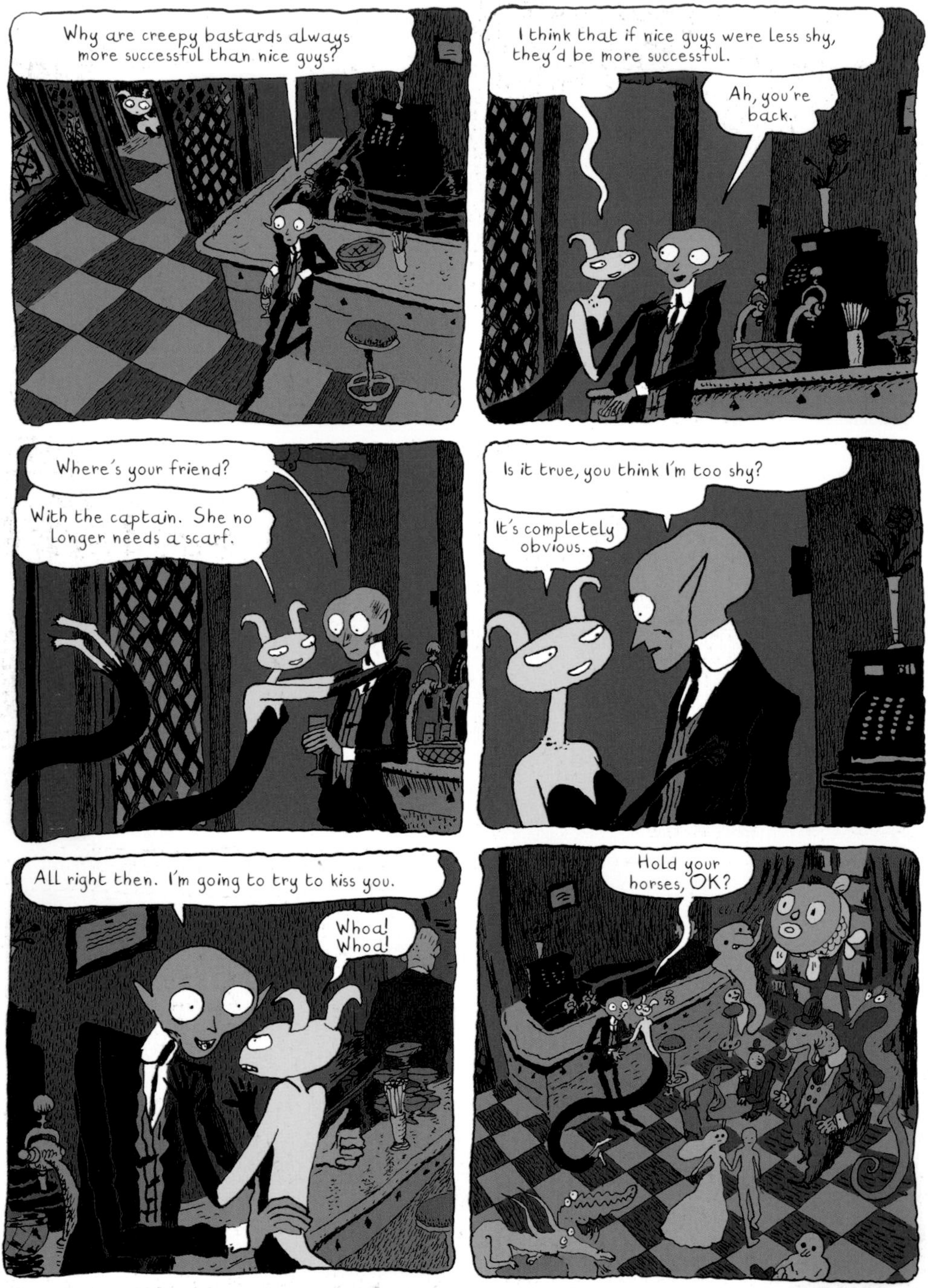
Why are creepy bastards always more successful than nice guys?
I think that if nice guys were less shy, they'd be more successful.
Ah, you're back.
Where's your friend?
With the captain. She no longer needs a scarf.
Is it true, you think I'm too shy?
It's completely obvious.
All right then. I'm going to try to kiss you.
Whoa! Whoa!
Hold your horses, OK?

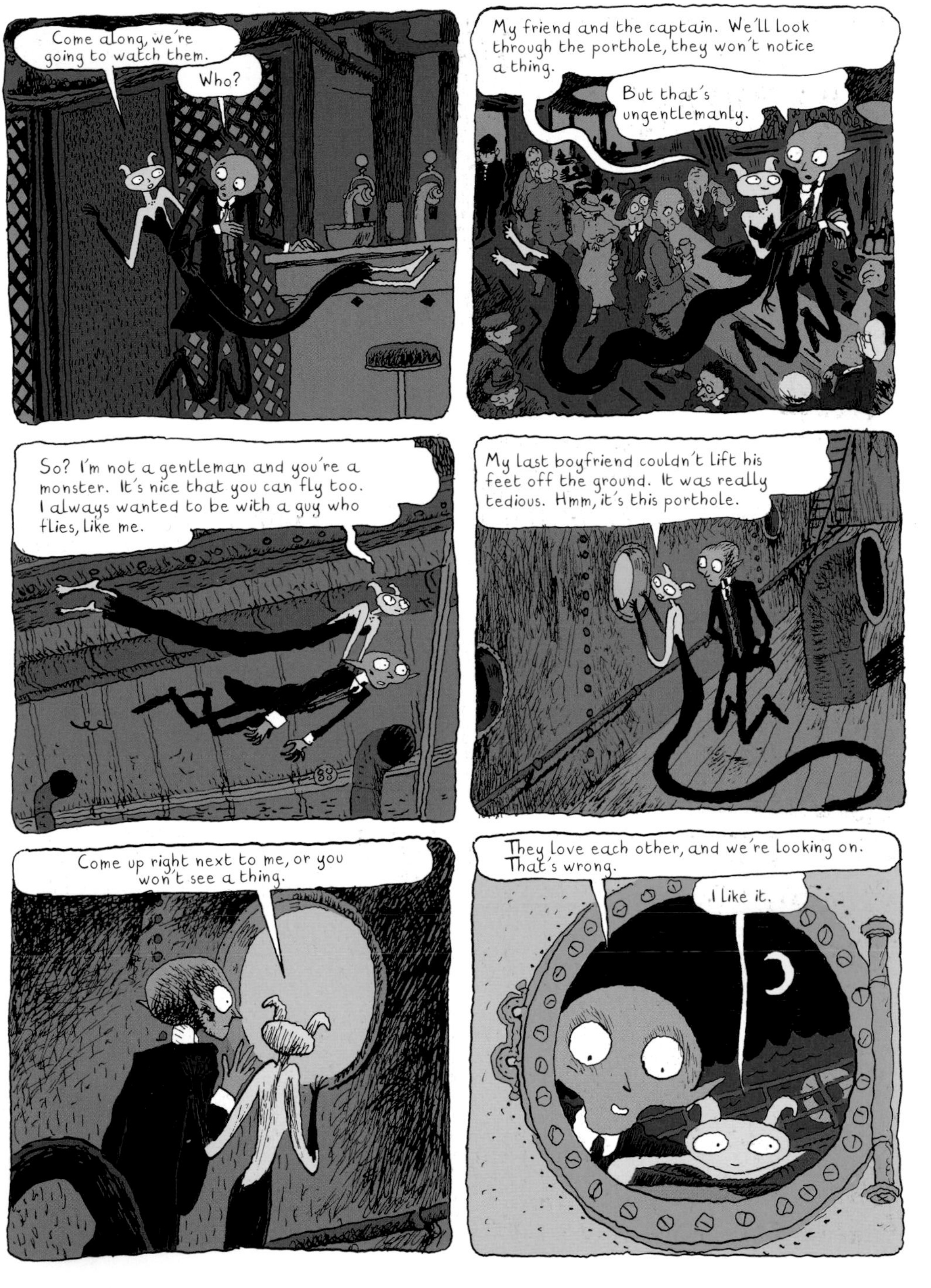
Come along, we're going to watch them.
Who?
My friend and the captain. We'll look through the porthole, they won't notice a thing.
But that's ungentlemanly.
So? I'm not a gentleman and you're a monster. It's nice that you can fly too. I always wanted to be with a guy who flies, like me.
My last boyfriend couldn't lift his feet off the ground. It was really tedious. Hmm, it's this porthole.
Come up right next to me, or you won't see a thing.
They love each other, and we're looking on. That's wrong.
I like it.

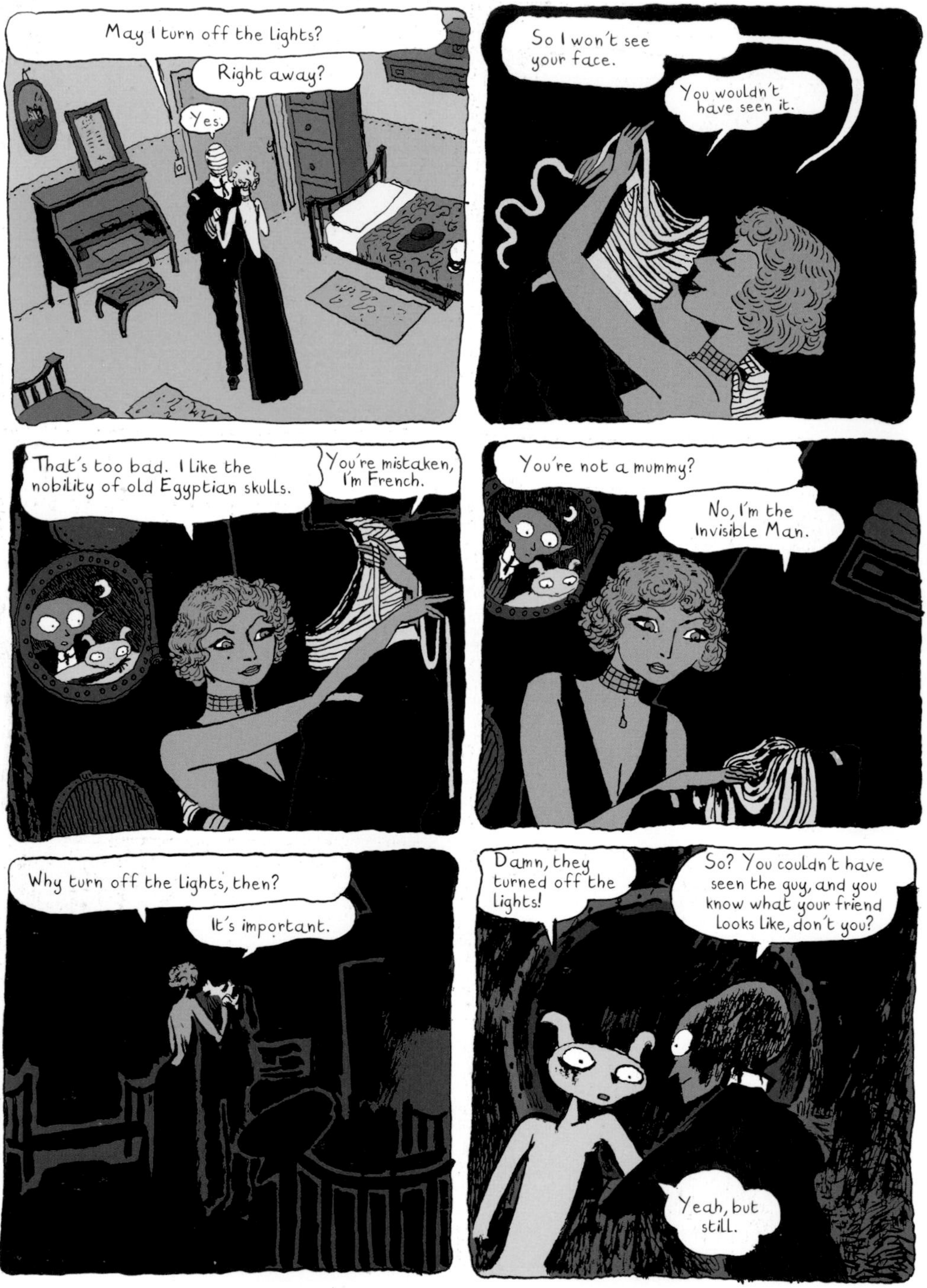
May I turn off the lights?
Right away?
Yes.
So I won't see your face.
You wouldn't have seen it.
That's too bad. I like the nobility of old Egyptian skulls.
You're mistaken, I'm French.
You're not a mummy?
No, I'm the Invisible Man.
Why turn off the lights, then?
It's important.
Damn, they turned off the lights!
So? You couldn't have seen the guy, and you know what your friend looks like, don't you?
Yeah, but still.

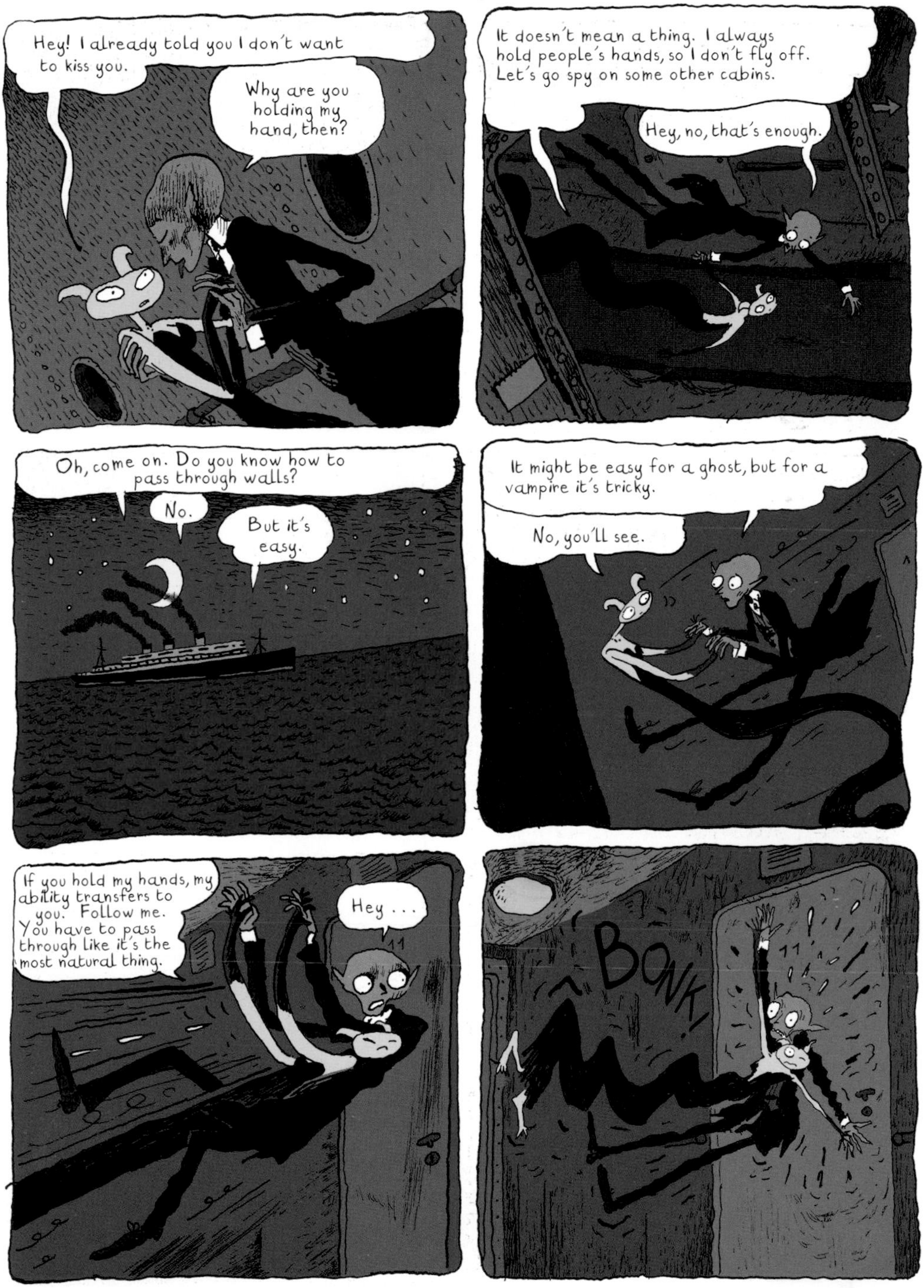

Hey! I already told you I don't want to kiss you.
Why are you holding my hand, then?
It doesn't mean a thing. I always hold people's hands, so I don't fly off. Let's go spy on some other cabins.
Hey, no, that's enough.
Oh, come on. Do you know how to pass through walls?
No.
But it's easy.
It might be easy for a ghost, but for a vampire it's tricky.
No, you'll see.
If you hold my hands, my ability transfers to you. Follow me. You have to pass through like it's the most natural thing.
Hey . . .
BONK!

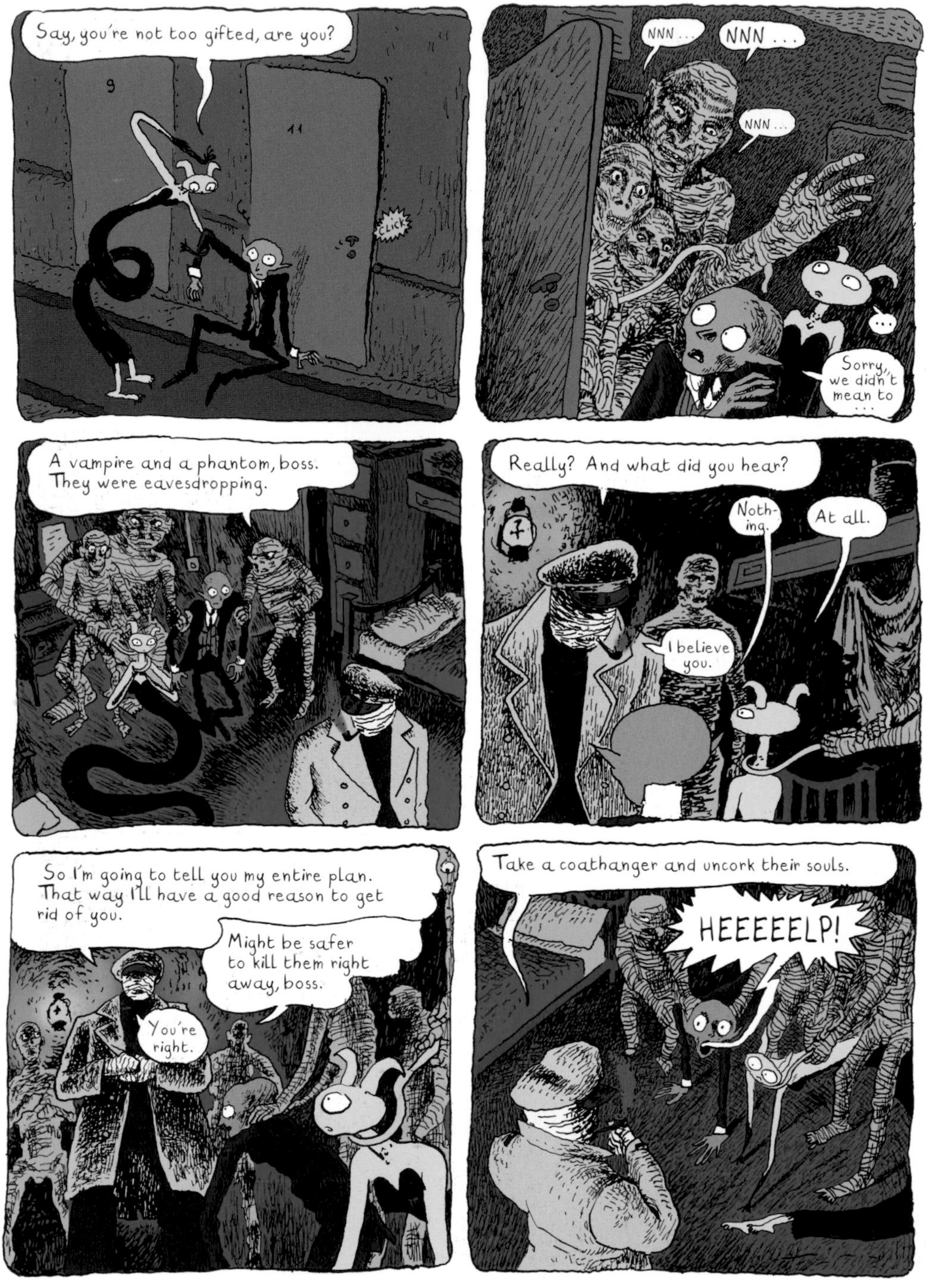
Say, you're not too gifted, are you?
CLICK
NNN...
NNN...
NNN...
...
Sorry, we didn't mean to ...
A vampire and a phantom, boss. They were eavesdropping.
Really? And what did you hear?
Noth-ing.
At all.
I believe you.
So I'm going to tell you my entire plan. That way I'll have a good reason to get rid of you.
Might be safer to kill them right away, boss.
You're right.
Take a coathanger and uncork their souls.
HEEEEELP!

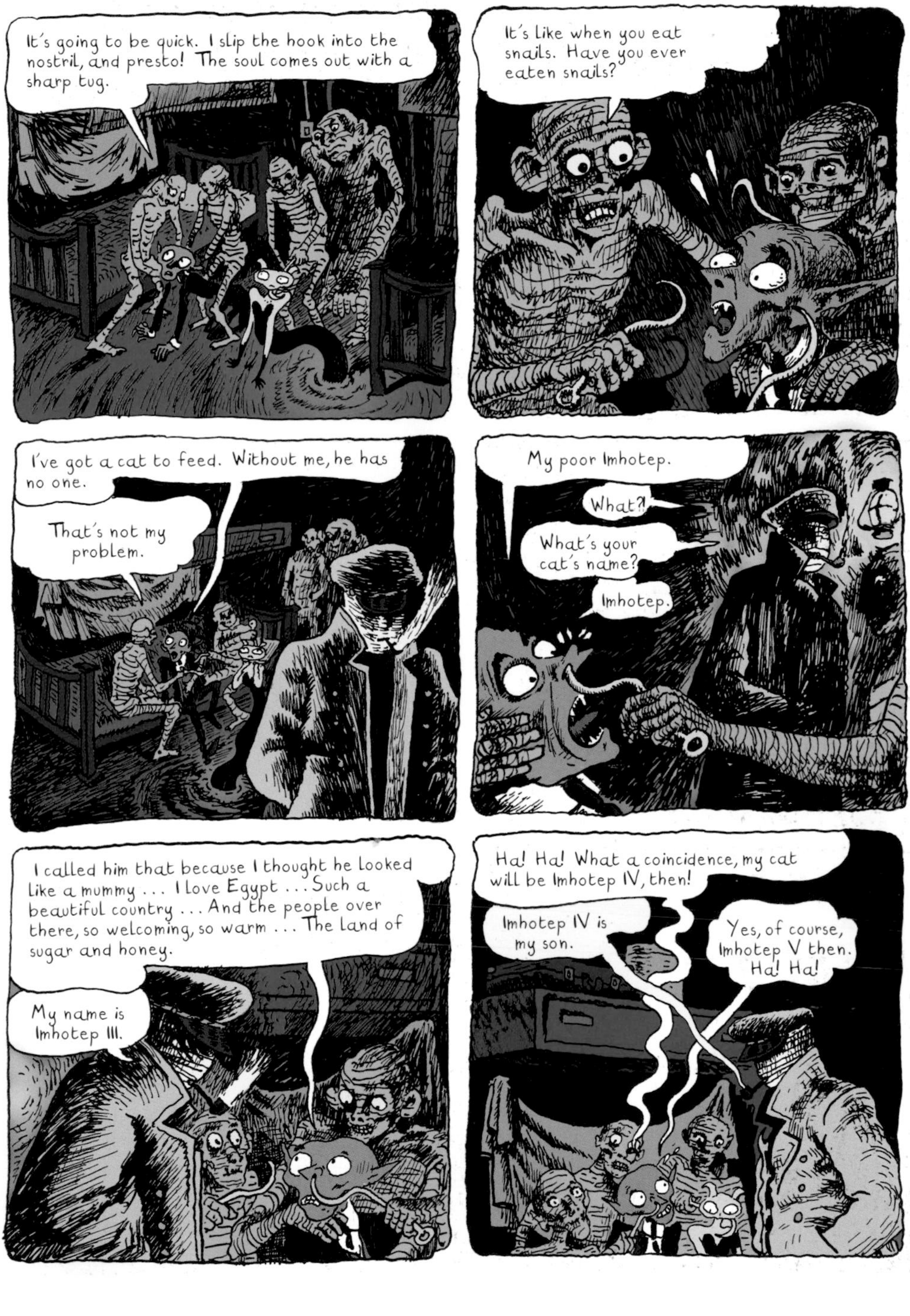
It's going to be quick. I slip the hook into the nostril, and presto! The soul comes out with a sharp tug.
It's like when you eat snails. Have you ever eaten snails?
I've got a cat to feed. Without me, he has no one.
That's not my problem.
My poor Imhotep.
What?!
What's your cat's name?
Imhotep.
I called him that because I thought he looked like a mummy . . . I love Egypt . . . Such a beautiful country . . . And the people over there, so welcoming, so warm . . . The land of sugar and honey.
My name is Imhotep III.
Ha! Ha! What a coincidence, my cat will be Imhotep IV, then!
Imhotep IV is my son.
Yes, of course, Imhotep V then. Ha! Ha!

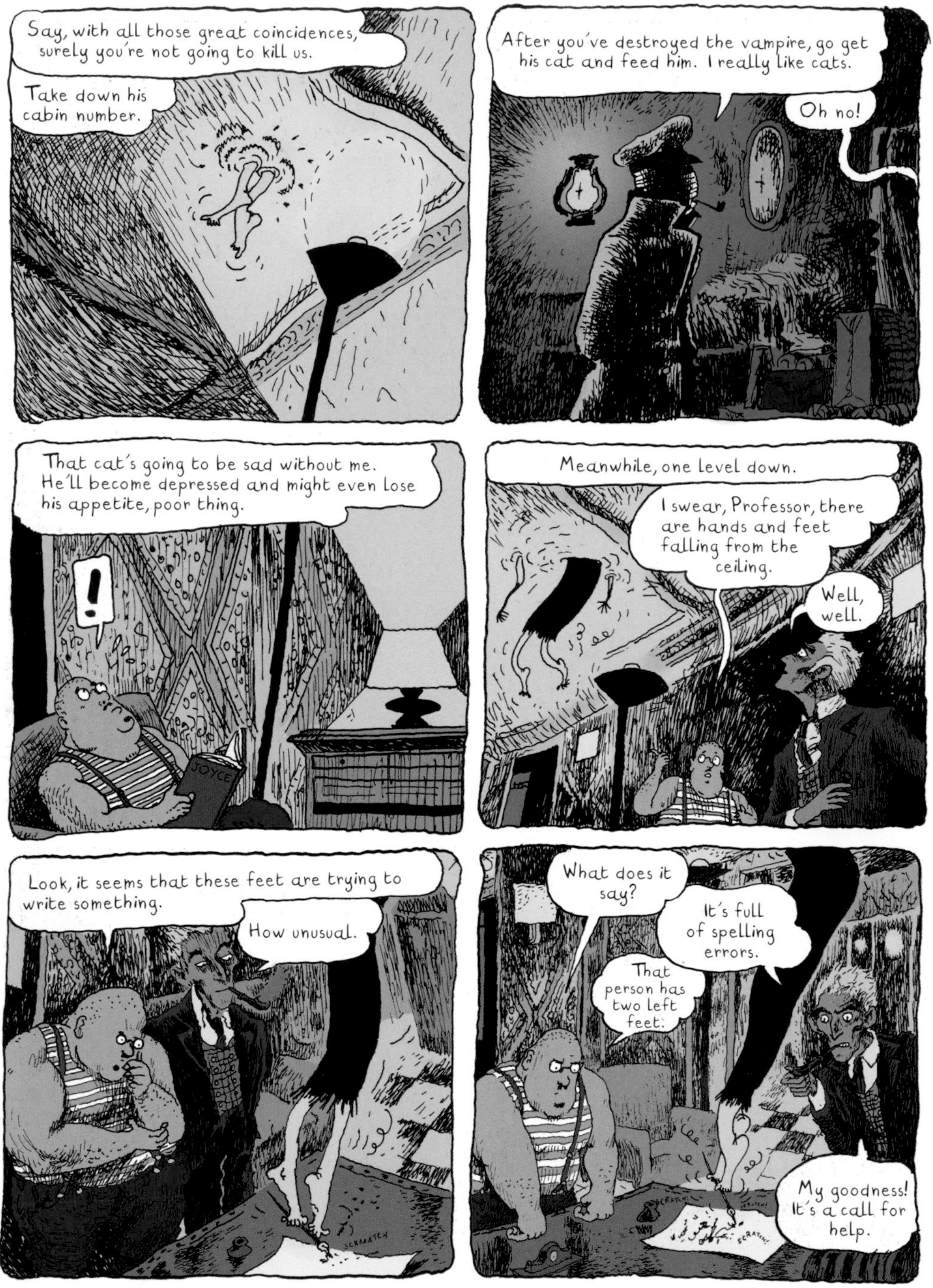
Say, with all those great coincidences, surely you're not going to kill us.
Take down his cabin number.
After you've destroyed the vampire, go get his cat and feed him. I really like cats.
Oh no!
That cat's going to be sad without me. He'll become depressed and might even lose his appetite, poor thing.
!
JOYCE
Meanwhile, one level down.
I swear, Professor, there are hands and feet falling from the ceiling.
Well, well.
Look, it seems that these feet are trying to write something.
How unusual.
SCRAAATCH
What does it say?
It's full of spelling errors.
That person has two left feet.
My goodness! It's a call for help.

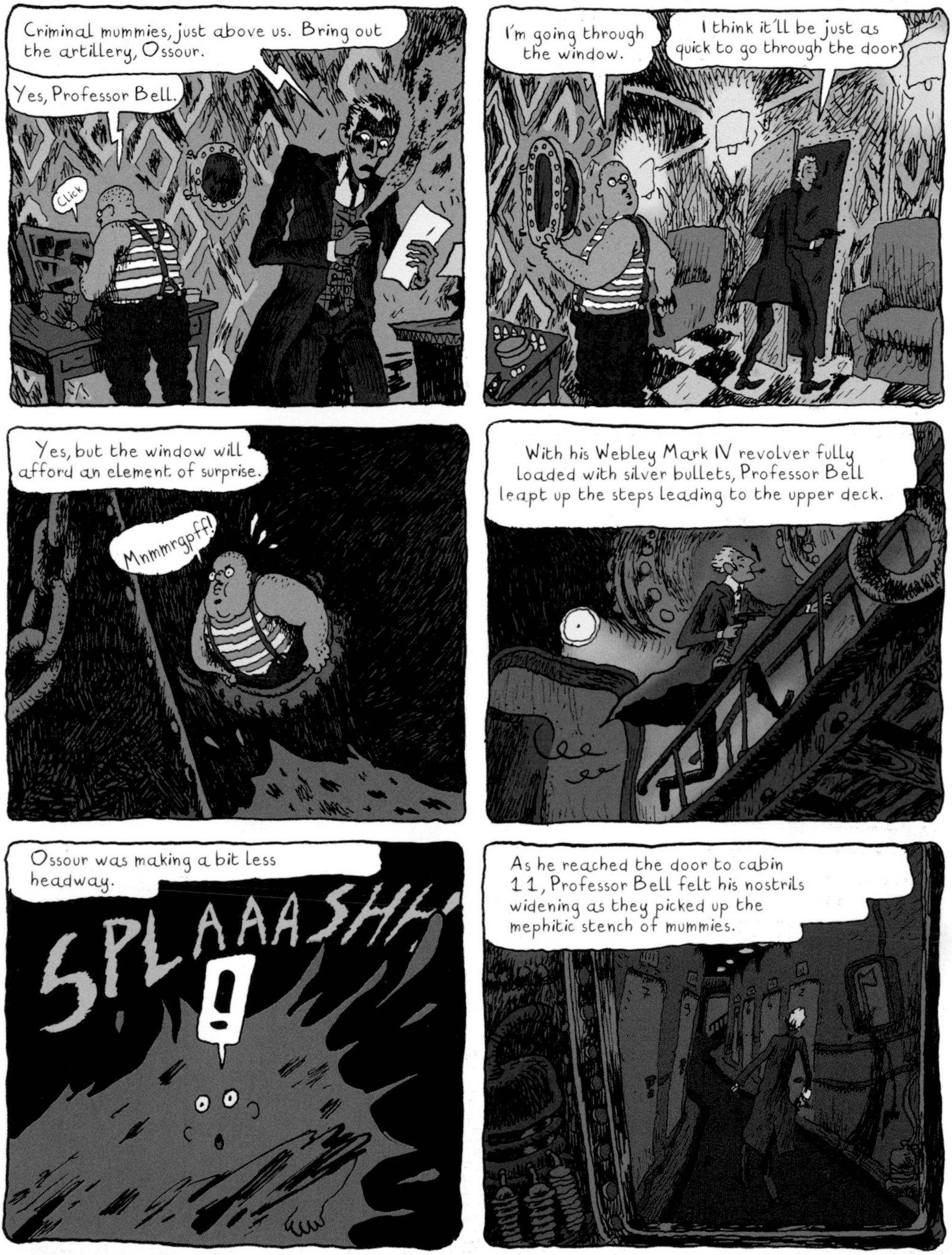
Criminal mummies, just above us. Bring out the artillery, Ossour.
Yes, Professor Bell.
Click
I'm going through the window.
I think it'll be just as quick to go through the door.
Yes, but the window will afford an element of surprise.
Mnmmrgpff!
With his Webley Mark IV revolver fully loaded with silver bullets, Professor Bell leapt up the steps leading to the upper deck.
Ossour was making a bit less headway.
SPLAAASH!
!
As he reached the door to cabin 11, Professor Bell felt his nostrils widening as they picked up the mephitic stench of mummies.

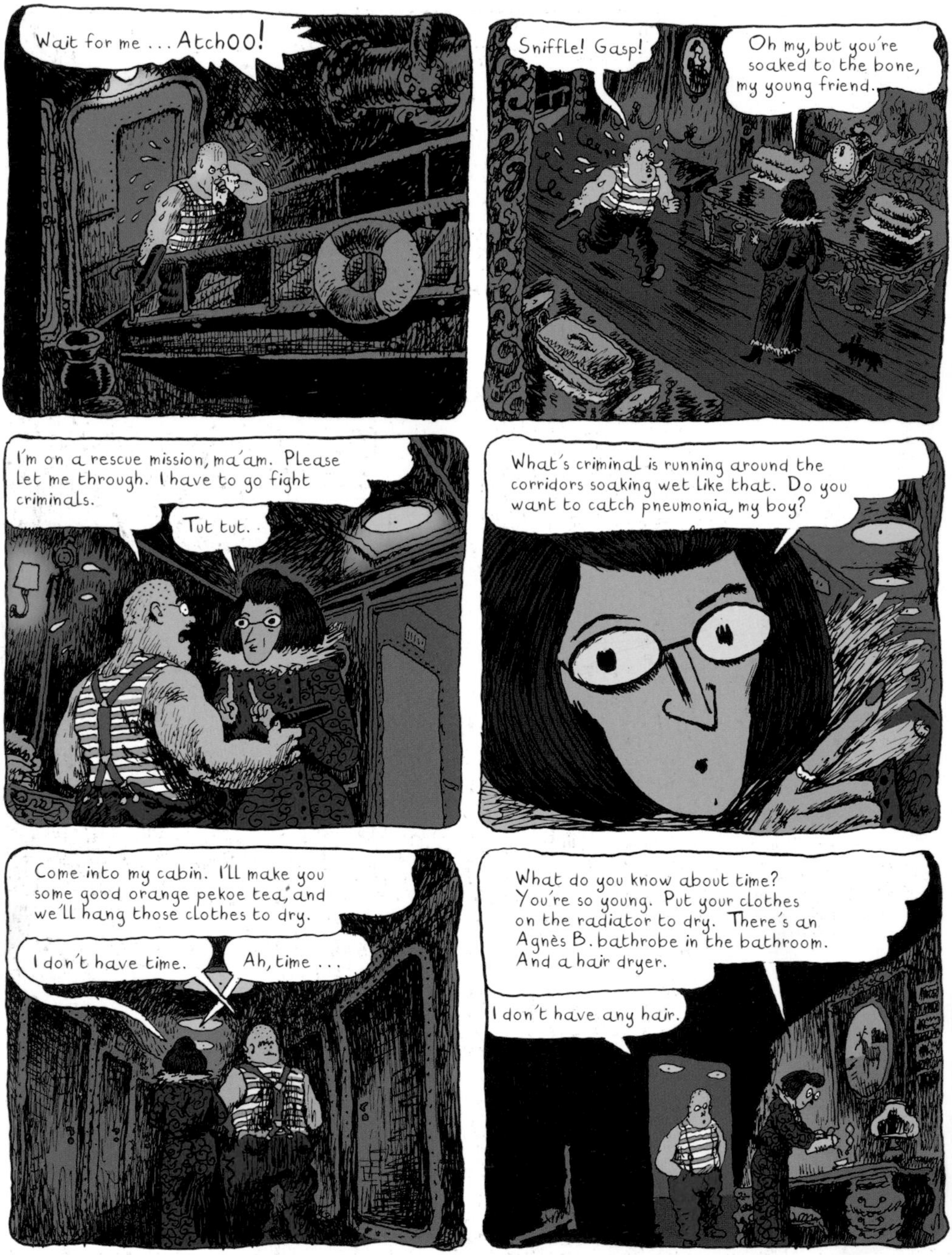
Wait for me . . . Atchoo!
Sniffle! Gasp!
Oh my, but you're soaked to the bone, my young friend.
I'm on a rescue mission, ma'am. Please let me through. I have to go fight criminals.
Tut tut.
What's criminal is running around the corridors soaking wet like that. Do you want to catch pneumonia, my boy?
Come into my cabin. I'll make you some good orange pekoe tea, and we'll hang those clothes to dry.
I don't have time.
Ah, time . . .
What do you know about time? You're so young. Put your clothes on the radiator to dry. There's an Agnès B. bathrobe in the bathroom. And a hair dryer.
I don't have any hair.

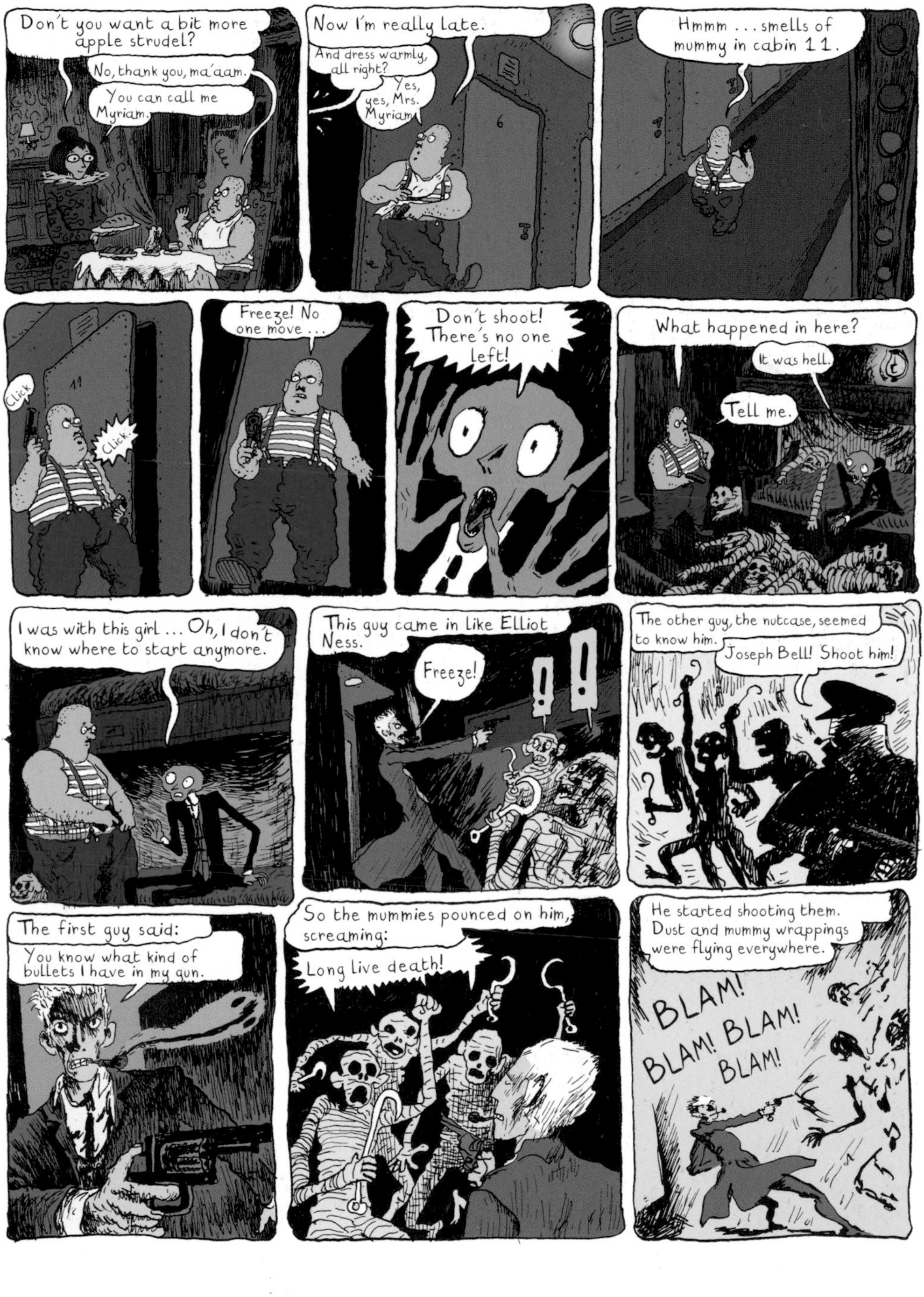

Don't you want a bit more apple strudel?
No, thank you, ma'aam.
You can call me Myriam.
Now I'm really late.
And dress warmly, all right?
Yes, yes, Mrs. Myriam.
Hmmm . . . smells of mummy in cabin 11.
Click
Click.
Freeze! No one move . . .
Don't shoot! There's no one left!
What happened in here?
It was hell.
Tell me.
I was with this girl . . . Oh, I don't know where to start anymore.
This guy came in like Elliot Ness.
Freeze!
!
!
The other guy, the nutcase, seemed to know him.
Joseph Bell! Shoot him!
The first guy said:
You know what kind of bullets I have in my gun.
So the mummies pounced on him, screaming:
Long live death!
He started shooting them. Dust and mummy wrappings were flying everywhere.
BLAM!
BLAM! BLAM!
BLAM!

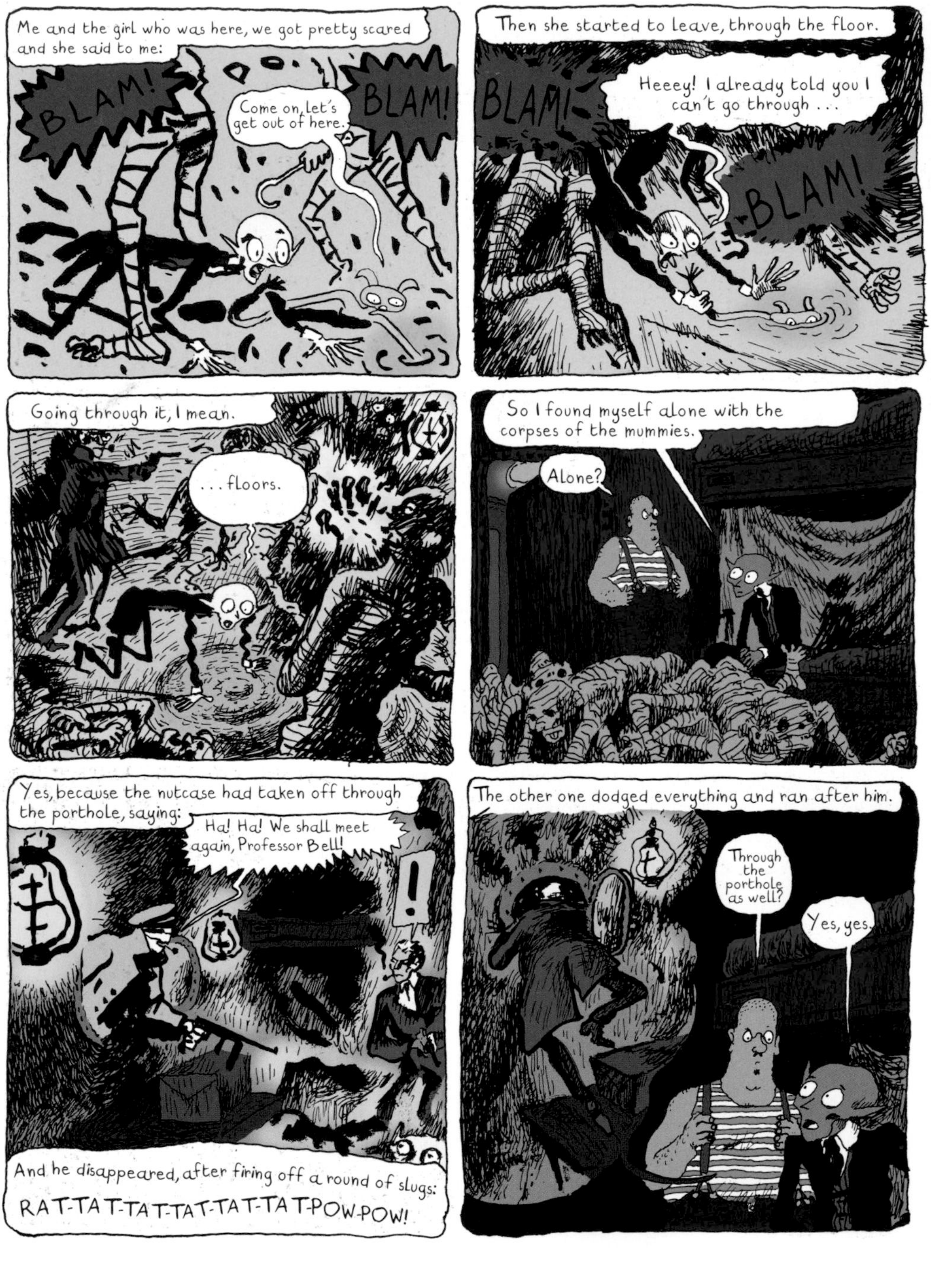
Me and the girl who was here, we got pretty scared and she said to me:
BLAM!
BLAM!
Come on, let's get out of here.
Then she started to leave, through the floor.
BLAM!
Heeey! I already told you I can't go through . . .
BLAM!
Going through it, I mean.
. . . floors.
So I found myself alone with the corpses of the mummies.
Alone?
Yes, because the nutcase had taken off through the porthole, saying:
Ha! Ha! We shall meet again, Professor Bell!
!
And he disappeared, after firing off a round of slugs:
RAT-TAT-TAT-TAT-TAT-TAT-POW-POW!
The other one dodged everything and ran after him.
Through the porthole as well?
Yes, yes.

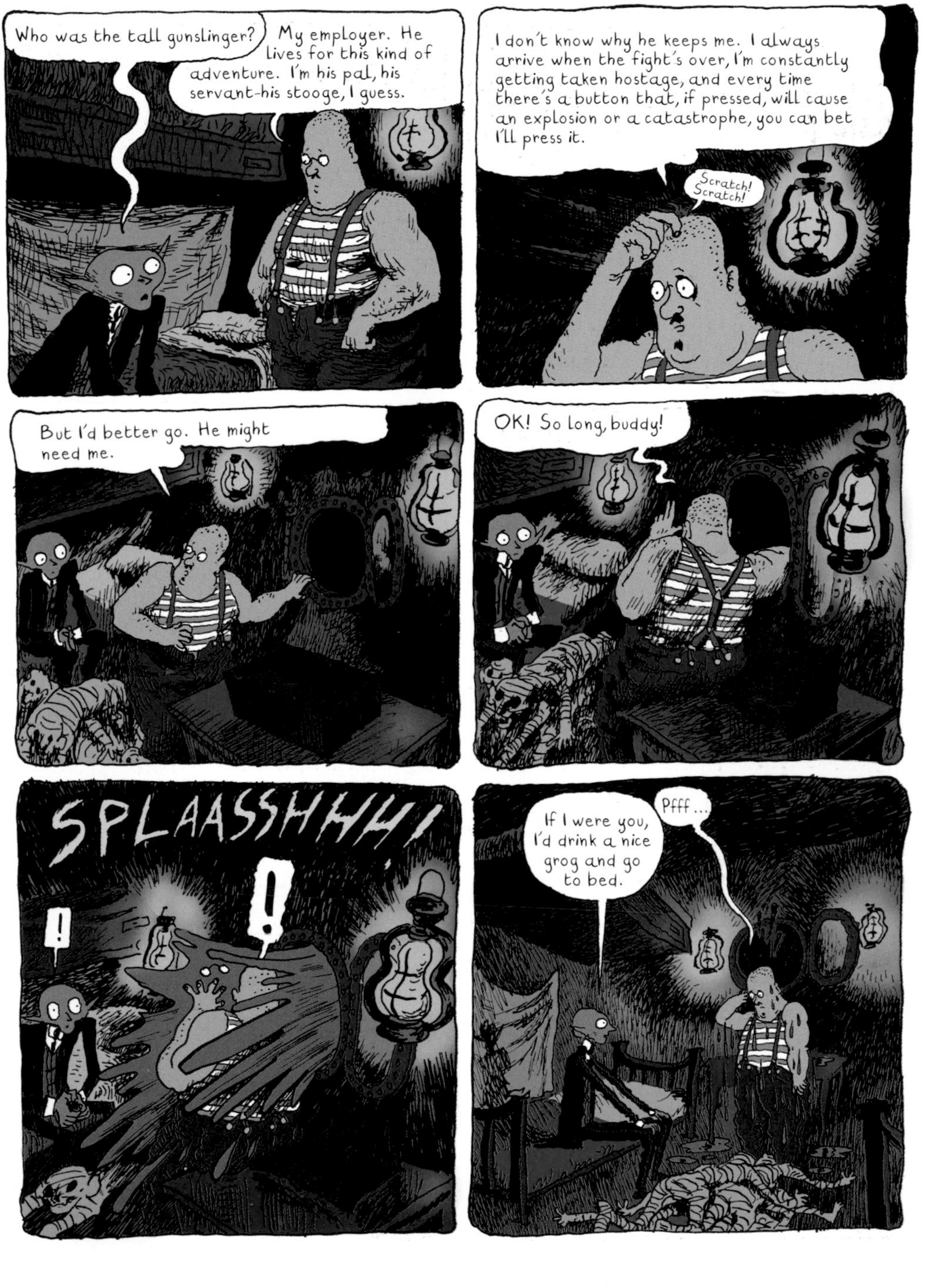
Who was the tall gunslinger?
My employer. He lives for this kind of adventure. I'm his pal, his servant-his stooge, I guess.
I don't know why he keeps me. I always arrive when the fight's over, I'm constantly getting taken hostage, and every time there's a button that, if pressed, will cause an explosion or a catastrophe, you can bet I'll press it.
Scratch! Scratch!
But I'd better go. He might need me.
OK! So long, buddy!
SPLAASSHHH!
!
!
If I were you, I'd drink a nice grog and go to bed.
Pfff...

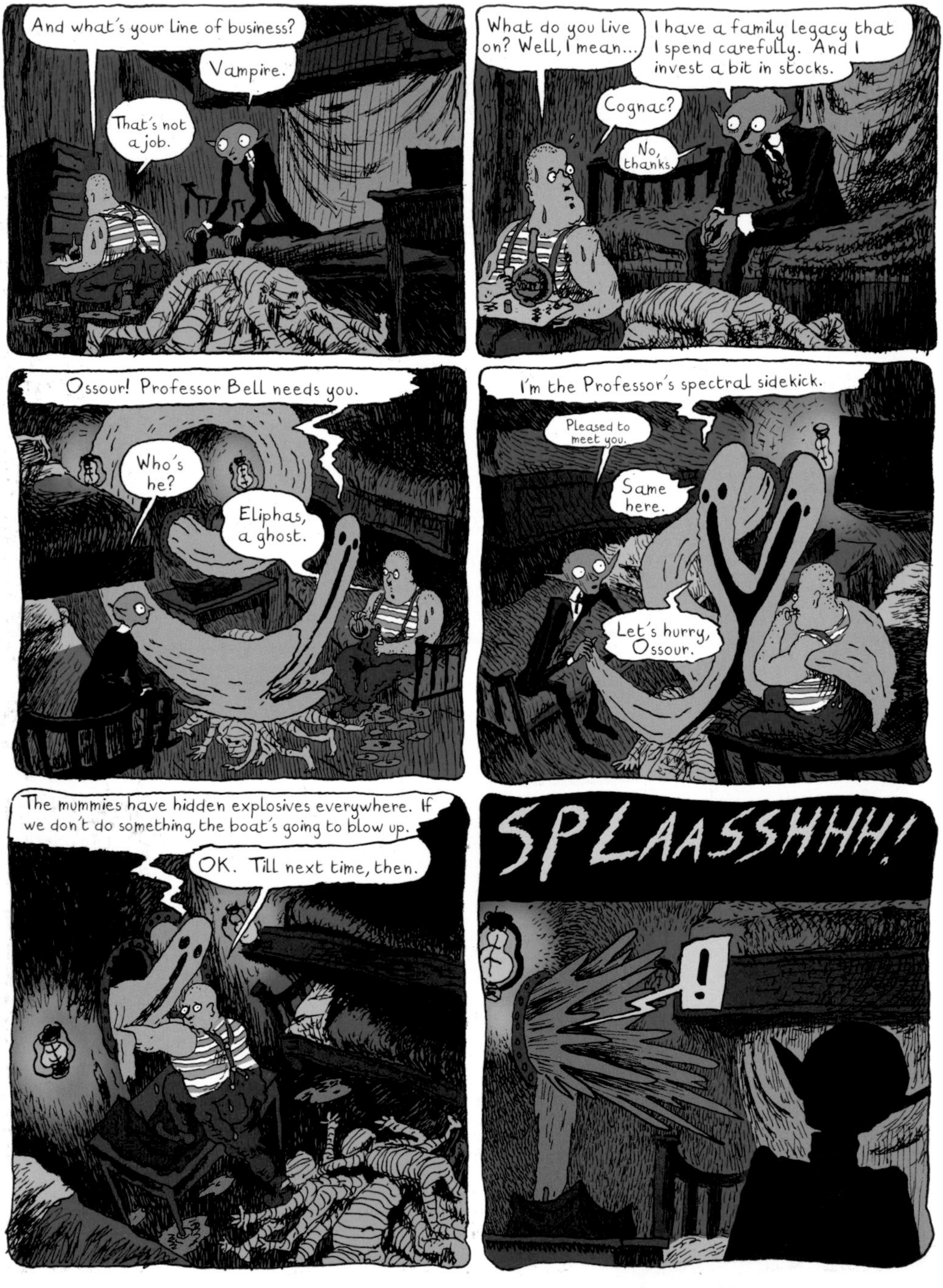
And what's your line of business?
Vampire.
That's not a job.
What do you live on? Well, I mean...
I have a family legacy that I spend carefully. And I invest a bit in stocks.
Cognac?
No, thanks.
Ossour! Professor Bell needs you.
Who's he?
Eliphas, a ghost.
I'm the Professor's spectral sidekick.
Pleased to meet you.
Same here.
Let's hurry, Ossour.
The mummies have hidden explosives everywhere. If we don't do something, the boat's going to blow up.
OK. Till next time, then.
SPLAASSHHH!
!

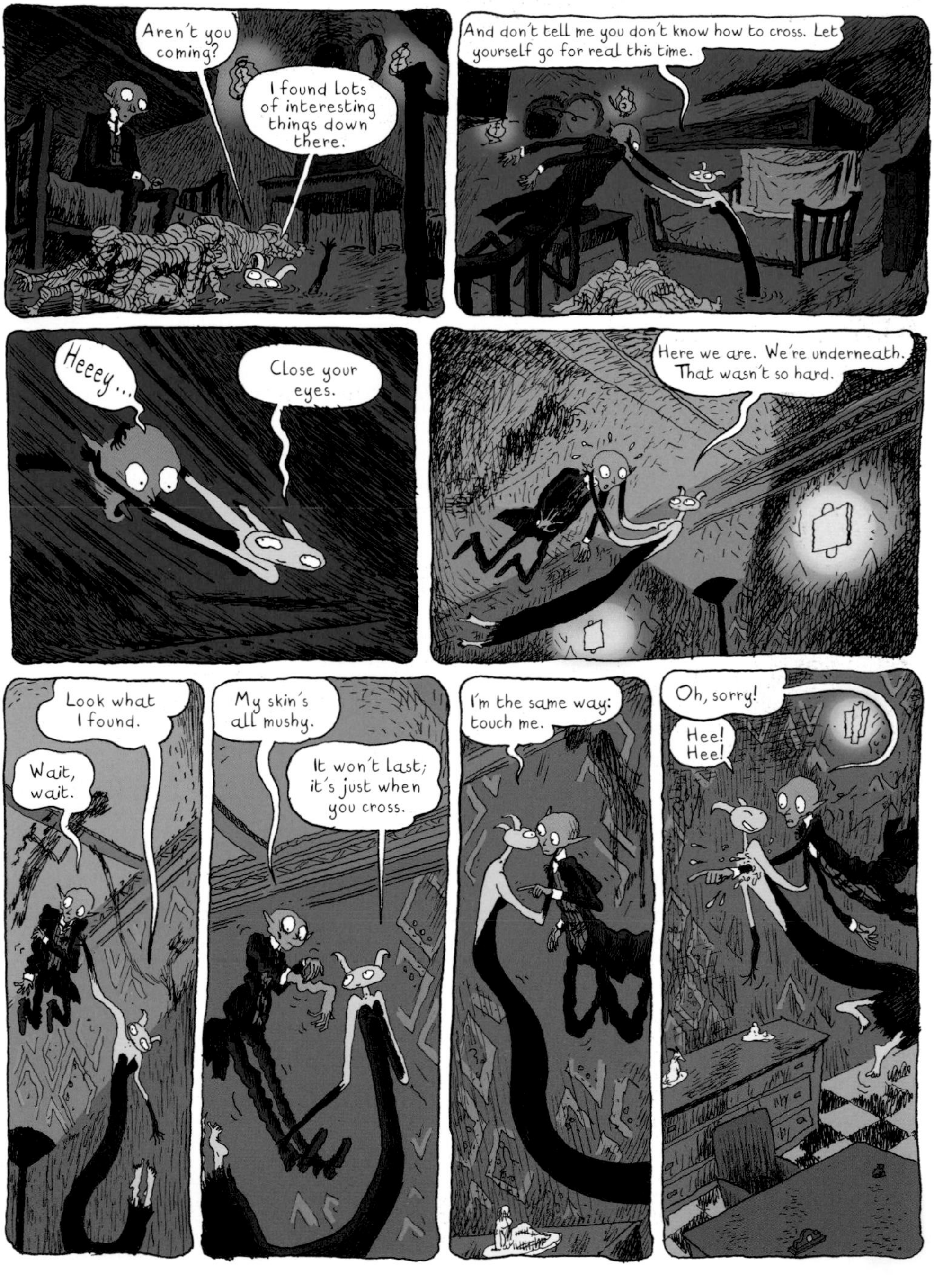

Aren't you coming?
I found lots of interesting things down there.
And don't tell me you don't know how to cross. Let yourself go for real this time.
Heeey...
Close your eyes.
Here we are. We're underneath. That wasn't so hard.
Look what I found.
Wait, wait.
My skin's all mushy.
It won't last; it's just when you cross.
I'm the same way: touch me.
Oh, sorry!
Hee! Hee!

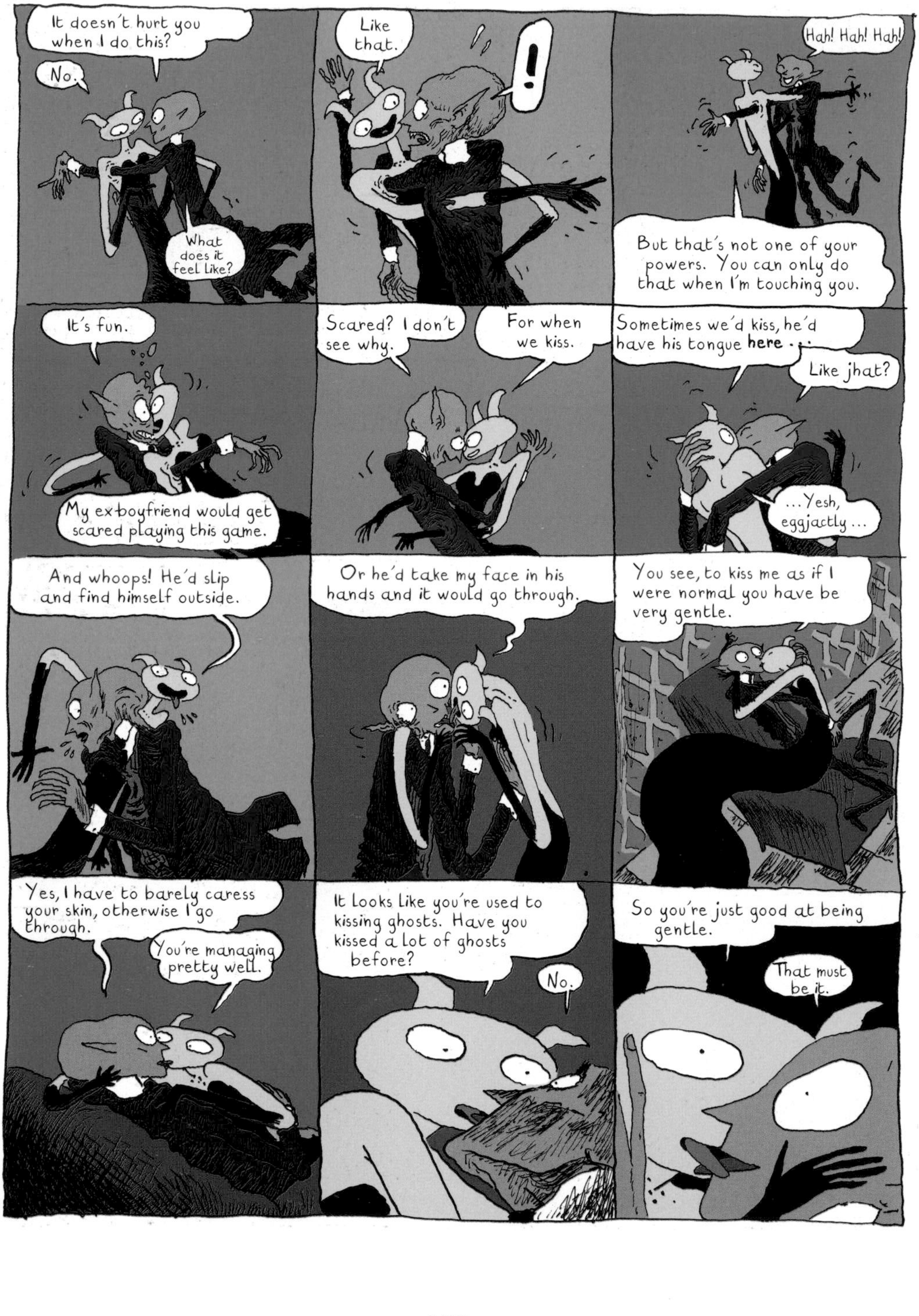
It doesn't hurt you when I do this?
No.
What does it feel like?
Like that.
!
Hah! Hah! Hah!
But that's not one of your powers. You can only do that when I'm touching you.
It's fun.
My exboyfriend would get scared playing this game.
Scared? I don't see why.
For when we kiss.
Sometimes we'd kiss, he'd have his tongue here . . .
Like jhat?
...Yesh, eggjactly ...
And whoops! He'd slip and find himself outside.
Or he'd take my face in his hands and it would go through.
You see, to kiss me as if I were normal you have be very gentle.
Yes, I have to barely caress your skin, otherwise I go through.
You're managing pretty well.
It looks like you're used to kissing ghosts. Have you kissed a lot of ghosts before?
No.
So you're just good at being gentle.
That must be it.

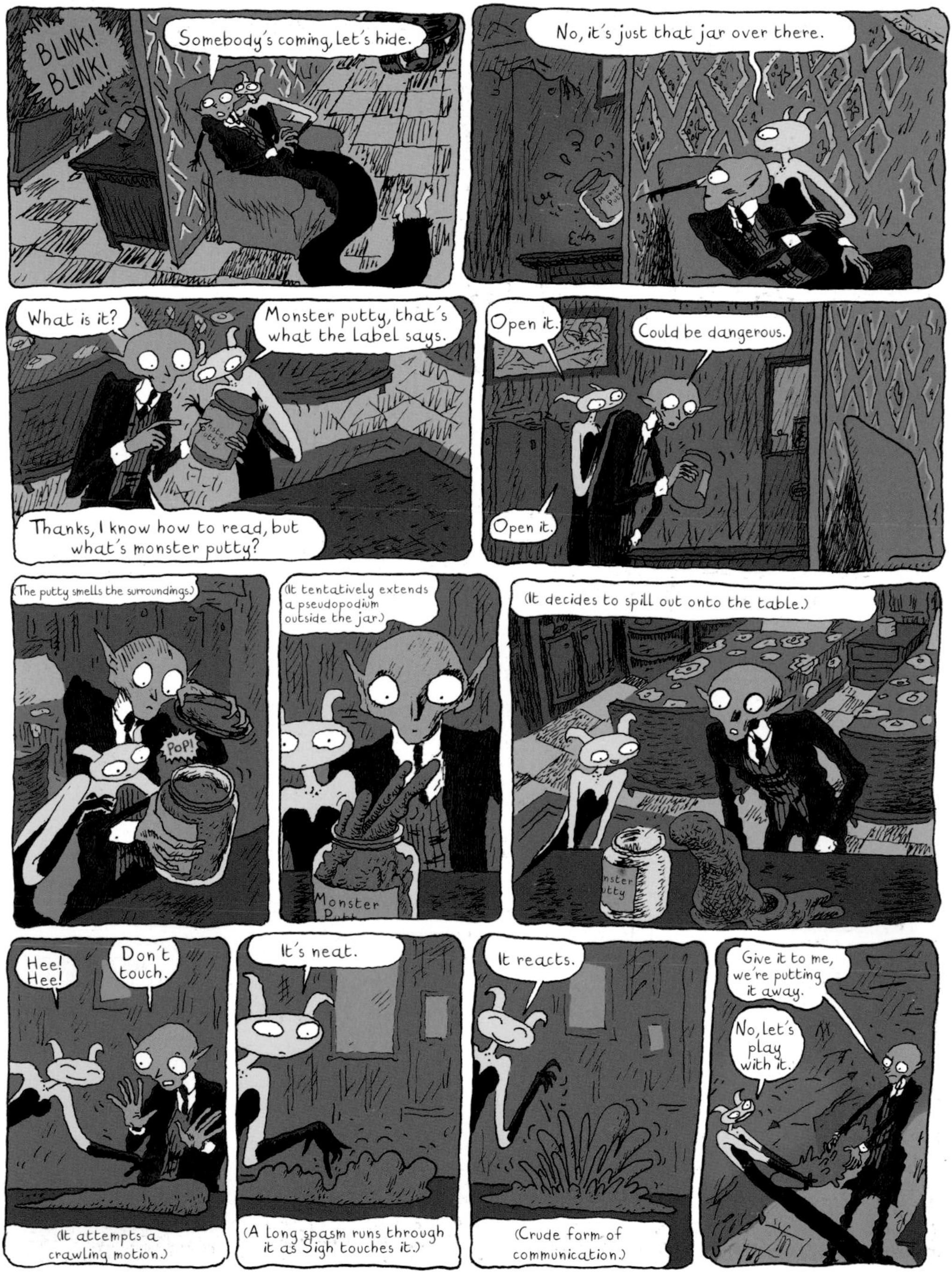
BLINK! BLINK!
Somebody's coming, let's hide.
No, it's just that jar over there.
Monster Putty
What is it?
Monster putty, that's what the label says.
Monster Putty
Thanks, I know how to read, but what's monster putty?
Open it.
Could be dangerous.
Open it.
(The putty smells the surroundings.)
POP!
(It tentatively extends a pseudopodium outside the jar.)
(It decides to spill out onto the table.)
Hee! Hee!
Don't touch.
(It attempts a crawling motion.)
It's neat.
(A long spasm runs through it as Sigh touches it.)
It reacts.
(Crude form of communication.)
Give it to me, we're putting it away.
No, let's play with it.

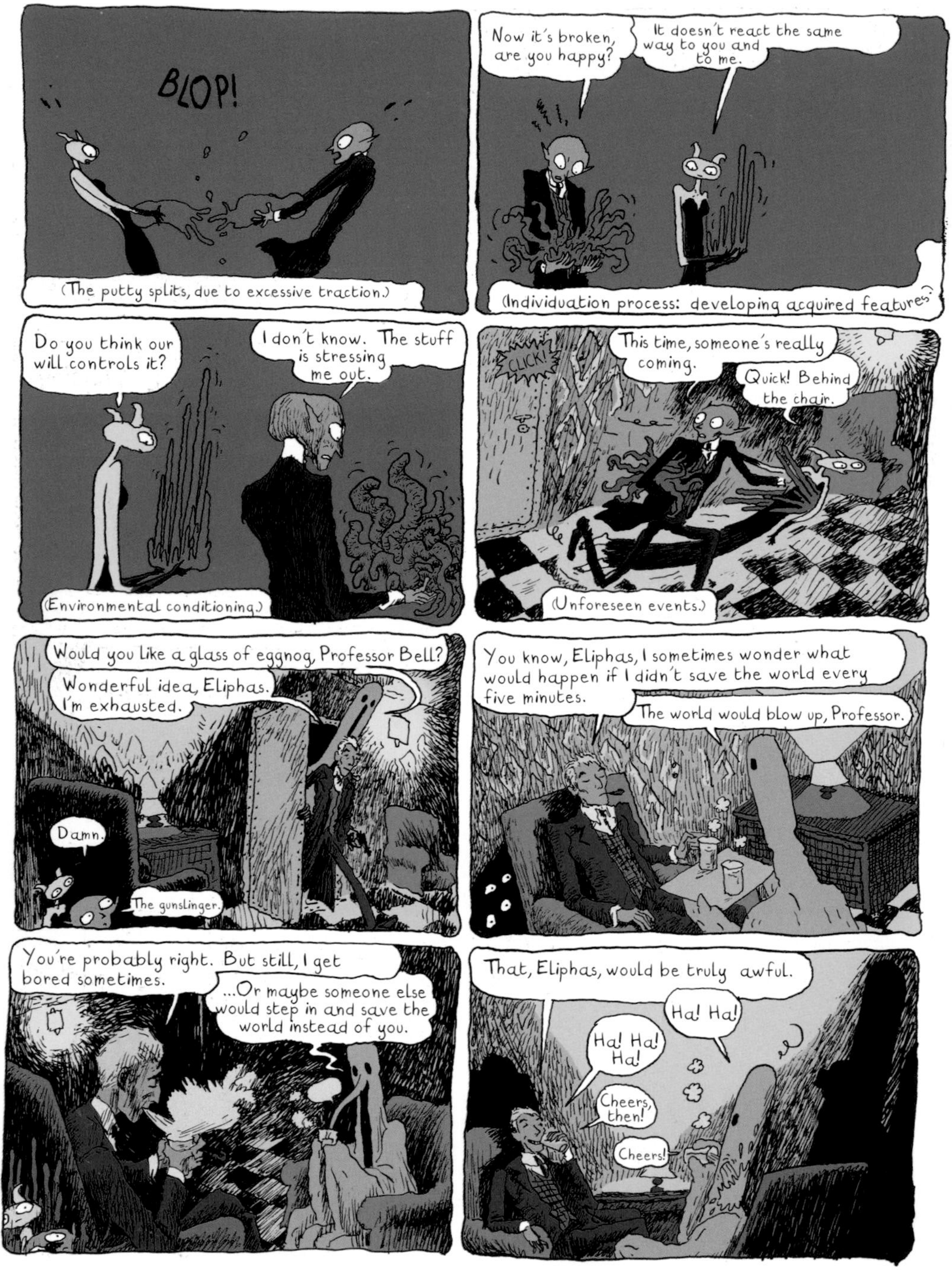
BLOP!
(The putty splits, due to excessive traction.)
Now it's broken, are you happy?
It doesn't react the same way to you and to me.
(Individuation process: developing acquired features.)
Do you think our will controls it?
I don't know. The stuff is stressing me out.
(Environmental conditioning.)
CLICK!
This time, someone's really coming.
Quick! Behind the chair.
(Unforeseen events.)
Would you like a glass of eggnog, Professor Bell?
Wonderful idea, Eliphas. I'm exhausted.
Damn.
The gunslinger.
You know, Eliphas, I sometimes wonder what would happen if I didn't save the world every five minutes.
The world would blow up, Professor.
You're probably right. But still, I get bored sometimes.
...Or maybe someone else would step in and save the world instead of you.
That, Eliphas, would be truly awful.
Ha! Ha!
Ha! Ha! Ha!
Cheers, then!
Cheers!

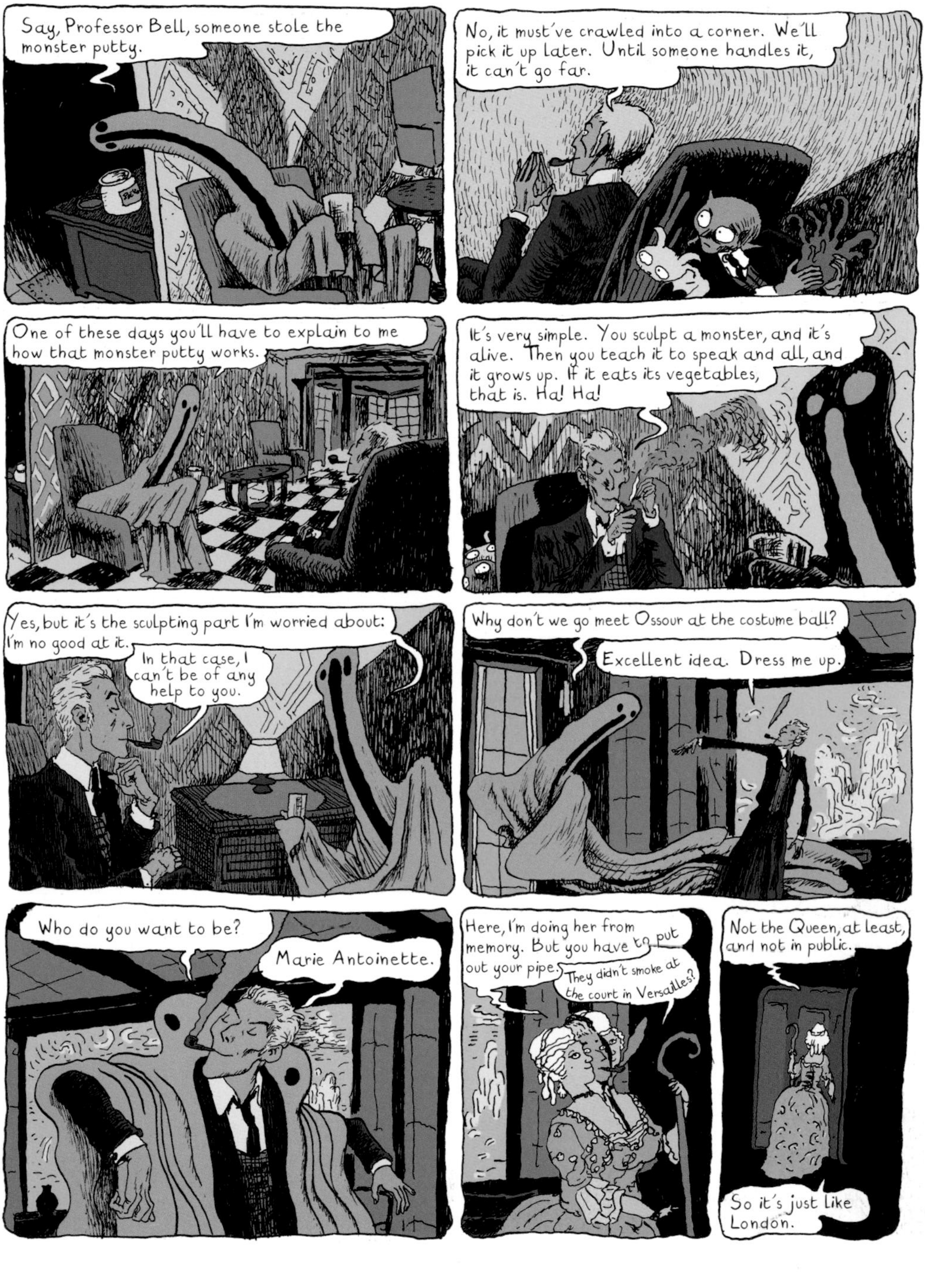
Say, Professor Bell, someone stole the monster putty.
No, it must've crawled into a corner. We'll pick it up later. Until someone handles it, it can't go far.
One of these days you'll have to explain to me how that monster putty works.
It's very simple. You sculpt a monster, and it's alive. Then you teach it to speak and all, and it grows up. If it eats its vegetables, that is. Ha! Ha!
Yes, but it's the sculpting part I'm worried about: I'm no good at it.
In that case, I can't be of any help to you.
Why don't we go meet Ossour at the costume ball?
Excellent idea. Dress me up.
Who do you want to be?
Marie Antoinette.
Here, I'm doing her from memory. But you have to put out your pipe.
They didn't smoke at the court in Versailles?
Not the Queen, at least, and not in public.
So it's just like London.

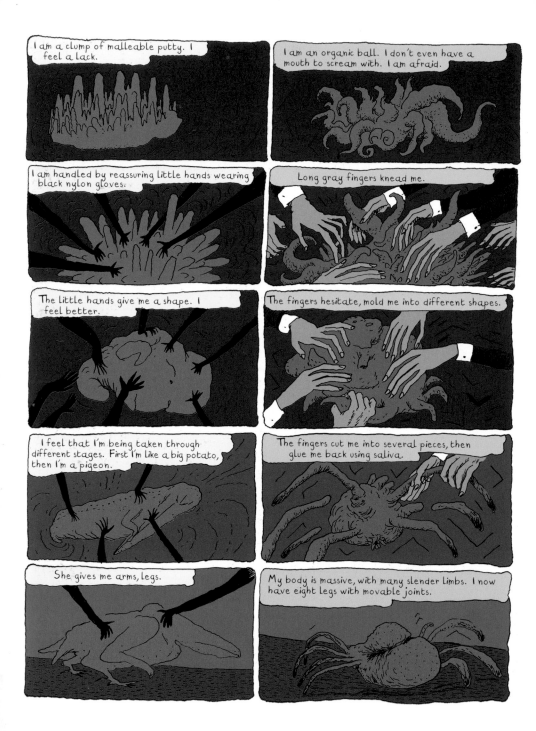

I am a clump of malleable putty. I feel a lack.

I am an organic ball. I don't even have a mouth to scream with. I am afraid.

I am handled by reassuring little hands wearing black nylon gloves.

Long gray fingers knead me.

The little hands give me a shape. I feel better.

The fingers hesitate, mold me into different shapes.

I feel that I'm being taken through different stages. First I'm like a big potato, then I'm a pigeon.

The fingers cut me into several pieces, then glue me back using saliva.

She gives me arms, legs.

My body is massive, with many slender limbs. I now have eight legs with movable joints.

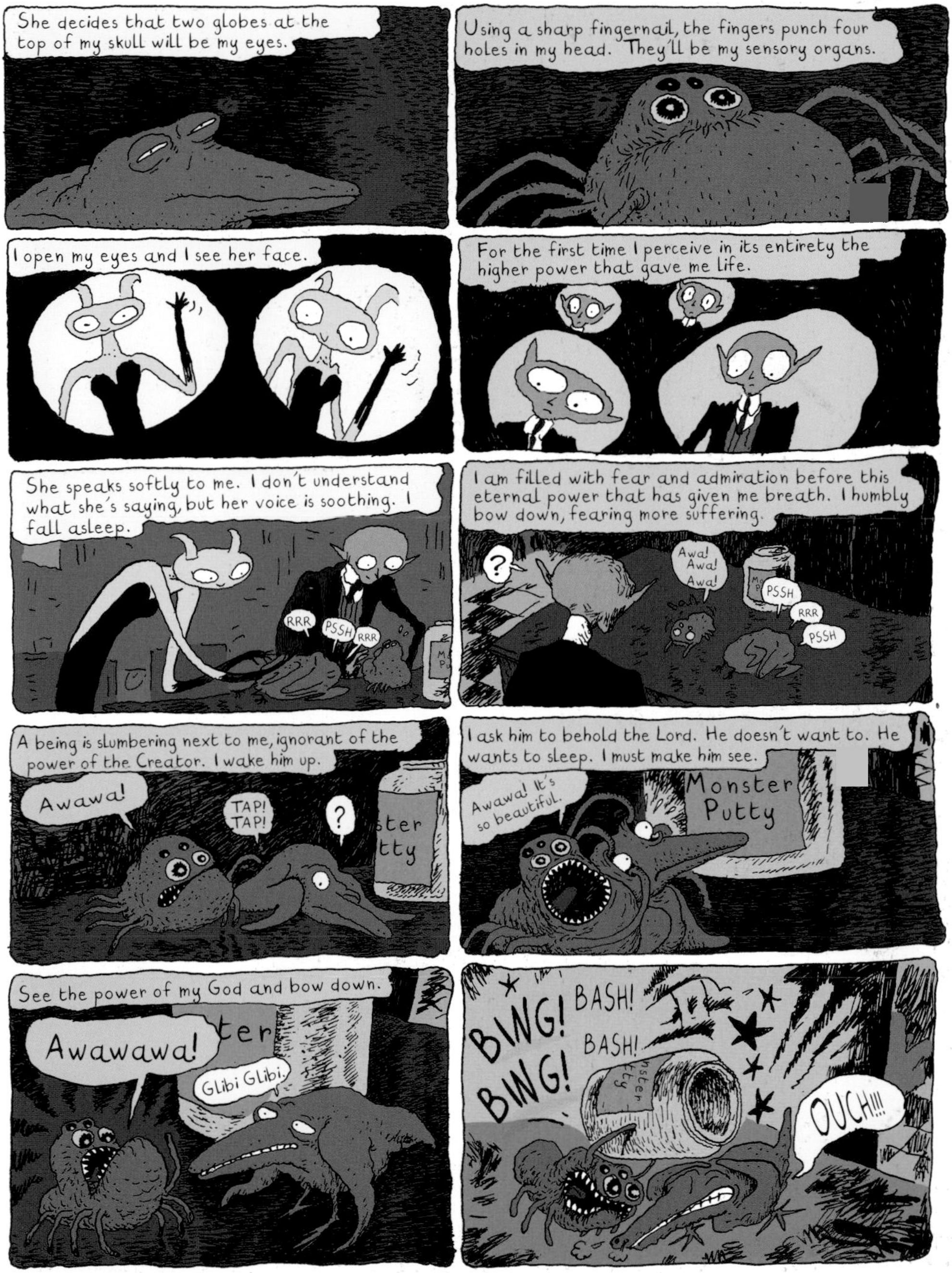

She decides that two globes at the top of my skull will be my eyes.
Using a sharp fingernail, the fingers punch four holes in my head. They'll be my sensory organs.
I open my eyes and I see her face.
For the first time I perceive in its entirety the higher power that gave me life.
She speaks softly to me. I don't understand what she's saying, but her voice is soothing. I fall asleep.
RRR
PSSH
RRR
I am filled with fear and admiration before this eternal power that has given me breath. I humbly bow down, fearing more suffering.
?
Awa! Awa! Awa!
PSSH
RRR
PSSH
A being is slumbering next to me, ignorant of the power of the Creator. I wake him up.
Awawa!
TAP! TAP!
?
I ask him to behold the Lord. He doesn't want to. He wants to sleep. I must make him see.
Awawa! It's so beautiful.
Monster Putty
See the power of my God and bow down.
Awawawa!
Glibi Glibi.
BING! BING!
BASH! BASH!
OUCH!!!

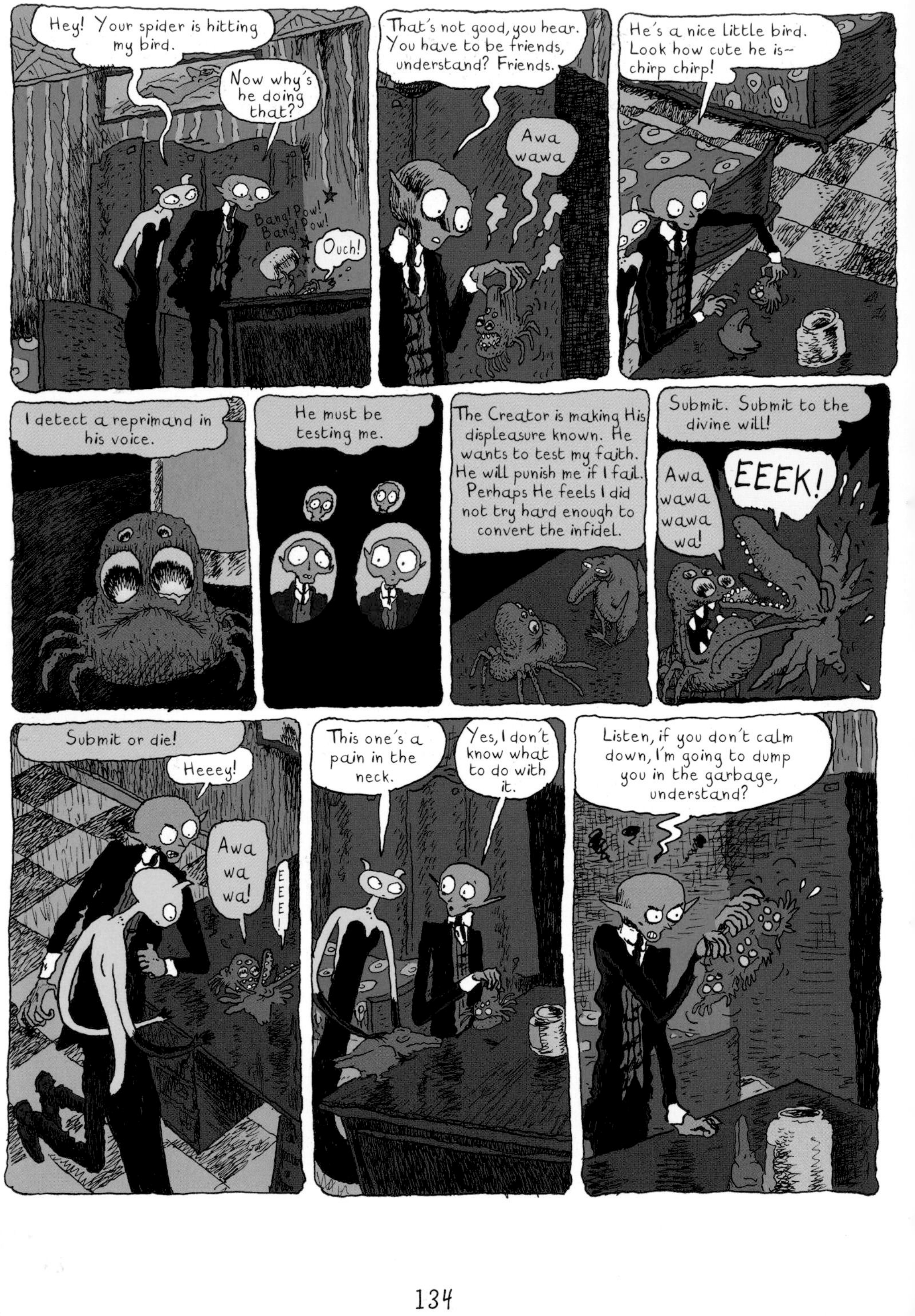
Hey! Your spider is hitting my bird.
Now why's he doing that?
Bang! Pow! Bang! Pow!
Ouch!
That's not good, you hear. You have to be friends, understand? Friends.
Awa wawa
He's a nice little bird. Look how cute he is— chirp chirp!
I detect a reprimand in his voice.
He must be testing me.
The Creator is making His displeasure known. He wants to test my faith. He will punish me if I fail. Perhaps He feels I did not try hard enough to convert the infidel.
Submit. Submit to the divine will!
Awa wawa wawa wa!
EEEK!
Submit or die!
Heeey!
Awa wa wa!
EEE!
This one's a pain in the neck.
Yes, I don't know what to do with it.
Listen, if you don't calm down, I'm going to dump you in the garbage, understand?

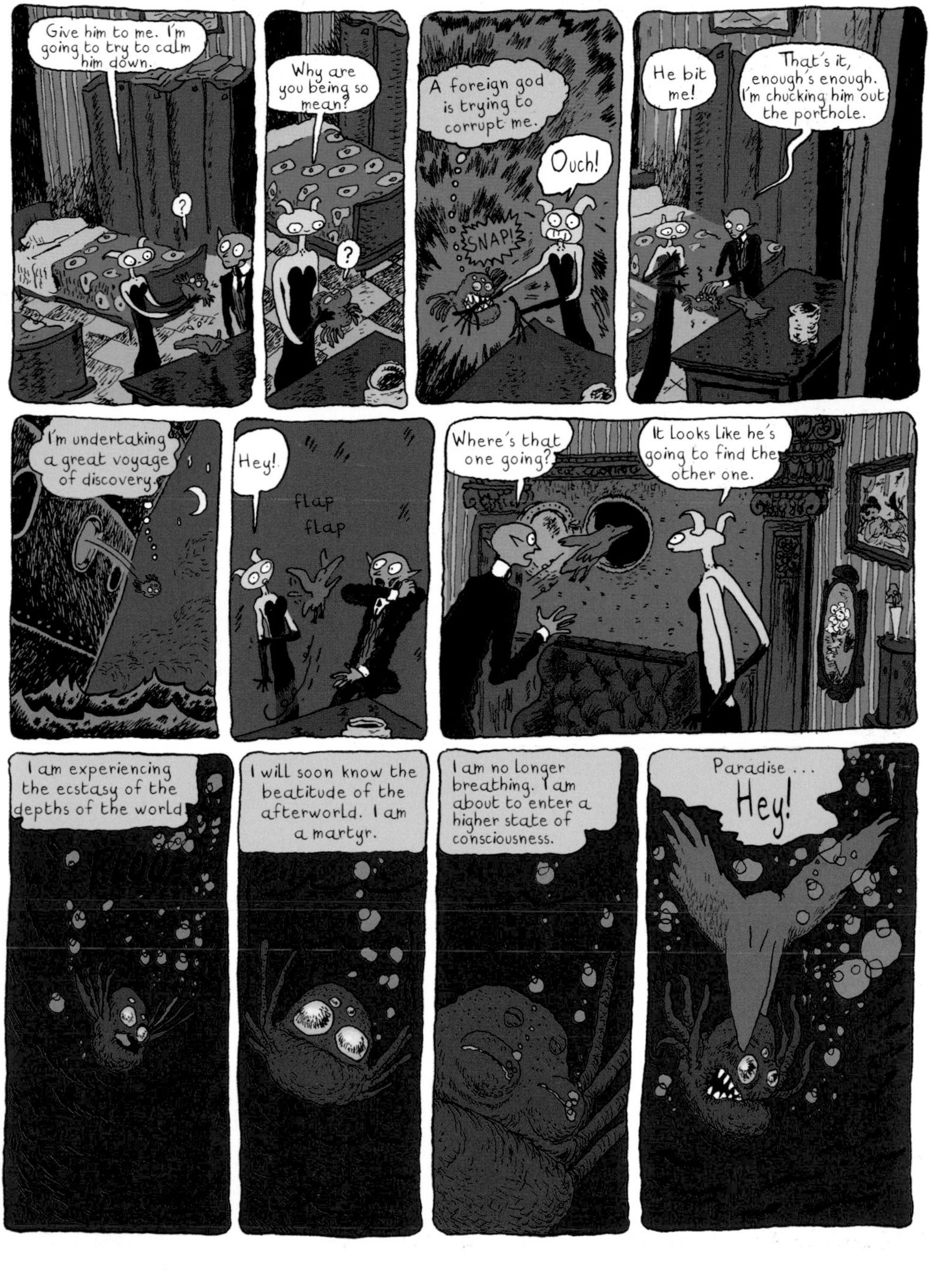
Give him to me. I'm going to try to calm him down.
?
Why are you being so mean?
?
A foreign god is trying to corrupt me.
SNAP!
Ouch!
He bit me!
That's it, enough's enough. I'm chucking him out the porthole.
I'm undertaking a great voyage of discovery.
Hey!
flap
flap
Where's that one going?
It looks like he's going to find the other one.
I am experiencing the ecstasy of the depths of the world.
I will soon know the beatitude of the afterworld. I am a martyr.
I am no longer breathing. I am about to enter a higher state of consciousness.
Paradise . . .
Hey!

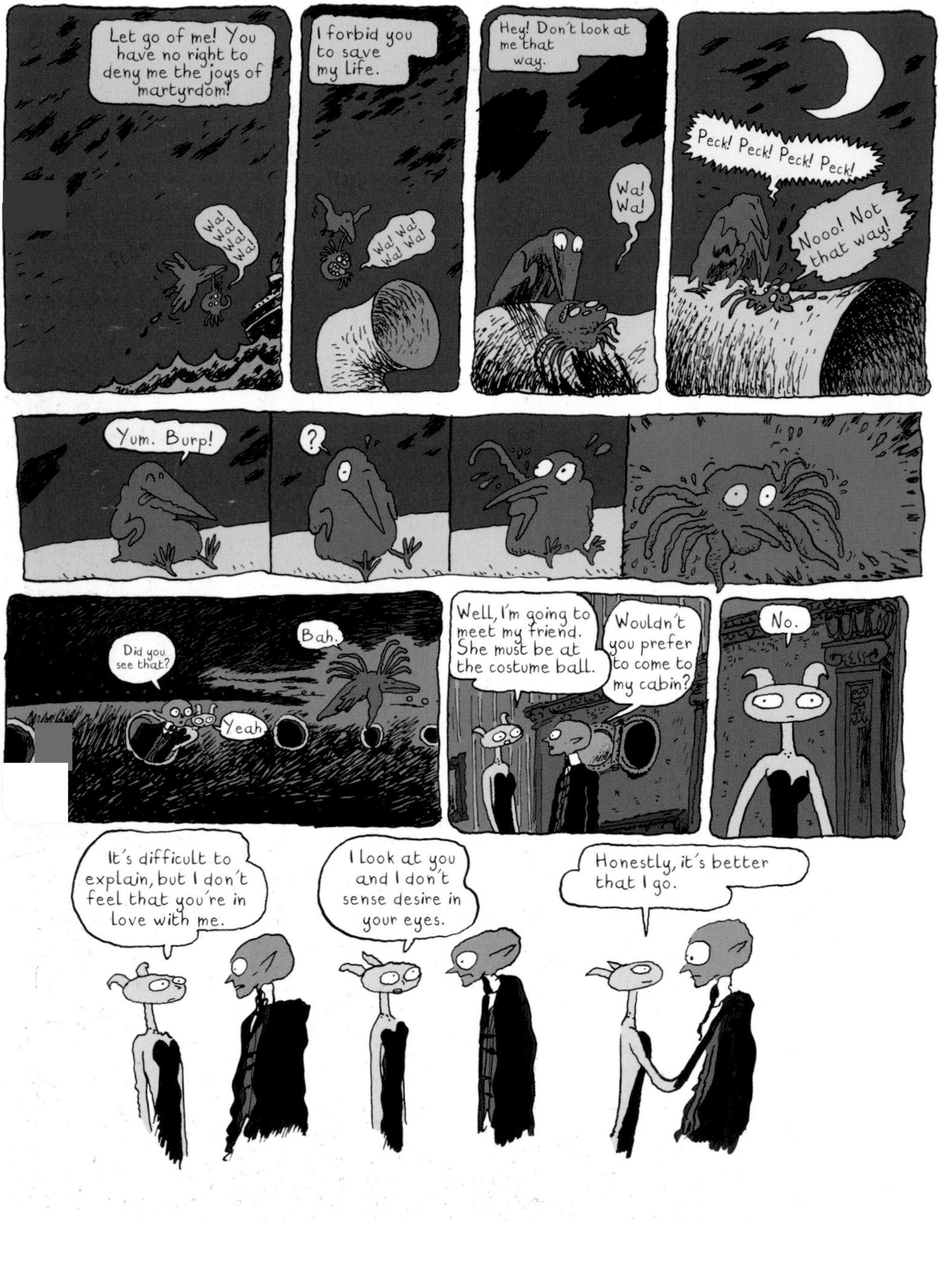

Let go of me! You have no right to deny me the joys of martyrdom!
Wa! Wa! Wa! Wa!
I forbid you to save my life.
Wa! Wa! Wa! Wa!
Hey! Don't look at me that way.
Wa! Wa!
Peck! Peck! Peck! Peck!
Nooo! Not that way!
Yum. Burp!
?
Did you see that?
Yeah.
Bah.
Well, I'm going to meet my friend. She must be at the costume ball.
Wouldn't you prefer to come to my cabin?
No.
It's difficult to explain, but I don't feel that you're in love with me.
I look at you and I don't sense desire in your eyes.
Honestly, it's better that I go.

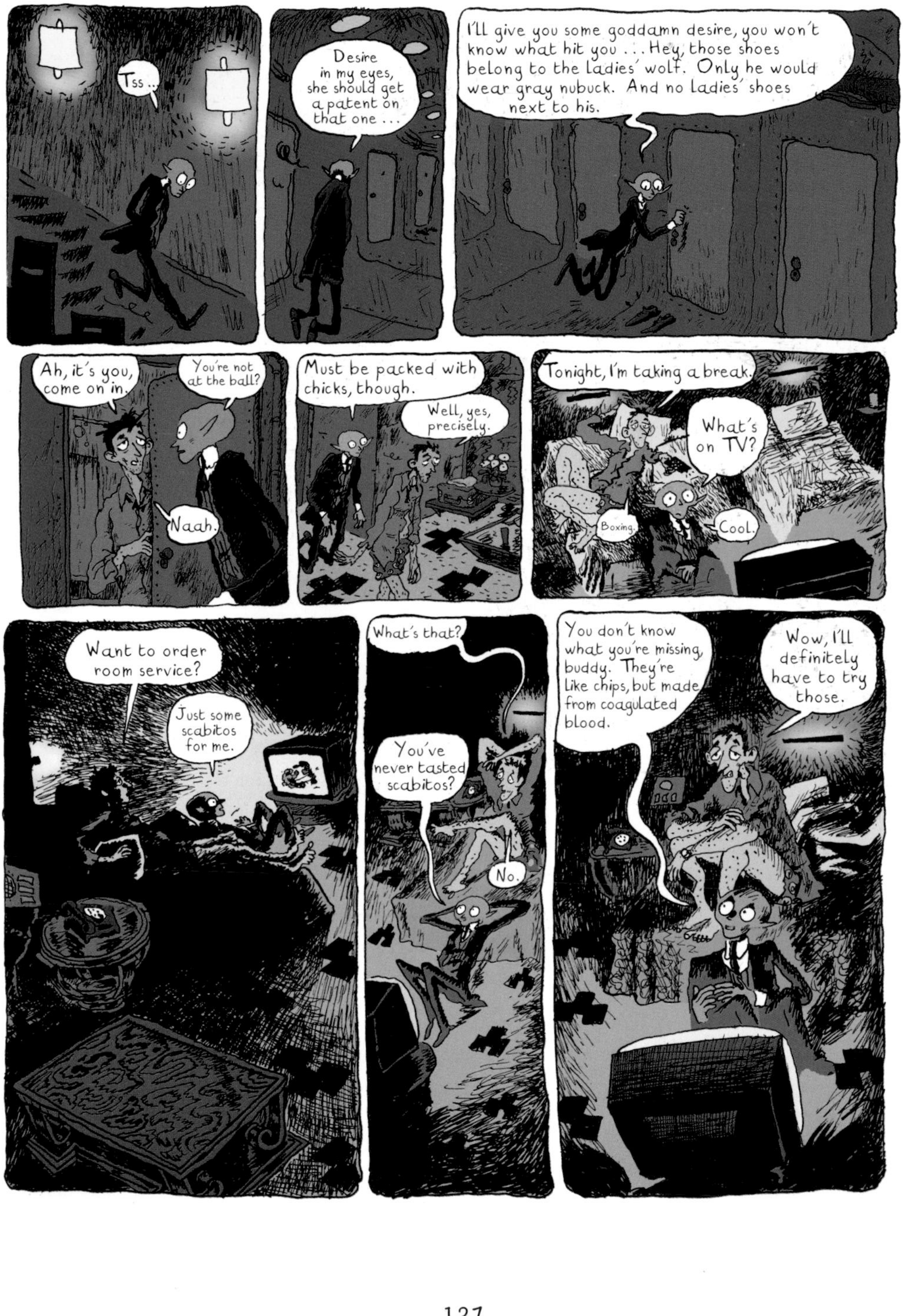
Tss...
Desire in my eyes, she should get a patent on that one...
I'll give you some goddamn desire, you won't know what hit you... Hey, those shoes belong to the ladies' wolf. Only he would wear gray nubuck. And no ladies' shoes next to his.
Ah, it's you, come on in.
You're not at the ball?
Naah.
Must be packed with chicks, though.
Well, yes, precisely.
Tonight, I'm taking a break.
What's on TV?
Boxing.
Cool.
Want to order room service?
Just some scabitos for me.
What's that?
You've never tasted scabitos?
No.
You don't know what you're missing, buddy. They're like chips, but made from coagulated blood.
Wow, I'll definitely have to try those.

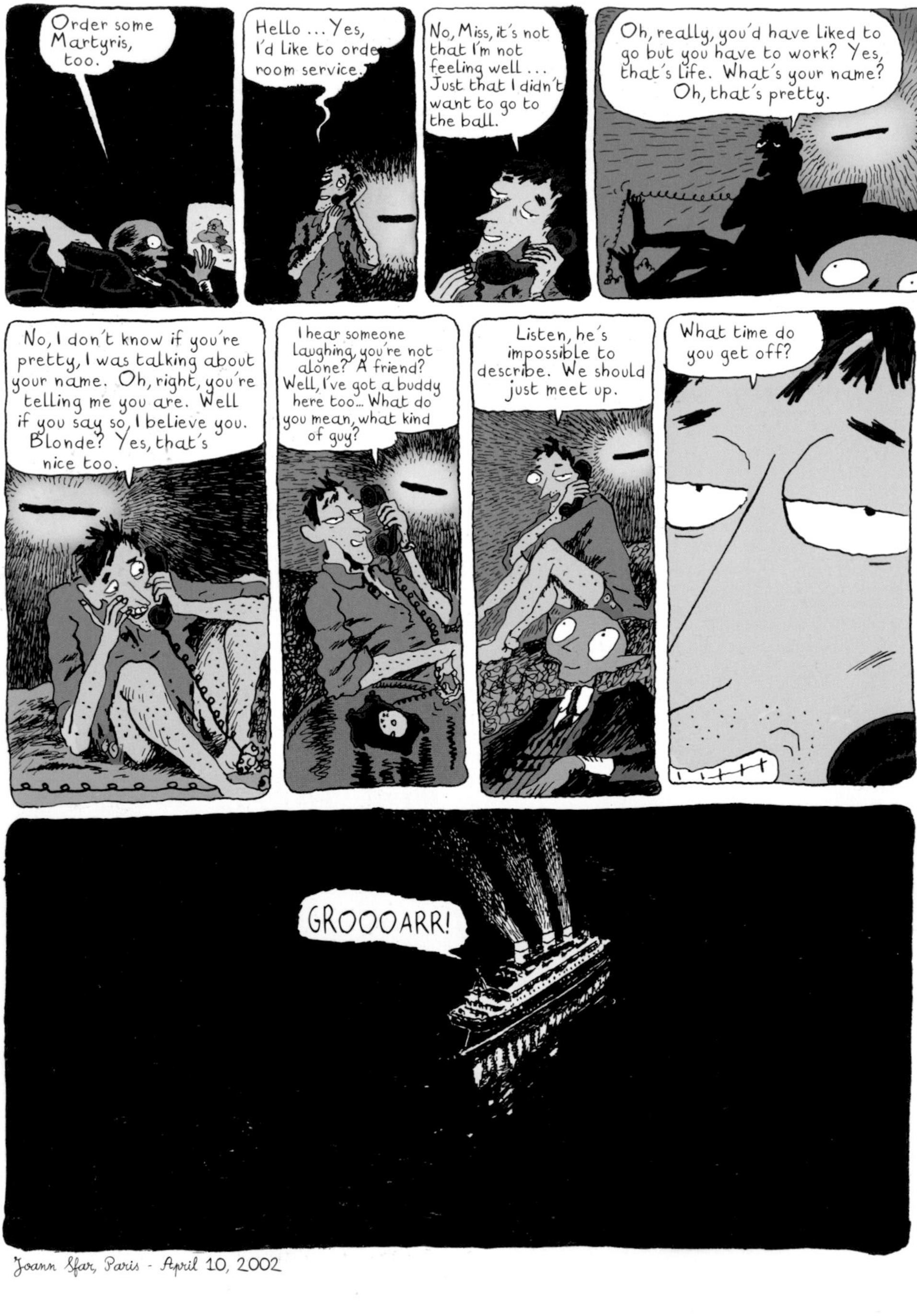
Order some Martyris, too.
Hello ... Yes, I'd like to order room service.
No, Miss, it's not that I'm not feeling well ... Just that I didn't want to go to the ball.
Oh, really, you'd have liked to go but you have to work? Yes, that's life. What's your name? Oh, that's pretty.
No, I don't know if you're pretty, I was talking about your name. Oh, right, you're telling me you are. Well if you say so, I believe you. Blonde? Yes, that's nice too.
I hear someone laughing, you're not alone? A friend? Well, I've got a buddy here too... What do you mean, what kind of guy?
Listen, he's impossible to describe. We should just meet up.
What time do you get off?
GROOOARR!

Joann Sfar, Paris - April 10, 2002

A few pointers on some of the characters of this story

Professor Bell: A Scottish surgeon and teratologist. A widower. His hair turned white over the course of one night when his wife died. He taught Arthur Conan Doyle and was a friend of J. M. Barrie and R. L. Stevenson. He is a pediatrician and logician. He practices sexual abstinence and heroism.

You can read about his adventures in Scotland, Jerusalem, and on the Riviera. He also appears in "The Professor's Daughter" under the name of "Bowell" and in "Paris-London," where he is called "Commander Crow."

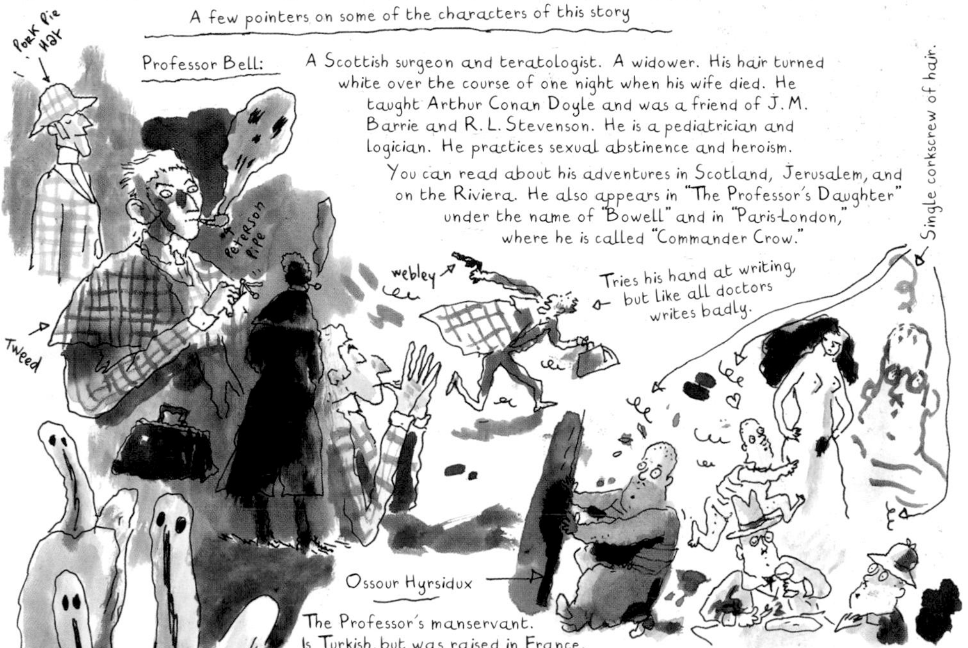

Pork Pie Hat
Tweed
Peterson Pipe
webley
Tries his hand at writing, but like all doctors writes badly.
Single corkscrew of hair.

Ossour Hyrsidux

The Professor's manservant. Is Turkish, but was raised in France. An orphan. Priapic. Well educated. Don Quijotish. Likes a tipple. Prone to verbal diarrhea. A writer. Deeply attached to secular values. Has a temper and a hearty appetite, and can be fairly infantile. He appears in "The Adventures of Ossour Hyrsidux," "Paris-London," and "Professor Bell."

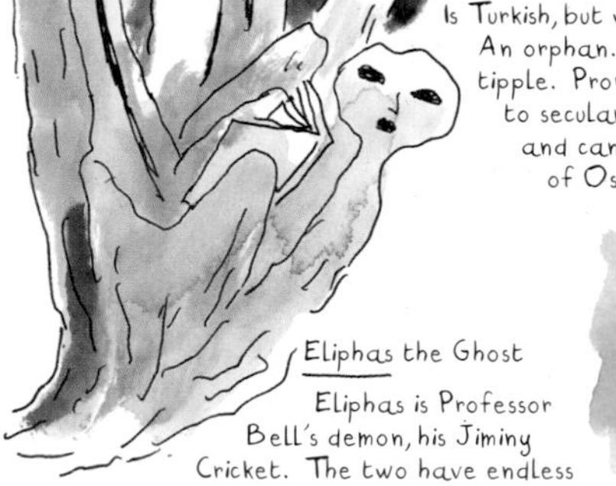

Eliphas the Ghost

Eliphas is Professor Bell's demon, his Jiminy Cricket. The two have endless talks. Eliphas is a conformist and a compulsive neurotic, like all ghosts. He can take on different forms, be visible or not, seem like a normal presence. Professor Bell has been trying to psychoanalyze him, but there's always the problem of the ante mortem barrier, which is like a goatskin drawn across a drum: rupturing that membrane would be like bursting an eardrum, you wouldn't hear a thing. Eliphas appears in the "Professor Bell" stories.

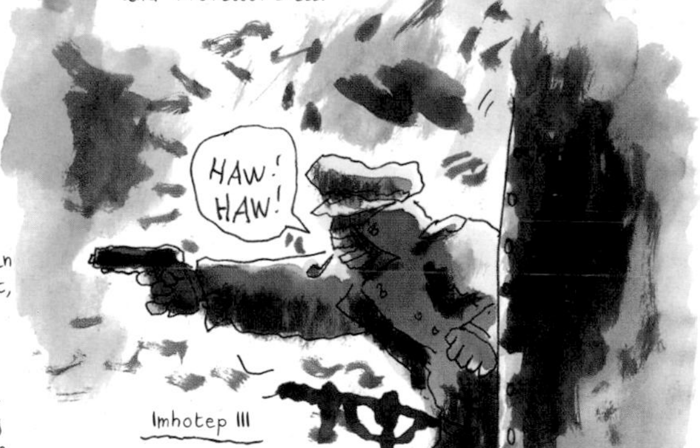

HAW! HAW!

Imhotep III

Bell's nemesis. The father of Imhotep IV. A dangerous madman, with manners alternately princely and filthy. Has undeniable charm. Is like noble rot. A devotee of the past, a romantic figure, and a poker champion. You'll find out more about him by reading "The Professor's Daughter."

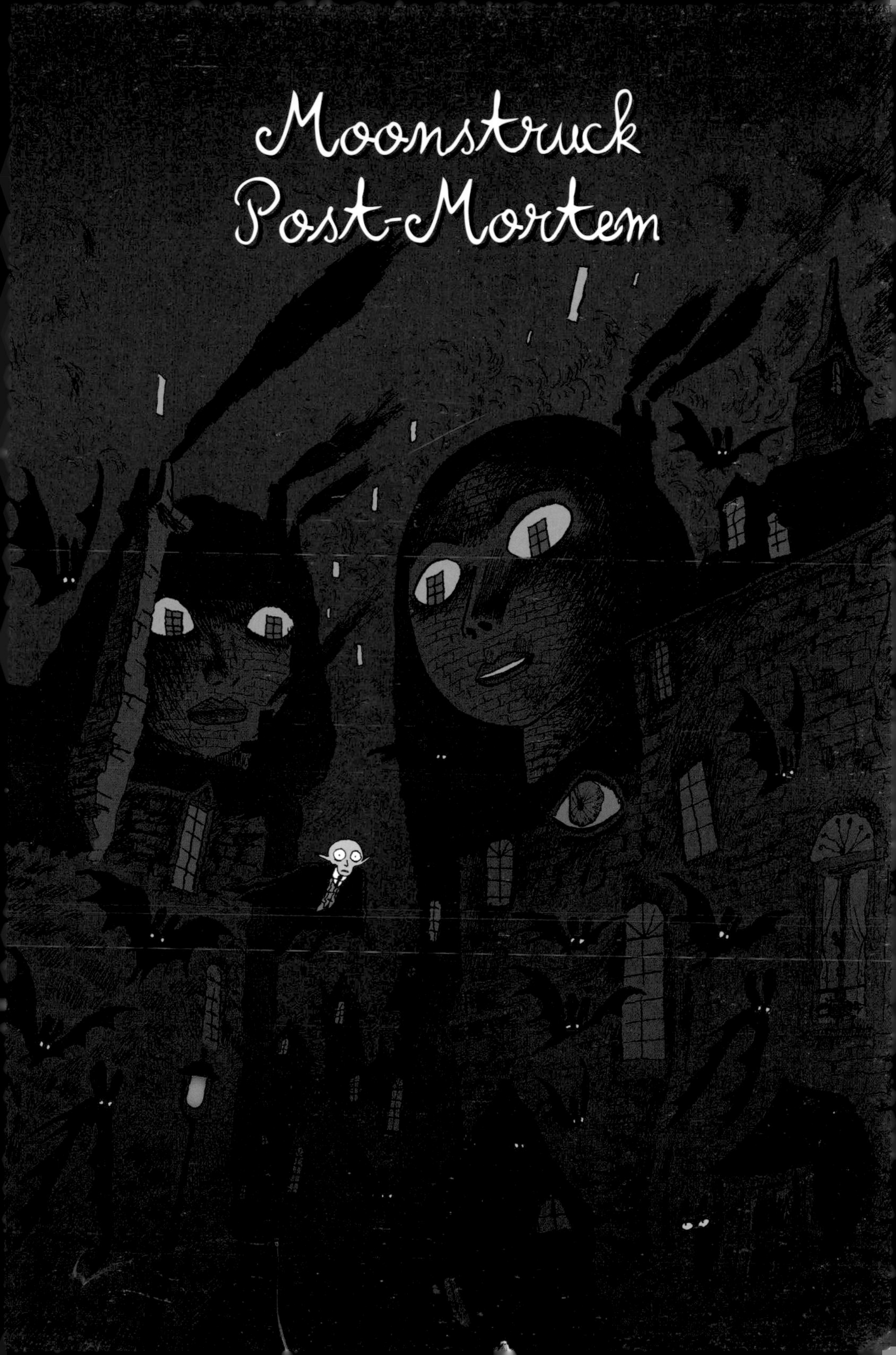
Moonstruck
Post-Mortem

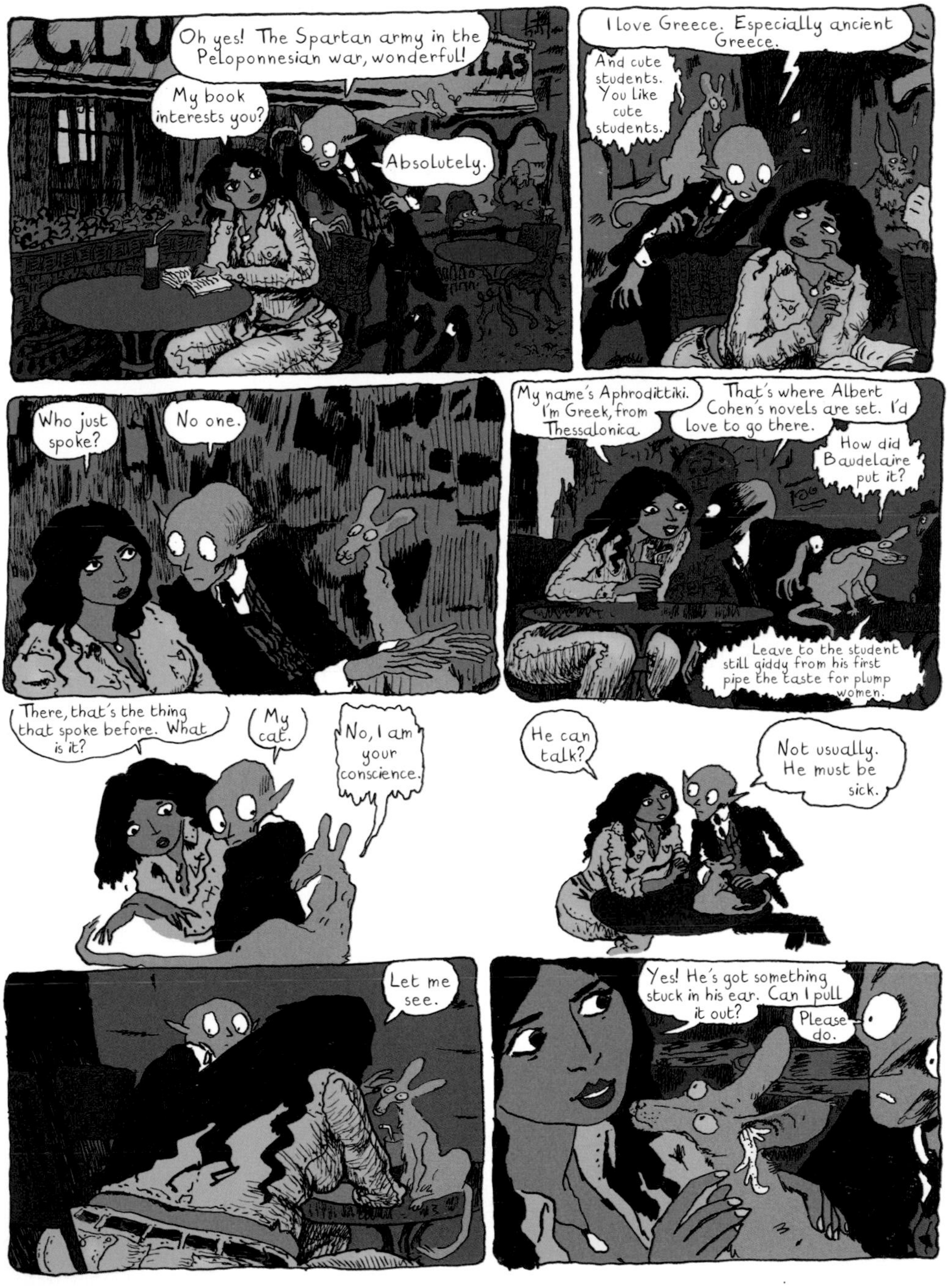
My book interests you?
Oh yes! The Spartan army in the Peloponnesian war, wonderful!
Absolutely.
I love Greece. Especially ancient Greece.
And cute students. You like cute students.
Who just spoke?
No one.
My name's Aphrodittiki. I'm Greek, from Thessalonica.
That's where Albert Cohen's novels are set. I'd love to go there.
How did Baudelaire put it?
Leave to the student still giddy from his first pipe the taste for plump women.
There, that's the thing that spoke before. What is it?
My cat.
No, I am your conscience.
He can talk?
Not usually. He must be sick.
Let me see.
Yes! He's got something stuck in his ear. Can I pull it out?
Please do.

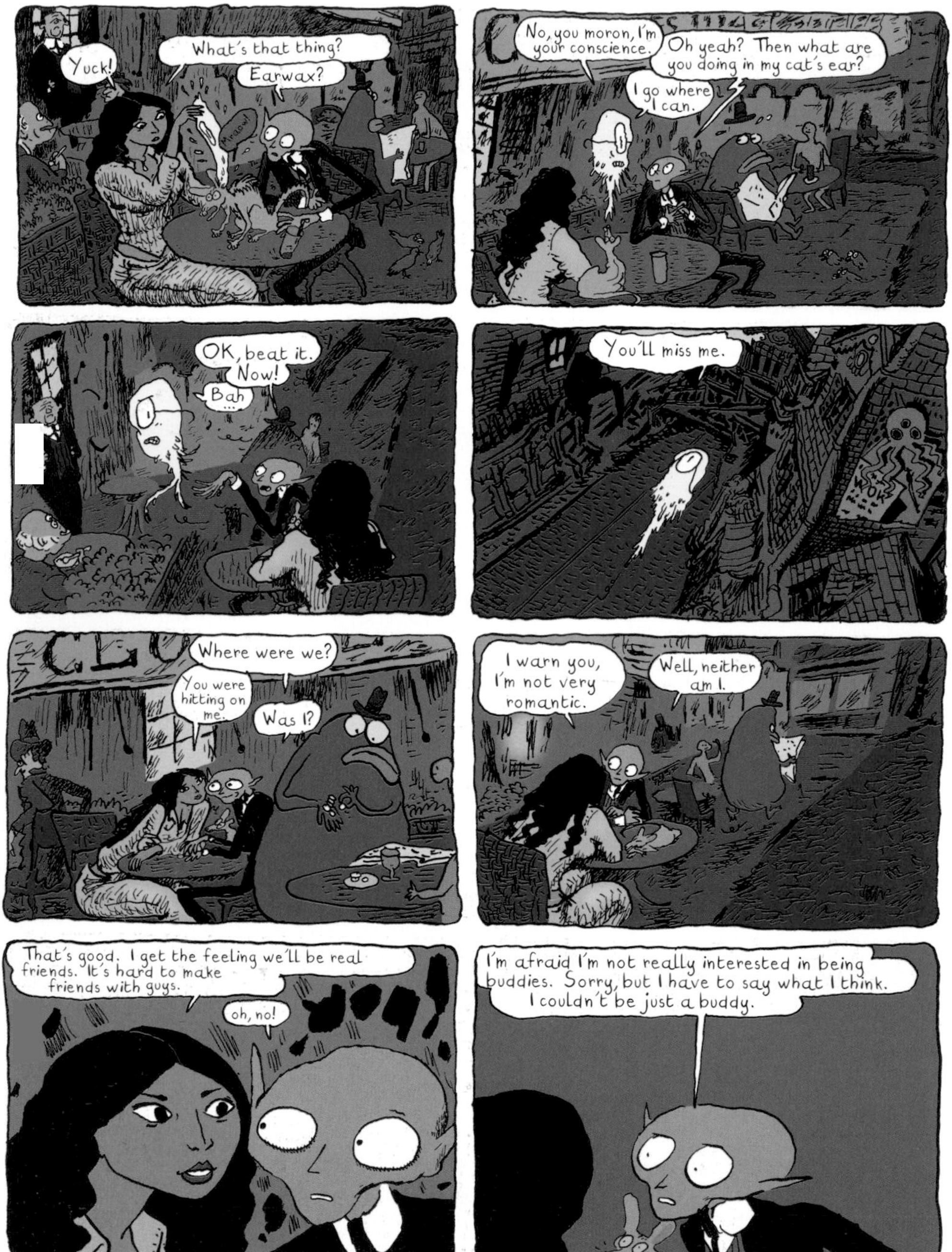
Yuck!
What's that thing?
Earwax?
No, you moron, I'm your conscience.
Oh yeah? Then what are you doing in my cat's ear?
I go where I can.
OK, beat it. Now!
Bah ...
You'll miss me.
Where were we?
You were hitting on me.
Was I?
I warn you, I'm not very romantic.
Well, neither am I.
That's good. I get the feeling we'll be real friends. It's hard to make friends with guys.
oh, no!
I'm afraid I'm not really interested in being buddies. Sorry, but I have to say what I think. I couldn't be just a buddy.

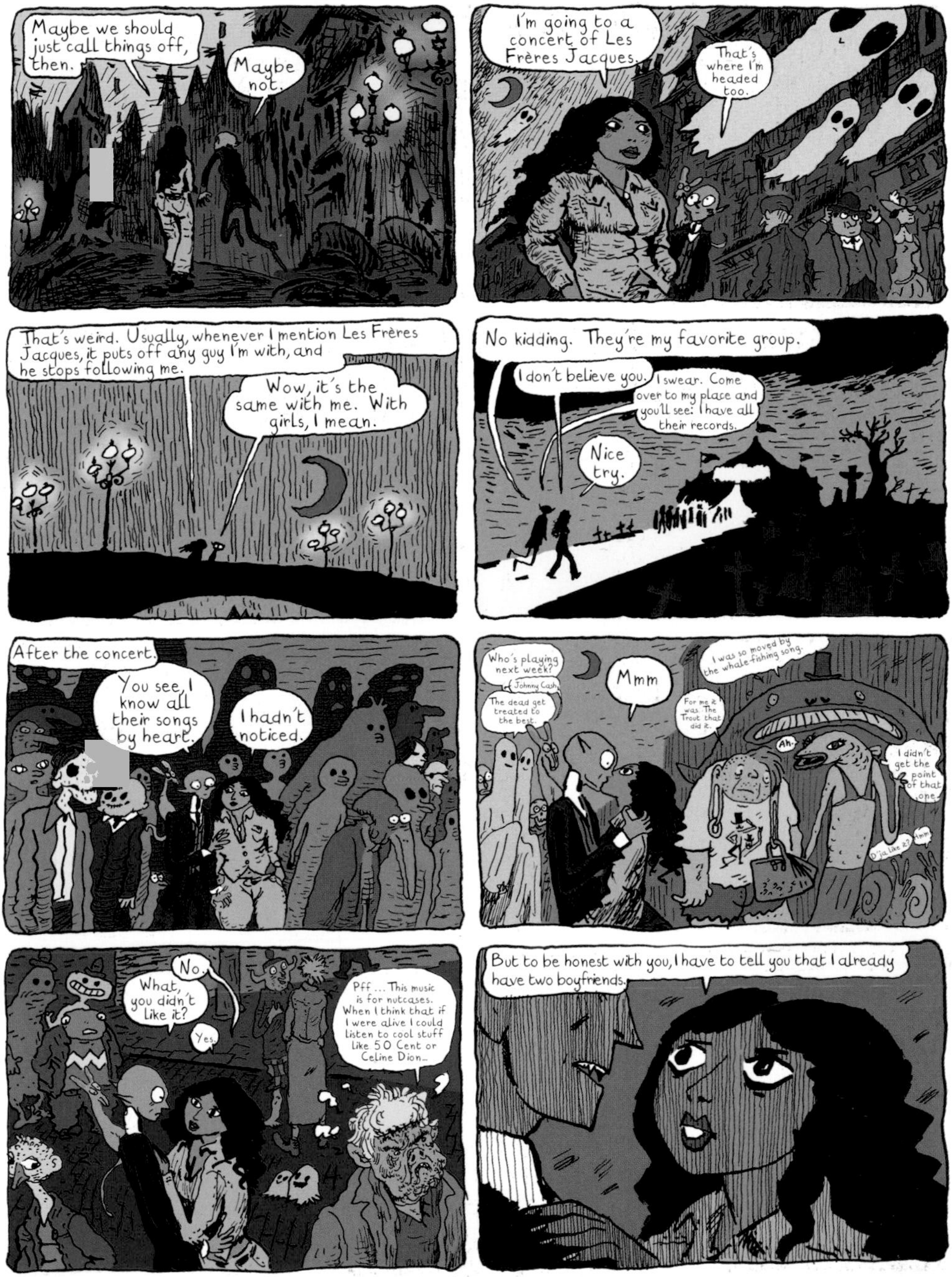
Maybe we should just call things off, then.
Maybe not.
I'm going to a concert of Les Frères Jacques.
That's where I'm headed too.
That's weird. Usually, whenever I mention Les Frères Jacques, it puts off any guy I'm with, and he stops following me.
Wow, it's the same with me. With girls, I mean.
No kidding. They're my favorite group.
I don't believe you.
I swear. Come over to my place and you'll see: I have all their records.
Nice try.
After the concert.
You see, I know all their songs by heart.
I hadn't noticed.
Who's playing next week?
Johnny Cash
The dead get treated to the best.
Mmm
I was so moved by the whale-fishing song.
For me it was The Trout that did it.
Ah.
I didn't get the point of that one.
D'ja like it?
Hmm
No.
What, you didn't like it?
Yes.
Pff ... This music is for nutcases. When I think that if I were alive I could listen to cool stuff like 50 Cent or Celine Dion...
But to be honest with you, I have to tell you that I already have two boyfriends.

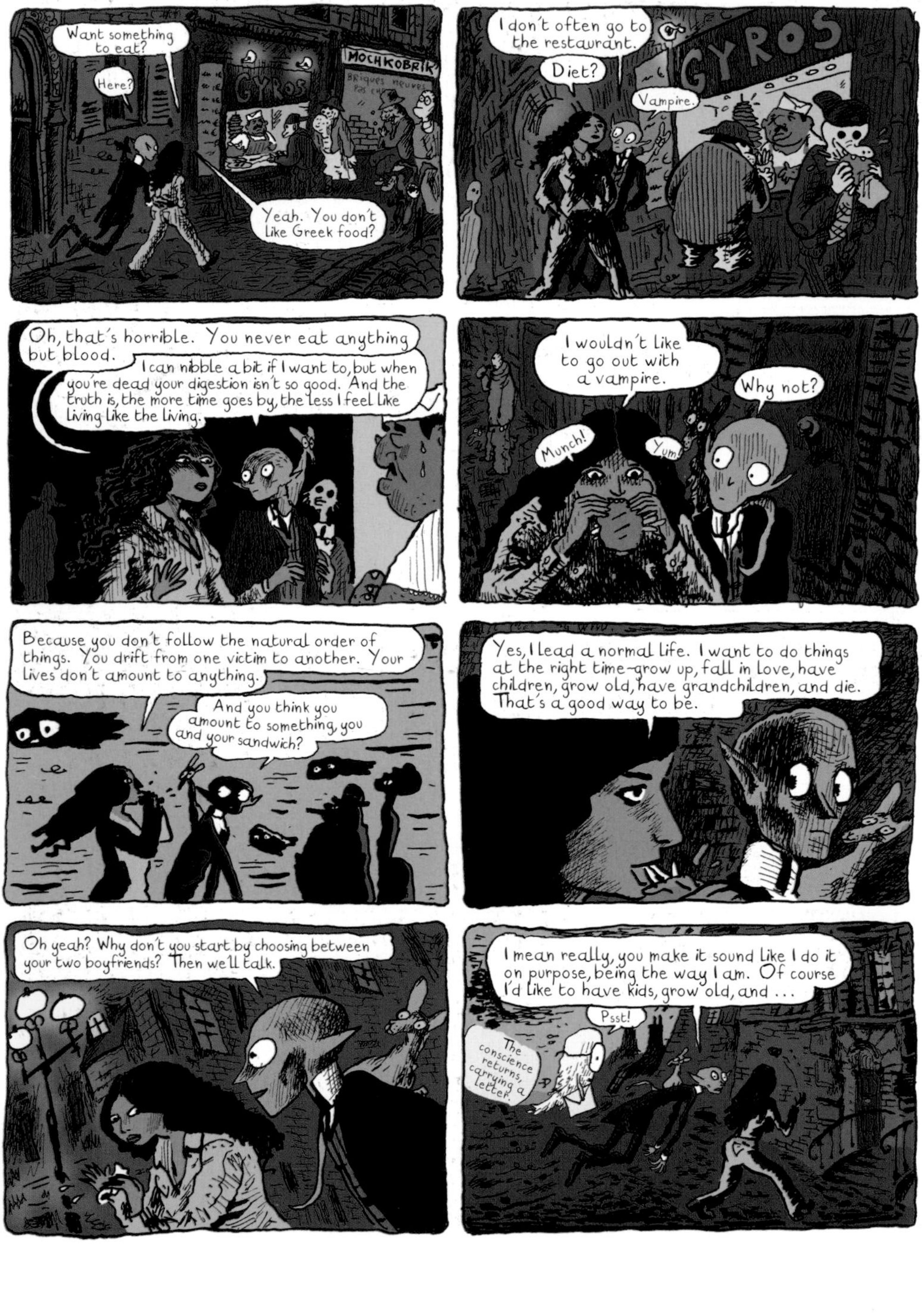
Want something to eat?
Here?
MOCHKOBRIK
Briques neuves
GYROS
Yeah. You don't like Greek food?
I don't often go to the restaurant.
Diet?
Vampire.
GYROS
Oh, that's horrible. You never eat anything but blood.
I can nibble a bit if I want to, but when you're dead your digestion isn't so good. And the truth is, the more time goes by, the less I feel like living like the living.
I wouldn't like to go out with a vampire.
Why not?
Munch!
Yum!
Because you don't follow the natural order of things. You drift from one victim to another. Your lives don't amount to anything.
And you think you amount to something, you and your sandwich?
Yes, I lead a normal life. I want to do things at the right time—grow up, fall in love, have children, grow old, have grandchildren, and die. That's a good way to be.
Oh yeah? Why don't you start by choosing between your two boyfriends? Then we'll talk.
I mean really, you make it sound like I do it on purpose, being the way I am. Of course I'd like to have kids, grow old, and ...
Psst!
The conscience returns, carrying a letter.

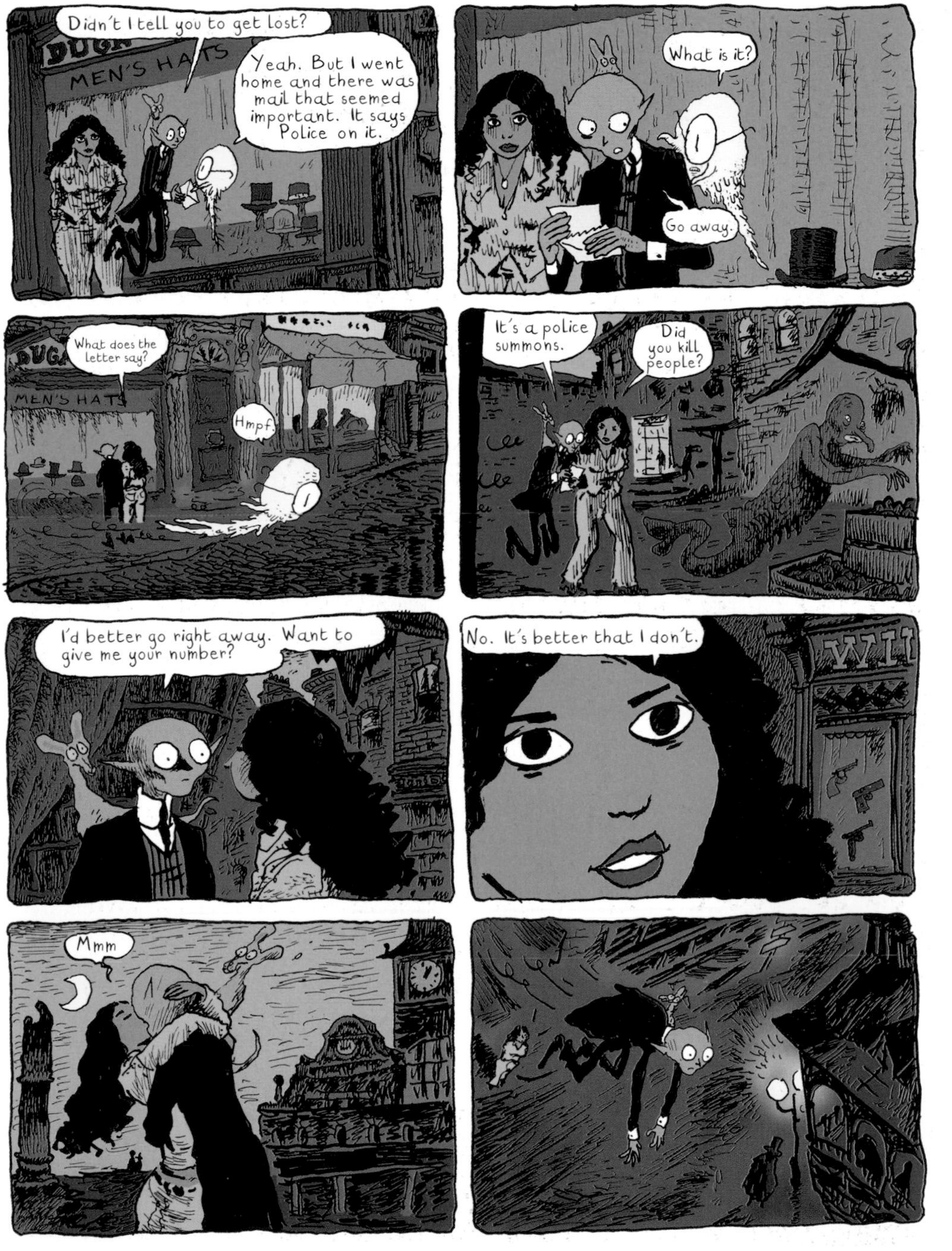
Didn't I tell you to get lost?
Yeah. But I went home and there was mail that seemed important. It says Police on it.
What is it?
Go away.
What does the letter say?
Hmpf.
It's a police summons.
Did you kill people?
I'd better go right away. Want to give me your number?
No. It's better that I don't.
Mmm

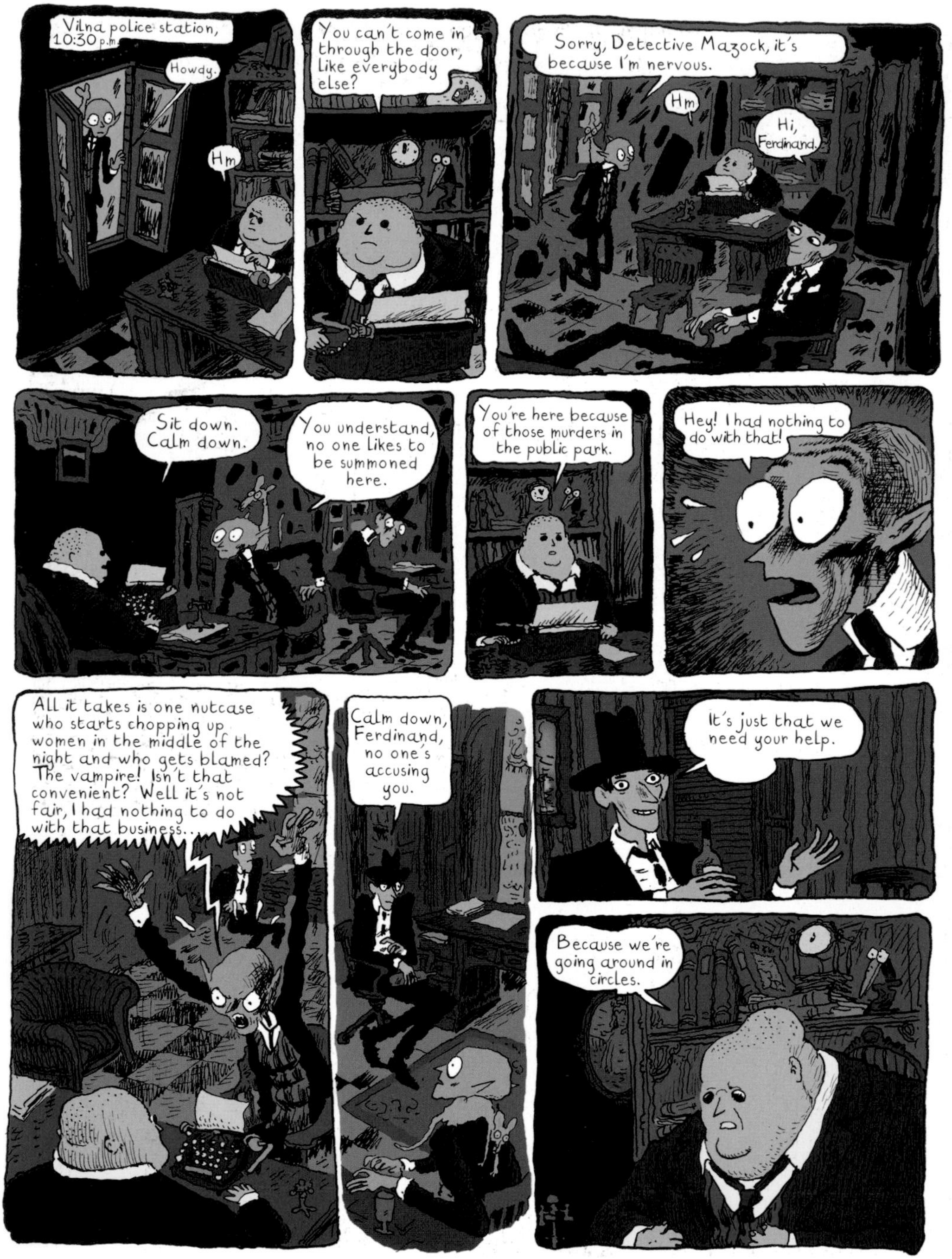

Vilna police station, 10:30 p.m.
Howdy.
Hm
You can't come in through the door, like everybody else?
Sorry, Detective Mazock, it's because I'm nervous.
Hm
Hi, Ferdinand.
Sit down. Calm down.
You understand, no one likes to be summoned here.
You're here because of those murders in the public park.
Hey! I had nothing to do with that!
All it takes is one nutcase who starts chopping up women in the middle of the night and who gets blamed? The vampire! Isn't that convenient? Well it's not fair, I had nothing to do with that business...
Calm down, Ferdinand, no one's accusing you.
It's just that we need your help.
Because we're going around in circles.

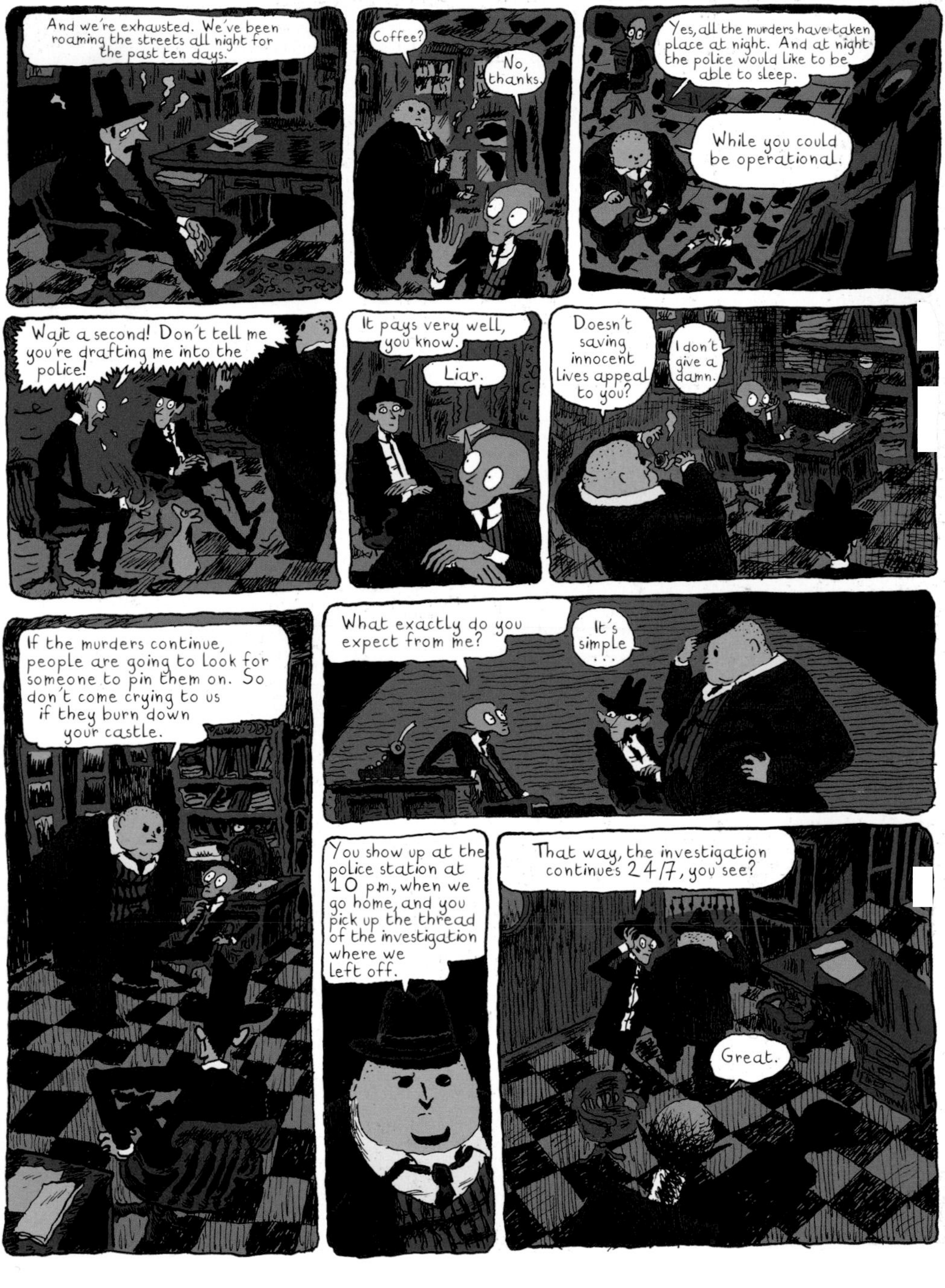

And we're exhausted. We've been roaming the streets all night for the past ten days.
Coffee?
No, thanks.
Yes, all the murders have taken place at night. And at night the police would like to be able to sleep.
While you could be operational.
Wait a second! Don't tell me you're drafting me into the police!
It pays very well, you know.
Liar.
Doesn't saving innocent lives appeal to you?
I don't give a damn.
If the murders continue, people are going to look for someone to pin them on. So don't come crying to us if they burn down your castle.
What exactly do you expect from me?
It's simple . . .
You show up at the police station at 10 p.m., when we go home, and you pick up the thread of the investigation where we left off.
That way, the investigation continues 24/7, you see?
Great.

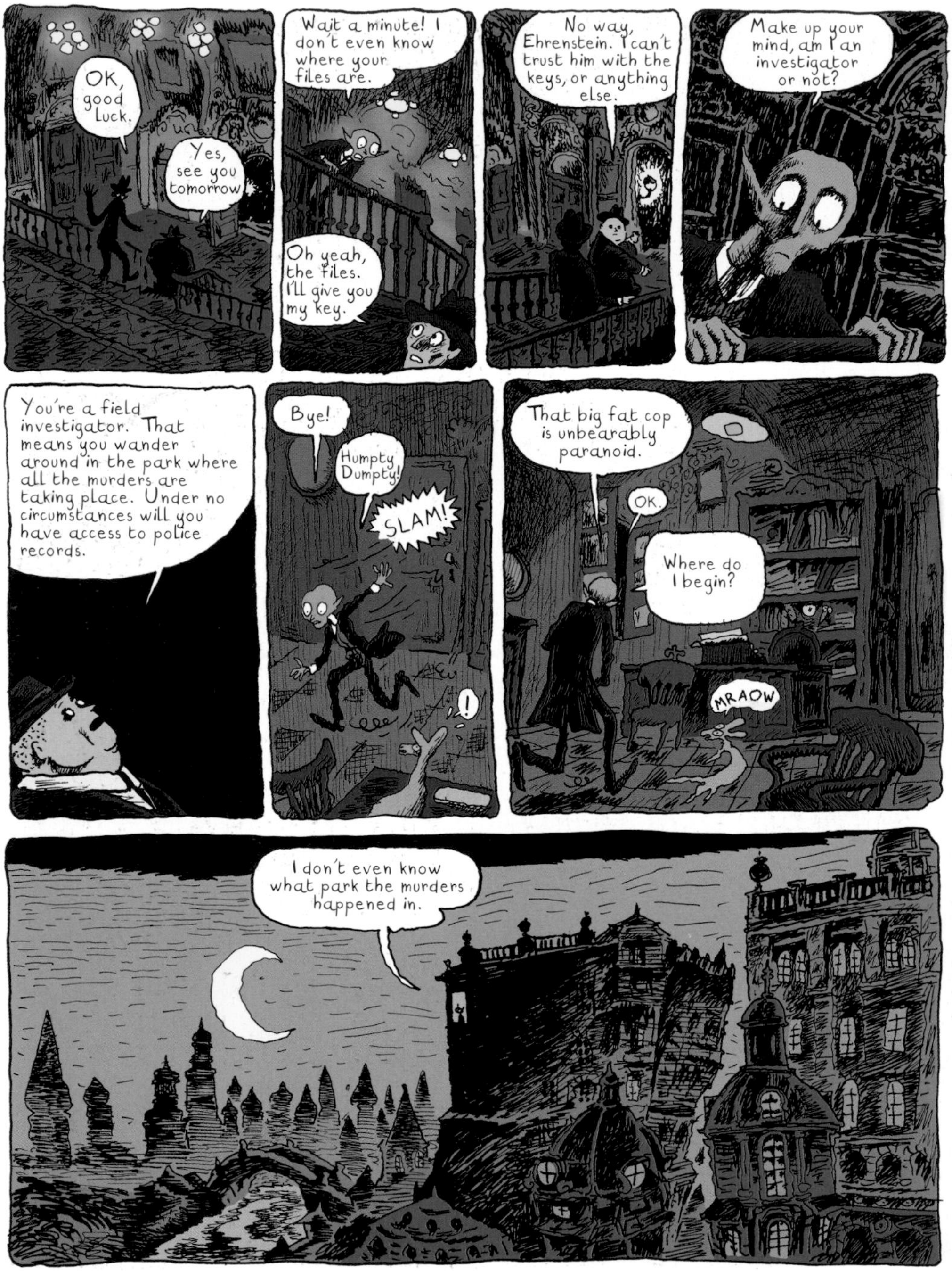
OK, good luck.
Yes, see you tomorrow
Wait a minute! I don't even know where your files are.
Oh yeah, the files. I'll give you my key.
No way, Ehrenstein. I can't trust him with the keys, or anything else.
Make up your mind, am I an investigator or not?
You're a field investigator. That means you wander around in the park where all the murders are taking place. Under no circumstances will you have access to police records.
Bye!
Humpty Dumpty!
SLAM!
!
That big fat cop is unbearably paranoid.
OK.
Where do I begin?
MRAOW
I don't even know what park the murders happened in.

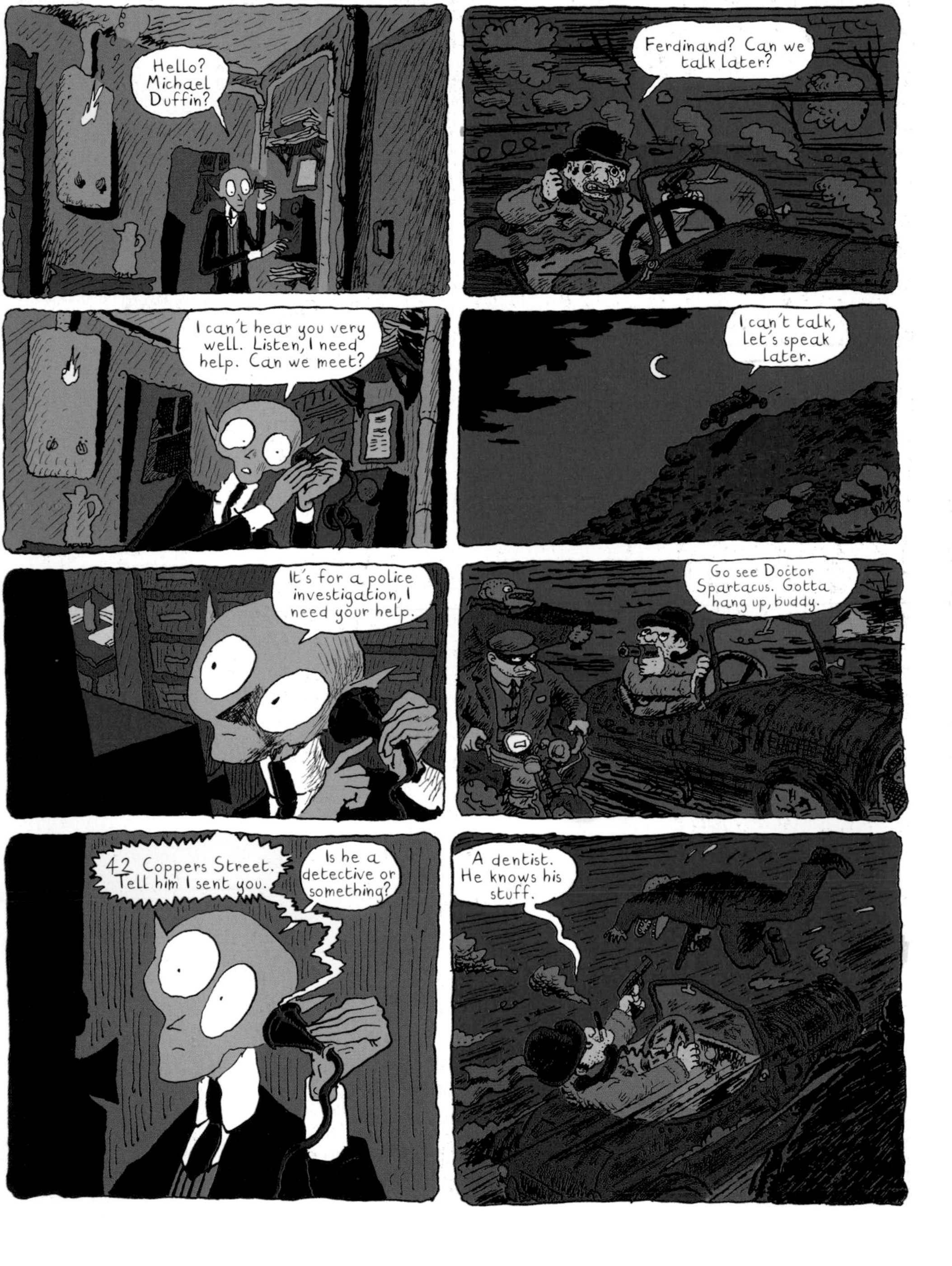
Hello? Michael Duffin?
Ferdinand? Can we talk later?
I can't hear you very well. Listen, I need help. Can we meet?
I can't talk, let's speak later.
It's for a police investigation, I need your help.
Go see Doctor Spartacus. Gotta hang up, buddy.
Is he a detective or something?
42 Coppers Street. Tell him I sent you.
A dentist. He knows his stuff.

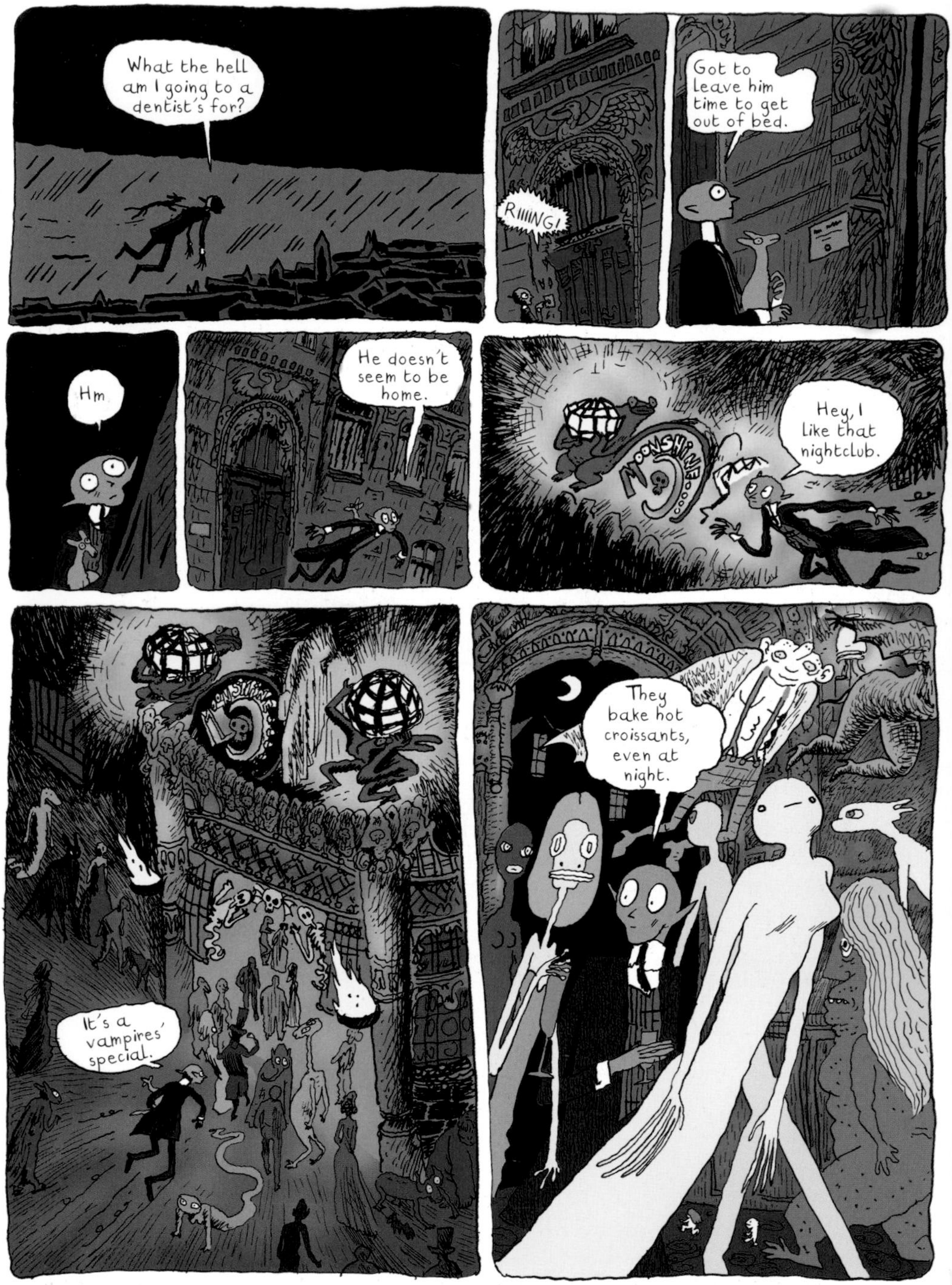
What the hell am I going to a dentist's for?
RIIING!
Got to leave him time to get out of bed.
Hm
He doesn't seem to be home.
Hey, I like that nightclub.
It's a vampires' special.
They bake hot croissants, even at night.

A few of Ferdinand's flops at the Moonshine Club (to pretty corny disco music).

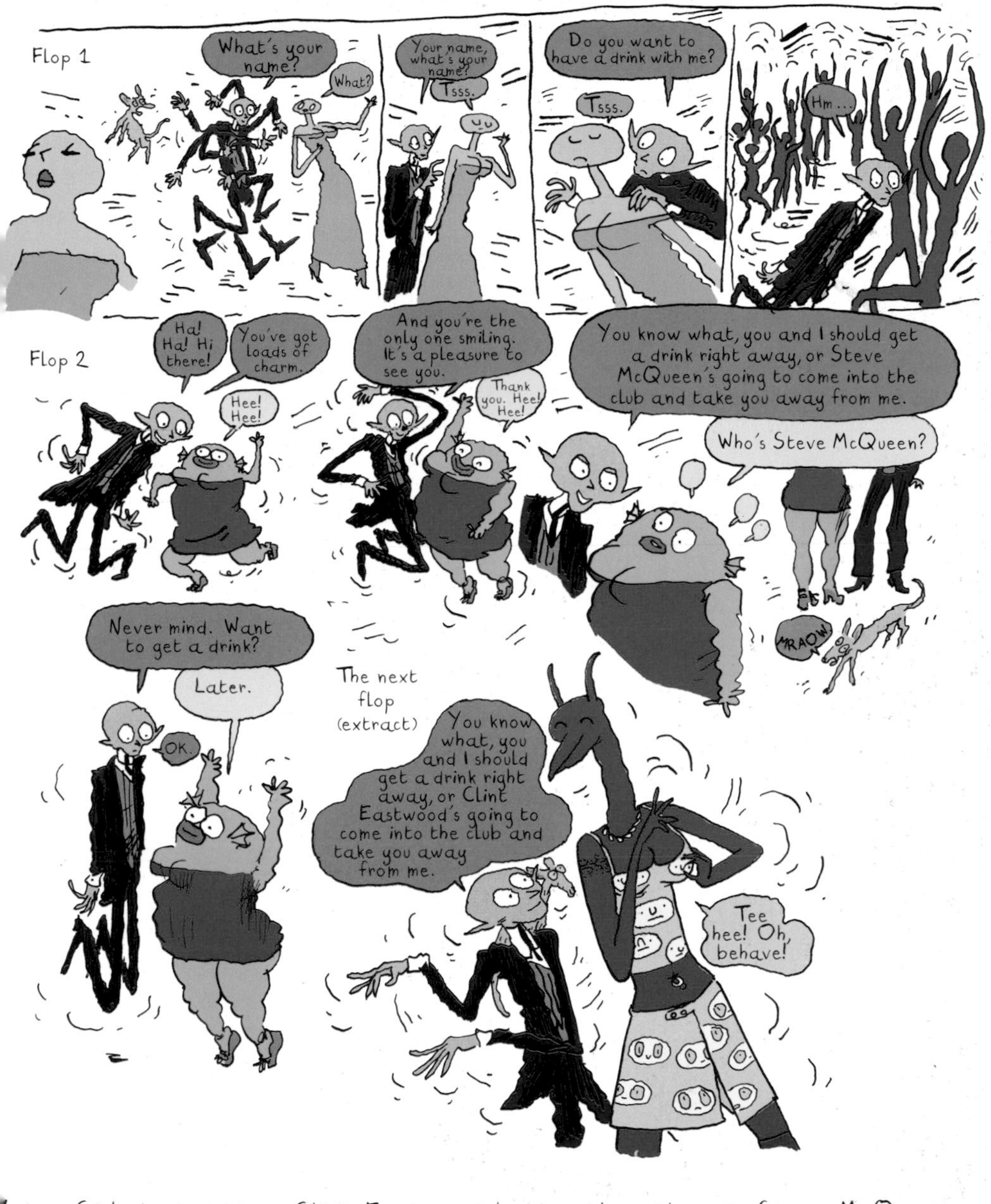
Flop 1
What's your name?
What?
Your name, what's your name?
Tsss.
Do you want to have a drink with me?
Tsss.
Hm...
Flop 2
Ha! Ha! Hi there!
You've got loads of charm.
Hee! Hee!
And you're the only one smiling. It's a pleasure to see you.
Thank you. Hee! Hee!
You know what, you and I should get a drink right away, or Steve McQueen's going to come into the club and take you away from me.
Who's Steve McQueen?
MRAOW
Never mind. Want to get a drink?
Later.
OK.
The next flop (extract)
You know what, you and I should get a drink right away, or Clint Eastwood's going to come into the club and take you away from me.
Tee hee! Oh, behave!

Note: Girls today know Clint Eastwood better than they do Steve McQueen.

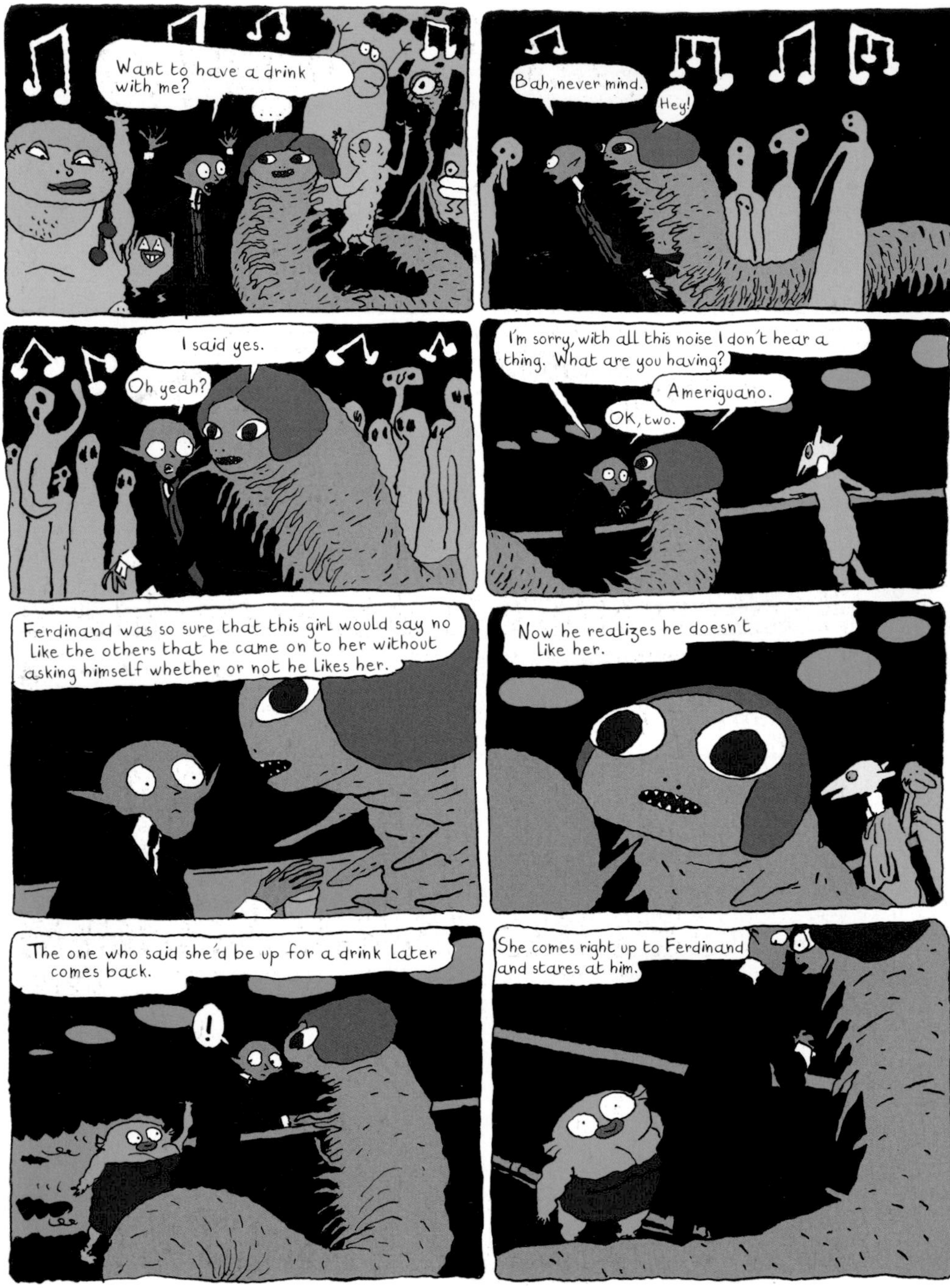
Want to have a drink with me?
...
Bah, never mind.
Hey!
I said yes.
Oh yeah?
I'm sorry, with all this noise I don't hear a thing. What are you having?
Ameriguano.
OK, two.
Ferdinand was so sure that this girl would say no like the others that he came on to her without asking himself whether or not he likes her.
Now he realizes he doesn't like her.
The one who said she'd be up for a drink later comes back.
!
She comes right up to Ferdinand and stares at him.

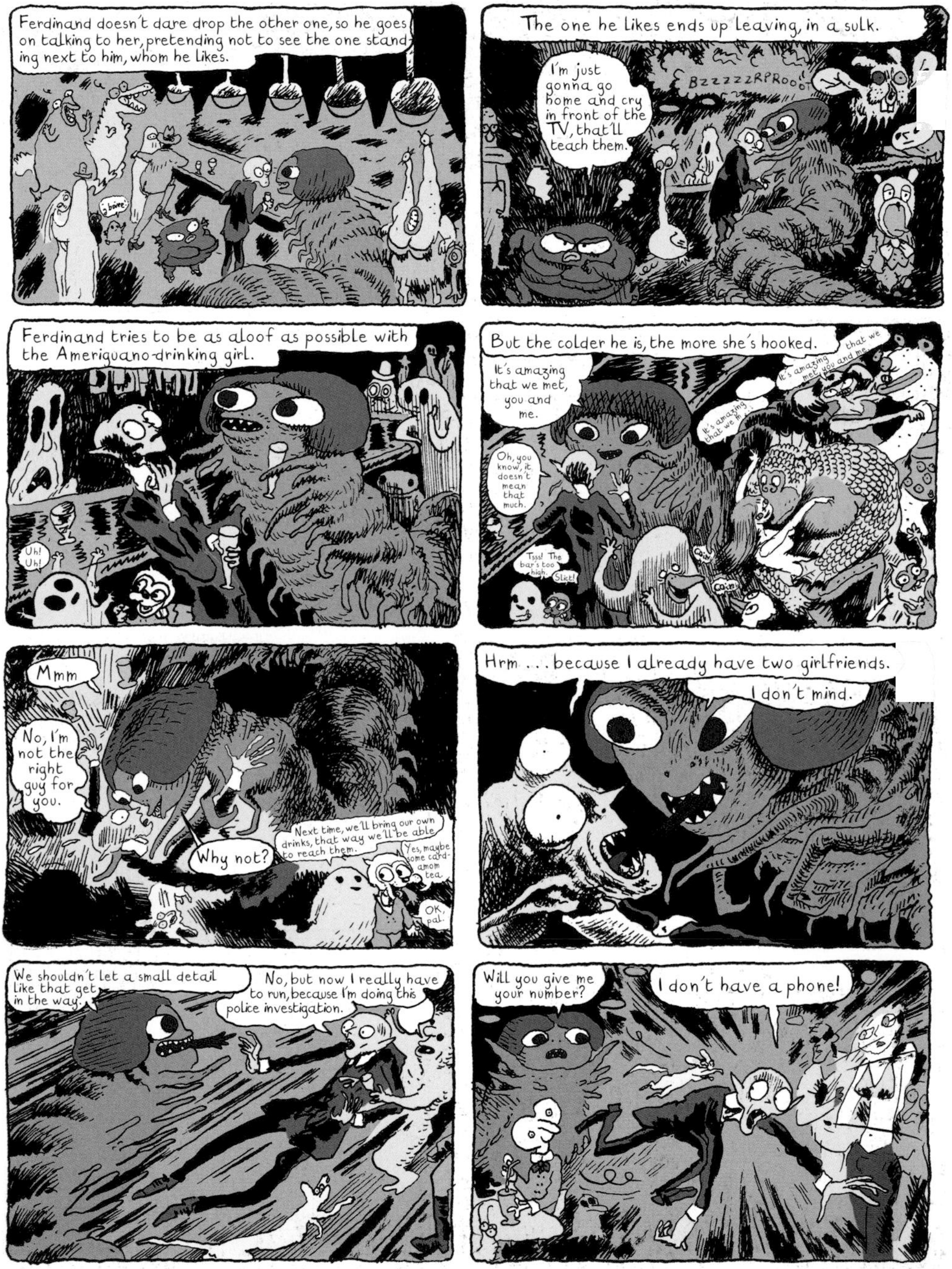
Ferdinand doesn't dare drop the other one, so he goes on talking to her, pretending not to see the one standing next to him, whom he likes.
à boire
The one he likes ends up leaving, in a sulk.
I'm just gonna go home and cry in front of the TV, that'll teach them.
BZZZZZRPROOO
Ferdinand tries to be as aloof as possible with the Ameriguano-drinking girl.
Uh! Uh!
But the colder he is, the more she's hooked.
It's amazing that we met, you and me.
Oh, you know, it doesn't mean that much.
It's amazing that we m...
It's amazing that we met, you and me.
Tsss! The bar's too high.
Slict!
Coin!
Coin!
Mmm
No, I'm not the right guy for you.
Why not?
Next time, we'll bring our own drinks, that way we'll be able to reach them.
Yes, maybe some cardamom tea.
OK, pal.
Hrm . . . . because I already have two girlfriends.
I don't mind.
We shouldn't let a small detail like that get in the way.
No, but now I really have to run, because I'm doing this police investigation.
Will you give me your number?
I don't have a phone!

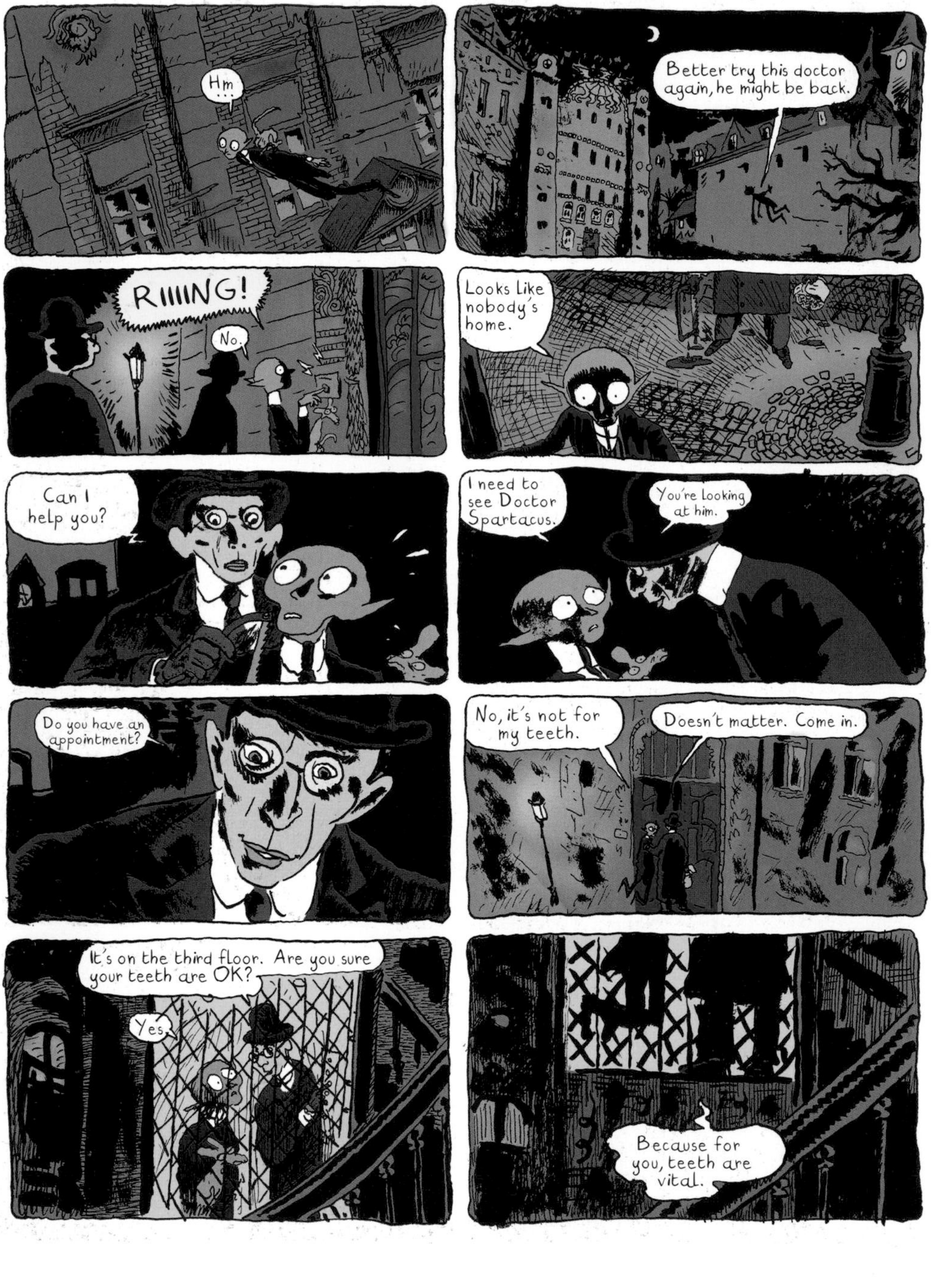
Hm
...
Better try this doctor again, he might be back.
RIIIING!
No.
Looks like nobody's home.
Can I help you?
I need to see Doctor Spartacus.
You're looking at him.
Do you have an appointment?
No, it's not for my teeth.
Doesn't matter. Come in.
It's on the third floor. Are you sure your teeth are OK?
Yes.
Because for you, teeth are vital.

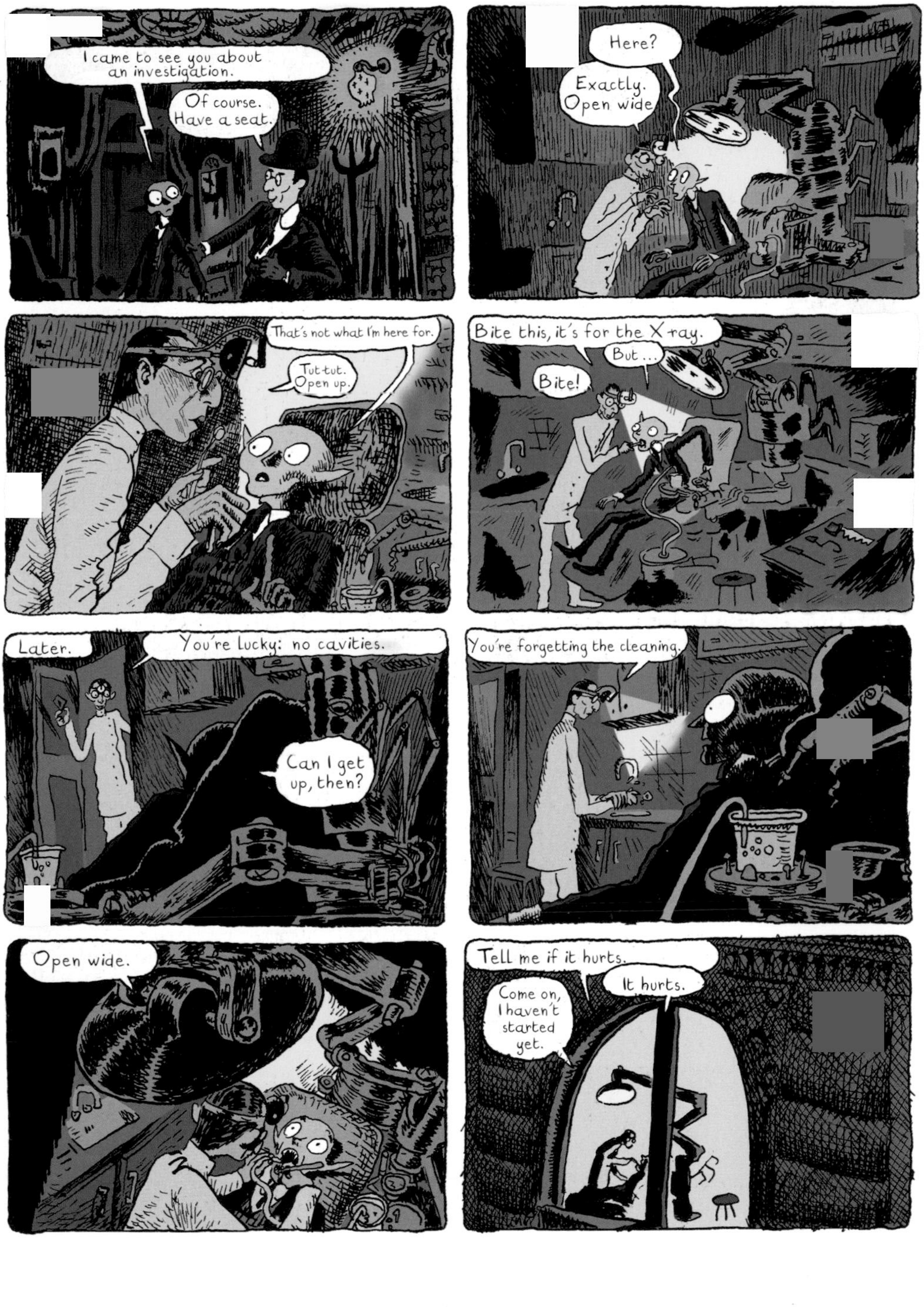
I came to see you about an investigation.
Of course. Have a seat.
Here?
Exactly. Open wide
That's not what I'm here for.
Tut-tut. Open up.
Bite this, it's for the X-ray.
But...
Bite!
Later.
You're lucky: no cavities.
Can I get up, then?
You're forgetting the cleaning.
Open wide.
Tell me if it hurts.
It hurts.
Come on, I haven't started yet.

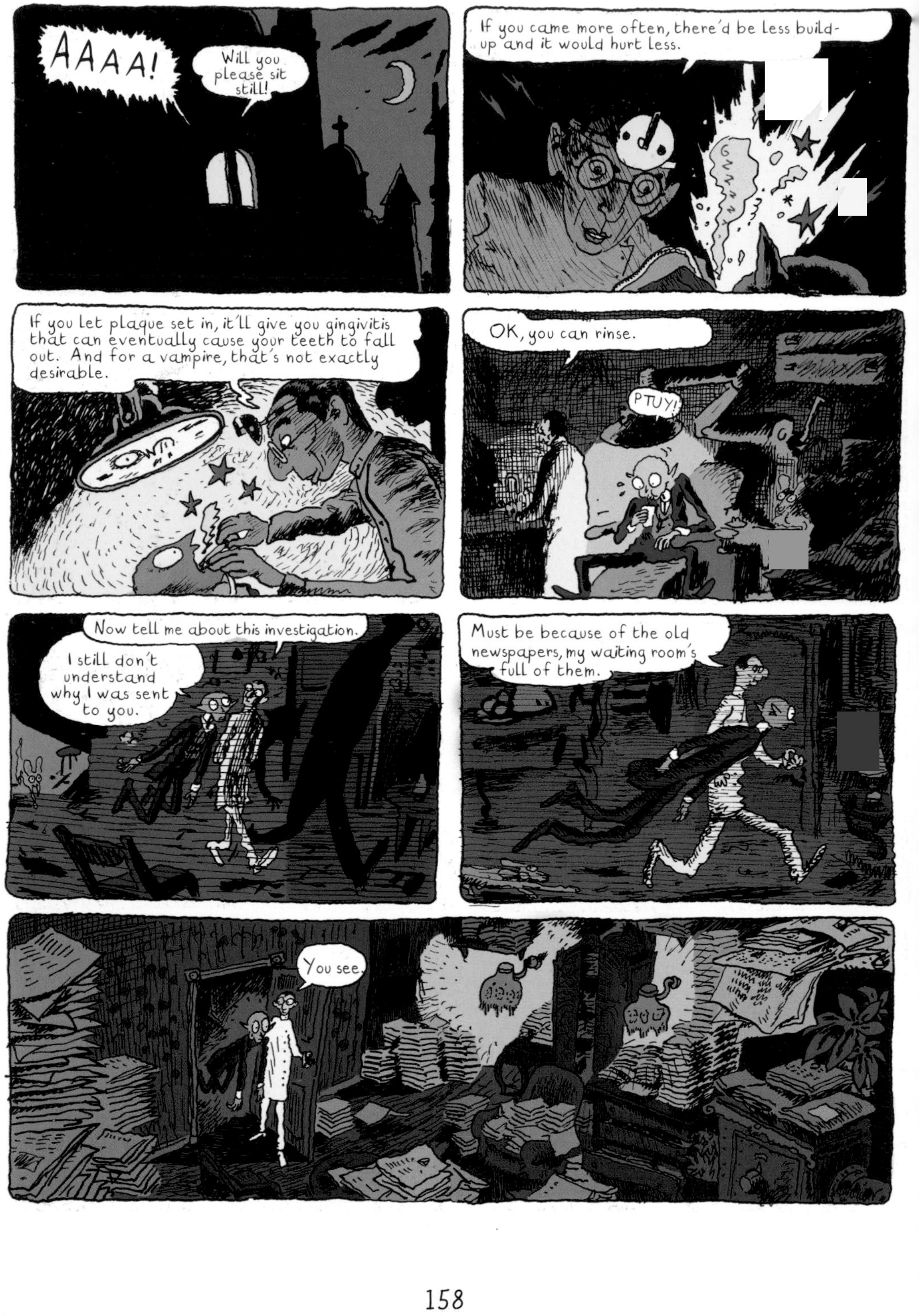
AAAA!
Will you please sit still!
If you came more often, there'd be less build-up and it would hurt less.
If you let plaque set in, it'll give you gingivitis that can eventually cause your teeth to fall out. And for a vampire, that's not exactly desirable.
OK, you can rinse.
PTUY!
Now tell me about this investigation.
I still don't understand why I was sent to you.
Must be because of the old newspapers, my waiting room's full of them.
You see.

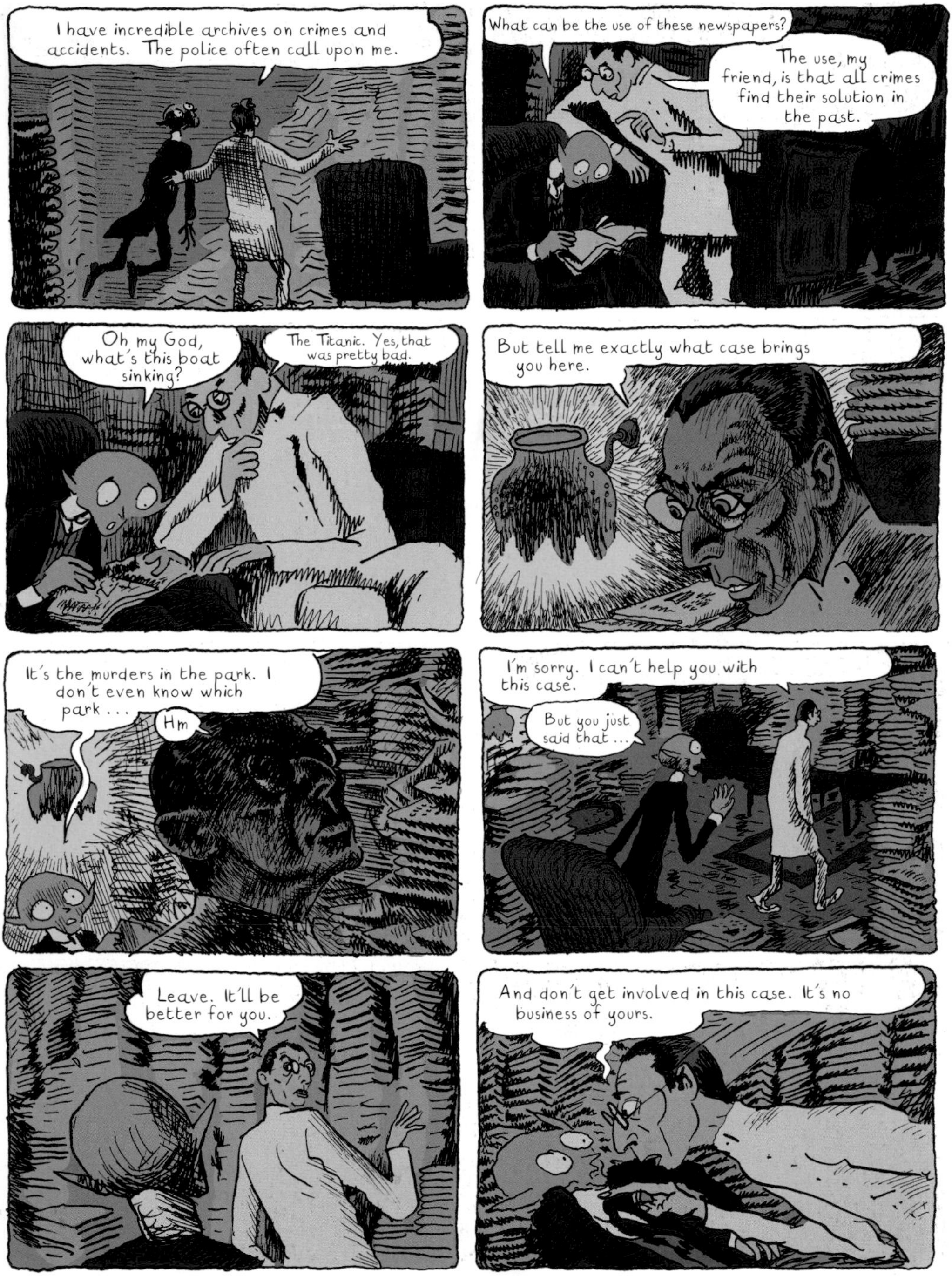
I have incredible archives on crimes and accidents. The police often call upon me.
What can be the use of these newspapers?
The use, my friend, is that all crimes find their solution in the past.
Oh my God, what's this boat sinking?
The Titanic. Yes, that was pretty bad.
But tell me exactly what case brings you here.
It's the murders in the park. I don't even know which park . . .
Hm
I'm sorry. I can't help you with this case.
But you just said that . . .
Leave. It'll be better for you.
And don't get involved in this case. It's no business of yours.

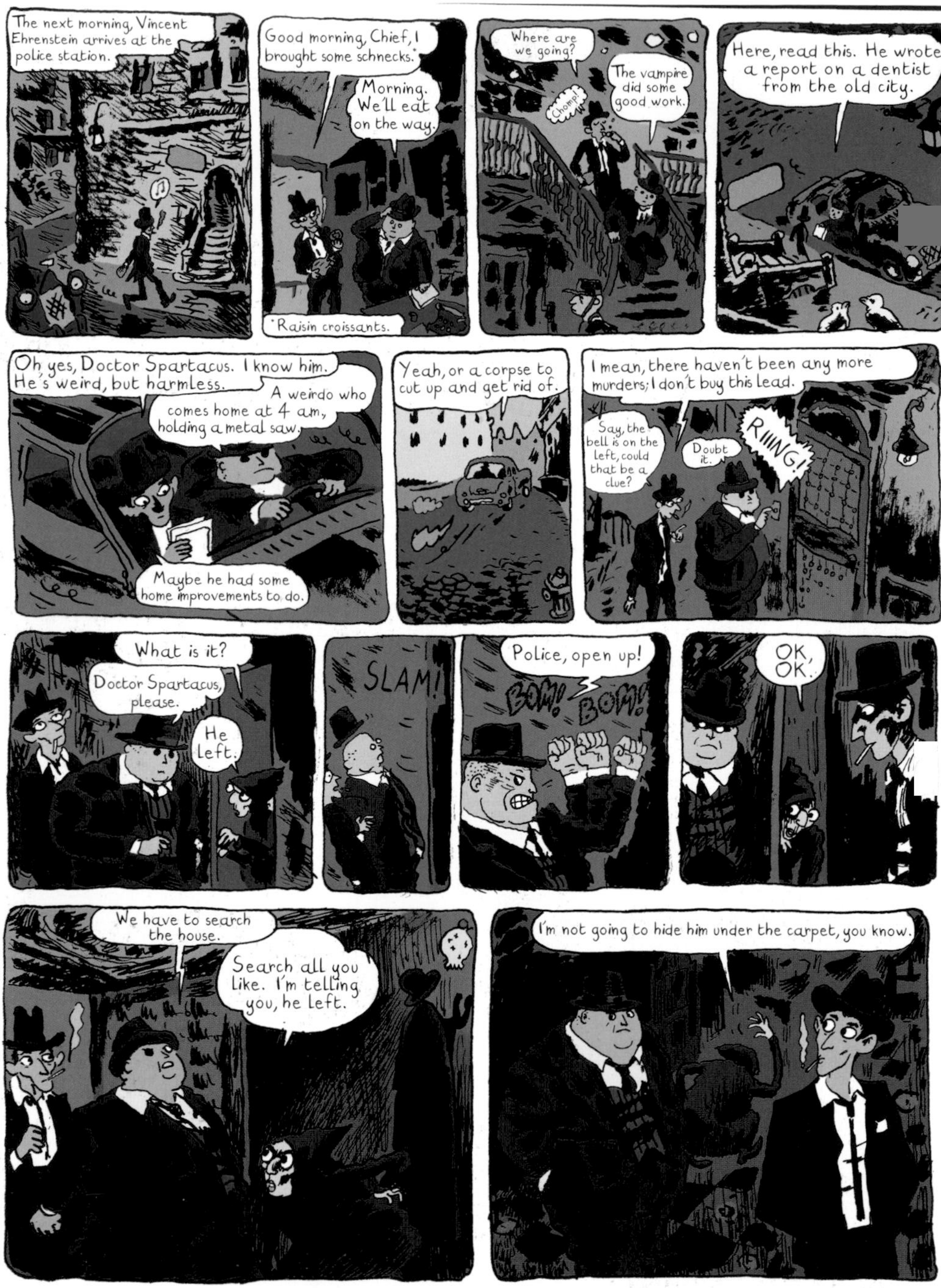

The next morning, Vincent Ehrenstein arrives at the police station.
Good morning, Chief, I brought some schnecks.*
Morning. We'll eat on the way.
*Raisin croissants.
Where are we going?
Chomp!
The vampire did some good work.
Here, read this. He wrote a report on a dentist from the old city.
Oh yes, Doctor Spartacus. I know him. He's weird, but harmless.
A weirdo who comes home at 4 am, holding a metal saw.
Maybe he had some home improvements to do.
Yeah, or a corpse to cut up and get rid of.
I mean, there haven't been any more murders; I don't buy this lead.
Say, the bell is on the left, could that be a clue?
Doubt it.
RIIING!
What is it?
Doctor Spartacus, please.
He left.
SLAM!
Police, open up!
BOM! BOM!
OK, OK.
We have to search the house.
Search all you like. I'm telling you, he left.
I'm not going to hide him under the carpet, you know.

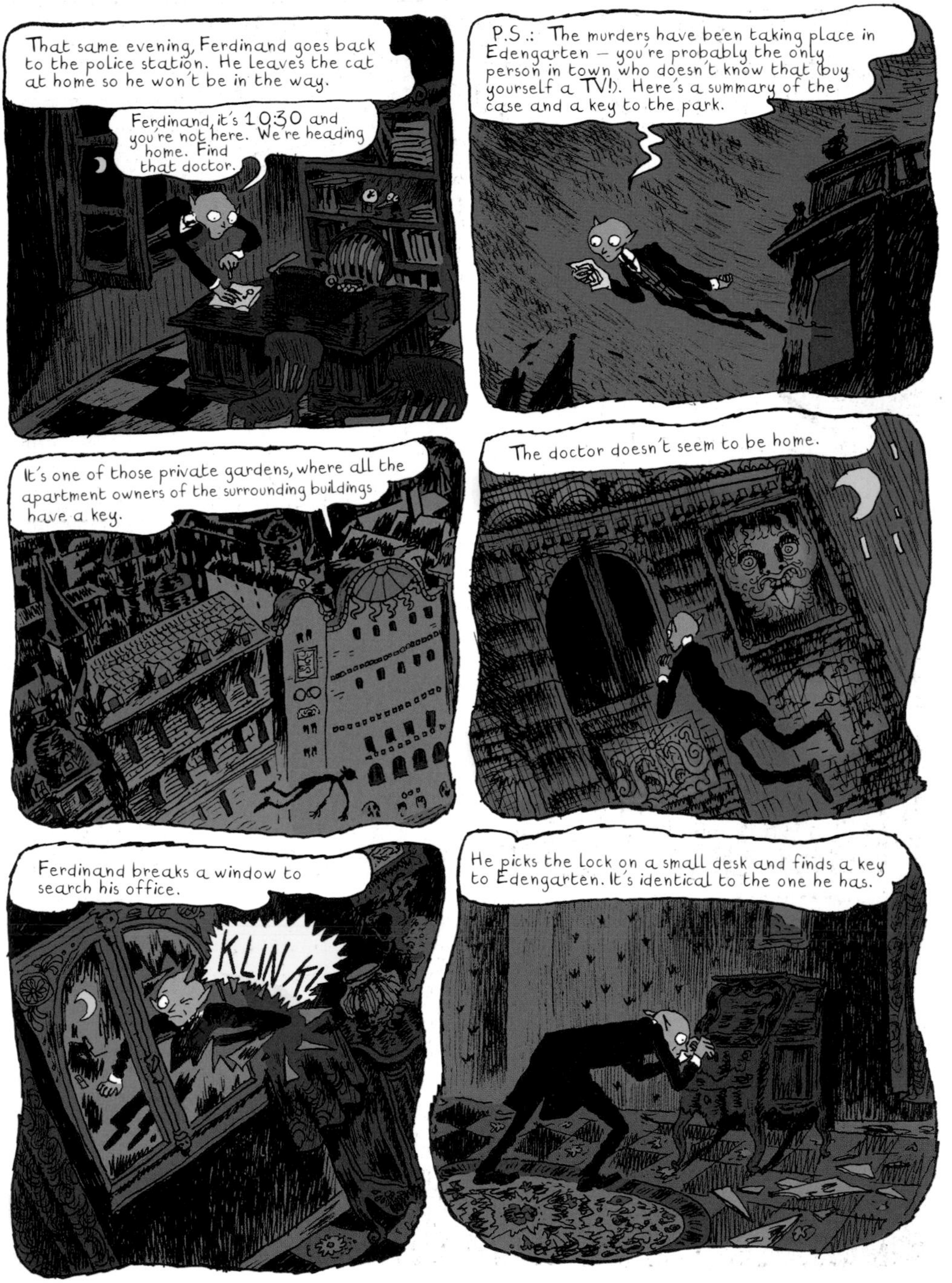

That same evening, Ferdinand goes back to the police station. He leaves the cat at home so he won't be in the way.
Ferdinand, it's 10:30 and you're not here. We're heading home. Find that doctor.
P.S.: The murders have been taking place in Edengarten — you're probably the only person in town who doesn't know that (buy yourself a TV!). Here's a summary of the case and a key to the park.
It's one of those private gardens, where all the apartment owners of the surrounding buildings have a key.
The doctor doesn't seem to be home.
Ferdinand breaks a window to search his office.
KLINK!
He picks the lock on a small desk and finds a key to Edengarten. It's identical to the one he has.

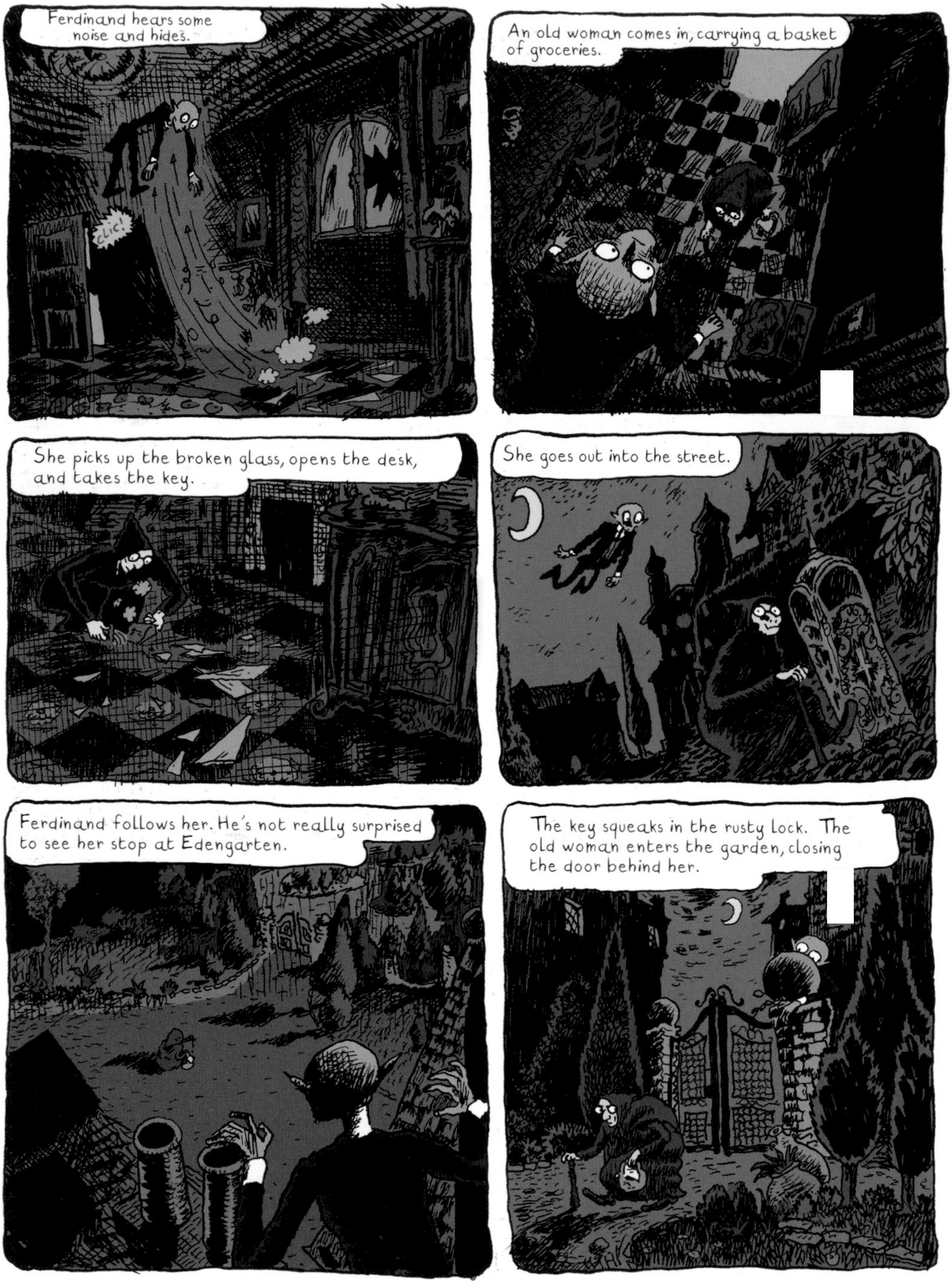

Ferdinand hears some noise and hides.
clic!
An old woman comes in, carrying a basket of groceries.
She picks up the broken glass, opens the desk, and takes the key.
She goes out into the street.
Ferdinand follows her. He's not really surprised to see her stop at Edengarten.
The key squeaks in the rusty lock. The old woman enters the garden, closing the door behind her.

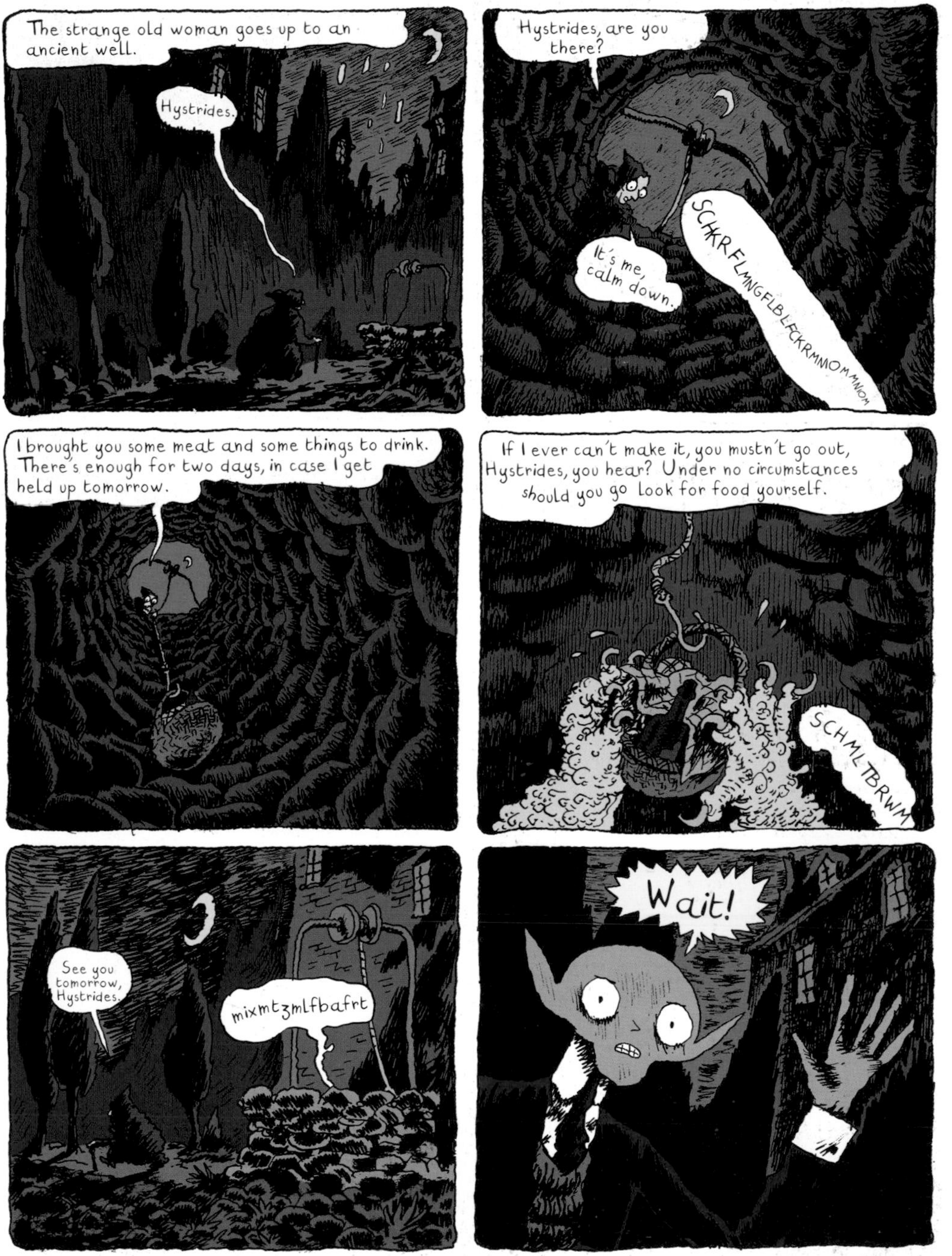
The strange old woman goes up to an ancient well.
Hystrides.
Hystrides, are you there?
It's me, calm down.
SCHKRFLMNGFLBLFCKRMMOMMNOM
I brought you some meat and some things to drink. There's enough for two days, in case I get held up tomorrow.
If I ever can't make it, you mustn't go out, Hystrides, you hear? Under no circumstances should you go look for food yourself.
SCHMLTBRWM
See you tomorrow, Hystrides.
mixmtzmlfbafrt
Wait!

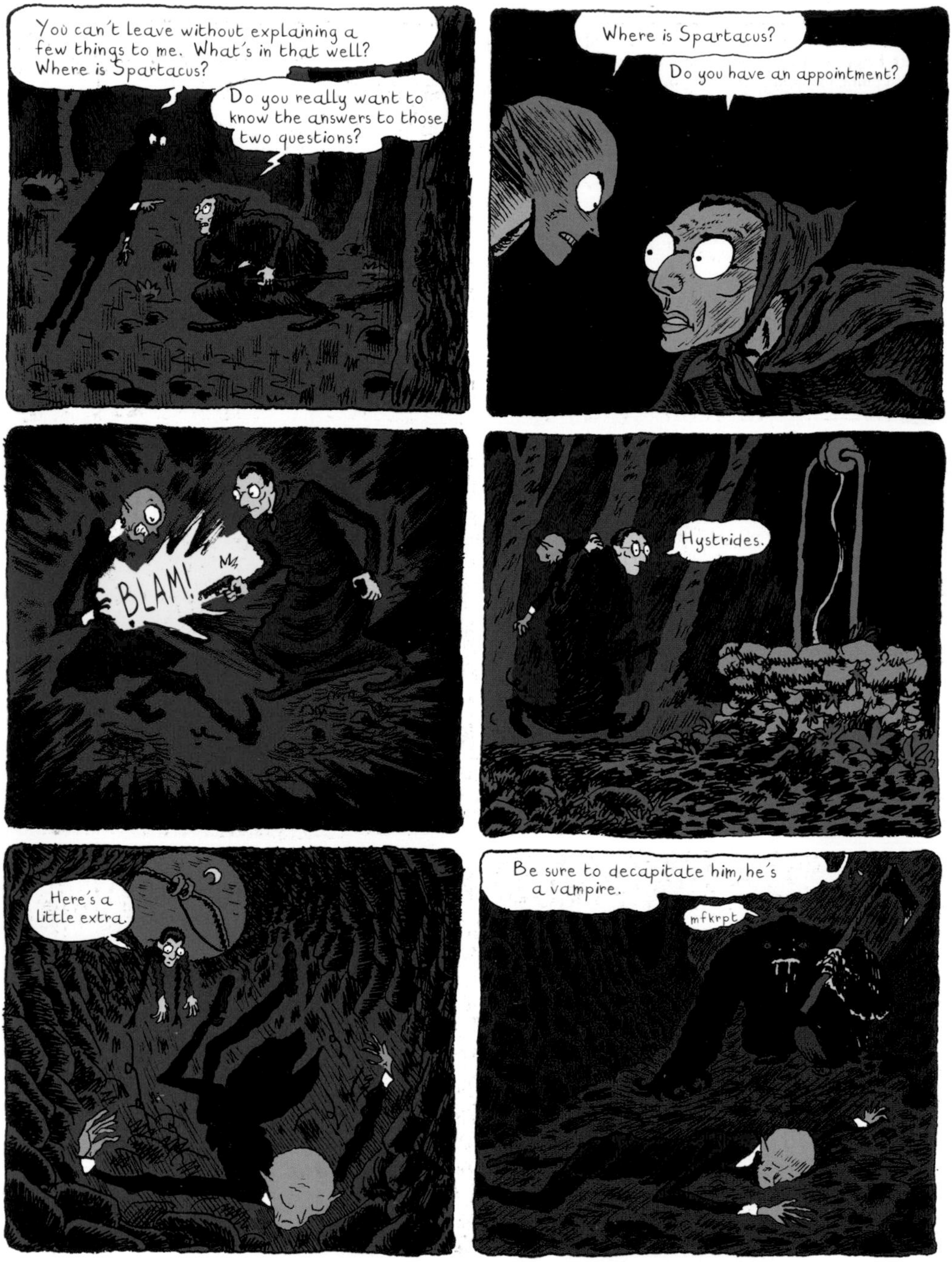
You can't leave without explaining a few things to me. What's in that well? Where is Spartacus?
Do you really want to know the answers to those two questions?
Where is Spartacus?
Do you have an appointment?
BLAM!
Hystrides.
Here's a little extra.
Be sure to decapitate him, he's a vampire.
mfkrpt

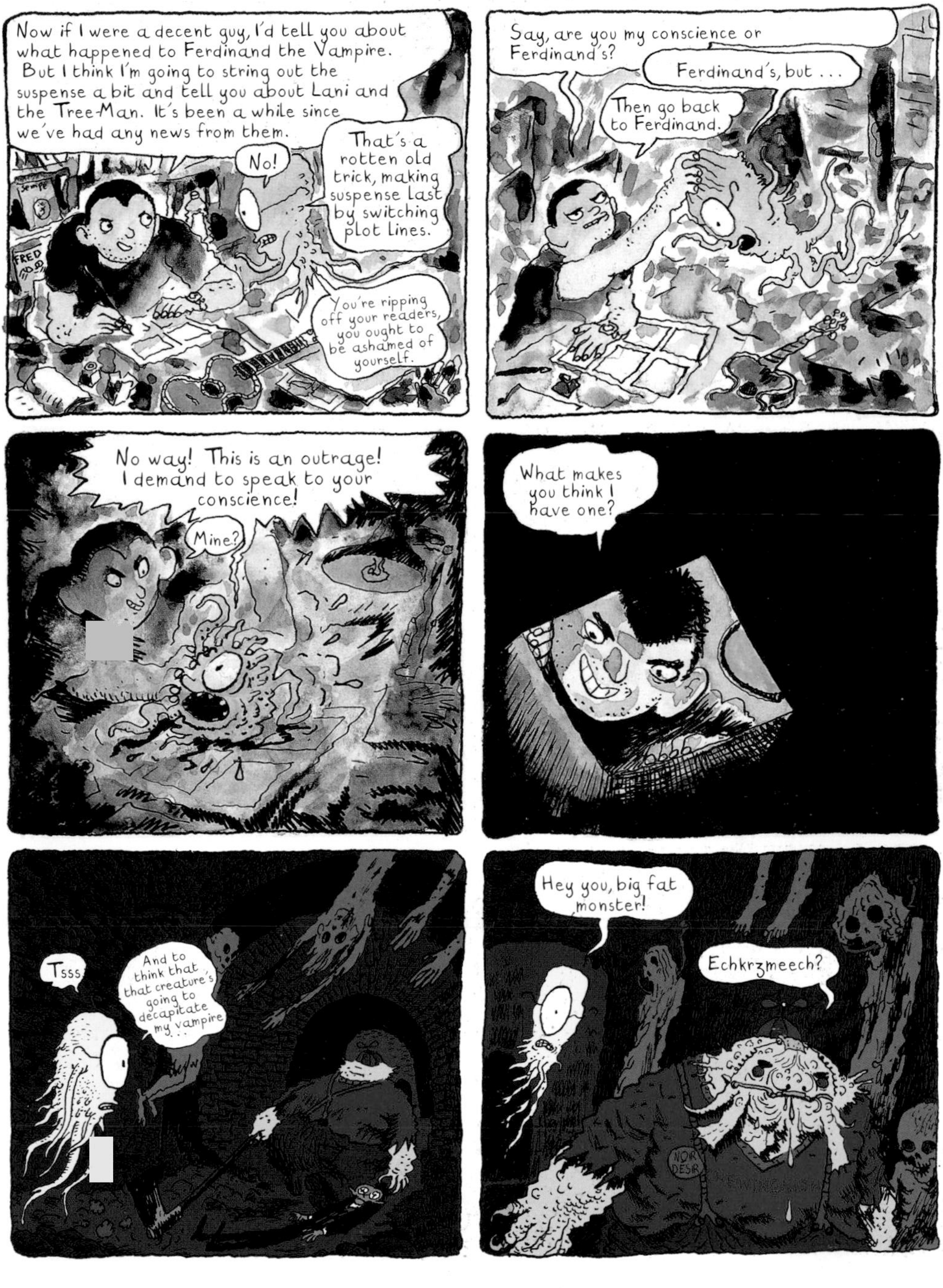
Now if I were a decent guy, I'd tell you about what happened to Ferdinand the Vampire. But I think I'm going to string out the suspense a bit and tell you about Lani and the Tree-Man. It's been a while since we've had any news from them.
No!
That's a rotten old trick, making suspense last by switching plot lines.
You're ripping off your readers, you ought to be ashamed of yourself.
Say, are you my conscience or Ferdinand's?
Ferdinand's, but . . .
Then go back to Ferdinand.
No way! This is an outrage! I demand to speak to your conscience!
Mine?
What makes you think I have one?
Tsss
And to think that that creature's going to decapitate my vampire . . .
Hey you, big fat monster!
Echkrzmeech?

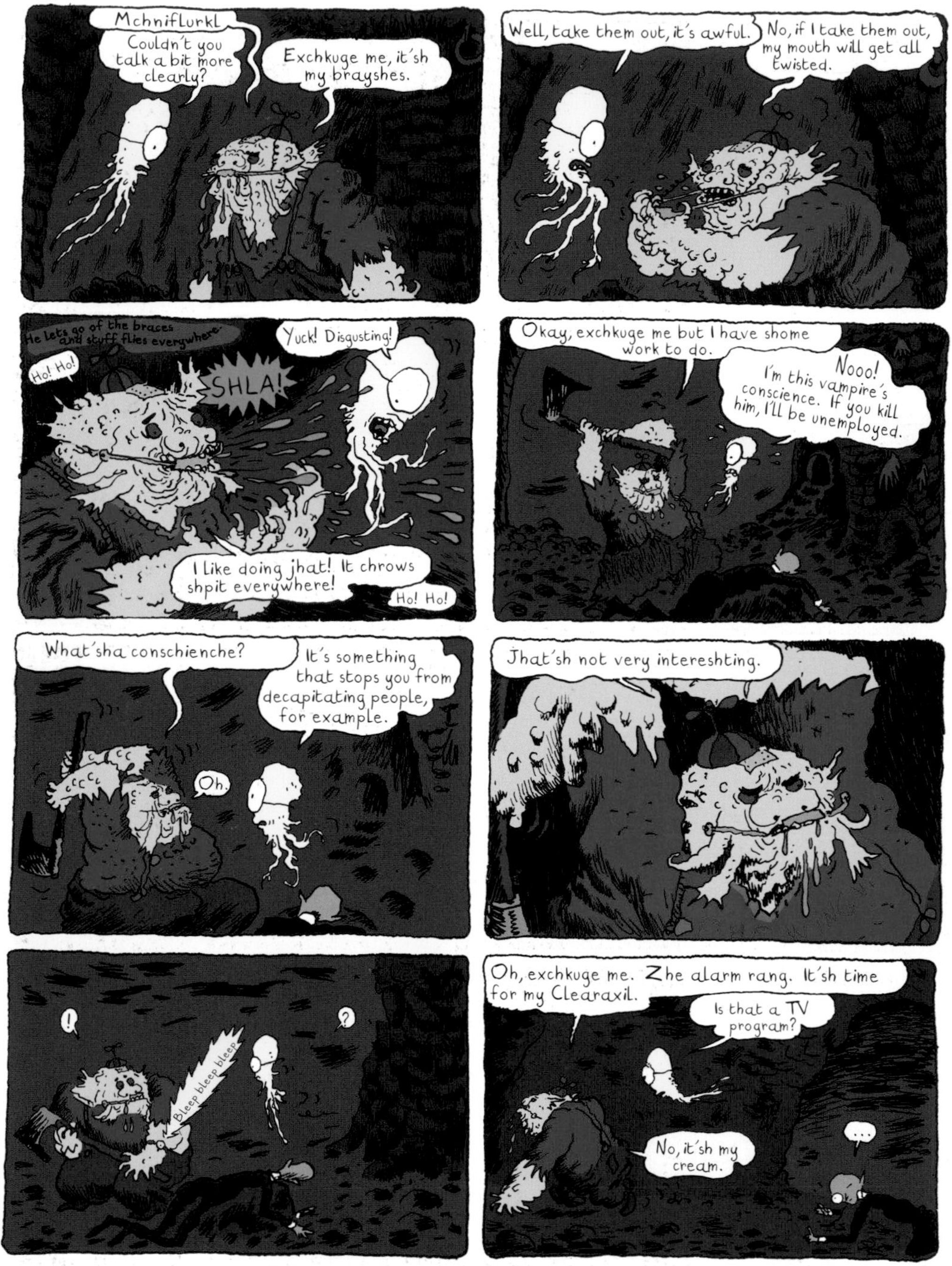
Mchniflurkl
Couldn't you talk a bit more clearly?
Exchkuge me, it'sh my brayshes.
Well, take them out, it's awful.
No, if I take them out, my mouth will get all twisted.
He lets go of the braces and stuff flies everywhere.
Ho! Ho!
SHLA!
Yuck! Disgusting!
I like doing jhat! It chrows shpit everywhere!
Ho! Ho!
Okay, exchkuge me but I have shome work to do.
Nooo! I'm this vampire's conscience. If you kill him, I'll be unemployed.
What'sha conschienche?
It's something that stops you from decapitating people, for example.
Oh.
Jhat'sh not very intereshting.
!
?
Bleep bleep bleep
Oh, exchkuge me. Zhe alarm rang. It'sh time for my Clearaxil.
Is that a TV program?
No, it'sh my cream.
...

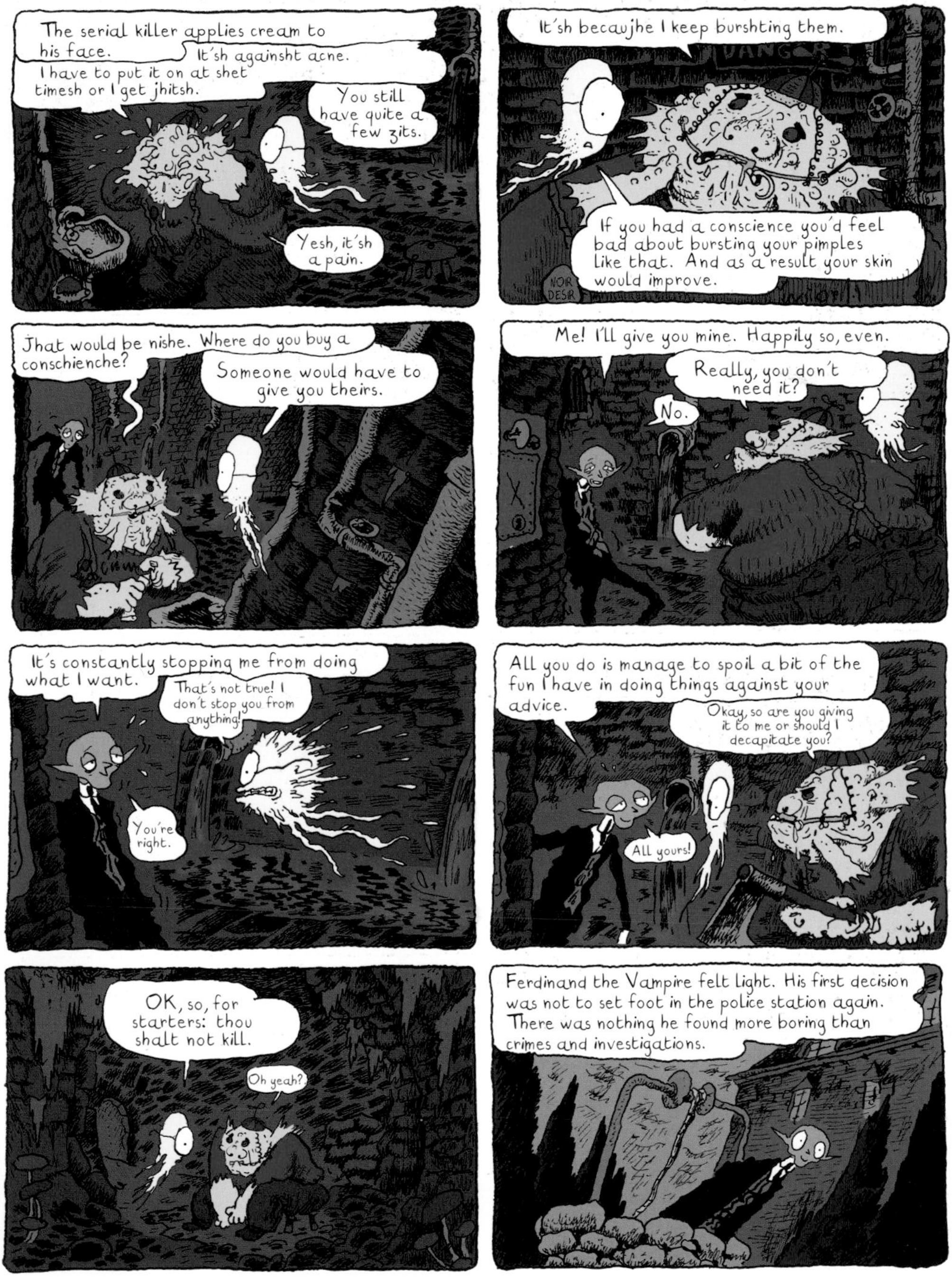
The serial killer applies cream to his face.
It'sh againsht acne. I have to put it on at shet timesh or I get jhitsh.
You still have quite a few zits.
Yesh, it'sh a pain.
It'sh becaujhe I keep burshting them.
If you had a conscience you'd feel bad about bursting your pimples like that. And as a result your skin would improve.
NOIR DESIR
Jhat would be nishe. Where do you buy a conschienche?
Someone would have to give you theirs.
Me! I'll give you mine. Happily so, even.
Really, you don't need it?
No.
It's constantly stopping me from doing what I want.
That's not true! I don't stop you from anything!
You're right.
All you do is manage to spoil a bit of the fun I have in doing things against your advice.
Okay, so are you giving it to me or should I decapitate you?
All yours!
OK, so, for starters: thou shalt not kill.
Oh yeah?
Ferdinand the Vampire felt light. His first decision was not to set foot in the police station again. There was nothing he found more boring than crimes and investigations.

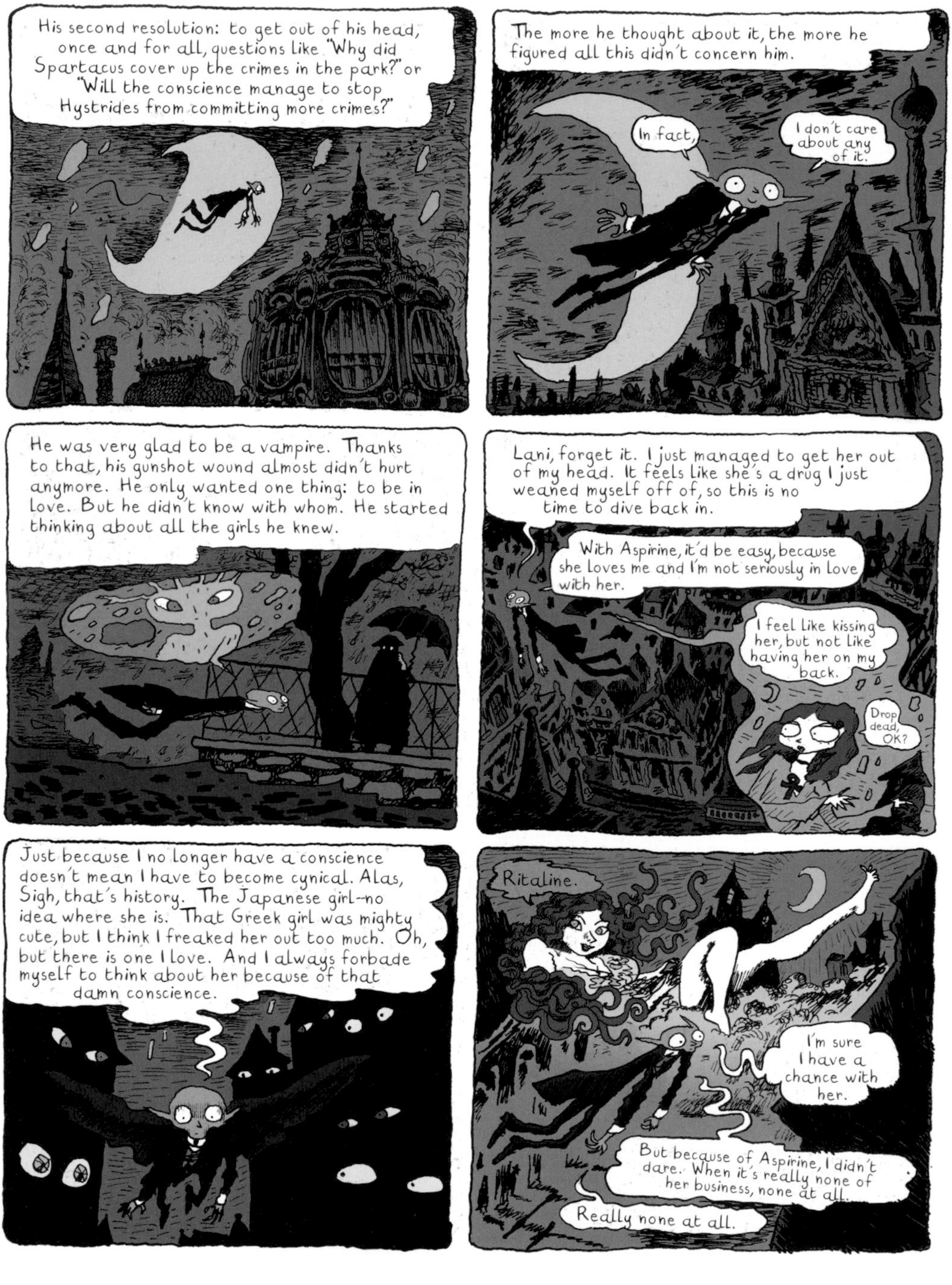
His second resolution: to get out of his head, once and for all, questions like "Why did Spartacus cover up the crimes in the park?" or "Will the conscience manage to stop Hystrides from committing more crimes?"
The more he thought about it, the more he figured all this didn't concern him.
In fact,
I don't care about any of it.
He was very glad to be a vampire. Thanks to that, his gunshot wound almost didn't hurt anymore. He only wanted one thing: to be in love. But he didn't know with whom. He started thinking about all the girls he knew.
Lani, forget it. I just managed to get her out of my head. It feels like she's a drug I just weaned myself off of, so this is no time to dive back in.
With Aspirine, it'd be easy, because she loves me and I'm not seriously in love with her.
I feel like kissing her, but not like having her on my back.
Drop dead, OK?
Just because I no longer have a conscience doesn't mean I have to become cynical. Alas, Sigh, that's history. The Japanese girl--no idea where she is. That Greek girl was mighty cute, but I think I freaked her out too much. Oh, but there is one I love. And I always forbade myself to think about her because of that damn conscience.
Ritaline.
I'm sure I have a chance with her.
But because of Aspirine, I didn't dare. When it's really none of her business, none at all.
Really none at all.

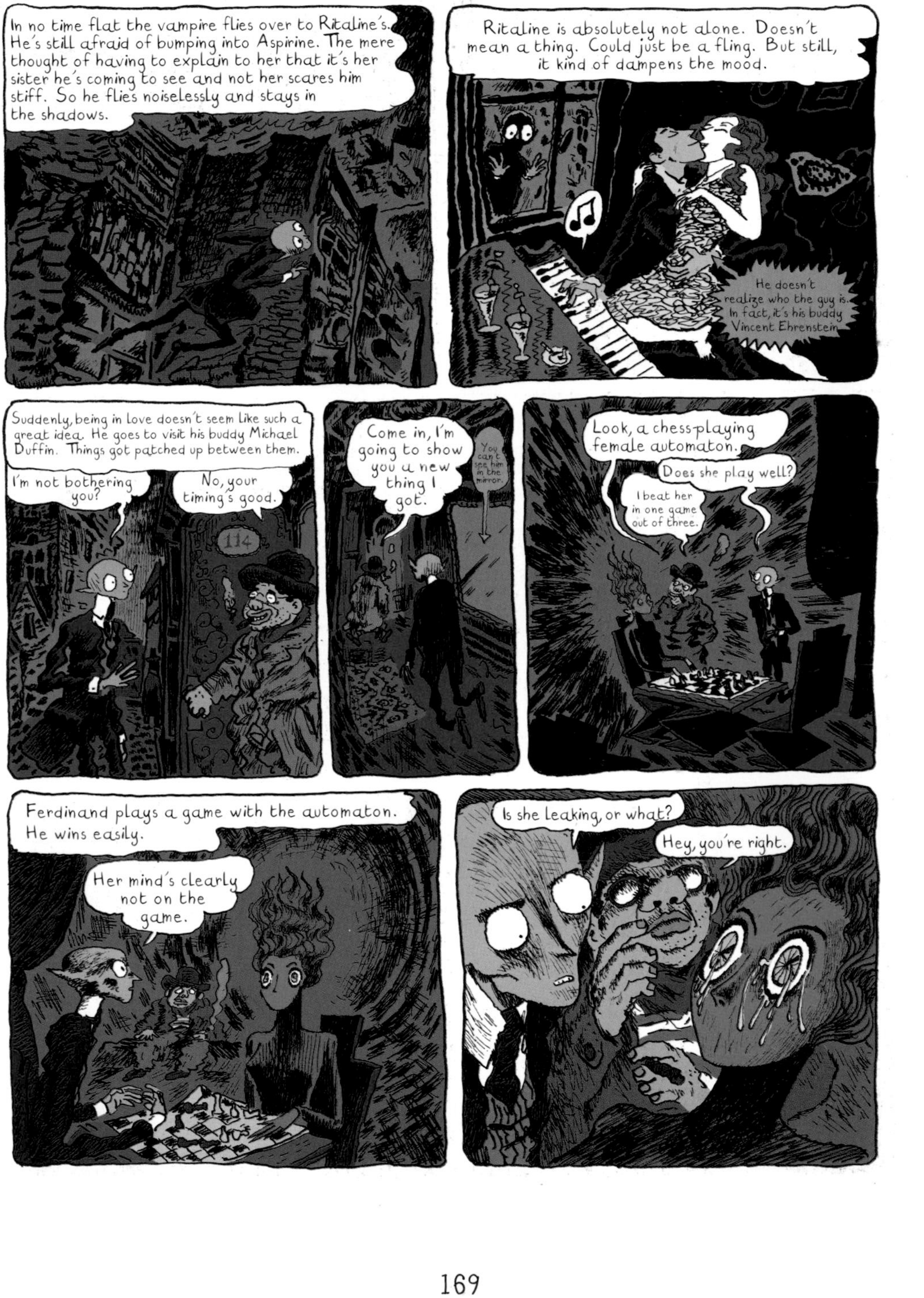

In no time flat the vampire flies over to Ritaline's. He's still afraid of bumping into Aspirine. The mere thought of having to explain to her that it's her sister he's coming to see and not her scares him stiff. So he flies noiselessly and stays in the shadows.
Ritaline is absolutely not alone. Doesn't mean a thing. Could just be a fling. But still, it kind of dampens the mood.
He doesn't realize who the guy is. In fact, it's his buddy Vincent Ehrenstein.
Suddenly, being in love doesn't seem like such a great idea. He goes to visit his buddy Michael Duffin. Things got patched up between them.
I'm not bothering you?
No, your timing's good.
114
Come in, I'm going to show you a new thing I got.
You can't see him in the mirror.
Look, a chess-playing female automaton.
Does she play well?
I beat her in one game out of three.
Ferdinand plays a game with the automaton. He wins easily.
Her mind's clearly not on the game.
Is she leaking, or what?
Hey, you're right.

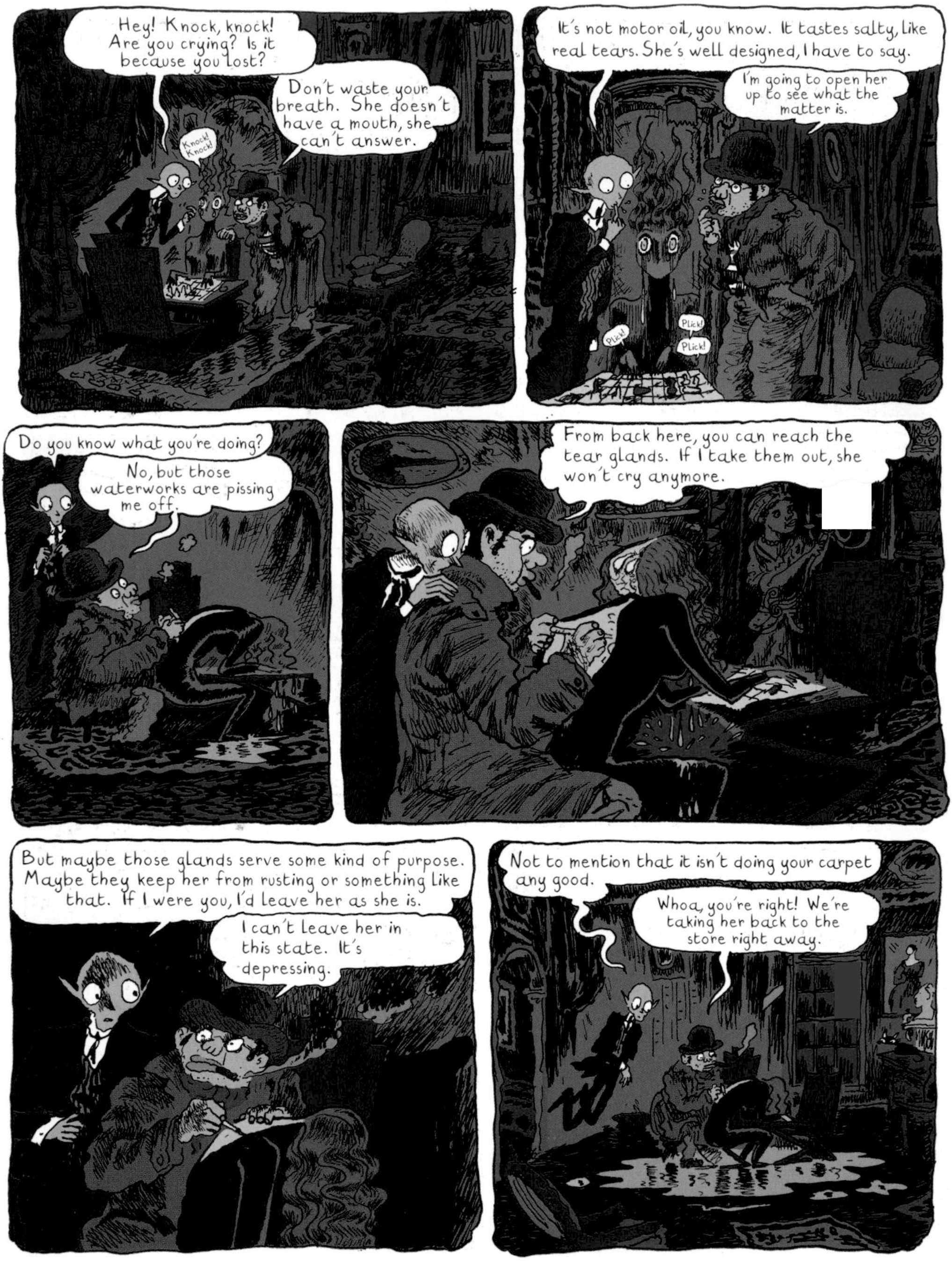
Hey! Knock, knock! Are you crying? Is it because you lost?
Knock! Knock!
Don't waste your breath. She doesn't have a mouth, she can't answer.
It's not motor oil, you know. It tastes salty, like real tears. She's well designed, I have to say.
I'm going to open her up to see what the matter is.
Plick!
Plick!
Plick!
Do you know what you're doing?
No, but those waterworks are pissing me off.
From back here, you can reach the tear glands. If I take them out, she won't cry anymore.
But maybe those glands serve some kind of purpose. Maybe they keep her from rusting or something like that. If I were you, I'd leave her as she is.
I can't leave her in this state. It's depressing.
Not to mention that it isn't doing your carpet any good.
Whoa, you're right! We're taking her back to the store right away.

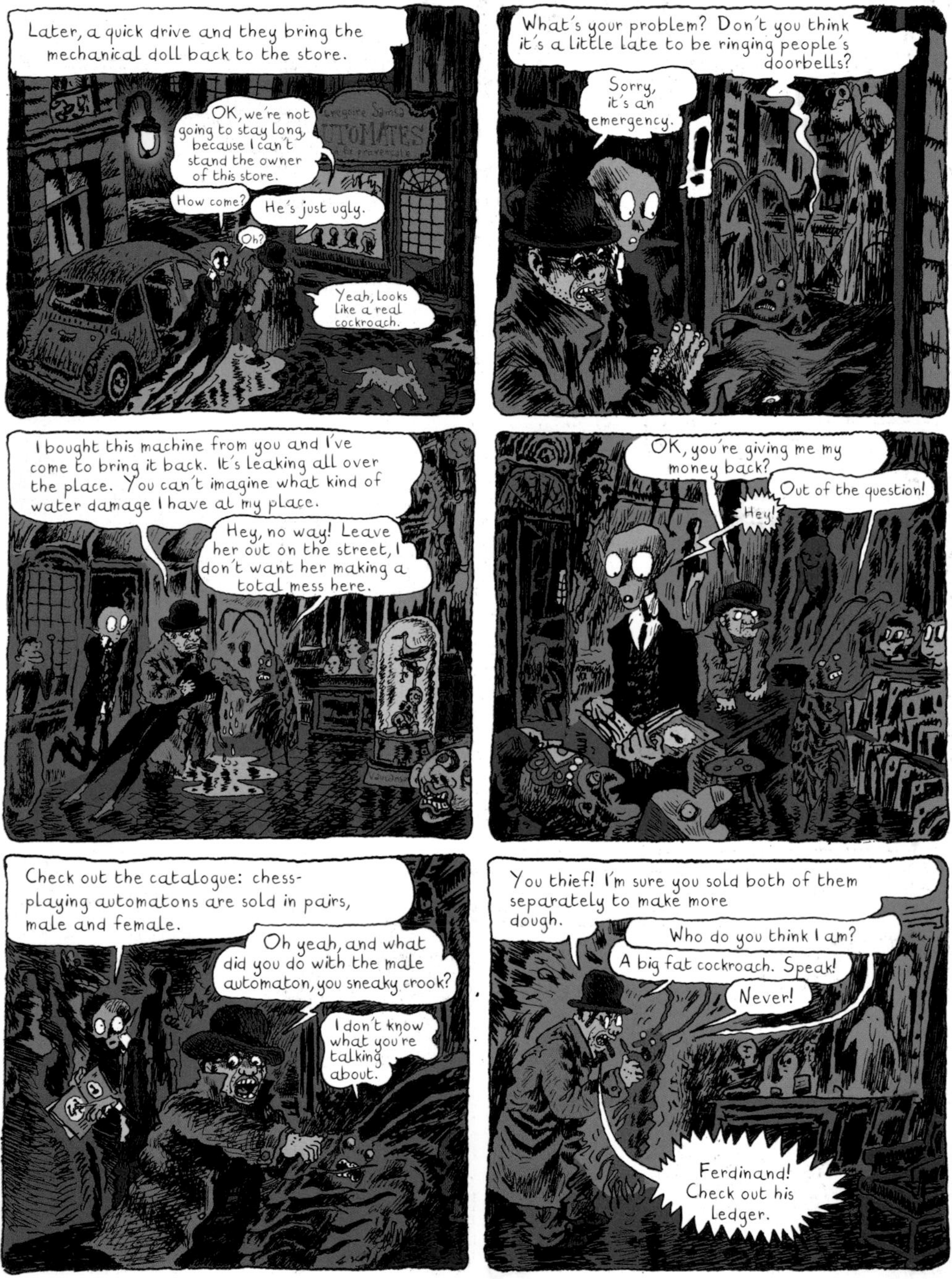
Later, a quick drive and they bring the mechanical doll back to the store.
OK, we're not going to stay long, because I can't stand the owner of this store.
How come?
He's just ugly.
Oh?
Yeah, looks like a real cockroach.
What's your problem? Don't you think it's a little late to be ringing people's doorbells?
Sorry, it's an emergency.
!
I bought this machine from you and I've come to bring it back. It's leaking all over the place. You can't imagine what kind of water damage I have at my place.
Hey, no way! Leave her out on the street, I don't want her making a total mess here.
OK, you're giving me my money back?
Out of the question!
Hey!
Check out the catalogue: chess-playing automatons are sold in pairs, male and female.
Oh yeah, and what did you do with the male automaton, you sneaky crook?
I don't know what you're talking about.
You thief! I'm sure you sold both of them separately to make more dough.
Who do you think I am?
A big fat cockroach. Speak!
Never!
Ferdinand! Check out his ledger.

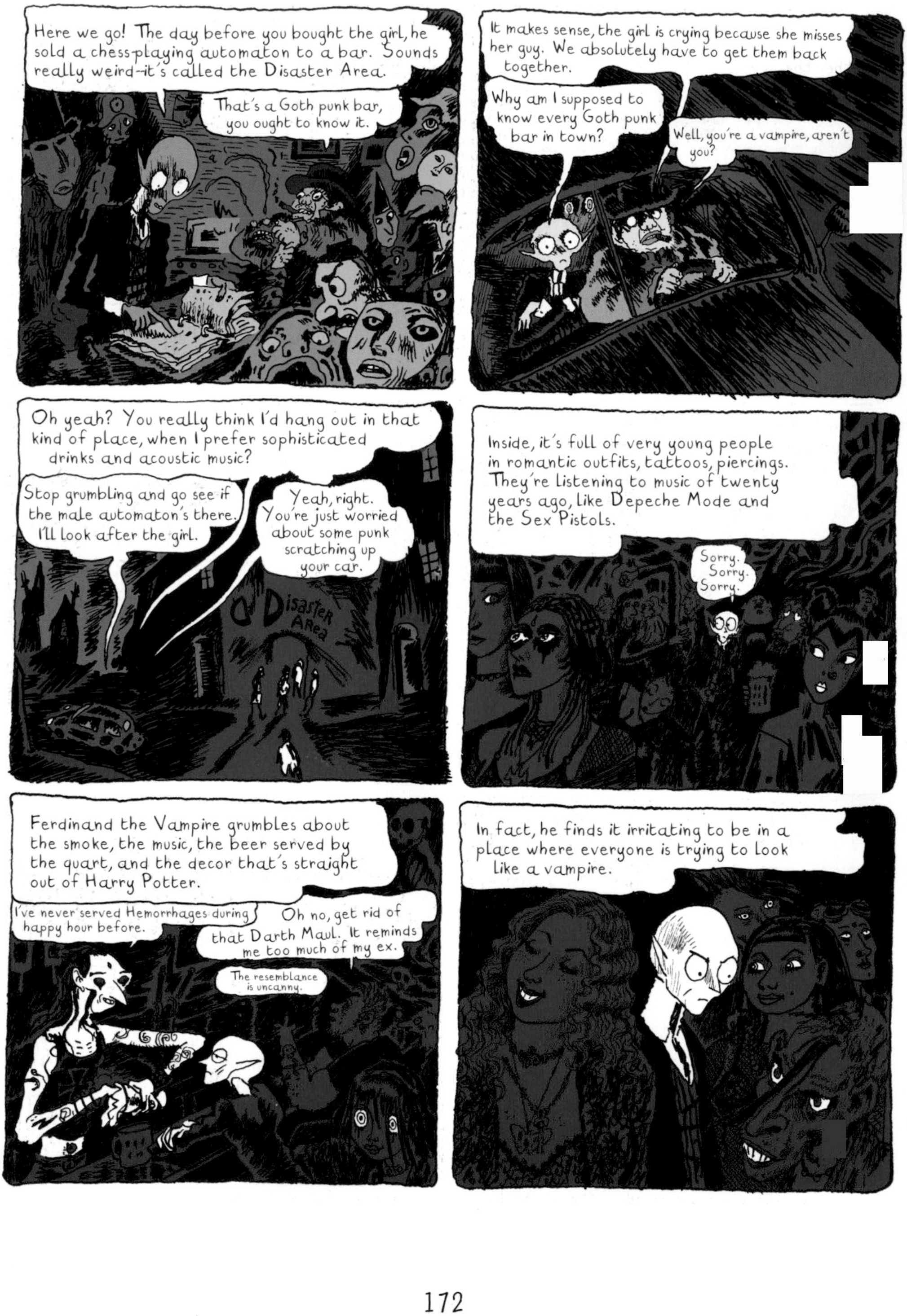
Here we go! The day before you bought the girl, he sold a chess-playing automaton to a bar. Sounds really weird–it's called the Disaster Area.
That's a Goth punk bar, you ought to know it.
It makes sense, the girl is crying because she misses her guy. We absolutely have to get them back together.
Why am I supposed to know every Goth punk bar in town?
Well, you're a vampire, aren't you?
Oh yeah? You really think I'd hang out in that kind of place, when I prefer sophisticated drinks and acoustic music?
Stop grumbling and go see if the male automaton's there. I'll look after the girl.
Yeah, right. You're just worried about some punk scratching up your car.
Disaster Area
Inside, it's full of very young people in romantic outfits, tattoos, piercings. They're listening to music of twenty years ago, like Depeche Mode and the Sex Pistols.
Sorry. Sorry. Sorry.
Ferdinand the Vampire grumbles about the smoke, the music, the beer served by the quart, and the decor that's straight out of Harry Potter.
I've never served Hemorrhages during happy hour before.
Oh no, get rid of that Darth Maul. It reminds me too much of my ex.
The resemblance is uncanny.
In fact, he finds it irritating to be in a place where everyone is trying to look like a vampire.

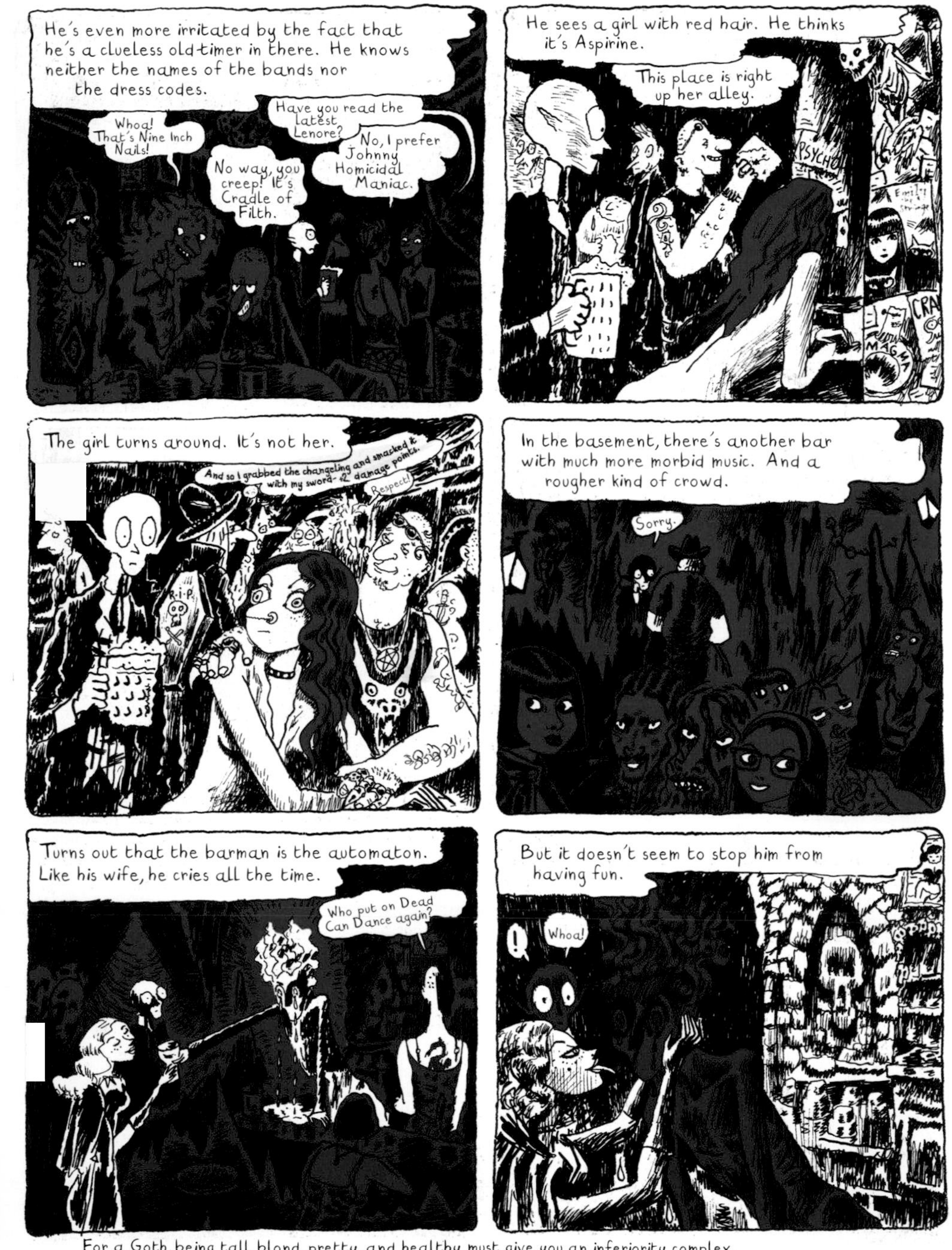
He's even more irritated by the fact that he's a clueless old-timer in there. He knows neither the names of the bands nor the dress codes.
Whoa! That's Nine Inch Nails!
No way, you creep! It's Cradle of Filth.
Have you read the latest Lenore?
No, I prefer Johnny Homicidal Maniac.
He sees a girl with red hair. He thinks it's Aspirine.
This place is right up her alley.
PSYCHO
MAGMA
The girl turns around. It's not her.
And so I grabbed the changeling and smacked it with my sword- +2 damage points.
Respect!
R.I.P.
In the basement, there's another bar with much more morbid music. And a rougher kind of crowd.
Sorry.
Turns out that the barman is the automaton. Like his wife, he cries all the time.
Who put on Dead Can Dance again?
But it doesn't seem to stop him from having fun.
!
Whoa!
For a Goth, being tall, blond, pretty, and healthy must give you an inferiority complex.

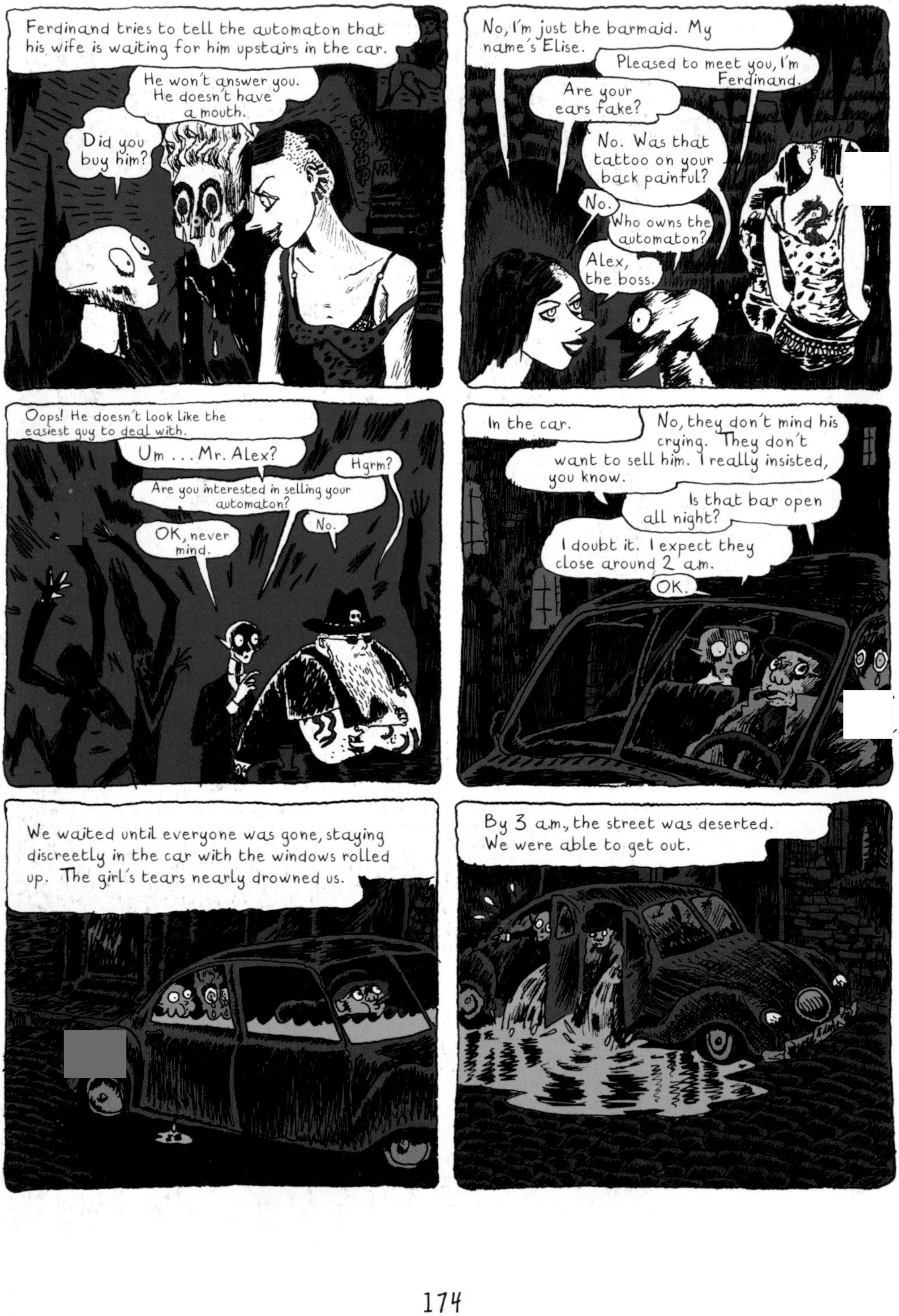
Ferdinand tries to tell the automaton that his wife is waiting for him upstairs in the car.
He won't answer you. He doesn't have a mouth.
Did you buy him?
No, I'm just the barmaid. My name's Elise.
Pleased to meet you, I'm Ferdinand.
Are your ears fake?
No. Was that tattoo on your back painful?
No.
Who owns the automaton?
Alex, the boss.
Oops! He doesn't look like the easiest guy to deal with.
Um . . . Mr. Alex?
Hgrm?
Are you interested in selling your automaton?
No.
OK, never mind.
In the car.
No, they don't mind his crying. They don't want to sell him. I really insisted, you know.
Is that bar open all night?
I doubt it. I expect they close around 2 a.m.
OK.
We waited until everyone was gone, staying discreetly in the car with the windows rolled up. The girl's tears nearly drowned us.
By 3 a.m., the street was deserted. We were able to get out.

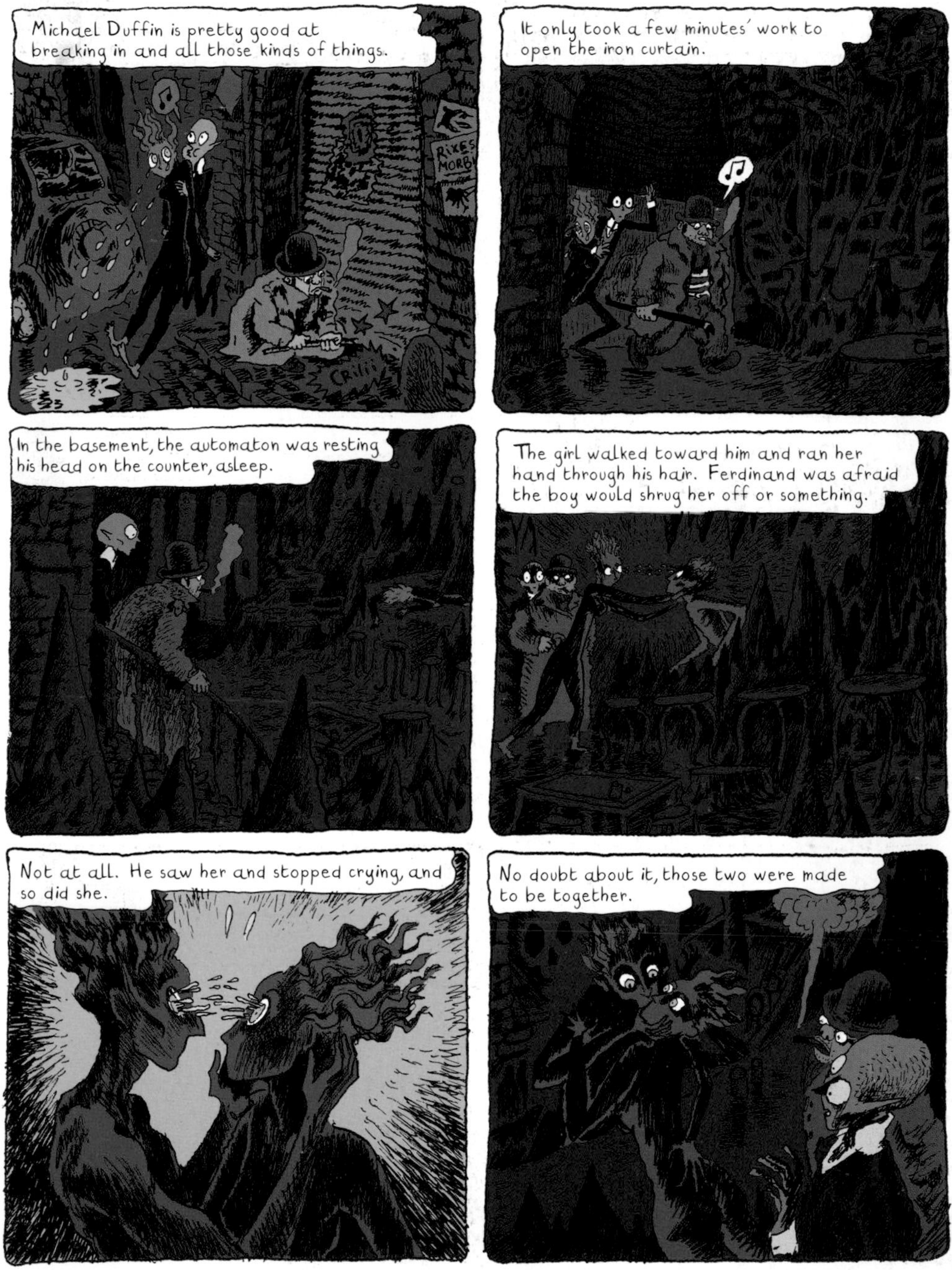
Michael Duffin is pretty good at breaking in and all those kinds of things.
It only took a few minutes' work to open the iron curtain.
In the basement, the automaton was resting his head on the counter, asleep.
The girl walked toward him and ran her hand through his hair. Ferdinand was afraid the boy would shrug her off or something.
Not at all. He saw her and stopped crying, and so did she.
No doubt about it, those two were made to be together.

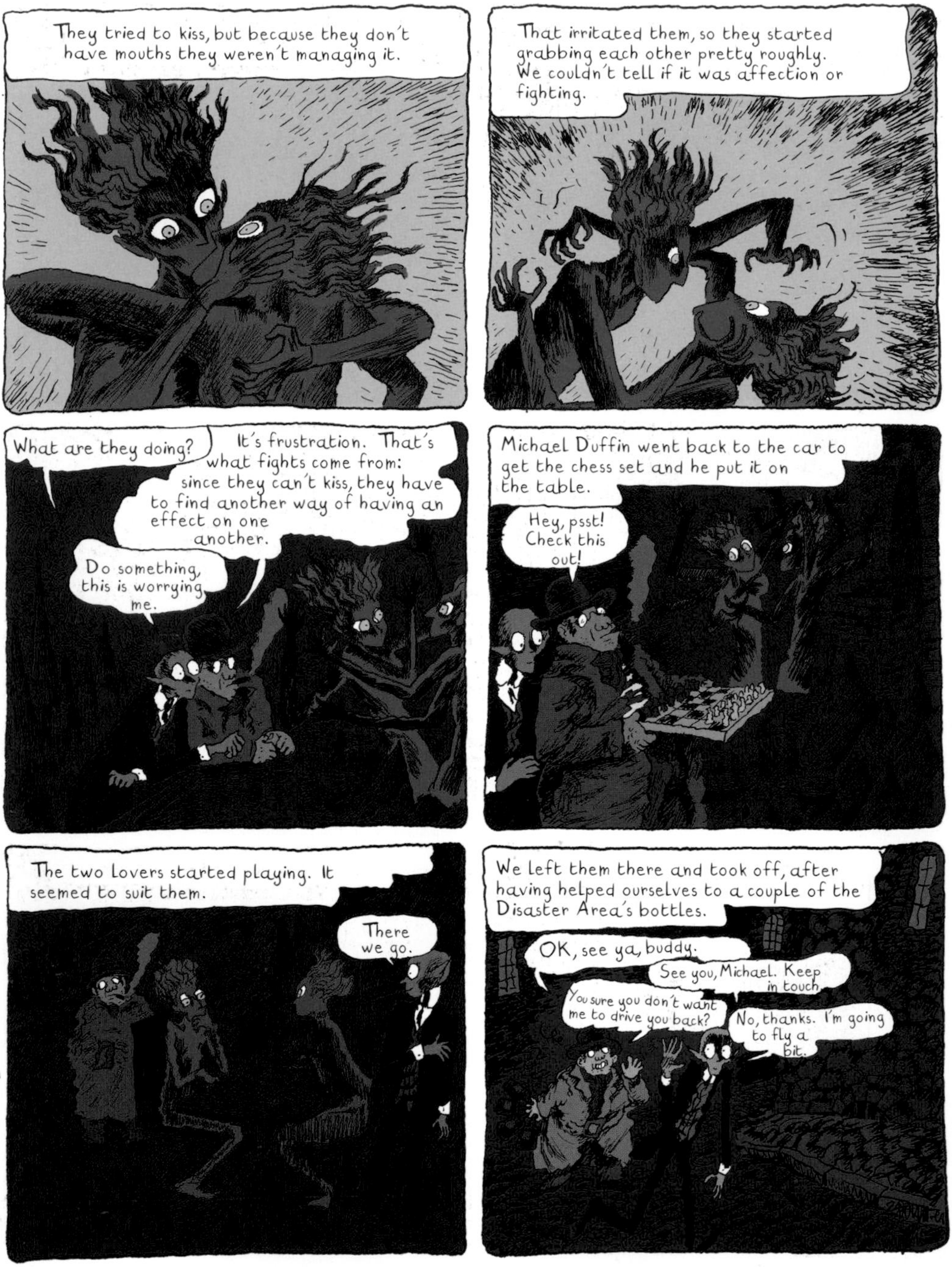
They tried to kiss, but because they don't have mouths they weren't managing it.
That irritated them, so they started grabbing each other pretty roughly. We couldn't tell if it was affection or fighting.
What are they doing?
It's frustration. That's what fights come from: since they can't kiss, they have to find another way of having an effect on one another.
Do something, this is worrying me.
Michael Duffin went back to the car to get the chess set and he put it on the table.
Hey, psst! Check this out!
The two lovers started playing. It seemed to suit them.
There we go.
We left them there and took off, after having helped ourselves to a couple of the Disaster Area's bottles.
OK, see ya, buddy.
See you, Michael. Keep in touch.
You sure you don't want me to drive you back?
No, thanks. I'm going to fly a bit.

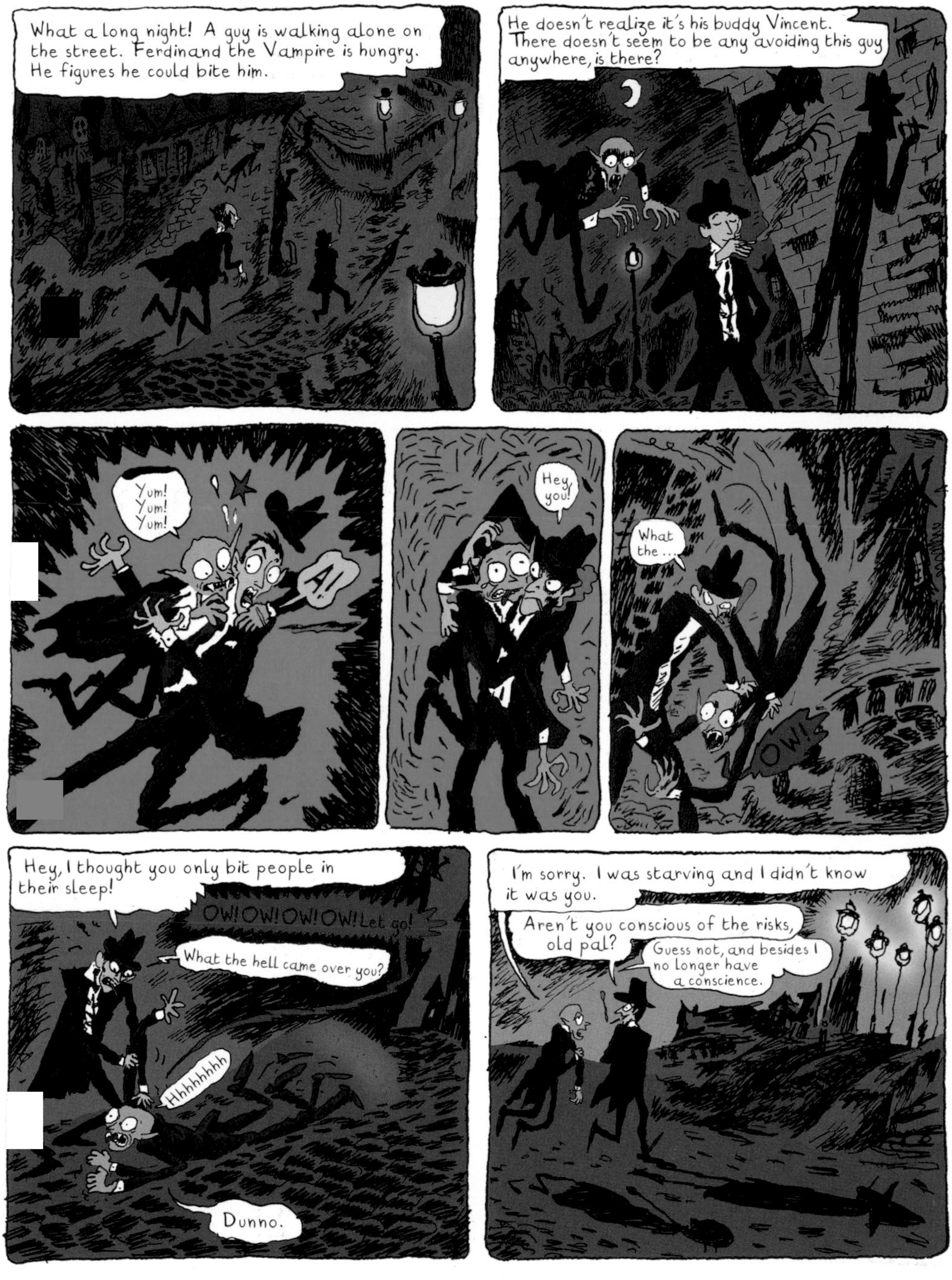
What a long night! A guy is walking alone on the street. Ferdinand the Vampire is hungry. He figures he could bite him.
He doesn't realize it's his buddy Vincent. There doesn't seem to be any avoiding this guy anywhere, is there?
Yum! Yum! Yum!
A!
Hey, you!
What the...
OW!
Hey, I thought you only bit people in their sleep!
OW! OW! OW! OW! Let go!
What the hell came over you?
Hhhhhhh
Dunno.
I'm sorry. I was starving and I didn't know it was you.
Aren't you conscious of the risks, old pal?
Guess not, and besides I no longer have a conscience.

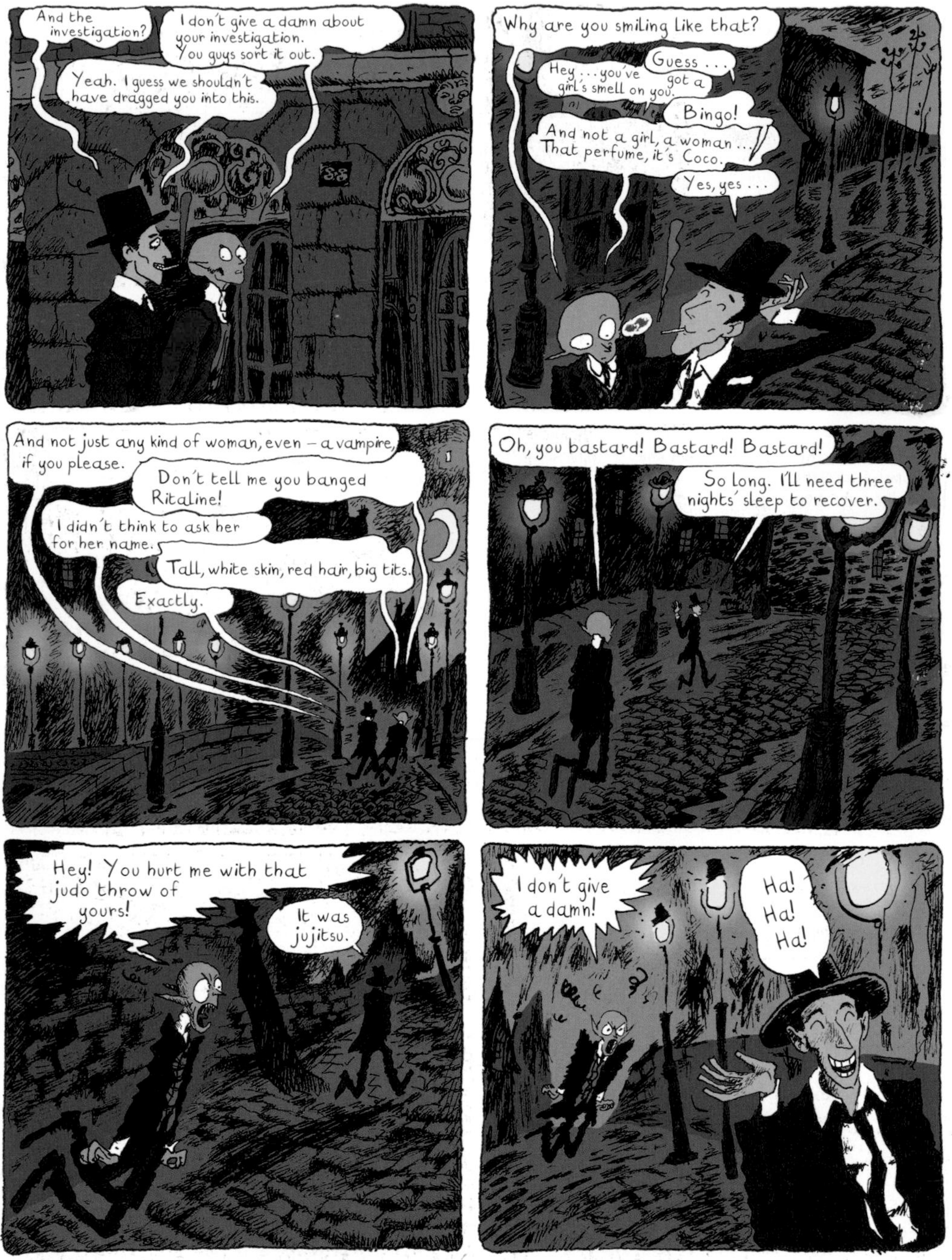

And the investigation?
I don't give a damn about your investigation. You guys sort it out.
Yeah. I guess we shouldn't have dragged you into this.
Why are you smiling like that?
Guess . . .
Hey . . . you've got a girl's smell on you.
Bingo!
And not a girl, a woman . . . That perfume, it's Coco.
Yes, yes . . .
And not just any kind of woman, even – a vampire, if you please.
Don't tell me you banged Ritaline!
I didn't think to ask her for her name.
Tall, white skin, red hair, big tits.
Exactly.
Oh, you bastard! Bastard! Bastard!
So long. I'll need three nights' sleep to recover.
Hey! You hurt me with that judo throw of yours!
It was jujitsu.
I don't give a damn!
Ha! Ha! Ha!

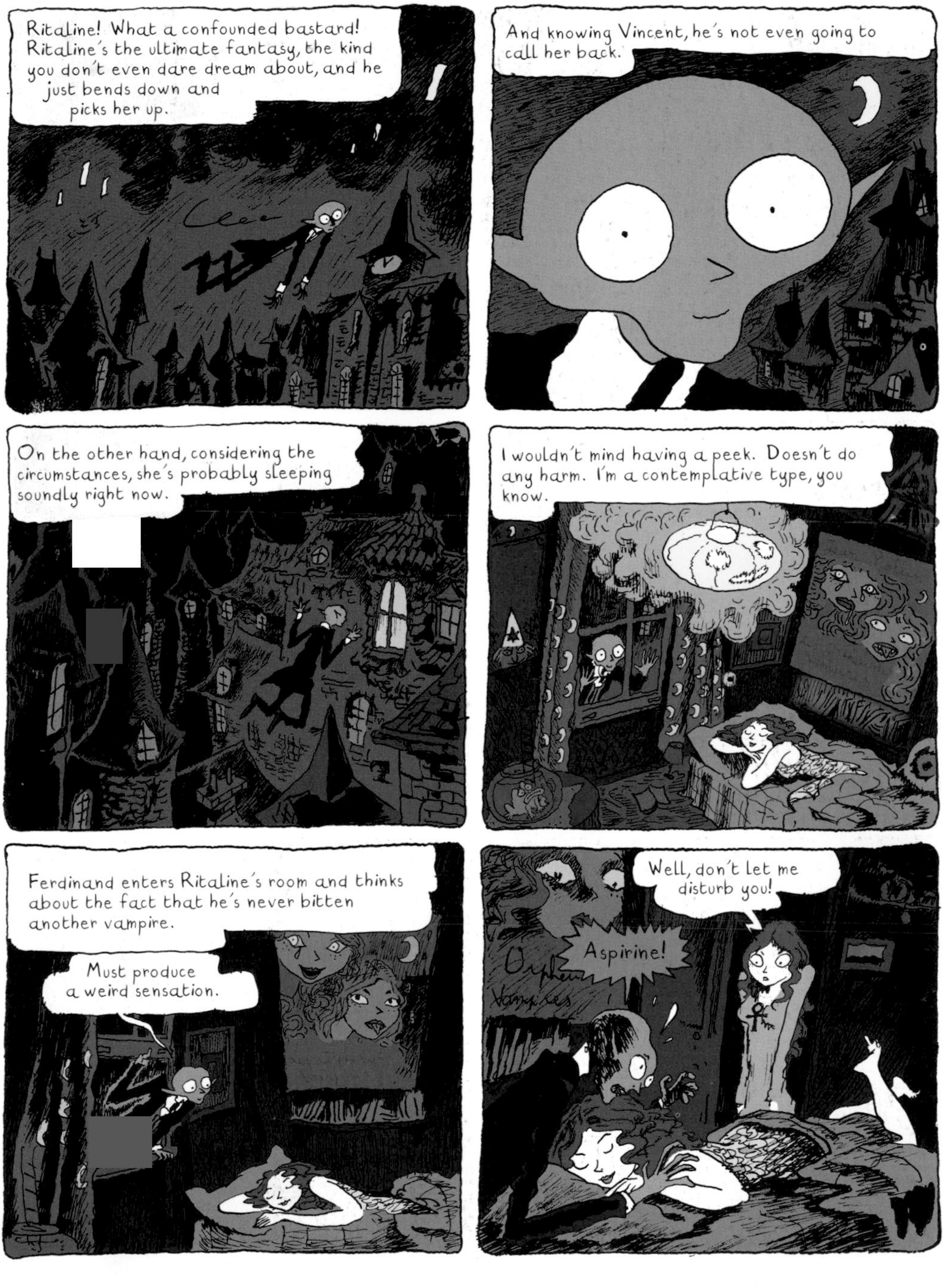
Ritaline! What a confounded bastard! Ritaline's the ultimate fantasy, the kind you don't even dare dream about, and he just bends down and picks her up.
And knowing Vincent, he's not even going to call her back.
On the other hand, considering the circumstances, she's probably sleeping soundly right now.
I wouldn't mind having a peek. Doesn't do any harm. I'm a contemplative type, you know.
Ferdinand enters Ritaline's room and thinks about the fact that he's never bitten another vampire.
Must produce a weird sensation.
Well, don't let me disturb you!
Aspirine!

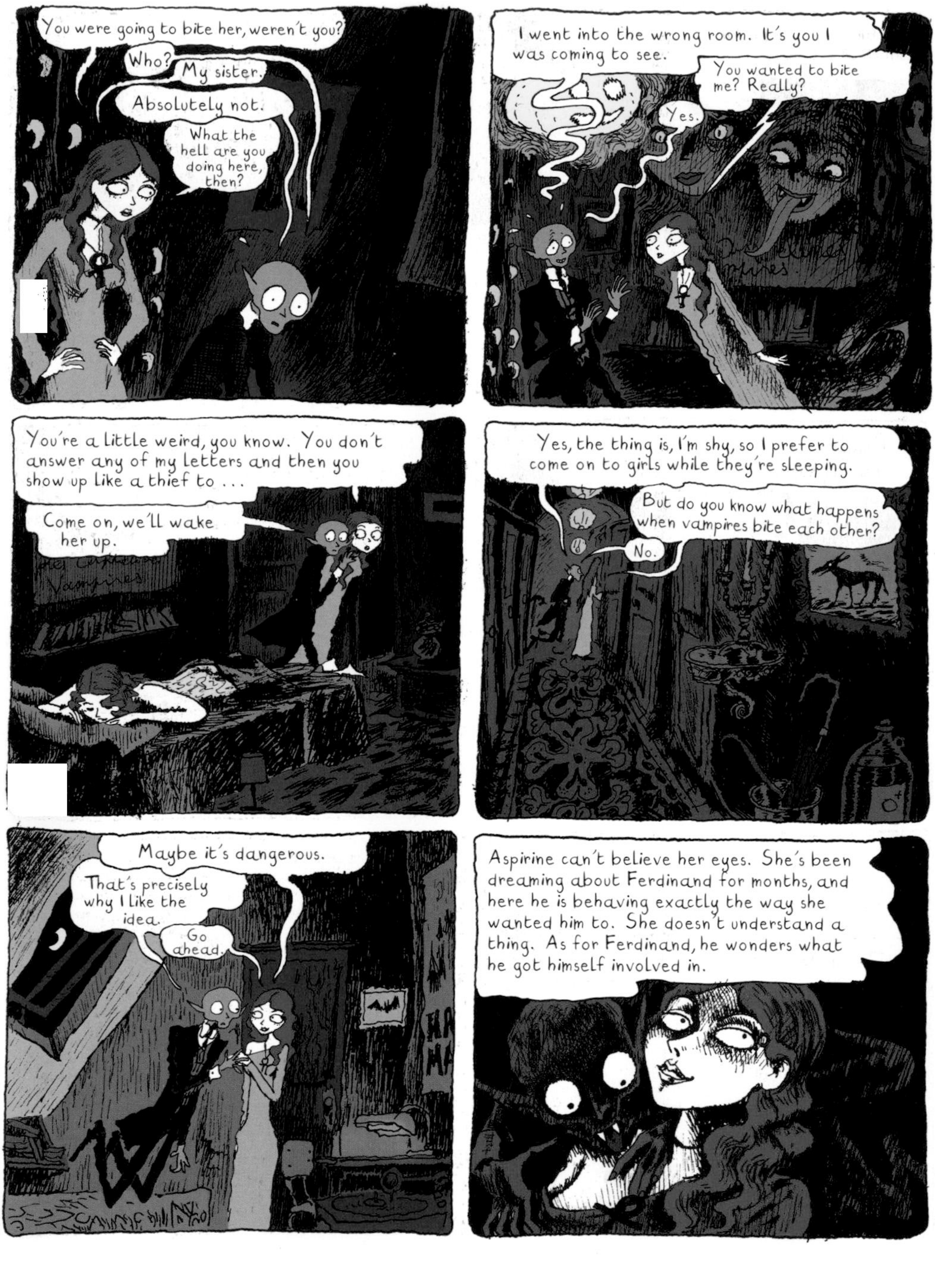
You were going to bite her, weren't you?
Who?
My sister.
Absolutely not.
What the hell are you doing here, then?
I went into the wrong room. It's you I was coming to see.
You wanted to bite me? Really?
Yes.
You're a little weird, you know. You don't answer any of my letters and then you show up like a thief to . . .
Come on, we'll wake her up.
Yes, the thing is, I'm shy, so I prefer to come on to girls while they're sleeping.
But do you know what happens when vampires bite each other?
No.
Maybe it's dangerous.
That's precisely why I like the idea.
Go ahead.
Aspirine can't believe her eyes. She's been dreaming about Ferdinand for months, and here he is behaving exactly the way she wanted him to. She doesn't understand a thing. As for Ferdinand, he wonders what he got himself involved in.

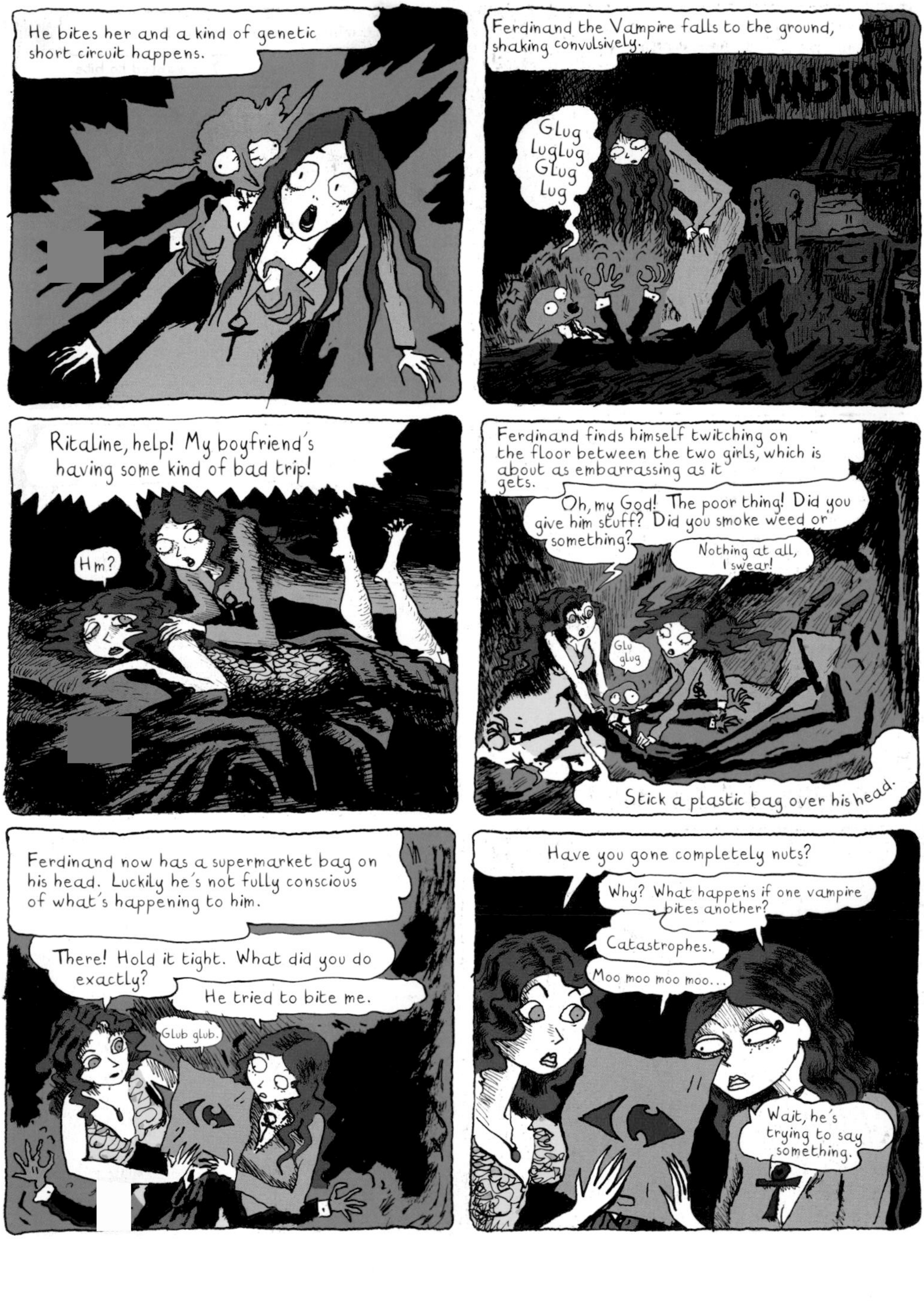
He bites her and a kind of genetic short circuit happens.
Ferdinand the Vampire falls to the ground, shaking convulsively.
MANSION
Glug LugLug Glug Lug
Ritaline, help! My boyfriend's having some kind of bad trip!
Hm?
Ferdinand finds himself twitching on the floor between the two girls, which is about as embarrassing as it gets.
Oh, my God! The poor thing! Did you give him stuff? Did you smoke weed or something?
Nothing at all, I swear!
Glu glug
Stick a plastic bag over his head.
Ferdinand now has a supermarket bag on his head. Luckily he's not fully conscious of what's happening to him.
There! Hold it tight. What did you do exactly?
He tried to bite me.
Glub glub.
Have you gone completely nuts?
Why? What happens if one vampire bites another?
Catastrophes.
Moo moo moo moo...
Wait, he's trying to say something.

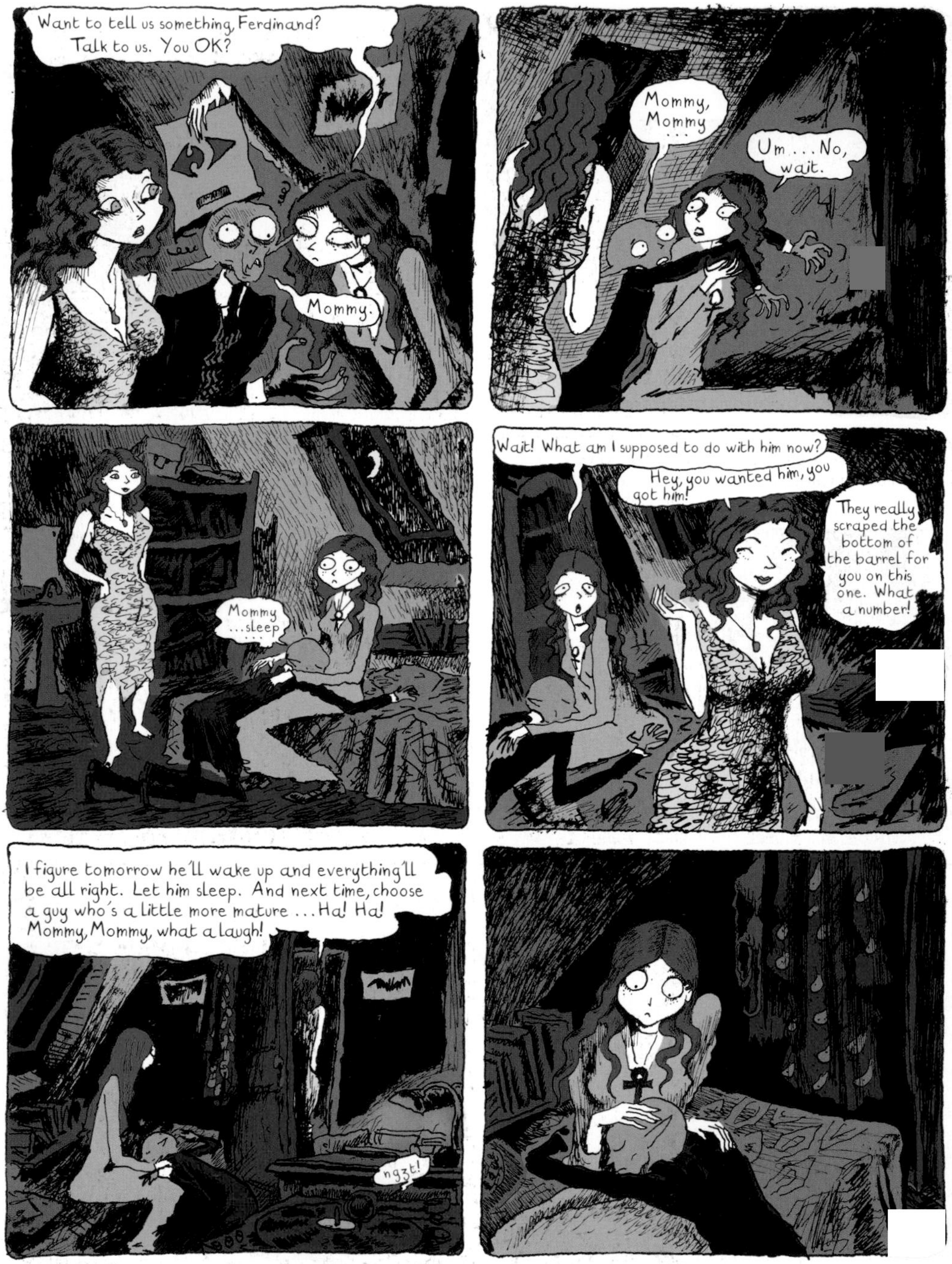

Want to tell us something, Ferdinand? Talk to us. You OK?
Mommy.
Mommy, Mommy . . .
Um . . . No, wait.
Mommy . . . sleep . . .
Wait! What am I supposed to do with him now?
Hey, you wanted him, you got him!
They really scraped the bottom of the barrel for you on this one. What a number!
I figure tomorrow he'll wake up and everything'll be all right. Let him sleep. And next time, choose a guy who's a little more mature . . . Ha! Ha! Mommy, Mommy, what a laugh!
ngzt!

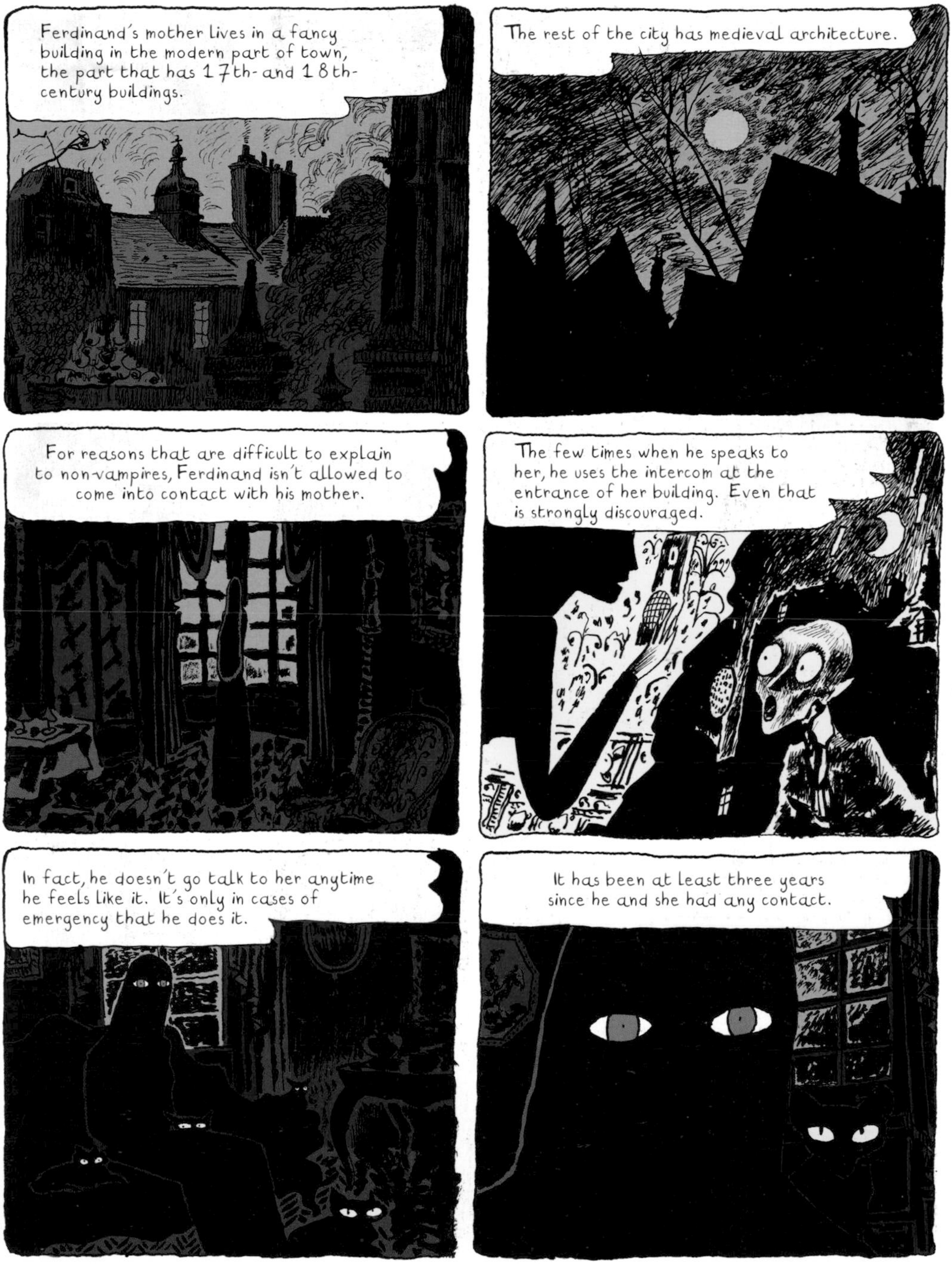
Ferdinand's mother lives in a fancy building in the modern part of town, the part that has 17th- and 18th-century buildings.
The rest of the city has medieval architecture.
For reasons that are difficult to explain to non-vampires, Ferdinand isn't allowed to come into contact with his mother.
The few times when he speaks to her, he uses the intercom at the entrance of her building. Even that is strongly discouraged.
In fact, he doesn't go talk to her anytime he feels like it. It's only in cases of emergency that he does it.
It has been at least three years since he and she had any contact.

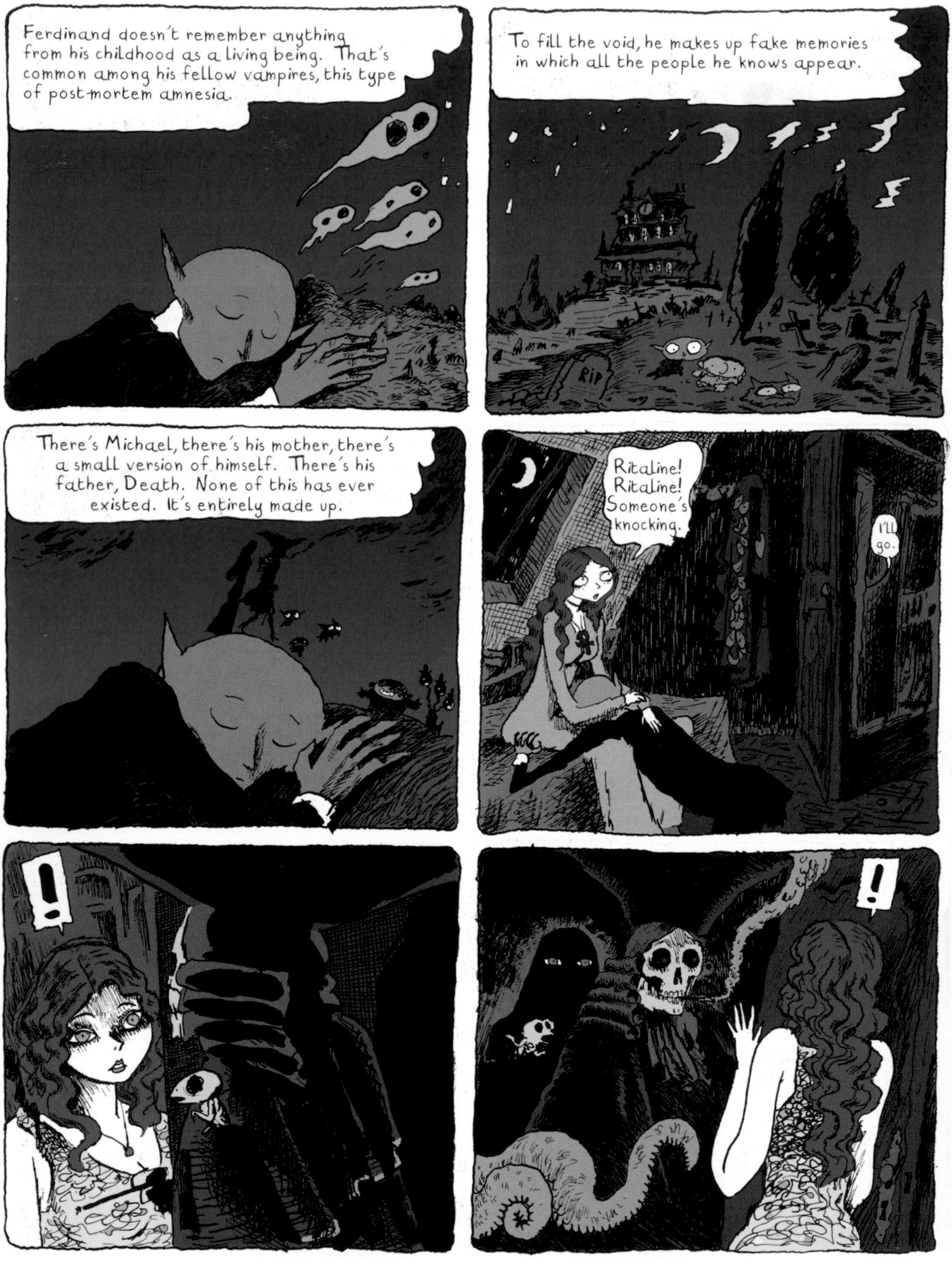
Ferdinand doesn't remember anything from his childhood as a living being. That's common among his fellow vampires, this type of post-mortem amnesia.
To fill the void, he makes up fake memories in which all the people he knows appear.
RIP
There's Michael, there's his mother, there's a small version of himself. There's his father, Death. None of this has ever existed. It's entirely made up.
Ritaline! Ritaline! Someone's knocking.
I'll go.
!
!

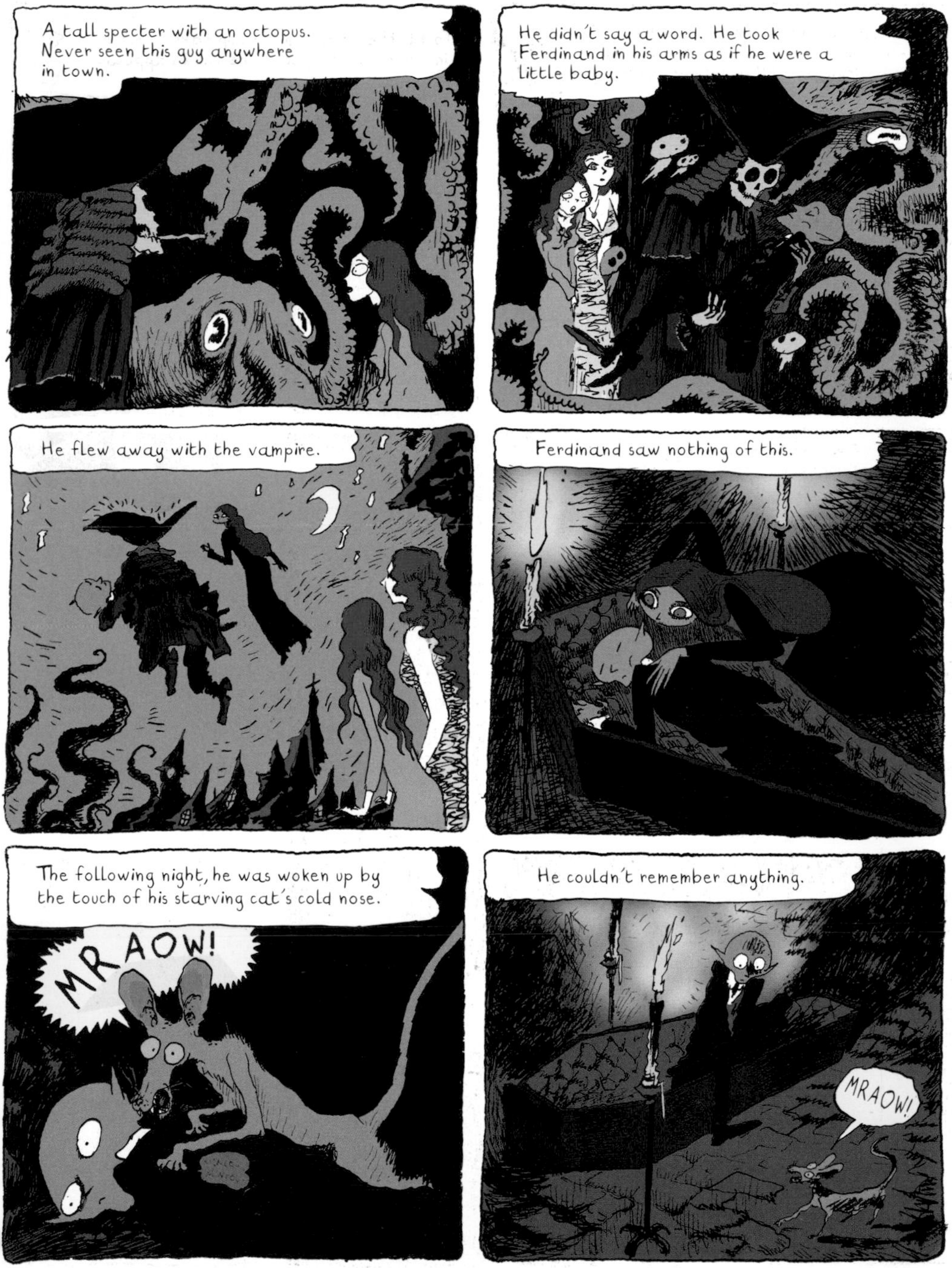
A tall specter with an octopus. Never seen this guy anywhere in town.
He didn't say a word. He took Ferdinand in his arms as if he were a little baby.
He flew away with the vampire.
Ferdinand saw nothing of this.
The following night, he was woken up by the touch of his starving cat's cold nose.
MRAOW!
He couldn't remember anything.
MRAOW!

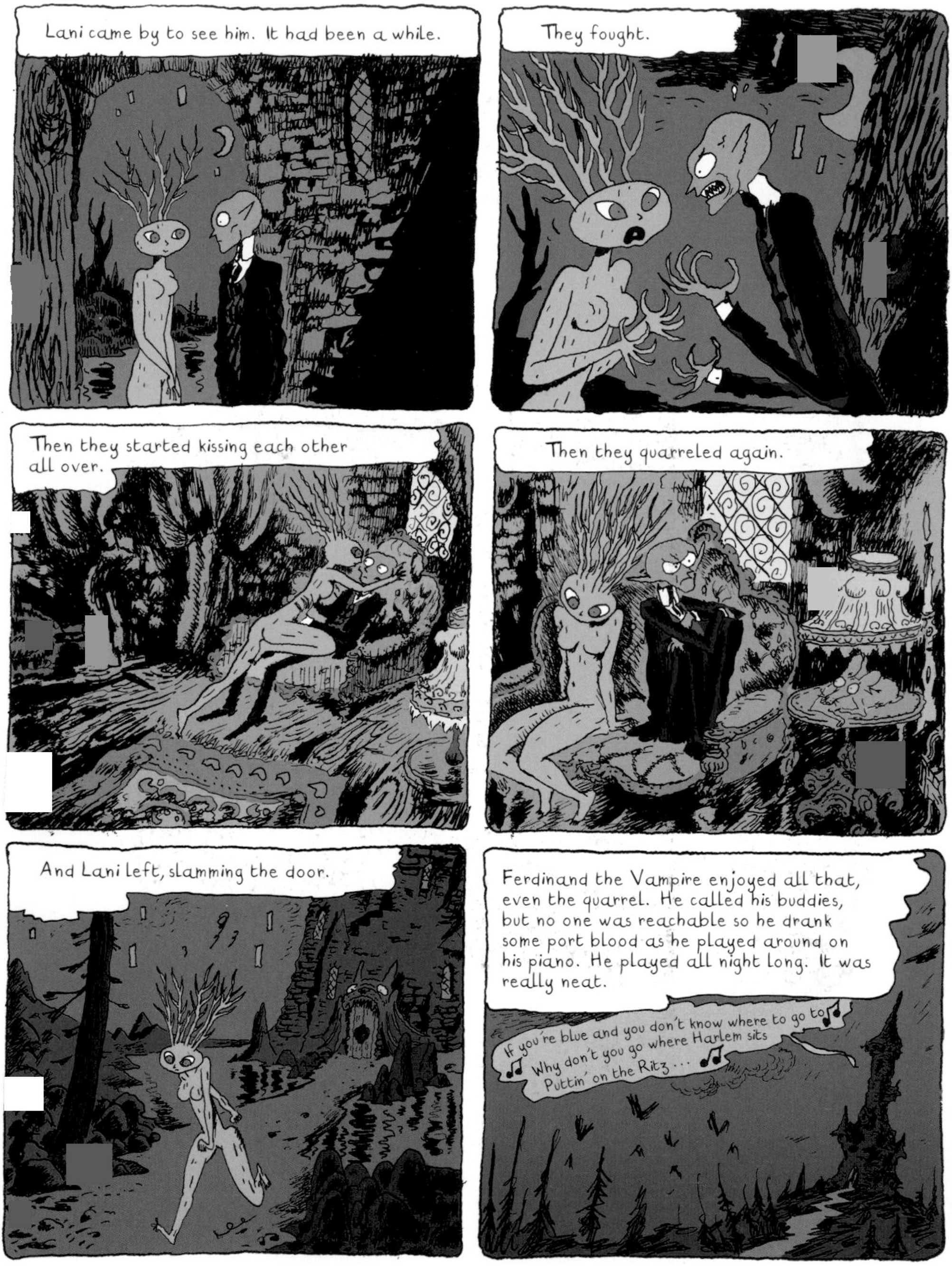

Lani came by to see him. It had been a while.
They fought.
Then they started kissing each other all over.
Then they quarreled again.
And Lani left, slamming the door.
Ferdinand the Vampire enjoyed all that, even the quarrel. He called his buddies, but no one was reachable so he drank some port blood as he played around on his piano. He played all night long. It was really neat.
If you're blue and you don't know where to go to
Why don't you go where Harlem sits
Puttin' on the Ritz . . .

Ritaline is fond of telling her lovers that she was the model for the young woman with her back turned in Watteau's painting The Two Cousins. So it's not far-fetched to imagine that Aspirine may have served as the model for the other one ... It is true that at the time people could powder their hair and thus conceal red hair. And as for the ghostly pallor of their skin, it was highly prized at the time.

Regardless, Aspirine shouldn't constantly poke fun at her older sister's old age, because the two of them are only eight years apart. And when you were born in the 18th century, that shouldn't make too big a difference. Except that for all eternity, Aspirine will be seventeen, and that's a painful age to be. The older sister is probably luckier.

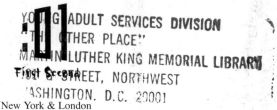
New York & London

Copyright © 2006 by Joann Sfar
English translation copyright © 2006 by First Second

Published by First Second
First Second is an imprint of Roaring Brook Press, a division of Holtzbrinck Publishing
Holdings Limited Partnership
175 Fifth Avenue, New York, NY 10010

Distributed in Canada by H. B. Fenn and Company Ltd.
Distributed in the United Kingdom by Macmillan Children's Books,
a division of Pan Macmillan.

Originally published in France under the title *Grand Vampire, tome 1: Cupidon s'en fout* (2001);
Grand Vampire, tome 2: Mortelles en tête (2002); *Grand Vampire, tome 3: Transatlantique en solitaire* (2002);
Grand Vampire, tome 4: Quai des brunes (2003) by Guy Delcourt Productions, Paris.

Design by Danica Novgorodoff

Library of Congress Cataloging-in-Publication Data

Sfar, Joann.
Vampire loves / story and art by Joann Sfar; coloring by Audré Jardel.—1st ed.
p.cm.
ISBN-13: 978-1-59643-093-8
ISBN-10: 1-59643-093-1

1. Graphic novels. I. Title.
PN6747.S48V36 2006
741.5'944—dc22

2005021498

First Second books are available for special promotions and premiums.
For details, contact: Director of Special Markets, Holtzbrinck Publishers.

First American Edition June 2006

Printed in China

10 9 8 7 6 5 4 3 2 1

BY ART
WE LIVE